JAZZ ODYSSEY

THE AUTOBIOGRAPHY OF
JOE DARENSBOURG

As told to
Peter Vacher

Supplementary material compiled by
Peter Vacher

LOUISIANA STATE UNIVERSITY PRESS
BATON ROUGE

For Patricia, Louise, Sarah and Amanda

First published in Great Britain by
The Macmillan Press Ltd
Basingstoke and London
under the title *Telling It Like It Is*

First published 1988 in the United States of America by
Louisiana State University Press
Baton Rouge

Typeset by Wessex Typesetters
(Division of The Eastern Press Ltd)
Frome, Somerset
in 10/11½pt Caledonia

Printed in Hong Kong

ISBN 0–8071–1442–1

Contents

Foreword

The greater part of Joe Darensbourg's reminiscences were recorded on cassette tapes during my stay at his home in Woodland Hills, California, in October 1979. Although I set out to build up a chronological account of his life, along the way there were many digressions and diversions, some omissions and a fair amount of repetition. A number of Joe's stories, when repeated, differed in details that were quite important and there were occasions when I had to guess which was the right version. Naturally there were topics that he preferred to hint at rather than explore, although Joe wanted, where possible, to be frank and direct. That is why we decided to give the book its title, *Telling it Like it is*.

We also spent time examining his personal papers, files and scrapbooks, to ensure that the career chronology was as complete as possible. In fact this filtering of data proved a far more involved task than I had anticipated, since Joe, unusually for a musician, had kept a lot of material. He had many of his recordings, too, and I listened to them all with him, cross-checking dates and personnel so that the discography would be reasonably comprehensive.

This book is the result of those days that we spent talking over his career, but its seed had been planted many years before. As far back as 1959, I had written to Joe at his house in North Hollywood, taking his address from Leonard Feather's *Encyclopaedia of Jazz*. To my surprise Joe replied promptly, asking whether I could help him organize a visit by his band to England and telling me that he intended sending me his latest records. These arrived and proved to be by the Dixie Flyers, the band that brought Joe some fame and a brush with fortune. Joe's touring possibilities came to nothing in my inexpert hands, but our friendship flourished despite this and we continued to exchange letters. We met for the first time in 1962 when Joe was touring Europe with the Louis Armstrong All Stars and, aside from the exceptional pleasure of meeting Satchmo and mingling with the Bob Scobey band, who were also backstage at the Odeon, Hammersmith, I was able to tape a lengthy interview with Joe, which later appeared in *Jazz Monthly* as "My Louisiana Story." This account of Joe's life was certainly the most complete to have been published up to that time, and made clear the varied circumstances of his musical wanderings.

After this Joe and I lost touch for a number of years, but our correspondence resumed in the early seventies and was followed by a cordial reunion in London, this time in March 1974, when Joe was a member of Barry Martyn's Legends of Jazz. I interviewed him for *Melody Maker* but it was obvious that Joe was quite ill. Fortunately trumpeter Andy Blakeney was on hand to take care of his old Ory colleague, but, more to the point, local enthusiast Dave Bennett was quick to take action and arranged Joe's admission to hospital. After two weeks' recuperation at Bennett's home Joe felt well enough to return to Los Angeles and continued his recovery, watched over by his wife, Helen. In August of the same year Joe brought Helen over to stay with the Bennetts for a holiday, before showing her a number of European countries where he had taken playing engagements.

It was during our conversations at the Bennetts' house that the idea of a book collaboration took root. Dave recorded those discussions and turned the tapes over to me; their contents were used to supplement the main flow of Joe's recollections. In 1975 Joe was in London once more, still with the Legends, restored to health but already tired of touring. I wrote about him again for *Melody Maker* and we continued to assemble interview material, starting to plan the book in earnest. Our exchanges of letters continued after Joe had left the Legends, but then Joe's poor health intervened and the anticipated series of trans-Atlantic tapes never quite materialized. Curiously, it was the recuperation period that followed his heart attacks that provided the impetus for the preparation of these tapes, and they started to arrive. Inevitably, recovery led to increased calls for Joe to work and the tapes slowed down, although some were sent in February 1978 and two more in early 1979. Their quality heartened me and also made clear Helen's clever questioning. Transcription confirmed that we had an excellent story to tell, but it was also obvious that detailed one-to-one interviews were needed to eliminate ambiguities and it was arranged that I would travel over in October 1979, just 20 years on from my first contact with Joe.

During our fortnight together I enjoyed the Darensbourgs' hospitality to the full. Joe was an outstanding cook and introduced me to all his favorite New Orleans dishes. I was able to hear him play – usually at private functions – and to meet a number of his musician friends, who were also remarkably hospitable. Joe took life fairly quietly following his heart attacks, but his lively anticipation of the gig and animation when at work belied his condition. His warm-toned clarinet style, for which he was well known, together with his easy-going personality, meant that he enjoyed the respect and admiration of his fellow musicians. The trombonist Herbie Harper put it well: "Joe's just wonderful. I have never heard anyone in this business say a word against him. He has friends everywhere."

I believe his story is uniquely American in its sense of movement and opportunism, a kind of picaresque journey that would be impossible to equal in today's world of music colleges and high-profile media hype. Joe worked with some of the greatest creative musicians in jazz, both black and white, straddling the line between art and entertainment, with the various phases of his career a partial mirror to the evolution of the music itself.

During his Louisiana childhood, Joe was fortunate to know some of the first great generation of Creole and black jazzmen before moving on to California, where many of the New Orleans pioneers had also journeyed. From Los Angeles he went on to the lively backwater of Seattle, which offered a low-life parallel to Pendergast's Kansas City with its "wide-open" status. Many readers, I think, will be interested in Joe's account of his participation in the Seattle scene, since this is a subject which has been overlooked by historians. He then took an active part in the New Orleans revival of the forties, the last major flowering of traditional jazz, and arguably Joe's finest hour.

No master plan attended his travels, just chance, and it is our good fortune that his remarkably accurate reminiscences bring back these lost eras with such vivacity. Joe was proud that he had always earned a living from music and seldom complained about past hardships. While often critical of others, he made no false claims for himself and he was refreshingly honest about the temptations that faced traveling musicians. If some of his stories sound apocryphal, then so be it.

Joe's most appropriate legacy must, of course, be his music, and I urge the reader to seek out his recordings, especially those of the early Ory period (from the mid-forties) and others by his Dixie Flyers and the Legends of Jazz. His style on these, as with his live performances, embodies the flowing arabesques of Creole clarinet, a tradition in itself, carrying forward the Picou and Tio lineage, with a hot attack allied to a warm, limpid tone quality.

Never an innovator, Joe brought the neglected skill of slap-tongue clarinet back to prominence; he was also an amusing vocalist, an occasional composer, a fine front man and bandleader, and a soprano saxophonist of genuine merit. Of his earlier alto and tenor saxophone we have no record, and it is one of my regrets that Joe's wanderings kept him away from the main centers of jazz recording during the classic pre-swing period. There is also a dearth of contemporary reference to his playing worth in those days, but I think it safe to argue that fine musicianship and good time jazz feeling would have been as evident then as they were in his more recent work. Joe waited a long time for recognition: happily, his later years were both successful and well documented.

The words and syntax throughout the book are in every way Joe's own and he was anxious that he should pay proper tribute to his many friends. Nearly 40 hours of recorded reminiscences have been compressed into an oral collage which we hope is both entertaining and informative. Even so, more could have been done had Joe survived long enough to allow additional interview time. Sadly, he died when only one chapter had been completed. Therefore any mistakes of interpretation are mine, but it is my hope that the unsentimental directness and wry sense of humor that were combined in Joe's observations will commend themselves to the reader. Even after the editing and shaping process, the voice that remains is truly that of Joe Darensbourg "telling it like it is."

Peter Vacher
London, February 1987

Acknowledgements

My main debt of gratitude is to Helen and Joe Darensbourg, whose friendship I have enjoyed for a quarter century or more and whose hospitality and patience when answering my questions took on saintly proportions. It remains a great sadness to me that Joe was unable to see the finished work for himself. Helen answered all my letters and filled in much essential detail, proving to be an excellent interviewer on the tapes that she made with Joe prior to my visit to Woodland Hills in 1979. She kept the project going even during the many illnesses that beset both Joe and herself in recent years. The existence of the book owes a lot to her persistent enthusiasm.

My thanks also go to Max Jones and John Chilton for their encouragement; to Floyd Levin for so generously providing photographs and sharing his files with me; and to Roger Jamieson and Sid Bailey who gave me much detailed information that has been incorporated in the discography and chronology. Frank Driggs allowed me to quote from his unpublished interviews with Joe; Karl Gert zur Heide gave me invaluable research assistance; Anne and Dave Bennett provided hospitality and help with cassette copies and photographs; my friend Denis Wynne-Jones painstakingly copied photographs lent to me by other enthusiasts. Others who helped with data or with pictures include Paul Affeldt (*Jazz Report*), Ray Avery, John Bentley, Andy Blakeney, Jonas Bernholm, Mary Corliss (MOMA, New York), Terry Dash (*Footnote*), David Griffiths, Gideon Honore, Larry Kiner (Aircheck Records), Joe Liggins, Terry Martin (JIC), David Meeker (BFI), Wayne Morris (Director Publications, Disney Consumer Products), Gene Norman (Crescendo Records), Brian Peerless, Archie Rosate, Brian Rust, Bo Scherman (*Orkester journalen*), Duncan Schiedt, Cy Shain, Bez Turner (*Juke Blues*), Patricia Willard, Val Wilmer, Laurie Wright (*Storyville*), and Theo Zwicky.

My special thanks go to my wife Patricia, who typed the manuscript and put up nobly with its editor's many variations of mood as the work forged ahead or lagged behind.

My publisher Alyn Shipton deserves his due in recognition of his encouragement, patience and faith in the book; it matters a lot to be working with someone who has genuine regard for the musical era epitomized by someone of Darensbourg's generation. I was lucky too, that his editorial team of Jannet King and Caroline Richmond were so understanding and professional.

Peter Vacher
London, February 1987

I think Joe's the most beautiful guy in the world.
You know why? He's honest.
He tells everything right like it is.
That's what I like about him.

Nick Fatool
Van Nuys, California

Prologue

I wanted this book to be written so that the people could get some insight into what musicians had to go through in those early days, especially mentioning about Prohibition. I don't want to hide that I drank. How I'm living today after going through that period, I'll never know. I had some rough times, like getting drunk and sick, having the DTs, jumping up in the middle of the night and almost having to be put in a strait-jacket. I wish I hadn't drunk so damn much. Any musician that's living now that went through Prohibition and drank all that bad liquor will know what I'm talking about. If I hadn't met my wife Helen, I'd probably have been gone by now; she cooled me down quite a bit. I've been lucky all my life, especially with women, even Gladys in Seattle and Margaret. I wasn't married to Gladys but I was married to Margaret and at the time I was very unhappy, but it was just one of those things where you don't hit it off for some reason. Everybody's not compatible, but Helen and I certainly are. She softened me up, changed the course of my life. Since I've been with her, she knows I haven't been tempted to do nothing. Once in a while I might get carried away with a few nips but nothing bothers me, so far as spending money, getting cars or chasing other broads goes. I just love to be home. Anyway, I think a reformed musician makes the best husband of all. I want to let people know about the insides and outs of musicians, that musicians are human beings just like anybody else and not bums like the great majority of people think. We have the same problems as you do. Like I said, Helen has helped me a helluva lot. I've seen so many musicians have headaches with women.

I think the music is changing. Like Louis Armstrong said, dixieland never went away, it just went to sleep for a little while. I think the greatest salvation for this type of music is the European musicians with their dedication to it. It's a known fact that we in America originated it but, like a lot of things, we miss the point and take it too much for granted. One of the biggest troubles with dixieland is that it's not a style but a feeling. People will tell you to play a dixieland tune, but when we was coming up you didn't pick out any special tunes. For instance, we played *Let me call you sweetheart* with a dixieland beat, although it was a waltz. It's the feeling that you put in it, not just the tune. The music didn't have that dixieland title to start with; they called it ragtime, and a lot of people didn't even want it in their houses – called it the Devil's music. To my idea, dixieland was at its best in Chicago. When I was on the boats you didn't hear much dixieland at all. You have to give Orson Welles a lot of credit 'cause he started reviving this stuff, along with Marili Morden, Nesuhi Ertegun, even Turk Murphy, Lu

Watters, Burt Bales and those guys in San Francisco. They really was in on the revival; they brought it back, helped to make your big period of dixieland.

I met so many great musicians. I'm talking about guys you never heard much about, like Evan Humphrey, the trumpet player that took Bobby Hackett's place with Katherine Dunham and Keith Purvis, the little drummer, that made the Johnny Wittwer Trio records – unsung guys. I've always said that the true musicians are the "head players"; guys that can't read but know how to play. I'm not boasting, but even if I never could have read a note of music I could have played jazz, because right to this day I play what I feel, what's in my head. I have great respect for symphony musicians, but they're very limited. You take the music away from them and they cannot play, like when the Mexican trumpet player Rafael Mendez came in the Beverly Cavern one time to sit in and couldn't cut it.

If you want to get into this music, be serious. It's all according to what you want to put in. You got thousands of musicians living here in Los Angeles, leading perfectly normal lives with wonderful families, but a lot of others, good guys, could have made it but they got drunk and threw all their money away. The best part of jazz to me is when you take a guy like Nick Fatool or Abe Lincoln or Mike DeLay, any of these good musicians, when they're feeling right at their peak on a job and it seems like everything is going well. We'll just start playing tunes and all night long it just goes great. The thing that bugs me about this kind of music is when you find some amateur musician getting in the way and screwing up the whole damn thing just when you're going so well. Still, when you see all these great musicians like Marvin Ash, Warren "Smitty" Smith, Eddie Miller, it don't get any better than them. And the thing about it is, the greater they are, the nicer they are.

When I'm playing clarinet I try to think of pretty things to play, but I don't want to do it the same way each time. I couldn't do that. When I'm playing a tune I don't know what's coming really; that was Bix Beiderbecke's idea, too. A lot of musicians do try to copy other players but I never remember one time when I wanted to do that. I used to hear guys like Isidore Fritz and my teacher Manuel Roque, who was pretty good, old Irving Fazola and Jimmie Noone; they all had something, but I never wanted to play like any of them. I respected them all and still do. I remember when Marili Morden owned the Jazzman Record Shop over on Santa Monica Boulevard. She used to live in the back of the shop; that's when she was with Nesuhi Ertegun. They had all these old records and we used to go over there after work a lot of times to drink and play records whenever we was in Hollywood. That was the first time I really remember the Hot Five records. I appreciated Johnny Dodds all right but I liked Jimmie Noone better, but even so I just had certain things in my mind I wanted to do, that's all.

I used to love it when Matty Matlock would come round with his clarinet and we'd do duets. Same with my old buddy Barney Bigard. We had a lot of fun making music together, playing beautiful solos like on *Mood Indigo* and *Creole Love Call*, anything like that. We had tunes where we did a lot of fast runs. I'd play my soprano, Barney his clarinet. Barney, to me, was a distinctive stylist. He played five notes and I knew it was him, unlike a lot of clarinet players where I have a lot of trouble distinguishing who they are. We worked very little together on jobs, except for a few things with Gordon Mitchell, one-shot deals for fund-raising purposes. There wasn't a helluva lot of money but we had a lot of fun. Barney made a wonderful contribution; he was the tops.

They brought Benny Goodman to Disneyland a couple of times. After one of the concerts they had a party with a big jam session. I remember Benny had to borrow some reeds from me. I enjoyed playing with him but he never really did anything for me. I'm not putting the guy down, you understand. Benny got a lot of his style from Jimmie Noone, but anybody had to like Jimmie, he had a pleasing style. Pete Fountain took a lot of his stuff from Louis Cottrell. He admits it and he says, "He taught me how to play a clarinet and he taught me how to be a gentleman." Cottrell was one of the good ones. I knew him in New Orleans in the later years only; I met him several times there, made it my business to talk to him. He had a beautiful style, made it look easy. He was capable of playing in anybody's band. Louis was entirely too fat though, nobody could live that long and work like that, packing that kinda weight; his stomach was just blubber. I think he was sick several years before he died. You know, he still played the old Albert system, and the last time I talked to him he said, "When you go back to California, find me a good Albert system clarinet. I need one." I said, "If you can get my old Selmer out of the New Orleans Jazz Museum you can have it." I didn't give it to them, I loaned it to them when they started the museum. Doc Souchon said I didn't have to give it to them, but I should have made him put it in writing. At the time I wanted to give it to them anyway. I thought the museum was going to amount to something but they just made it a commercial venture, made a mess out of it. Now they fixing to change it again. You got to have that clarinet according to my idea. Clarinet is such a versatile instrument, it can do so many things. It can get way up there, raise a lot of hell, and then it can play sweet.

I would sum all this up by saying I don't think anybody could have had a greater life. I don't know if I would want to change anything. I had a wonderful family with my mother, as much as I knew her, and my father. I just wish he could have lived longer 'cause he loved music so much. I think music would have been his life had he not married young; I'm sure he would have been one helluva good musician. He was very slick and he loved life. I hated to practice but Poppa said, "I bought you a clarinet, you gonna play it." I might be outside playing baseball and then I'd think about my uncle which was on the circus, make a bee-line inside and grab my clarinet. "Damn, I gotta get this shit over with, I've gotta learn how to blow this thing." So that's what motivated me. From that and loving to be round animals, the glamor of the circus parade, I went on to meet all these wonderful musicians and fabulous people all over the world. Nothing will ever top the thrill of playing with Louis Armstrong or even the first time I played with Papa Mutt Carey; but if it wasn't for loving the circus, I'd probably have been a bricklayer or wound up with a shoe shop like the rest of them. Instead I got to see the Pope in Rome, Westminster Abbey in London, St Peter's Square, the Orient – all through the clarinet. It gave me a wonderful life.

What more can you ask? I'm still playing, still cooking, still eating red beans and rice! Not bad for a guy who's well up in age. I only have one regret. One of the things I thought about, and Louis wanted to do it, was to open a restaurant called Satchmo's. Every time I got the chance on the road I would cook, so Louis used to say, "Me and you will open a restaurant, one in New York, one in Los Angeles, call them Satchmo's. We'll play and you'll be back in that kitchen. I don't want you to cook but I want you to show the cats *how* to cook. We'll just play when we feel like it, and one thing, we'll have a lot to eat, we won't be hungry."

It's a shame Louis had to leave us so soon.

Joseph Wilmer Darensbourg, born in Baton Rouge, Louisiana, died of cardiac arrest at the Valley Hospital Medical Center in Van Nuys, California, late on 24th May 1985. He had been in intensive care for some weeks following a stroke sustained on 5th February. Thus came the end of Joe Darensbourg, a fine New Orleans-style clarinetist, a warm-hearted friend and a splendid storyteller. He had no enemies and was an enthusiastic performer on clarinet and soprano saxophone, always carrying the torch for the best musical values.

ONE

Every little town in Louisiana had some kind of band

As far back as I can remember I used to love the family picnics and gatherings that we had in Louisiana in those early days. One of the big things in my life was to look forward to going to the picnics and cotton-picking parties out there in the country districts. All my family and the other people would get together and everybody would fix picnic baskets with all kinds of different cold meats, cakes, and things like that. Sometimes they would have moonlight picnics, too.

And usually they would hire a band. Most of the time it was string bands. In fact that's the first music I can remember. It was beautiful. They played the pretty tunes of the day, everything that was popular in that time. I guess that was when I fell in love with music. The string bands usually had mandolin, guitar, bass, and a violin in there. Sometimes you'd see an accordion or a banjo. Guitar and mandolin was a great thing then. A mandolin is a beautiful instrument. Those bands played so pretty. Some of the guys would make their instruments, but primarily it was the regular instruments that they played. A lot of guys used bows with the string bass. Really, they used a bow more than anything.

To me, these are your first jazz bands. Hell, none of those fellows could read notes. Maybe the violin player could spell a little. It was improvising, that's mostly all that they did. They was natural musicians; whatever they could hear or come to their mind, they would play it. That's your greatest musicians.

Most of the musicians that played those picnics was my relatives. Guitar and mandolin players. Then there was my uncle Zephus, who was the world's greatest zither player at the time. He could really play that zither. Later on my dad would send me and my brother out to the country to play music with a cousin that was a wonderful guitar player. I had another cousin, Truell Darensbourg, only we called him Sayou, who was an outstanding violinist. He lived out in the country and I know he couldn't play nothing from music. He was a baker by trade and he moved eventually to Baton Rouge, where he appeared on a little radio show. People always tried to get him to leave town. Even Paul Whiteman wanted to get him in his band. He had his chance, but he wouldn't leave. I think he was better than Eddie South, Joe Venuti or any of those top men. He just had that ear, could play anything, but hated to leave home. There's a lot of Louisiana musicians like that.

My father was an amateur cornet player and he was crazy about music. Him and some of my cousins got them a little band together for parties and picnics. He'd bring his little E flat cornet to the picnics. He carried it in a sack and sometimes, when he'd pull it out, Sayou and them would say, "No, Henry, we don't want that thing." A lot of them didn't want no part of a brass horn. Papa was ready to bang that cornet over Sayou's head after that. Most of the time they did let him sit in. Other times he had his harp, which is a harmonica, and he could wail on that, too. In a way he was a frustrated musician, and, to come right down to it, he would have liked to have been good enough to go down to New Orleans and play in the pit for the French Opera. I don't know whether he could have been a professional, and he never found out because he got married when he was young and started having children. His family came first, that's all there was to it.

One thing I do know is that he loved music and musicians. He really wanted all of us kids to be musicians. It was a way of life down there in Louisiana. Whenever they had a gathering of people they had a band. Hell, after you was born they'd baptize you, and they had somebody playing music there. When you was christened they'd have a party, and, surely, when they planted you, why, you didn't amount to much if you didn't have music. That's no doubt why so many great musicians come from Louisiana in the first place.

My great-grandfather and his two brothers, that's the beginning of the Darensbourgs in Louisiana. They came from France well before 1900. One of my cousins had traced the whole thing and he told me something about the Gold Rush and how they came over in those days. All of them was shoemakers way back. My cousin and I would sit down and get to talking about them, but we'd never finish because we'd start drinking and forget all about what we was talking about. We was going to have the whole family history translated, but then he died so we never did finish it. Later on some woman came up to me when I was working with Kid Ory, and her hobby was tracing family trees. She said, "You know, you come from royalty. Your people were the Comtes d'Arensbourg. I read that name in history." Well, it could be true! Still, Darensbourg is a pretty common name in Louisiana. You pick up a phone book in my home town of Baton Rouge and there must be half a page of Darensbourgs. In New Orleans you got two pages of them.

Funny thing is that I don't remember nothing about my father's parents. None of my sisters and brothers know anything about them. They must have been long gone, or else they died when I was very young. All I do know is that they died in a small town called Chenal, which is about 20 miles from Baton Rouge; Glen was the name of the place really. It was just a whistle stop, out there by New Roads, north of Baton Rouge. That's where an obituary came out ten years ago about a Joe Darensbourg, saying that the funeral would be in The Chenal. The news services and everybody got that all mixed up, thinking it was me.

Still, I remember my father's sisters and brothers. We had a slew of relatives and some of them had plantations and farms out there. I had two uncles that owned big plantations and they owned slaves. My dad told me that, but he didn't believe in nothing like that; he used to say how his grandpa was nice to the slaves but how he thought what they did was wrong. For those days my dad was a very liberal man. He liked everybody.

On my mother's side I remember my grandfather and my grandmother. His name was Anatole Bageron and his people also came from France. He spoke nothing else but French – real French. Some of my other relatives spoke the broken or Cajun French. Grandpa Anatole lived out in the country, a few miles from Baton Rouge. He had a great big farm – called it a plantation. My mother had a couple of sisters and a brother there. Grandpa had a long beard and he wore a big hat and high boots. He could pass for Buffalo Bill. He looked just like a typical plantation owner. He had a horse and buggy, and once every two weeks he'd come and get Mama and take her out to the country. She would always take me or one of my brothers and sisters. I loved it out there.

My grandfather used to raise watermelon, canteloupes, stuff like that, and he had a lot of plum and peach trees. Land was cheap there and he lived good. He was comfortable for those days. He just loved us kids. Later on he bought all this property on the outskirts of Baton Rouge and he built a house for every one of us: six houses. He said, "This is in case anything happens. As you grow up, one of these houses is yours."

Like I said, my father's name was Henry. My mother's name was Alice. I used to have their wedding picture, and, of all things, my father was sitting down, holding a little derby, and my mother was the one standing up. She used to laugh about that. A guy who was a prominent artist was going to make a hand-painted copy of it for me, but he and his wife started drinking like hell and fighting. That way they lost the picture. It was the only one. My sisters could have killed me.

Papa made shoes and he fixed shoes. He had all the lathes and everything but he made shoes strictly by hand. The average guy couldn't afford to have them made because it would cost ten or fifteen dollars for a pair. Papa knew almost every prominent person in town because he had one of the first shoe shops and he was the best shoemaker in Baton Rouge. People like the five Ringling brothers came to the shop to have their shoes fixed. He made shoes for John Ringling himself. He autographed a picture to my dad as "The Best Shoemaker in the World," and one time he took us all out to the special car he had on the railroad for his traveling. The cowboys on the circus would bring their cowboy boots to get them fixed. My dad knew a lot of circus people. It was a thrill for us to meet a guy like John Ringling who owned a circus. We all loved circuses.

So my father was a shoemaker; he wasn't only a shoe repairer. It was handed down from all of his relatives. He taught half of the shoemakers that come out of Louisiana. They just came there to learn, stayed at the house. A lot of my cousins and relatives was shoemakers and some are still living in California. Naturally, Papa insisted his kids learn the shoemaker's trade before we even learned music. I guess I had a shoe in my hand when I was born. All the boys was shoemakers and shoe repairers.

Other kids would be out on the street playing and, naturally, we would want to play, but we had to do a certain amount of work before we went to school. I didn't think that was good, but it set us straight, because I seen so many of those kids that I went to school with never amount to anything. But me and my brothers always had this trade. After I was grown I could literally make a pair of shoes myself, and I'd fix my own shoes. I liked to do it. We had to learn that trade first. We all got to start out at that shoe shop, doing something. My dad said, "I want you to have a trade. You learn this and you can have your music, too." Music wasn't an established thing you can depend on like it is now. His idea was, if you didn't make it in music, you could always get a job fixing shoes!

My mother was devoted to her father and her sister. She had two brothers, too: one named Val, and Joe, who was my godfather. We called him Parain, and I was named after him. She was a very strong-willed woman and she had a horrible temper. Yet she was the most gentle-looking woman and very beautiful. If I did something wrong I would much rather Papa would get hold of me, because she'd half-kill you. I remember one time I did something and she was ironing, using one of them old-time flat irons that you put in a hot fire to heat 'em up. She called me and I said something cheeky to her. I got close to her and she swung that iron at me. If she'd connected, she'd have probably killed me.

Mama died in 1912. She was sick for a long time and she wasn't over 35 when she passed. I think it was the TB. Once you got consumption so many people died. They never said it was that, but I remember she coughed a lot. I was about six and my youngest sister wasn't even one year old. In those days, when a person died, the undertaker would come to the house. They didn't take you to the mortuary. They had a kind of portable stand that was strong enough to support a coffin, set up like an ironing board, and that's the way they put the body on display. That's one thing I can still see as plain as day. I remember thinking when she was laying there that, if I went over and pinched her or took a pin, would she wake up? Honest to God, ain't that silly?

At the cemetery, Grandpa Anatole was holding me by the hand, telling me to say goodbye to Mama, right there in the grave. And the way you did that, you'd pick up a piece of dirt and throw it in the grave before they covered it. I don't remember being really sad. It didn't register. I was too young. But when I threw that dirt in the ground, that was something to be sad about.

There was no music at the funeral. We was Catholics and Catholic people didn't have music. Only time you seen any music was when some black lodge guy that belonged to the Oddfellows died and they had music for his funeral.

Later on all my father's relatives said that Papa couldn't raise us children by himself. They were saying, "You got to give these children away, you can't raise them like this." And Papa would say, "Nobody is getting any of the children. I never will give them away. I'm going to raise them myself." We would have had nice homes, but he wanted to keep us all together, even though we was all pretty young. It wasn't as bad as you might think. My dad hired a lady housekeeper to take care of us and, like I said, we had oodles of relatives and there was always some of them around there. Even so, Papa had friends, people that liked him and us, who said, "Henry, you can't carry them children and the shoe shop." But we managed pretty good and we never wanted for anything. We older children always had our chores to do. We worked around the house and the housekeeper would do the cooking and the housework. She lived with us. And we had aunts that would come over. Aunts Adele and Laura would come and stay, and Aunt Nana, who lived to be over a hundred years old. She only died a few years ago. So we was well taken care of. Then we'd ask to go and stay with our relatives and Papa let us go to the country, to Uncle Prosper, Aunt Edna and Aunt Denise.

And then there was always some broad trying to spark Papa and move in. He was a good catch, so they would come sashaying around, saying, "Mr Henry, you must get pretty lonesome around here. You got these children running around the street. You need somebody to take care of them." Hinting around, you know. They figured he had a lot more money than he did. He did have the six houses, close to the Mississippi River, near where Louisiana State University is built right now. He used to rent them. They wasn't worth much. Papa would look at these old gals and arch his eyes, then look at us sitting there, as if to say, "I know what you're after, you bitch, but it ain't gonna work." But those old broads was always after him. He had a nice house, some property and the business.

See, Papa himself was a good-looking guy. He was a sport, a sharp cat. When he went out he had a derby on and he always carried an umbrella, like the English people. He'd dress up. He had a mustache, beautiful black hair and very distinct eyes. He had some cousins in New Orleans and he used to go up there to visit the French Opera. They brought musicians over from France to play at the French Opera House. My dad was in New Orleans, it look like every week. He'd have to go there for supplies, too. He'd visit the big suppliers to buy leather or to buy second-hand shoes. He used to sell shoes in the shop. One time he came home and all his pocket was cut out. Some guy took a razor and cut half the seat off his pants and lifted his wallet. Papa was always telling us to be careful, and I know he had his money pinned in the pocket, but they still picked his pocket.

I don't remember my family going down to New Orleans together. We'd go down individually with my dad; never went with my mother. All her relatives lived in Baton Rouge. One thing I remember from my mother's time was when my Grandpa Anatole got one of those old Edison phonographs that played cylinder records. They had a little box compartment that came with them, and when me and my brother Frank first heard this music and singing coming out of this phonograph we was very curious about it. Somebody was crazy enough to tell us it was little people in there playing these instruments and singing. We wanted to see these little men and women, so when everybody was in the other room we decided to open up the phonograph. We got a hammer and chisel and we was hammering on this thing when my mother came back. Luckily we hadn't broken it open. I think a phonograph cost 50 dollars then, and we had this thing on the floor, ready to massacre it. She took the hammer and swung it at my brother. She'd have laid him out if she'd connected. Between her and my grandfather, I think it was the worst beating we ever had in our lives. We never tried that again.

Our house and the shoe shop were on North Boulevard in Baton Rouge. That's one of the main streets. It was just a dirt road then, wasn't even paved. We never had any electric lights until later on. We had outside open toilets. We had a cow and got milk, used to make our own butter. That's how small a town Baton Rouge was then. It had only 25,000 people but that was considered a fair-sized city in those days. It was the third city in Louisiana in size. Shreveport was next to New Orleans, which, of course, was the biggest.

We had a horse. He was beautiful and I remember he had a white blaze on his face. Somebody stole our horse and I went on many trips around Louisiana with my dad looking for him. A guy would come and say, "Mr Henry, I think I seen your horse at Denham Springs." That's ten miles from Baton Rouge. That's all they needed to tell him. Papa always hoped to find that horse but we never did.

We usually traveled on the train in those days. Some of our people had an old piece of a car but we never had one when I was a kid. We had this little train, across the river at Port Allen, called The Plug. It ran like a plug, too, but all of us would load up on that train, carry a little lunch and go on out to the country.

We'd go visiting my Uncle Prosper, who had a big farm out there. He was a kinda shady uncle. My dad didn't get along with him at all. He had this big house, horses, and everything, but that wasn't how he made his money. He had a private road that run in front of his property leading to the next town. A lot of people used to make it for a short cut. My uncle had dug a great big hole and put water in it. This was in the early days of automobiles, and every time one of them would hit that hole they'd get stuck. Even if it hadn't rained for six months, you always found water in the mud-hole. People wouldn't expect a mud-hole to be there on a bright sunny day in the summertime, so naturally they didn't carry no chains to put on their wheels. He'd be there in front of his house, sitting in the shade, maybe drinking some lemonade or some wine, with a couple of mules all ready. The guy would come over and ask about some help. The guy would say he hadn't much money and my uncle would ask how much he had. Usually he'd charge five dollars. Then he'd get up and pull the guy's automobile out of the mud-hole. On a good day he'd make about 50 or 60 dollars. My dad didn't like that. He used to tell Uncle Prosper, "You gonna go to hell for sure, you're just robbing these people." Papa would tell us that he was never going to have any good luck at all, behaving like that. Still and all, my uncle got to be a very wealthy man and his children had lots nicer clothes than we did. He left his sons a lot of money and he had a nice smile on his face when he was laid out there.

Papa remarried about five years after my mother died. I had a wonderful stepmother, a beautiful woman, just like my own mother. Her name was Amalie, and she was a Darensbourg, too – a very distant relative, maybe a fourth cousin, which don't mean nothing. I think the Catholic Church tells you not to marry anybody like a second cousin; below that there's no restriction. She was French, too, had a French prayer-book that she used; couldn't say her prayers in English. Our French at home was a little off-beat. It wasn't the real French – more like a mixture. They still have people in New Orleans that talk the real French. Then there's Creole French, like on Ory's record of *Eh là bas*.

We all knew each other, even before she and my dad got married. I remembered her being at the funeral and me sitting on her lap. She helped out a little after Mama died. She was younger than my father. Anyway, she and Papa decided to get married. I can't remember anything about the wedding but I know she was a very wonderful woman, wasn't like a stepmother, no different from our real mother. She never made any attempt to discipline us. My father always took care of that after Mama died. He was kinda strict and I think I got more lickings than any of the others. He had a great big strap that he made – being a shoemaker – and I was always finding it and hiding it, putting it away. So he was always making a new one and saying, "This is for you." I hated that.

When it came to music, my father wanted us all to play. He didn't have good teeth in later days and I think it hurt him to play his cornet, so he didn't fool with it too much. But he'd get his harmonica and play along with us. He just loved to hear us play. He didn't want me to touch a horn until I learned my music. A lot of teachers was that way. Tio was one. They want you to learn the notes before you touched the horn.

My brother Frank played the violin. He started before I did. We had a German guy used to come to the house to give him lessons. Papa would tell me to sneak in the room and listen, so we could get two lessons for one. So I would go in, and it got so I could fool with the thing. That way the violin was my first instrument, though I didn't particularly like it to start with. Then I got to know some people that had pianos. Fooling with a piano, that's what I really liked. We had a neighbor that had a piano, so we used to go over next door and she'd give me lessons on the side. That was fun.

Now my father had a brother, Uncle Willie, that was a trombone player on the circus. He played originally on the Hagenbeck–Wallace Circus, which was one of the big circuses, and then he was on the Ringling Brothers Circus. He worked on the big top and you had to be a good musician, a helluva reader, to hold down that kind of job. He was the black sheep of the family really, just like they considered me later on. He used to like to drink and gamble, and, even worse, he never went to church! I guess I take a lot after him. He told everybody on the circus to come to the shop if they wanted their shoes fixed. That's how we all got to be good friends with John Ringling himself. He had this special railroad car and they say it was the finest private railroad car in the world. The reason why I remember it so good is that he took my dad and my brothers, Henry and Frank, and me on a visit to the car. The name of it was The Jomar and they had a big double brass bed, a kitchen, and two colored waiters that took care of the car. Naturally, they gave us all free passes for the circus. It's a funny thing but John Ringling looked a lot like my father. He was heavy-set and he had mustaches like my dad.

I was always bugging my uncle about going on a circus. My life ambition was to play on a circus parade. Circuses, to me, had the most tremendous musicians in the world. In fact they was my idols. Looking back, I don't think I would have been dedicated enough to be a musician without the idea of playing on the circus.

My uncle said I would have to learn something besides the violin or the piano. He said, "Piano or violin is out if you want to go with a circus. Only thing close to a piano on a circus is the steam calliope and that goddam thing is liable to explode." Which they did sometimes, which is why they put the calliope at the end of the circus parade. Actually the calliope wasn't nothing but a bunch of steel whistles that was pitched in tune. You could hear a calliope for miles. All the riverboats had them, and that's the way they advertised they was coming into town. I lived about two miles from the Mississippi waterfront and we could hear the calliopes right there. We'd run down to the river and watch the boats coming in.

I love to think about my days as a little boy on the levee by the Mississippi River, watching the boats and traffic moving up and down the river. It was real exciting to watch the big barges and the steamboats and stern-wheelers going up and down. We would sit there, me and the other kids, watching those boats and thinking about where they came from and hoping we'd go to some of these places some time. Another thing was the great floating palaces that had the shows and the excursion boats like the *Capitol*, the *Sydney* and the *St Paul*, owned by the Streckfus Line. They all docked at Baton Rouge and you'd know they was coming when you heard the calliope.

So I didn't want to play no damn calliope. Too loud, for one thing. The last wagon was always the calliope because it was so dangerous. That and the elephants.

Uncle Willie suggested that I play a cornet, a clarinet or one of the reed instruments. So I got a clarinet and I started fooling with it, without knowing too much about the notes. My dad wanted me to learn to read music. He couldn't read it himself but he wanted us to learn right. Frank was supposed to go to Boston Conservatory and he started to go, but then he changed his mind. Papa had bought him a fiddle for 300 dollars, which in those days was a fabulous amount of money. I settled for the clarinet and I started taking lessons from Manuel Roque. I was about ten years old. There must have been a dozen kids played the clarinet, some of them even had two clarinets. In Baton Rouge almost every kid tried to play an instrument, it was the way of life. People would hear me practicing, they'd hear my brother practicing: in a small town like that everybody knew what was happening with everybody.

My dad paid ten dollars for an old Albert system clarinet that he bought from my teacher. That was my first clarinet. Then after that, seeing I was going to learn, he bought me a new one, a C. G. Conn, for 25 dollars. That was an Albert system, too. In fact I didn't change to Boehm until 1950, when I was playing with Kid Ory.

It seems like I learned pretty fast, and once in a while my teacher would let me play along with him in his band. They would play dances at my school. We had a Catholic school and they had a little auditorium where the band would come and play. After I got to play well enough he would let me play along with them. Roque himself also played the C-melody saxophone. I hated to practice. But every time I went to put the horn down I'd think, "Better learn how to play if you want to be on that circus. Time is getting later than you think." God knows, I needed something like that.

We played music around school, too. Holy Family Academy was the name of the school. They had a big convent in New Orleans and schools all over Louisiana. I had one teacher there, her name was Sister Thomas, and had she lived I think I would have been a helluva lot better musician. She was a good musician herself, played piano. She would teach by sight and give us the tone. With her I was getting so I could read the notes by sight and sing them. I'd have had perfect pitch if I'd kept that up. You got so you could identify the sound, that is if you had any talent. As you read it, she'd write it up on the blackboard. I guess she seen I did have a little talent, so she'd keep me sometimes after school, with my clarinet, and talk to me. That was when I became really interested. If I could have went from there, I might have been an arranger. She was a wonderful teacher. We had Sister Thomas for about a year, but she was such a fine teacher they would want to spread her around. That way she'd teach one year in Baton Rouge, and then they'd send her to Lafayette, and so on. Consequently we got very little of her teaching. That was one of the bad things about Catholic schools to my idea. They would transfer those teachers back and forth; they didn't have too many good ones so they kinda spread them around. Some of the nuns from my school would even work at the leper colony at Carville. That's the only leprosy colony in the USA.

That year with Sister Thomas was the only time I can remember that I liked to go to school. Really, I hated school; I just didn't like all the book stuff. All I wanted to do was learn that damn clarinet so I could leave home. My dad always said, "As soon as you learn how to play good, I'll let you go with your uncle."

I went to Catholic school all my life, except for the last two years, when I went to public school. I had two years of high school up to the tenth grade. I always had good teachers but I don't think the nuns was as good as the public-school teachers, but they did have a certain amount of discipline.

About this time I was the head altar boy at the church. My job was to prepare the altar for the priest and our deal was to go in on a Saturday night and get it ready for Sunday morning mass. I had a cousin named Jerome, he tried to play clarinet too, and he'd help me. We'd go in the sanctuary where they kept that wine and fill the little decanters. The wine was in a big barrel, and for a long time we wouldn't touch that wine, because they said it was blessed and we'd be committing a mortal sin. Then some guy said the wine wasn't blessed until the priest got it up there at the altar and then blessed and drank it. So we said, "Lord have mercy, we have been missing something here for sure!" So me and Jerome started taking a little nip, and it was delightful tasting stuff. When the priest, Father Slater, came in there about seven o'clock on the Saturday night, the two of us was laid out like pieces of linoleum, sicker than a dog, drunker than a hooting owl. Boy, did we get a licking from Father Slater, and when I got home I got another one. This was about the time I was getting out of the eighth grade and I was going to get a little gold medal and a certificate. It was Sister Thomas that went to bat for us and she kept them from expelling us. That's the first time I got drunk – in church!

When I was about 11 or 12 years old I'd go visit an aunt that lived in New Orleans. This was every summer. Somehow Papa talked Alphonse Picou into giving me lessons when I went to New Orleans. See, Picou would come to Baton Rouge once in a while with Papa Celestin's band. Every time he came to do a parade he'd talk to my dad and come and have a few beers. Picou wasn't really interested in teaching me; it was just a favor to my dad. Usually he would never teach anybody; he never wanted to be bothered. He liked his juice, you know. He always had a bunch of women around him. Never had much time for me, but he'd give me a lesson whenever he could get away from them broads that he was going with. He had a lot of money at one time. Picou lived not far from one of my cousins. He had several children. The first time I went there he told me to come back. He said, "I can't see you right now, you come back here later on this afternoon." He had some woman in the room. I think I had about half a dozen lessons from him. He'd pick up the clarinet and show me, or show me in a book, but I never really learned much from him. The guy that really taught me was Manuel Roque. He was a bricklayer in Baton Rouge and quite a fair musician himself.

New Orleans was a jumping city then. Always has been a seaport, and then there was all those boats that came down the Mississippi River, big ocean liners, ships from all over the world. Oil tankers used to come up as far as Baton Rouge and pick up oil from the Standard Oil refineries. All the big ferry boats coming from as far as St Louis or Memphis, they'd come right by Baton Rouge to go to New Orleans, which was the last port before you hit the Gulf.

I didn't play with any bands there in New Orleans, but we used to have parties where we played. There wasn't no big musicians there, just other kids that was coming up but who never made it as pros. I was too young to go in the cabarets and those places. Picou never would take me in. I heard some bands at a club that the Creole guys had called the Autocrat Club, which is still going in New Orleans.

A little later on I met all the great guys, or heard them at one time or another at Perseverance Hall or marching down the street in a parade. All the guys used to rehearse at the hall. It was a little old dance hall and they had a gallery around it; actually it was a porch, but down in Louisiana they call that a gallery. They'd sit out there, blowing their horns, and you could hear them all over the place. I'd go over there because I just loved to listen to them play. They was also so nice to me. I never knew them too well because I was so young, but I was there every day. I met Joe Oliver, Sam Morgan, every last one of them. They all used to come there. I heard all the guys that was around then, like Tio, Big Eye Louis Nelson and Willie Humphrey. And they had a clarinet player named George Baquet that was a helluva musician. I hadn't heard Jimmie Noone at that time. Later on, when I heard Jimmie, he was the one. If I could say any clarinet player influenced me, it was Jimmie. More so than Johnny Dodds or any of those others. But, you know, I didn't never want to copy anybody. I listened to them but I wanted to develop my own style.

Hell, every day you walk out on the street in New Orleans you're liable to see two or three bands at one time or another.

My sister used to crochet and knit yokes that women wore over their nightgowns. This was to make extra money. Me and my brother would go down to the red-light district in Baton Rouge and we'd love to go selling these yokes to the prostitutes. They'd be sitting out there without hardly any clothes on, and, even as kids, we kinda enjoyed these scenes. We sold those yokes for two dollars and my sister would give us a quarter. My dad didn't know about this because he would have been pretty mad if he'd known us kids were going down to the red-light district. The district consisted only of three blocks around Carruthers Street and Palmer Street, known as Red Stick Alley. Papa did some work for all them whores. On top of that they'd come by and try to trade some pussy for some shoe-work, too. He would say, "I couldn't handle all of that. I can't buy no leather with that kind of stuff." And we knew what he was talking about.

Thinking about New Orleans in those days, one of the great things when I was a kid was the French Opera. They brought the big shows over from France and the great musicians, too. Some stayed on and had such a great effect on the music that came later. A lot of the old French musicians taught the slaves how to play.

On the other side, there was a regular circuit for colored actors known as TOBA, which meant the Theater Owners' Booking Association. So many things happened on this damn circuit they nicknamed it "Tough on Black Artists." The guys wouldn't be paid because the promoters ran off with the money. They had some of your top stars on those shows. The Lyric Theater in New Orleans was probably the best house they played down South. They had a good band in there led by a left-hand violin player named John Robichaux. One of the features of this band was a terrific little drummer named Happy Bolton. He was the forerunner of all your trick drummers. They called them trap drummers in those days. He used to juggle the sticks and he was first drummer I seen use a blank pistol that he'd shoot in time. And he'd jump around and run all over the theater, beating on chairs and doing all these acrobatic things on the drums. I remember when I first seen his act on *Tiger Rag*. He'd take the drum off the stand and imitate that tiger roar by blowing into the back of the drums where those snares are. He was a good part of the show and people would go to the Lyric just to see him juggle. All your great performers, such as Ethel Waters, Mamie Smith, Bessie Smith, Ma Rainey, the big minstrel shows like the Georgia Smart Set, and comedians like Pigmeat Markham, they all came there.

New Orleans was a great place for those funeral parades, and down there they had some horses at the Geddes and Moss Funeral Home that used to cry. Yes, crying horses! People had to have these crying horses: cost you ten dollars extra. They had this brother in front with a great big towel, wiping their eyes out. As the horses would cry, he would just wipe their eyes. And this went on until somebody discovered this guy had a couple of onions cut up in the towel. The more he'd wipe their eyes, the more they'd cry. That's how it was done. He got away with it for about 20 years before they discovered what he was doing. I think he died and they found they didn't have no crying horses any more.

Geddes and Moss undertaking parlor had a sign which was a picture of a great big eye. Whoever set that eye up was a genius. Wherever you would look, from any angle across the street, the way it was focussed, that eye would be looking at you. You could never duck that eye. The caption underneath said "We'll get you in the end."

Now the bands that I was hearing in those days in New Orleans didn't classify styles. Everybody was playing ragtime, as they called it then. They didn't call it dixieland or anything like that. Ragtime wasn't a matter of certain tunes, like some people think; you played anything. We had a lot of waltzes in those days. At a dance every third number was a waltz. Now if you play a waltz, people look at you real funny and wonder what the hell you're doing. They don't know how waltzes was a very important part of ragtime. One of the first tunes I remember was *Over the Waves*, which was originally a waltz. Then there was *Listen to the Mocking Bird*. Didn't have to be *Muskrat Ramble* or *Fidgety Feet*.

Some bands had solos, but mostly you didn't see guys laying out. In other words, if a guy was playing a solo, the other musicians was playing right along with him. Not like these bands where each man plays a solo; no, they play something behind it. You might see a band with two trumpets, maybe a cornet and a trumpet, maybe a saxophone, before they got organized. Most of the bands had a banjo and some of them had a violin to play the lead and start off a waltz. String bass was always there and sometimes they'd have a guitar and a banjo. They didn't have pianos. Then I remember Piron's band. His was the first band in New Orleans that used sections. He came up with three saxophones.

Every little town in Louisiana had some kind of band. There was a good band in Alexandria led by a left-hand violin player named John Tonkin, and there was the Banner Band out of New Iberia that had Evan Thomas, a trumpet player. He was out of this world, great! He made a trumpet sound like a violin. I played with him later on. They also had a left-hand trumpet player named Victor Spencer who was very good. I played with him later in the twenties. There was another band in Lafayette and the Martel Band out of Opelousas. I worked with them, too. And they had the Black Eagles out of Crowley, that was one of the best.

Donaldsonville was where the Claiborne Williams band came from. They didn't play any jazz but it was a great band. All young kids. Williams was a fine teacher and he used to take these kids and turn them into one of the best marching bands in Louisiana, maybe 30 or 40 pieces. This was one of your top bands. Every year in Baton Rouge we had a fireman's parade, and Claiborne would bring his band from Donaldsonville, which is across the river from Baton Rouge, just for that parade. Claiborne was a good musician himself and he taught a lot of musicians. He has a son, Claiborne Williams, Jr, plays piano and lives right here in Los Angeles. These marching bands would come to Baton Rouge all the time. That was the music I heard even before I went to New Orleans. We had no kid marching bands, no school bands of our own in Baton Rouge, and I never played in a marching band.

Even in a small town like Baton Rouge, you always had a lot of music. Two or three times a week you seen a funeral parade. If a cat amounted to anything or if he had any quality about him, he had a band playing at his funeral. You'd see those bands in any part of town. They had those lodges like the Oddfellows that was affiliated with each other. If a prominent brother would cut out, they might have two marching bands for his funeral parade. They had a marching band in Baton Rouge led by Charlie Vidal. He was a violin player, a concert violinist really. His dad was a dentist and he had a brother that was a dentist, too. They sent Charlie to the Boston Conservatory to study music. He became a teacher and a bricklayer by trade. Oh yes, he could play. He would never leave Louisiana, though. They had a cemetery right at the end of North Boulevard, about eight blocks from my house. The undertaking parlor was close to my house so they'd all start from there. I couldn't hardly miss them because they passed right in front of my house. They would go maybe two miles to the cemetery and it look like it would take them three hours to do it. The one tune they would play was *Nearer my God to Thee*, with the drums beating "boom, boom, boom." Everybody marching, just like that, with the horses right along with them. Needless to say we kids would make a second line and follow the parade all the way. That's according to what kind of band was playing. A lot of good musicians came from New Orleans to work in these jobs, like Buddy Petit and even Freddie Keppard. Then Papa Celestin's band would come there, that Tuxedo band. He was in Baton Rouge all the time. Anytime they had a big parade, he'd bring the Tuxedo band there. I would notice the difference between the Tuxedo band and the local bands, because in the first place they would march regularly. These other bands, they would only march sometimes, and when they played a funeral they always added a few pieces. Those funeral bands would be eight or ten pieces, so they'd put somebody extra on there. But the Tuxedo was precisely known as a marching band, and a good band. I remember LSU would have their big marching band in these parades and Papa Celestin would cut them to ribbons. The first time I seen Louis, he was with the Tuxedo band. This was before I even knew who he was. You could hear that damn cornet two blocks away – I never heard a cornet like it. I'll never forget it. That's one of the things that really made me want to be a musician, hearing a sound like that. What a man!

They had about three jazz bands in Baton Rouge itself. There was Toots Johnson's band, another led by a trombone player named Gistain and another by a tenor saxophone player named Tody Harris. Gistain was very good but Tody didn't play a damn. He had played saxophone in Toots's band, but then he got a band of his own musicians. He was a promoter really. The best known band, and the best for jazz, was Toots Johnson. He was every bit as good as any of the bands in New Orleans, and that goes for Papa Celestin and all of them. He just had a good band with good guys. Toots was the first band that started using saxophones, with the old Tody Harris on tenor saxophone. People used to say that Toots was the only guy in the band that couldn't read music. He was a great big fat guy, a good natured guy, strumming his banjo. He kept his band going for years.

Toots used to work all the time. He had a lot of jobs and he played almost every night. He'd go down to New Orleans and hold his own, too. Toots could play with any of them. The other bands was only fair. They mostly played for dances and once in a while they'd get together and play for a funeral parade. But they wasn't in the class of Toots. Toots had a helluva clarinet player named Art Green. I know he couldn't read music. He was a real dark, heavy-set fellow, and I don't know where he came from, but I never heard a guy that could play clarinet like him. I remember I used to watch his fingers all the time. He'd pass in front of the house and I'd say, "How come your fingers ain't moving, clarinet player?" Ain't that a dumb question? Anyway, Green used to come to my dad's shop and get his shoes fixed. Sometimes he'd have his clarinet with him and Papa would talk him into taking it out and then he'd play it. And Papa would play his cornet and then I'd go get my clarinet and try to play right along with them. Green could play *Tiger Rag* and things like that like nobody's business. He was the one guy that made me say, "I'm really gonna learn to play that clarinet." He was the greatest of them all, in my eyes. Green played with Toots for a while and then Toots had another guy named Isidore Fritz who was very good. He was a bricklayer. A lot of those musicians was bricklayers and carpenters, trades like that.

Fritz was another that came to my father's shop, and he'd play as well. He was one helluva clarinet player, but today you never hear nothing about him. He was a keen family man and a lot of them guys wouldn't leave home for nothing, for no kind of money. I think he's supposed to have come from some other little town, but I know he had been living in New Orleans. My teacher Manuel Roque had come from New Orleans, too. That's the way a lot of these good musicians came to Baton Rouge – by way of New Orleans. And these guys seemed to kinda like me. Later on, when I was 14, I went on jobs with Toots. These guys were so nice to me. Musicians would come from New Orleans and play for Toots because he made good money. You had more competition in New Orleans, so they came to Baton Rouge and worked with Toots, and I used to hear them say they was making 30 or 40 dollars a week. That was when you could get a suit of clothes for two dollars, and a room for a dollar a week.

Buddy Petit came to live in Baton Rouge. He was hired to play with Toots. He was a likeable guy, always half-loaded, but he could handle his liquor. Really he drank an awful lot. Most of the musicians did, for that matter. Buddy was a little guy, had a white mark on his lip where you could see he'd hold his horn. He played so pretty, always melodic. He played tunes like *Sister Kate, St Louis Blues, No, No, Nora* and *Panama Rag*. If he was living today, he would be in the style of Bobby Hackett; he wasn't a powerhouse like Sam Morgan. Louis said he was the sweetest trumpeter that ever was. Buddy was in a class of his own. For some particular reason he used to like me. He would get little jobs on the side on his night off and he'd come and ask my dad, "Can Joe play?" To pick me out like that, when there must have been a half a dozen other kids to choose from, that told me I was better than the rest of them. Hell, I was just a kid taking lessons. Papa always had a bottle handy for when Buddy would come round. My dad wasn't a big drinking man himself, not for hard liquor, but he had wine all the time, just like a Frenchman. But he'd take a little nip with Buddy once in a while.

When I'd go out with Buddy or Toots I got paid maybe a dollar and a half, and then I'd have to spend all that money on drinks for them. They'd always say, "Well, you young guys, we old men show you things, buy us a little drink." So when I got home I didn't have a nickel left; spent it all on them.

And Buddy was the one that encouraged me to sit in with Toots's band. He must have stayed in Baton Rouge about three or four years before he went back to New Orleans. He always had some broads, some whores, making money for him on the side in the District. I heard that Buddy came to California later, but he didn't stay around here too long: just turned around and went back to Louisiana. A lot of musicians are like that, they miss that food and everything. Of course, the average musician that left when Storyville closed didn't have much choice if they wanted to play music; they didn't have nothing to go back to.

Buddy never did record that I know. He died fairly young, too. When he left Toots's band, Guy Kelly, who was just a young kid at the time, replaced him. Guy was born in Baton Rouge and he was just a little bit older than me, but he was so much bigger than me and so much ahead of me in music – so much ahead of anybody, for that matter. He's another guy that was outstanding. Even when he was young he sounded a lot like Louis; he could play closer to Louis than anybody I ever heard. Guy mimicked Louis in every kind of way. Naturally, Louis left an influence on every trumpet player after they heard him once. I guarantee that every kid that had an ear for music knew all about guys like Louis Armstrong and exactly what they was doing.

Guy was in high school when I was in grade school and I think he'd have been one of the greatest trumpet players if he'd lived. I think he left Baton Rouge around '26, after I left, and I think he was playing around Chicago in '28. He didn't make too many records, I know that. He was born in Scotland, that's a suburb of Baton Rouge, where Southern University is now. He would sit down and play at the drop of a hat. Just like me, he always had his horn with him. He was a drinking man, no question; he'd always drink a lot. He sat in with me and my brother. We'd play deals at schools and different things. But he died young, in 1940.

After Guy, Toots had Kid Dimes, another good trumpet player, remind you of something of Alvin Alcorn, on that style, and Kid Shots Madison played trumpet around Baton Rouge for a while. They were from New Orleans, too. Then they had another good trumpet player in town named Spider, but I don't remember his last name. All of these different musicians worked with Toots at one time or another.

I'll try to give you an idea of just how good Toots's band was. Whenever LSU played Tulane University, Tulane would bring their big marching band with them. They was the inter-sectional rivals. LSU would have their band, too, and they'd have a big rally down-town. Somebody set up Toots's band this one time to advertise some kind of dance. When LSU got through playing people would be there watching old Toots, and sometimes he'd break in there and just start playing. When he did that, the people would leave the LSU and Tulane bands just stood there playing and go over and listen to Toots. He had a one-eyed guy singing, using one of those big horns like megaphones. He'd be singing up a breeze on *Sister Kate* or one of those tunes. When those guys were playing the blues it sounded better to me than other bands. That's why I say black musicians was so supreme, because they outplayed one hundred LSU musicians.

There was always a great rivalry between the musicians of Baton Rouge and New Orleans. New Orleans is a big city and its people would try to look down on us small-town guys, call us country folk. When the top bands came up Toots would be ready for them. I remember when Kid Ory used to bring his band to town to play in a place called Bernard Hall. Toots would be waiting for him outside the saloon next to Jim Bernard's restaurant, and while Ory's men were in the saloon Toots figured to slip his wagon in there. They had a guy who used to "lock the wheels," and he took a big heavy chain, drove the wagon right alongside and locked the two wagons together. The idea was, whoever you was playing against, if they figured they couldn't outplay you they would light out and run away, so when Ory came out he couldn't leave because them wheels was locked. All hell would break loose. Old Tram, that's Toots's trombonist, he hated Ory and Ory hated Tram, so they'd just hook up there and fight. Tram used to call Ory "that goddamned yeller sonofabitch." I think Ory had worked for Toots one time and I know that he had taken one of Tram's gals, so that's why they was rivals there. As trombone players, they was about equal.

Buddy Petit and Art Green was playing for Toots that day, along with Tram, and a club-footed piano player named Lawrence Martin. He was good, and they had a guy named Booster on drums. He used to sing and do all them funny things on the drums. He had things he'd blow into, and whistles, all that stuff. Those guys could wail, and that day Ory couldn't leave because them wheels was locked. I know Ed Garland was with Ory and it could have been Johnny Dodds, Baby Dodds or King Oliver there, too. The result was, Toots run Ory's band out of town that day. That's the first battle of music as I remember. These cutting contests started right there on the street, to see who was best. One would roll up besides the other one and they'd start blasting at each other. This band would play a tune then the other would reply.

Incidentally, Ory was another of the musicians who used to come to Papa's shop to get his shoes fixed. That's how I first came to know Ory.

Toots Johnson was a promoter, too. He'd promote all these dances, exactly like New Orleans but on a smaller scale. Whenever they played to ballyhoo a dance they'd usually rent a furniture wagon. Furniture stores in those days had flat bed wagons drawn by horses, and they would put banners on the side telling where the band was going to play. They'd rent that wagon for about an hour and the sign would say the dance was being held at Bernard Hall. Toots and them would start touring town. They'd stop in front of every saloon, play a tune, and the people would bring some beer out. It was a regular dixieland band, had a piano on it, tailgate trombone, everything. Just like them early bands in New Orleans. Only thing, they called it ragtime then. Needless to say, we kids followed those wagons all over Baton Rouge to listen to them play. I guess that was the beginning of the second line, although we didn't call it that at the time.

When they played the dance old Toots and his band would be in a band uniform. A lot of those bands had uniforms, it was all according to how many pieces they used. As to how they lined up on the stand, Toots would be on the left, then the clarinet, which would be Green or Manuel Roque, then sometimes they'd have two saxophones, while the trombone and trumpet would sit together with the bass in the back. If they could spread out, the reeds would sit on the end and the drums would be in the center. When the bands wanted to play soft, the bandleader would holler that he wanted to hear the people's feet shuffling on the dance floor. And when they'd get ready to close you stomp off and hit it. The nearest thing on records would be that Preservation Hall Jazz Band or the early George Lewis band. It was very, very primitive, though.

About this time it just became a natural thing to form our own band. I guess we started that band when my brother Frank was about 14 and I was 12. Jazz was in our mind from the go, because we patterned ourselves after Toots Johnson and those others that we heard. We had some other friends, slightly older, that joined us. Our drummer's name was Edmond Hebert and then he had a brother that played a banjo. This guy was probably the worst banjo player that ever lived, but he was in this band. His name was Stanley. We called him Sugar Dude and this cat could only play in one key. Now me and my brother played in all the keys, and when we played something in the key of C, we'd let him play. We tried to learn a lot of tunes in C so as to let him play. We rehearsed the band in a little room in the back of my brother Henry's shoe shop on Government Street.

That was the combo, just four of us. We also had a good bass player that we used, although he didn't play with us all the time. His name was Skeets and he played real good guitar, too. In fact he played a helluva lot better than Sugar Dude. We had a pretty good little band.

The first time where we actually made money was at a little lawn party. Some people had a birthday party for a kid. When we played for the church, we did it for nothing. People would hire us for christenings. The Italians were great for that: they'd give us a dollar apiece, sometimes two dollars. Then we'd play little house parties and school dances, usually making about 50 cents or a dollar. We'd try whatever was popular in those days, songs like *Margie*, or go back further than that to tunes like *Over the Waves* and *Golden Slipper*, or to a few of those spirituals that had been around a long time. Naturally, we included *When the saints go marching in*. If it was a current tune of the day, we'd play it. We'd do *Tiger Rag* and all those things. I remember the first time we played *Who's sorry now*, which was one of the great tunes of that time. This was in 1923. It was originally a waltz and that's how we used to play it at first. I told my brother, he was the leader, "Let's jazz it up a little. D'you think we can do that?" We were playing at a party, so we started playing it in foxtrot time. It look like from the very first it went good, and right until today it's one of my favorite songs.

By the time I was 14 I could play good, and we started to do pretty well around Baton Rouge. Buddy Petit came round a couple of times and sat in with our band.

Of course, Frank put his violin down later and concentrated on his shoe shop. Anyway, we thought we was the greatest musicians in the world. Cousin Truell the great jazz violinist, he used to sit in with us, too, and he give us a lot of encouragement.

Across the street from Papa's shoe shop was a saloon run by Joe Abrahams, and next to the saloon was a restaurant called Jim Bernard's. That was the headquarters for all of the musicians. That's where they went to eat, so any time you wanted to see any of them, it was between Jim Bernard's and the saloon next door.

Some of the specialties at Jim Bernard's would make your mouth water. You'd get oyster loaves and chicken loaves. An oyster loaf is made out of oysters fried in deep fat on a large loaf of French bread, a little over a foot long. This was 50 cents or, for a half loaf, 25 cents, all prepared with pickles and ketchup. Or you could get a chicken loaf for a dollar, with a whole chicken in it and a loaf of French bread. Then you could get a great big plate of red beans and rice, with ham skins for seasoning, all for a nickel – with all the bread you could eat. Louis always said that without red beans and rice there wouldn't be any Louisiana people, because there wouldn't have been anything else to eat.

You ever eaten possum and sweet potatoes? That was a great delicacy in Louisiana. This Jim Bernard was a resourceful guy, so he figured out a clever idea to tell people whenever he got a couple of possum. He rigged up a steam whistle on top of his place, like a train, and when he had possum and sweet potatoes he'd give it three toots. Everybody in Baton Rouge got so that they knew that whistle, and when they heard it guys would be running from every part of town. I think it sold for 15 cents and that was a high-price meal in those days.

In this restaurant they had a real belligerent cook called Crackshot. He was always getting into fights with the customers. This particular day, some guy that had worked with him in the sawmill across the river came in and ordered a plate of red beans and rice. Crackshot gave him the order with a piece of ham skin in it, and the guy asked Crackshot for another piece of ham skin because he was hungry. Crackshot says, "I'm giving you what you supposed to have and I ain't giving you any more." One word led to another, so Crackshot got mad and hit him on the head with one of those big iron skillets. The guy pulled out a .45, they called them "Saturday Night Harrisons" in those days, and he put it right up there to Crackshot's head and blasted him. The bullet must have been kinda defective because it went only part way into Crackshot's skull. There was a quarter of an inch hanging out. Naturally, this knocked Crackshot down and he hit the floor saying, "Lord, have mercy, my head's hurtin'."

Somebody ran down to get Dr Murray. He had a little office right down the block. So he jumped into the horse and buggy he rode around in. He was always running down there for Crackshot because of the fights, but this was serious.

This time he saw Crackshot sitting on the floor shaking his head, and he wanted to know what the hell was going on. Doc Murray was quite a character himself. He says, "You ain't got no damn sense. I told you this was going to happen, you're always getting into arguments with these people. How do you feel anyway?" Crackshot says, "My head is hurtin'. I gotta headache." Doc Murray pulled out his eyeglasses and looks down and says, "This is the most unusual thing I ever seen. I never seen a guy with a head so hard. I know you had a hard head but I thought at least a bullet would penetrate it. I'll give you a couple of aspirins and set you up on a chair."

So they set Crackshot up on a chair and some guy hollers, "Why don't you get a pair of pliers and pull that bullet out?" Doc says, "Crackshot ain't got no brains as it is. If I pull that bullet out, the little brain he's got will probably fall out all over the floor." And he just kept repeating that, and then he asked for a piece of sandpaper. Somebody went and got some sandpaper and Doc Murray started to level that bullet off. In the meantime it had stopped bleeding. It looked like a silver dime, like a little headlight up there right in the middle of his forehead. And then Crackshot says, "I feel pretty good now. Anybody got a looking glass to let me see how this thing look?" Somebody gets a mirror and he looked and he says, "Hey, Doc, I'm glad you didn't pull this thing out. Anyway, can I shine it up?" They got some polish and shined it up. Crackshot fixed the Doc some oyster loaf for his trouble and started on cooking again. Proudest thing in the world, that bullet stickin' half out of his head. He just left it there and eventually he had it monogrammed "C. S." for Crackshot. No kidding. That was the biggest conversation piece in Baton Rouge. That gives you an idea of the type of town I came from.

Every Sunday morning, after the excursion boat came in from New Orleans, they'd have some kind of celebration at Bernard Hall, right around the corner from my house. That's where Charlie Vidal was playing. All the musicians would go there and play. Papa would take his horn and play with them. He didn't want it to be known too much because he thought Mama would kill him. And I'd play, too.

Another man I played with was Tody Harris. I remember we played a big prom at LSU and a couple of little parties around there. He had a big book with saxophone parts. I think he had Sammy, a girl piano player, and either Buddy Petit or Guy Kelly. Bernard Hall was the top dance hall, just about two blocks from my house, and then they had a place called Catfish Town and another they called the Trash Pile. The minstrel shows would come to Bernard Hall and so would the TOBA deals. Like I remember they had a show called Billy Mack's Merrymakers, out of New Orleans. A lot of New Orleans musicians worked for them. Old Billy Mack was May Mack's husband and the comedian of the show. She used to sing. All of these shows had little side novelty acts, and they had a guy called Strawberry Russell that played a one-string violin using a bow – and he played the hell out of it, too. Billy Mack heard me practicing and he tried to talk my dad into letting me go on the show. My dad said, "No, Billy, no chance. He's too little for one of those rough minstrel shows."

Then I remember Ma Rainey. The first time I heard her was when she came to Baton Rouge on Ed Lee's minstrel show. Lee was one of the few colored guys that owned a minstrel show. They came out of Alexandria, Louisiana. You had to have a little money to own one of those shows. You had to have a railroad car, all the equipment and the big canvas tent. Ma Rainey came in with that show. Later I seen her when she was singing on a show. I also seen Mamie Smith, Bessie Smith, every last one of them. I heard Ethel Waters when I was a young musician. She came around a little later. She was the prettiest woman you ever seen.

They had the big production companies, like the Georgia Smart Set which carried maybe 40 people, and for those days that was a helluva show. J. Holmer Tutt and Salem Whitney was the two guys that owned that show. They had comedians like Butterbeans and Susie, people that would be big-time actors today. They'd come down to Baton Rouge and then go on the TOBA and play the big places in the East – New York and the rest.

They didn't have a music director at Bernard Hall. These shows would come in there and bring their own men. Some would have just three pieces, some would come in with a piano player and a saxophone player, some with a piano player and a drummer. Some didn't even have a piano – just a bass and guitar, or a banjo.

One musician I do remember around the shows was Johnny Sturdivant. I later run into him in California, where he was a prominent saxophone player; he wasn't a big name when I first knew him.

Like I said before, I wanted nothing more than to be around a circus. From the moment I was born I wanted to play on a circus. Actually I didn't so much want to be a musician when I was a kid as I wanted to be a performer. If only we'd had someone to teach us, I'd probably have been a big-time circus performer instead of a lousy clarinet player. These days the kids can go to the school they have in Florida where they teach them to be performers. We didn't have that but we used to have a little show of our own. We'd make trapezes and Frank used to walk the tightrope wire. I got so I was a pretty good acrobat on the trapeze. Cousin Jerome used to ride in a circle on a bicycle, and I would pretend that he was one of the big circus horses and jump up on his back and on to his shoulders.

One time we decided to build our own circus tent out of gunny sacks. We had an Italian grocery store next to our house owned by a guy named Joe Romana, and he gave us some empty wooden barrels that used to have lard in. As it was kinda cold, we started a fire in the backyard to warm this tent up. Now lard is inflammable as hell, and it's almost like setting a match to gasoline. Anyway, the tent caught fire like to set the whole damn neighborhood alight. So that ended our circus careers for the time being.

The circuses always managed to come to Baton Rouge in the fall, like in September and October, just about the time they was ready to go into winter quarters. Circuses didn't travel in the wintertime. If you're playing under canvas, you don't travel when it's cold or when it would rain a lot. I'd start asking Papa in the middle of summer, when were the circuses coming. He knew all of them. See, he loved circuses as much as we did. There was Dan Rice's circus, for instance. He was the greatest clown in the world at that time. He got paid a thousand dollars a week and had played with all the biggest circuses. Then he formed his own circus. He brought it to Baton Rouge by boat.

The circus grounds was only about six blocks away from my house. All the big circus parades went past our shoe shop. I specially remember Ringling Brothers & Barnum & Bailey's Circus, because they had one of the greatest circus bands. That was P. G. Lowery's band. He was a concert cornetist and that's the guy I admired. Usually the black musicians only played in the sideshow, but P. G. Lowery was the exception. His was the only black band that every played in the Hippodrome. He was a part of the main circus – the big spectacle, in other words. He used all black musicians most of the time. I met up with him much later on in Seattle and he was still playing pretty good. The last time I seen P. G. I was working with a black piano player out of Chicago named Oscar Holden that knew him and some of the guys that played on the circus. P. G. was a virtuoso and a good one.

The night before the circus came to town we kids couldn't go to sleep. We'd make all kinds of arrangements. I lived closest to the railroad yard in Baton Rouge. North Boulevard, the street I lived on, if you took it straight ahead you passed by the Governor's Mansion and then if you went on about eight blocks you were right at the railroad station and the railroad yards, on the Mississippi River. That's where the circuses came in. They had their own trains.

Our house was right on the street and I would sleep in the front room. The bedroom in the house was right next to the shoe shop. Some of my cousins that lived far away in the country would come spend the night, so we'd sleep maybe three or four of us in that one room. We'd tie a string around one of the toes, and this kid that lived furthest away, his mother would have an alarm clock and she'd wake him up and tell him, "Now, hurry up. Don't forget to go in and pull that string and wake Doty and them up." Doty was my nickname then. So he'd come by and pull that string about four or five o'clock in the morning. That's when the circuses got into town to unload, before daybreak, just before the sun was coming up, because they didn't want to unload all those big wagons in the dark.

So we'd light out to that railroad station and watch them unload. I just loved that. In those days the big circuses would travel on flat cars with the wagons on top of the cars. They had great big beautiful draught horses to pull the wagons. It was all manually done. The circus is mechanized now and they use tractors or trucks to pull the wagons; you don't see the horses now and you don't have the big circus parades like we had. That's what I liked. They say, once you been on a circus you never forget it.

I'd be there, watching the circus guys work, hanging around the horses or bringing water to the elephants so as to get a pass for the show. We got to know Floto; he was a colored guy that was one of the roustabouts on the circus, a stake-driver. The circuses used to compete every year as to who had the greatest stake-driving team. That was an art in itself. You'd put six or seven guys on one stake, and one after the other the stakes would go in. It was the goddamnedest rhythm. And the team that could drive it the fastest and the most accurate, they would win the prize.

It was always my idea to get away from home. I wasn't thinking only of Baton Rouge: I had higher ideas than that. In fact I ran off from home even before I could play, just to be on the circus. I was about 12 or 13 years old. I was working around there as a roustabout, all the way clear to California. The particular circus

I wanted to play on was the Al G. Barnes Circus. This was because it was a predominantly wild-animal circus. I loved to be around animals. Their winter quarters were in Los Angeles and at the time they had the biggest elephant in the world. This elephant was called Tusko and he could throw a rock like a guy pitches a baseball. Anyway, the story goes that somebody annoyed Tusko, and when this guy started running away Tusko picked up a rock. The guy thought he'd duck down the side of a tent but Tusko pitched that rock and put a little English on it. Tusko curled it around the side of the tent and flattened him. That's true, so don't do nothing to Tusko!

Naturally, my dad had me come back home as soon as he found out where I'd gone. Soon after I ran off again, this time with my cousin Jerome.

When I was 16 I ran off from home again and went back to Los Angeles. I was still strong-minded about being in show business so I ran away to California, partly to catch up with the circus again and just to come to California. I got ready to leave, had my stuff all fixed up, and I caught the Santa Fe train one night at 11 o'clock. I just slipped out of the house – to come to join the circus. I knew where every circus had their winter quarters in Los Angeles. The Al G. Barnes Circus had theirs at Culver City.

Papa always used to send for me but this time I got stuck. I had run off before and he got sick of that. He said, "You make it back the best you can." I started staying with my Aunt Nana, the one that lived to be a hundred. One of my cousins had a bicycle, so I looked through the ads in the paper, where it seemed the Federal Telegraph Company in down-town Los Angeles wanted some messenger boys to deliver telegrams. So I said to myself, "Hell, I don't want to go back, I'll stay with my aunt." She was feeding me and everything.

And I had a girl that came to Los Angeles, too, that was a little side deal. Her name was Mabel and she came here for a visit because she had some people here. Her people hated me, but that's another story. Her father was a big contractor in Baton Rouge, and he told Mabel I was going to be nothing but a lousy musician all my life and would never be able to support her. One day she told me, "Mama and Papa don't think you're going to be anything but a musician; you don't want to fix shoes, you just want to play music. They say if you was a bricklayer or something, it would be different." So I said, "Shit, I'll learn the goddam bricklayer's trade." I had a cousin named Theodore Darensbourg, he was learning to be a bricklayer, and I had another distant cousin named Tony de Quiere who was a big contractor, so I asked him about learning the bricklayer's trade.

This was before I ran off from home. I had all kinds of jobs in Los Angeles. One of my first jobs was washing dishes. I got hungry and I went into this restaurant and ate a big meal. I couldn't pay for it so the owner says I gotta wash the dishes or go to jail. I go back there in the kitchen and it was just my luck that the cook was from New Orleans and that he knew my people from Baton Rouge. He even knew Papa. After that he just loaded me up with food. And I stayed around there getting my money and I didn't do hardly any work at all.

Another time I worked in a factory as a pattern-maker, making patterns for pleating skirts, and then I worked in a pressing shop. I knew how to press clothes from a guy that had a pressing shop next to my older brother Henry's shop in

Baton Rouge. This Mr Cotton taught me how to use a steam machine, so I got into that for a while.

Los Angeles was a small town at that time. Ory was around there working then; I remember he was working in a small club on Central Avenue. I played with a couple of Mexican bands around there. My cousin knew this Mexican guy, so I brought my clarinet and played around with them. It was just little church socials. They didn't know anything about jazz.

Then I had another cousin named Joe Darensbourg who came to Los Angeles. He was my first cousin and his mother's name was Aunt Lo-Lo. He had heard about the glamor of California. He came from a little town named Maringouin, Louisiana. Had a good jazz band there, all of them little towns had bands. Both of us was working at this place, making patterns for pleating skirts, and the next thing Joe was disappointed with Los Angeles and he wanted to go home. By that time I was kinda sick of Los Angeles, too, and I wanted to come on back home. I had been there about six months.

In the meantime the authorities had got after the circuses and said not to hire any kids on a circus without strict permission. If you were under age, they couldn't use you. I went out to the winter quarters but it was out of the question. I never worked.

During that time *Shuffle Along*, the great musical comedy, came to Los Angeles. I went backstage and asked them for a job, to play. I talked to the old Man Tan Moreland, the comedian that was on the show. He says, "You're too young. Besides, we don't use white boys on this show; this is a colored show." He told me that. I said, "How do you know I'm a white boy?" He says, "You look white. Get the hell out of here. You can't play anyway." I was kinda cheeky all right. I had to be.

Papa wouldn't help me to get home. He wanted to teach me a lesson. But cousin Joe was going back anyway, so he says, "I'm getting my ticket and I'm leaving." Now I had went to the Traveler's Aid Society one time and they said, "We can't give you a ticket outright but we'll give you a ticket for half-price." Charity rates, they call it. My cousin don't know nothing about this, so when he says he's gonna buy a ticket, a bell rang. So we go up to the TAS and I says, "Now, we'll get two tickets on your money. Don't tell the people you got any more money; you tell them you're broke." Joe was a little older than me and he was tight with a buck. He wanted me to promise that my father would pay him the money. So I said, "Joe, you ought to be glad to do this. Didn't Papa teach you the shoemaker's trade?" He says, "Yeah, but that's a lot of money." He couldn't figure that out, but we got two tickets, got on the train and went on back to Baton Rouge.

When I got back Papa said, "I see you don't want to go back to school, so come and work in the shoe shop." I was nearly 17 by then, so I started back to work in the shop. In the meantime me and Frank was still playing around there with our little band. That's when me and Mabel got together and I started this damn bricklaying. My cousin Tony had me working for a dollar a day. You don't start out laying bricks, that would be too easy: you're carrying mortar or making nails out of lumber, everything else but bricklaying. See, these contractors are going to get all the labor out of you for nothing before they teach you. You could learn actually laying bricks in two or three months, but they wouldn't allow that.

Anyway, when I got through fooling with them goddam bricks I was too tired to go see Mabel. All along my cousin Theodore was making time with her, and just about when I learned to lay bricks pretty good she announced her engagement to him. Her people beat it into her. She really still loved me, so I said to hell with it.

I got my clarinet for *real* then.

TWO

Doc Moon could sell an icebox to an Eskimo

In the meantime everything looked like it just fit into place, like my whole life was being laid out. We started getting more band jobs and taking out-of-town deals at colorful little towns like Bayou Sarah, or we'd play along the Mississippi River. Sometimes the people would hire a boat, pull out of the docks at Baton Rouge, and we'd play for their little excursions. It was still the same cats in the band: Sugar Dude, Edmond and Skeets. They was all white boys – well, their father was white and their mother was colored.

Then, when I was about 17 years old, my brother got a job for us to go and play for a Knights of Columbus convention in Opelousas, Louisiana. It was one of those things that went on for three days. The job came through one of the nuns that taught at my school. The Knights of Columbus is a big Catholic organization. The Catholic religion is very liberal and the Knights had clubrooms in the various cities where you could go and shoot pool, drink and every other thing. We had our no-good banjo player Sugar Dude, Edmond on drums, and me and my brother. I think we took Skeets with us, too. When we got there the people wanted a bigger band than that. We asked around to see who was there. We couldn't find a trombone player and we didn't have no trumpet player in Baton Rouge that could play anything.

They had a family orchestra over there called the Martel Orchestra, which was working three or four days a week in that part of the country. Frank knew about them, and, before we even left Baton Rouge, I think he called Dayton Martel and asked them, would they play with us as we needed two extra pieces. They was playing the convention along with us and another band. Our jobs was in the daytime and the Martels was playing for the dances at night. We hired Bert and Dayton Martel, one playing trumpet and the other trombone. The whole Martel family came to hear our band, and as old man Martel needed a clarinet player he asked me to sit in with them that night. I think he also used Frank, but not Sugar Dude or Edmond. So we played with them for the dance. Along with Bert and Dayton they had the daughter Hillary, who was playing a banjo, and Willard, who also played a banjo. I think Hillary did play a piano and I know Willard sometimes played drums. A brother named Chesley played bass, and their father, old man Albert Martel, who was the leader, he played a B flat soprano sax.

After he heard me play the old man asked me to stay on and play with the band. He didn't want Frank. I played a couple of jobs and then I went back home. I talked to my dad and he said, "I guess it's all right with me if you want to go. You'll probably run off and do it anyway if I tell you, no, so go ahead." So I went back there and I started playing with the Martels' band. Who was in the band playing with them, but Manuel Manetta and Barney's brother, Alex Bigard. That's the last time I seen Alex. Otherwise it was a real family band. They played quite a few jobs. Manuel and Alex only stayed there for about two or three weeks but I was with them for about a year. They had a pretty good little band.

Darn right, they was playing jazz. None of them was outstanding musicians but old man Martel was damn good on that soprano. They might have been better if they'd left there, but they was like some others that didn't ever want to leave home. A lot of these young guys won't leave home, or they're afraid to leave the security of home. But that was the furthest thing from my mind. I wanted to get the hell out of that place and as quick as I could.

They was playing *Tiger Rag*, *Sister Kate* and all those tunes. I didn't play any saxophone with the Martels, just clarinet. We never wore no uniforms, we just dressed ordinary: all of those bands, they had the same pattern. The only guy in the group that fooled with any music was the old man. He'd get a lead sheet, a piano copy – ordered it from New Orleans – and transpose it. Then he'd write out a part in B flat for soprano saxophone, and, between him and his son Bert, they'd alternate on the lead. We had a full band but no piano. That is, none of the kids could really play piano so they figured to have Manuel. Same with drums. The youngest son was too small to play drums well – that's why they added Alex. About two months in all and he and Manuel was gone. Perhaps the old man couldn't afford to pay them the money they wanted. And then this other kid, Mills was his name, he started to play drums. None of them ever got that good, although maybe they could have if they'd had the incentive like I had. I wanted to get going.

Working with the Martels was considered a good job. I was making 25 dollars a week during that time, when it was considered a lot of money – more like 300 dollars now. This was in 1923. I heard a lot of bands while I was staying in Opelousas. They used to come there to play for dances once a week and I would go sit in with them. Bunk Johnson played in Opelousas. He was living in New Iberia then, along with Evan Thomas and them. There was a dance hall in Lafayette that they all came to, but mostly we heard them in Opelousas. I remember the Blue Devils, out of Plaquemine, another band called the Black Devils and a band out of Crowley called the Black Eagle Band. The first time I met Victor Spencer the trumpet player, he was with the Black Devils, and I think he played with the Banner, too. The personnels of these bands changed quite a bit; the guys went around. Like Evan Thomas, they got him with the Banner Band but he had his own band. I heard him several times. He drank like a fish; all of them was big drinkers. First time I heard Evan it was in Opelousas, the next time it was in Lafayette. That's where Bunk and a lot of the bands from New Orleans would come and play. Their transportation was usually two Ford cars. During that time old Bunk could kinda play some. He knew old man Martel very well but never worked with the band as far as I know.

About the time I first went to Opelousas Papa had a stroke and he was partially paralyzed on his left side. After he got sick my oldest brother Henry closed the shoe shop he had on Government Street in Baton Rouge and took over my father's shop. Papa then moved into one of his houses, but later on he improved so much that he got able to work part of the time. But in 1925 he died. He was about 54. At the time I came back for the funeral Henry was still in Baton Rouge, but Frank, who had been working in the shoe shop with my dad, had married a girl in New Orleans and was living there. The rest of the family was intact. After the funeral they knew I was going to go. They knew all the time what I wanted to do; I had been attempting to run away from home all that time and they knew why. We had all that property but I wasn't bothered with that. I used to tell the kids in school that I was learning to play clarinet so that I could play on a circus. We idolized circus musicians; we thought they were so damn great. Papa understood that and he always used to drill it in my head about practicing. I would have done anything to get out of Baton Rouge and play on a circus. I'd have maybe committed murder if that was the way. Papa used to say, "Go ahead, do whatever you want to do." He just loved music and was for anybody that could do anything in the entertainment world. He always wanted to know their stories, especially if they had been to California. If mother had not got sick he would probably have come to California. He always looked ahead more than I did. I didn't think about the money angle to playing music. I wanted to learn to play to get on the circus and travel. I would have went for nothing, but my father knew that if you was a good musician you would always be able to make a living.

A lot of performers wouldn't ever have any money so my dad would fix their shoes on credit. Leadbelly was one of the guys that used to come to the shop. He was in prison down there in Angola, Louisiana, on the outskirts of Baton Rouge. They wore stripes then, and they had them out on road gangs with the ball and chain on their legs. Another old musician that my dad knew was Buddy Bolden, who was in the insane asylum at Jackson, up north of Baton Rouge. My dad would go up there and get shoes and then bring them back. Jackson was one of the places we played when we had our little band. I don't know if he fixed shoes for the prisoners, but he did for the officials and the keepers. He knew about Buddy Bolden and that he was a good musician at one time. He always talked about the crazy musician up at the insane asylum.

Alton Redd, the drummer that was with Kid Ory, used to live right round the corner from my house in Baton Rouge. I remember his mother and him coming in to have their shoes fixed. Papa was a soft touch, and entertainers would get a free pair of rubber heels in exchange for their stories. Even so, he always said that one of the worst things in the world was credit. He had a big, thick book called his credit ledger, and he said that he lost many friends because he gave them credit. They wouldn't pay him, so they'd take their shoes to a worse shoemaker. That way everybody lost out. He'd say, "If you can help it, don't give credit." I've always remembered that.

Right after the funeral I went back to Opelousas, on account of playing music with the Martels, and I also went to work in Chapman's Shoe Shop for 25 dollars a week. Good money!

Hillary Martel was about ten years older than I was, and way before Papa died she took a liking to me, so we start fiddling around there. Anyway, she got pregnant. That was a helluva thing when you got a girl pregnant in those days. I called my dad and he says, "You got her that way, you just marry her, that's all." Anyway, the whole family knew the situation and they knew I wasn't in love with her. See, she was older than me and she literally came and got in bed with me. She had a little money and she bought me a watch and things like that. We got married but we didn't stay together. She had the kid and he's near 60 now. I still hear from him now and then. His name is Joe Darensbourg, too, and he lives in Cincinnati. He fiddled around with guitar and he had a lot of talent. He'd have been a great guitar player if he'd kept it up.

After I left the band we separated. We never got divorced. Right after that I heard Hillary got killed in an automobile accident going to a job. The boy lived with his grandparents for a while, and then he went to New Orleans and lived with my sister and then he lived with Frank. In the meantime I was traveling and I never heard from him. I guess I didn't see him again until about 1950. He lived with me for a while and that's when I got him the guitar. Got him a job, too. He worked and fooled around here, but he never did play professionally.

The Martels were Creoles, nice people. It was an understanding that the main reason for getting married was to give the kid a name. Hillary knew it, too. She said, "I know you don't love me and you won't stay." My wife Helen understands. She knows little Joe. It was just one of those things.

Back in the Martels' band we was playing a lot of these small towns, places like New Iberia and Lafayette. One time we played a dance hall in Ville Platte when it was illegal to sell liquor. They would bring a big coffeepot on the stand with some coffee cups and people would think we was drinking coffee when really we was drinking liquor. Called it "Mountain Dew" or "White Lightning." It was about 200 degrees proof. You could really get loaded.

You got some old Frenchmen in those little Louisiana towns like Ville Platte who think all the French people in France migrated there from Louisiana. That's true. There's a place called Plaisance where they got the prettiest people in the world. It's all intermarriage, with guys marrying their first cousins and all that kinda stuff. Everybody's related. It's not that big a town, perhaps a couple of thousand people, so if a person dies everybody goes to the funeral. I went there and played one time. They got a language of their own they talk down there, just like in Ville Platte, New Iberia, Big Mamou and Little Mamou, where they talk French all the time.

During this time *It ain't gonna rain no more* was a heck of a popular tune. We used to have to play it about seven or eight times a night. By some kind of coincidence they had a big drought in Louisiana. This was in the summertime and it didn't rain for two or three months. We'd have to drive on dirt roads and the dust would be six inches deep. The crops was dying and the cotton was dying, so, being superstitious, the Louisiana people thought a song like *It ain't gonna rain no more* was causing the drought. They got the idea of passing a law, and believe it or not, it was made illegal to play that tune. Several times musicians and bands got put in jail when they got caught playing that tune.

Opelousas was a very small town, with 10,000 population or maybe less. The main industry at that time was Standard Oil. A lot of people out there raised cotton, and, in order to get some cotton picked without paying for it, they would have these cotton-picking parties. They'd have lots of eats and drinks and we'd play a little. They'd invite fellows to come out there to one of these small cotton farms, but mostly they didn't do much cotton picking because we'd start out down the cotton row with a girl and wind up in the bushes most of the time – if you know what I mean. We'd pick a little cotton and do a lot of loving.

Like I said, the Martels played in Ville Platte every week at this one dance hall they had there. One time we was gonna play the day afterwards but we went there the day before, and that's the day I witnessed a public hanging. I never want to see anything like that again. It was a white man; his name was Pierre Vidrine and he had killed a whole flock of guys all over Louisiana. His victims was mostly cab drivers. He'd get a taxi-cab, say he wanted to go someplace, get the guy out of town and shoot him in the back of the head. He was from Ville Platte, all his family lived there. Anyway, he was back in Ville Platte, and just about that time the sheriff's son had bought a new automobile and gone out driving down one of the country roads. They found him dead in the car. Naturally, they started a big man-hunt to find out who killed him, and this Vidrine, who was really the killer, joined the posse. Of course, he had changed his clothes, but the tracks was still alive and the bloodhounds led them right back to Vidrine's house. After the killing he went back home and pulled off his clothes and hid them somewhere in the house. When the dogs found the clothes the people couldn't bring themselves to believe that Pierre Vidrine was the killer. But after all the facts was found they knew it was him, so they had nothing to do but arrest him. They tried and convicted him and the sheriff gave permission to have a public hanging. I guess the sheriff wanted everyone to see the man that killed his son. Even so, it was pretty unusual, because when I was a kid in Baton Rouge my school was across from the penitentiary on Florida Street and that's where every other hanging in Louisiana took place.

They built the gallows right across the street from the dance hall. The guy that owned the dance hall said, in order to get a ringside seat, we could climb on top of the building. That way we could look right over and see everything. Consequently, everybody that could climb up there got up on this roof. It was full of people before the hanging. I've played in circuses and carnivals but I never seen anything like that before or since. It was just like a big victory celebration, like after World War I. They had guys selling balloons and hot dog stands and souvenirs. See, they had allowed Vidrine to write a book while he was in jail to help pay the lawyer's bills and that was on sale, too. They was selling tags with Vidrine's name on them and little ropes with hangman's knots in them. It was a carnival atmosphere.

It made me sick the rest of the day to see him dropping through the trapdoor and hanging there, just swinging. It looked like it took him five minutes to die. Doctor walked up and put a stethoscope to his heart. When they cut him down they had him laid out there so you could see his face. His face was black and his tongue was hanging out. Yet the people was there with their kids on their shoulders so they could see it better. I know I'll never forget it.

Some of those southern people are the cruellest people in the world. One of the things they would do was to block off a road when a band was traveling home. They never did stop the Martels because old man Martel was a kinda tough character, but they'd make the black bands stop and have them play until they felt like letting them leave. Usually there'd be nothing but one little old dirt road to get out of town, so you was trapped. I remember another musician telling me about a band which had played a dance, got through about one o'clock in the morning, and the crackers got them on the outskirts of town. They seen this bunch of lights and a circle of cars, and these guys stopped the band, made them take out their instruments and play right out there on the road for nothing. It happened to me one time when I was with a white band out of Memphis when we was in Mississippi. Makes you ashamed to be white.

Not only that: some of those little places, a long time ago, they had what they called "laughin' barrels," especially for black guys, Indians or poor Mexicans, if they had any around there. You'd be walking around one of these towns and probably somebody made a remark or seen something funny, enough to make you want to laugh real loud. You had to go stick your head in the barrel and mute that sound. That way you wouldn't disturb anyone. They had these barrels where there was houses around, and they'd be lined with felt or moss. If you were 40 or 50 feet from that barrel, you better hold off that laugh until you could get in there and dive head-first into it and start laughing. They had them all down South, and I talked to some musicians that said they had to use them. This was just done to black guys to show them who was boss. Those people was bastards. You had more good white people than you had bad, otherwise there wouldn't have been a black man alive, but some of them would kill colored people for the fun of it. You ask where the term "alligator bait" comes from, and that's where they'd cut the eyes out and use them as bait. All kinds of cruel things.

One time, when Frank and I had our band, we went to play in Shreveport and we saw all these people standing on a dirt road, out of town, and we wondered what it was. Turned out they had lynched a colored guy, put a big chain around his neck and drug him around town, right past a colored school. Doesn't that sicken you?

Rogers's Sunshine Minstrels was out of a little town called Florence, Alabama, and in those days minstrel shows was one of your great attractions, especially in the smaller towns. I wanted to get on this goddam show because I was after one of the little chicks in the chorus line. See, all of these shows had eight to ten chorus girls, just like a musical comedy. This was when I was working around Oppelousas, and I quit the shoe shop to go with Rogers. I know this was only for a short time but all this is kinda hazy now.

Herman Grimes the great trumpet player was the bandleader, and he's the only big-time musician that I remember from the Minstrels. He was one of your top trumpet players, one of your real powerhouse men, and later played with Duke Ellington. I ran into him again in Seattle and played with him in a small combo for a long time. This was after he had been with Duke. He was capable of playing with anybody. A great big guy. He knew his music. I don't know where he was from but he was very knowledgeable. All of these bands had top musicians that could read music and knew everything about leading a band. They played get-off solos, too. Sure, they also had some guys in the band that couldn't read.

I met one of the musicians and he tried to get me on the show. Mr Rogers says, "I don't want this guy on the show. I don't want no white guys." A lot of people want to pass for white but I had to try to pass for colored to get on this damn show. Anyway, I got over that.

The tent was set up just like a theater. They had a stage and the musicians played in a pit. Outside you did about a 30-minute concert in front of the tent before the show started. Anyway, I'm sitting down there playing and pretty soon something hit me in the back of the neck. They had these guys in the audience using sling-shots; used to call them "nigger-shooters," and a lot of times them guys would come with rocks and shoot them at you. They had a guy on the show, a white fellow, used to sell hard candy, and when he found out what the audience were doing with his candy he started saying, "All right, here's some candy for you to shoot the musicians." That was a helluva deal, never knowing when somebody would hit you in the back of the neck. After four days on the show I told Grimes, who was leading the band, "Why do you guys put up with this shit, man? Why don't you do something about it?" So Grimes went after old man Rogers and they made some little shields to go behind your necks. He was the first one to do that.

One time we was playing at a little place in either Mississippi or Tennessee. All of them was the same as far as rules go. We was living in a place where you could cook, and Sundays was usually chicken day. They had markets there, so the guys went and picked up a chicken for dinner. They happened to pick out a white chicken. It seemed to me the guy that sold it to them should have told them, or they should have known better and put that damn chicken in a sack where nobody could see it. They passed in front of a fire station where some white firemen was sitting outside. They called them over, "Where you going with that chicken, boy?" It's a wonder that Herman Grimes didn't hit one of them and really go to jail. Instead he said, "We gonna cook him and have him for dinner." The firemen said, "No, not this white chicken. You take him back down and get a black one. You boys ain't gonna eat no white chicken." They did all kind of crazy things then.

That was Grimes and he was with Trombone Red, a real good trombone player from Durham, North Carolina. He was one of the first guys I ever seen do what they called "echo trombone." We would be playing a concert in a town square and he would walk across the street. The band would make a certain passage and Red would answer them, make the same thing, like an echo. They had a whole bunch of tunes they just used to feature a trombone on, classics like *Lassus Trombone*. That was really a show-off instrument, and Trombone Red was very good.

They must have had two dozen minstrel shows in those days, and they was always coming through Oppelousas. Neil O'Brian was one, another was Honey Melody, also Al G. Fields – that was the white minstrels that did blackface, which, needless to say, didn't compare with the natural black actors. The exception to black actors doing blackface was the team of Moran and Mack, called the Two Black Crows. Now they was funny guys. I've seen them. Amos and Andy started out as Sam and Henry in Chicago; that was their original name. Then I remember the funny black comedians like Strawberry Russell, Butterbeans and Susie, Sweet Papa Snowball, Sugarfoot Green from New Orleans and Silas Green from New Orleans. They had Lee's Minstrels, out of Alexandria, Louisiana, and I once played on their show while they was in town. Then there was the Florida Blossom Minstrels out of Florida, and the Georgia Smart Set which Andy Blakeney played on.

The shows all used to have street parades on the day they came into town. You would have the band parading and some of the performers marching with them. They didn't have wagons like a regular circus. The street drummers were a show on their own and the greatest of them was Manzie Campbell, who was with the Florida Blossom Minstrels. He was the first street drummer that I ever seen juggle sticks while he was marching. I think he had been with our show at one time.

You had this railroad car you traveled in, and it had sleepers on there. You carried all your equipment in one part of the car and the entertainers stayed in the other part. It was a special railroad car that you hooked on to a train to pull it. You'd go off on to a siding; that was all taken care of in advance, and from there is where your parade started. You got off the cars in the morning and you had to parade to the town square. Most of these small towns in the South had a town square, and you would have a concert advertising the attractions. You'd walk a mile – you always had nice uniforms – and you'd parade down the street playing with people following you.

Pretty often we'd date another show. Two of the minstrel shows would be playing the same day, in the same town or maybe five miles apart, and that always called for a carnival party – get-acquainted day. The show lasted from eight to ten or maybe 10.30, and every one of these towns had some bootlegging joints. That's where you'd hear Ma Rainey or some of the other entertainers do some singing. Everybody would have a full-time jam session after the show. You'd get drunk and sing and play and every other thing. Ma Rainey was really going down then. She was on the Florida Blossom Minstrels, and then I used to see her on Ed Lee's and Rogers's shows. I think Chippie Hill played on some of those shows. Most entertainers are nice people, otherwise they wouldn't be entertainers. They like a good time. I know Chippie liked her liquor, just like Bessie Smith and Mamie Smith and all the rest of them. I met Bessie Smith, too, in Alabama, back at one of those TOBA shows. They tell me she was a pretty good drinker. It's true she drank all the time.

People in those small towns, the only time they ever heard any music or got any entertainment was when those minstrel shows or a medicine show, a circus or a carnival came through.

About this time I borrowed a saxophone from this barber friend of mine. We was at a house one Sunday fooling around and he was playing this C-melody sax and I asked him, could I play it. Saxophones was something more-or-less new then. When I was a kid, saxophone was a novelty; you didn't see many of them. The first saxophone I remember was this guy Tody, that played with Toots Johnson, slap-tonguing on his damn tenor. I guess he thought that was the way it should be played. In fact I had fiddled around with a saxophone before, because my teacher Manuel Roque played C-melody back in Baton Rouge.

I started playing saxophone around town at the little bootlegging joints after I got off from work. There was always places where guys would meet and where they had a piano. The guys would congregate and play a little music. This one night I wasn't working with the Martels, and Doc Moon's Medicine Show had come to town. After the show was finished I was drinking with some musicians from Doc Moon's show. I had the C-melody saxophone with me and soon we was having a little session. In comes this guitar player named Big Boy, which was a pretty good guitar player, and some other guy that was singing with them called

Blue Coat. I can't remember what Blue Coat did, if he played an instrument. Anyway, he didn't stay with the show too long. We had a little jam session and I pulled out this saxophone. Big Boy says, "Hey, man, you play good. I didn't think I'd find somebody who could play as good as you in this jerkwater town. Would you like to go with the show?"

The next day I was back working in the shoe shop and Doc Moon came to see me, along with Big Boy. The owner of Chapman's Shoe Shop was a Jewish fellow and he gave me the run of the shop. In fact this guy almost cried when I left, no kidding. He says, "Joe, I want you to stay here." Like he was going to make me a partner in the business. I was the best shoemaker he ever had, but I told him, "No, Mr Chapman, this ain't for me." Doc wanted me to go with the show as a saxophone player and I had to tell him, "I don't have a saxophone." He said he'd buy me one. I asked him where the show was going and he told me they was eventually going to St Louis. Medicine shows didn't play in the big cities proper but mostly in the smaller towns. They was working their way up through Louisiana, Arkansas, up into Missouri, on to Illinois, and then we were supposed to play Gary, Indiana, on the outskirts of Chicago. I had a couple of pupils that I was teaching clarinet and I got in touch with them to tell them I was leaving. They was little boys then. They cried, "Oh, Joe, who's gonna teach us?" One of them was Lionel Gill and he turned out to be a pretty good saxophone player. Later on he came to Los Angeles.

I had known of Doc Moon's Medicine Show before, because the headquarters was in Baton Rouge. I used to see the show all the time. A medicine show was a big thing in those days. You didn't have much entertainment then. Maybe you'd go to a moving picture but you didn't have radio. If you wanted to listen to music then it was on the phonograph. But to hear live music on the stage . . .. They didn't have a music store in Oppelousas that had a saxophone, but Lafayette, which was about 20 miles away, was the show's next stop and they had a store there which had a saxophone. On the show we had a comedian and another guy that played a clarinet, can't remember his name, along with Big Boy on guitar and another comedian named Stave. We was playing with two clarinets until we got to Lafayette and went to the music store. The only saxophone they had was a nickel-plated Conn E flat alto, and Doc Moon put up the money to buy it for me. It cost about 125 dollars and I was supposed to pay him back two dollars per week out of my salary, which was 25 dollars a week. So that's how I started playing saxophone full-time. Kind of an accident really. Hell, I never had a lesson on the saxophone. I stayed with Doc Moon for only about four or five months and I never did pay him for that alto. It's long gone now.

Moon's was one of the biggest medicine shows touring the USA at that time and was a great attraction. Doc Moon was practically a millionaire himself from selling that medicine. Doc was white and he wasn't a doctor – none of these guys was doctors – he just had a good line in bullshit. We had a great big bus, cost 30,000 dollars then, like a big railroad car with sleeping quarters; more like a house on wheels. It was special made, the size of a Greyhound bus. It had a medicine room with vats where we mixed up and bottled the stuff. On the back of the bus was a stage or platform, like the observation platform on railroad cars, where we would stand and play; it had a little railing around it.

When we hit a little town, this is what would happen. We'd put out signs on the street corners telling them where we were going to play and then go round the town advertising the show. We'd have a banner on the side of the bus giving the location of the empty lot where we was gonna set up. "FREE MEDICINE SHOW: Moon's Medicine Show will give a performance starting at eight o'clock at . . ." such and such a location. Then we'd strike up the band; ballyhoo, they called it. Had two clarinets at first, with Big Boy on guitar and some gal singing with us for a while. Had a banjo and guitar player, and a bass. This was a class act for that time. Soon as you start playing in those little old towns, you got a zillion people coming out there watching. Doc Moon would make a speech telling them where the show was gonna be and we'd proceed over to the lot. We put up our portable platform, no top over it. This was a first-class deal with a big stage, about the size of a room. Then we had these gas lights that you pump up and light.

Doc Moon would get up there and start his spiel. The thing that got those country people was that he'd say, "Look, I want you people to know that I'm not doing this to make money. I'm here because I love you people and I want to heal your suffering. I love you all." He'd go on through his story about loving people and wanting to cure them until he'd say, "If you think I'm here to make money off you, then I want you to get the hell off this lot right now. I don't need your money. I got money to throw away. Here . . . ." He always had a handful of change, three or four dollars in nickels and dimes, and he'd just throw it all out into the audience. The people, seeing this money, they about killed each other trying to get hold of it. That part of the psychology would get these people right off the bat. They'd say, "Jeez, if this guy's throwing money away like that, this medicine must be something." He'd proceed, "OK, the band will strike up a tune here and entertain us." We'd do part of the show, with the other vocalist and me doing some vocals. I had some kind of a clown suit that I put on. Then Doc Moon would talk some more.

Before the show we'd go down to town and pick up the town bum, take a bunch of bandages, take off his clothes and bandage him all up. Then we'd put him in a wheelchair and wheel him up on stage. We'd rehearsed him and told him what he's supposed to do. Paid him a dollar for it. So this guy would be shaking and trembling like he was real sick. Doc would say, "Now, to show you how this medicine works, I have a poor, unfortunate fellow here that's been sick for 40 years. Look at him. He's had gall bladder, cancer, TB, every disease you can imagine, and he hasn't walked in 20 years. If my tonic can cure him, it should cure anything. Now, we'll give him a shot of the tonic." Doc would ask the fellow how he felt and he'd say, "I feel awful, Doc, I don't think I'm going to make it," and he's shaking his head. This bum would probably win an Academy Award for acting. Some of them were so real. He'd take a big swig of the tonic and start coming to life. Often these guys would say they'd only do it if Doc put real liquor in the bottle, and Doc would do that. He'd ask the guy how he was feeling and the guy would start tearing the bandages off and shouting, "Doc, I feel great. I wanna cut a few steps." We'd light into *Tiger Rag* or *12th Street Rag* and this cat would jump up and do a dance. Then Doc says, "OK, you can see how I cured this poor soul here. Just think what Moon's Tonic can do for you. If you want to buy a bottle of this medicine, it's one dollar a bottle, and the boys will be out there ready to sell it to you." I think everybody that had a dollar would buy a bottle. You have to remember a dollar was considered a lot of money in those days, but that's the way Doc Moon became a millionaire. He was one of the biggest con men that ever lived, but he had the right bait and the gift of the gab. He could sell an icebox to an Eskimo. This didn't only appeal to colored people but right across the whole South. Near as I can figure it out, Moon's tonic consisted of about 60 percent alcohol, some tincture of green soap, which made it all-purpose so you could shave and bathe with it, and some red grenadine syrup for coloring. I think it did have some vitamins. It would take the corns off your feet and it had a strong laxative which would make your bowels move, like Louis's Swiss Kriss.

The shows lasted one hour: you got maybe 30 minutes of entertainment and 30 minutes of selling medicine. Actually medicine-show work was one of the easiest jobs in show business. You worked from eight to nine and you got all night free. And all day. The show lasted until you got to sell all that medicine. Then you're finished, long gone.

We never played directly in the big towns themselves but on the outskirts, in the suburbs. We usually stayed in a town a week and we never played on a Sunday night. When we got to a town I wasn't particular about staying on that damn bus so I'd get me a room. I couldn't bring no gals on the bus so I had to pay for a room. See, I had to have some chicks coming in to see me. On the 25 dollars I made on the show as a salary I'd get me some bottles and make up some of the medicine right there in my room. I'd get on those vats and help bottle some of that stuff. Then I'd take out some of the labels, go out in the daytime and hide a dozen bottles in the weeds around the lot. When I got through selling Moon's, I'd go sneak and get my pack and sell it as extra. When you were through you gotta say, "Sold out Doc," and hold up the money. Old Doc would be hollering, "Hey, Joe, where are you?" and I'd be out in the weeds getting my medicine to sell.

During this period with the medicine show we was in Rayne, Louisiana, a little chicken-shit town, and I got with this girl that lived out in the country. Her place didn't even have any inside toilet, just a faucet in the yard where you'd draw the water, take it inside in a bucket and heat it up. She had just moved to this house, didn't have a bit of furniture, only an old mattress on the floor. And she had a little bag of cosmetics.

Naturally, we gonna get a little high, so I pull off my clothes. It was hotter than hell in the summertime. I was trying to get in but she was just like a virgin. She's saying, "It hurts. You gonna hurt me." She used to call me Dody and her name was Dudie. So I says, "Goddam, Dudie, ain't you got no fucking grease around here, a little Vaseline, so that we can loosen that up?" She says, "No, I just moved in, the only thing I got is . . . ." She had some hairdressing stuff that girls used. This was a jig broad and she used a hair straightener called Poro, which was a big-name brand for these black gals. You had to use a hot comb with it, so undoubtedly they had lye in it, but it was greasy, so when you first put it on you didn't feel it.

So I doused myself real good and she stuck a lot round her gash. I got ready to start again and I began to feel this burning sensation. Pretty soon my dick got to smoking, it was so goddam hot. Then she says, "Lord, my pussy's on fire." Ain't no water in the house, it's out there in the front yard. Day was breaking and luckily they only had about three or four houses around there. So both of us made a bee-line for the bucket, trying to cool our ass off a little; we look like we was fighting each other to get to this bucket. Anyway, somebody from the house across the street must have seen us and they called the sheriff's office. In the meantime Dudie had grabbed the bucket and was sitting on top of it rinsing herself, while I'm trying to get her off the top so that I could get a little of that cool water, when here come the fucking cops and this old country sheriff. He says, "Somebody called up and says a bunch of you people was round here fighting. What the hell you doing out here without no clothes? You must be crazy." He's fixing to arrest us, but when I unfolded the story he starts laughing. He laughed so much he rolled on the ground. Then he says, "You guys go on inside, we ain't gonna do nothing to you. I can see you suffering enough, son, and it looks like it gonna be a while before you can handle any more pussy."

I'd just started on the medicine show when we hit this town. What a helluva way to start. This Dudie had told me, "Hey, Joe, I used to see you at those parties. I always did like you but you never paid no attention to me." Hell, I wasn't crazy about her but I seen I could get a little pussy, so I told her, "Yeah, I was always crazy about you, you was the gal for me but I didn't think you liked me." I wished I had left her alone because this Poro left me in pretty bad shape and I was out of action for about three or four weeks.

Another time the medicine show was in Centralia, Illinois, and I met a little girl named Ruby. She was only about 16 years old and her dad was an engineer on the New York Central Railroad. He went out and stayed away for two or three days, so we had to have a signal for when I'd come by her house. We was planning it for a whole week. We had it fixed for *Sleepy Time Gal*. I was to whistle this tune and she'd come out on the little gallery of the house, shimmy down a post and meet me. She lived on the second floor and they had some woman taking care of the house. I didn't know her father was in this particular night, but apparently he had got wind of his daughter fooling with one of these medicine-show fellows and he was waiting for me. When I hit *Sleepy Time Gal* that front door flew open and he rushed out of there with a baseball bat. The race was on. I had my saxophone case in my hand and, believe me, I set some world records that night.

One thing about a medicine show, you could play extra jobs. After we worked our way up through these small towns we got to St Louis and we stayed around there, just playing on the outskirts. We played across the river in a little town called Blueport, Illinois – that's outside East St Louis. We lived in St Louis itself and that's how I happened to go into Jazzland, which was Charlie Creath's club, at 22nd and Market, with the Booker T. Washington Theater on the corner. I had a room right off Market Street, which was where all the action was. That's how I started to work with Charlie Creath.

The way I got the job, I walked in there on a Sunday afternoon, met the musicians and had a couple of drinks with them. A guy said, "What you doin'?" And that was it. It was easy to get a job; they was always looking for somebody. Creath was one of the big names, I knew that. He was Zutty Singleton's brother-in-law. Zutty married Marge, Charlie's sister. I didn't get to meet Zutty at the time, but I think he had been there and just left. Charlie was a cornet player himself and every time he'd come in the place we'd have to play *Clap hands, here comes Charlie*. He never showed up until ten or 11 o'clock but whenever he came in, whatever tune we was playing, we'd have to stop right in the middle of it. He didn't play with that band, at least not often while I was there. He'd come in the club a couple of times a week and just once in a while he'd pick up his horn and play a few tunes. We used to play a Sunday matinee deal and then we'd play on Sunday nights. Did this off and on, for three or four months. Charlie was all right. We had a lot of fun during that time.

I made records with Charlie Creath in St Louis at Jazzland, I know that. This was the summer of 1925. I never heard 'em, but I remember *Spanish Shawl, Dinah, Ballin' the Jack* and an old tune that a couple of guys in the band used to sing, *Don't bring me posies*. Could have been for the Okeh label. I don't remember none of the guys now. It was just a pick-up band. These recording things would come up and you'd just go and do them. I played with so many combos, names never did mean much to me, especially when I wasn't with them that long. I know the drums didn't register in those days. I made a record with some other guy, also for Okeh, this was a singer out of a little town named Brooklyn, Illinois. I can't think of his name and it never was released. I met him when I was on the medicine show.

They had a place around the corner from the Booker T. Washington Theater where a bootlegger operated up on the second floor. He never would let you up there, but he had a little tin cup with a string on it that he would let down from his window. You had to haul it up if you wanted a drink. It was always hanging down and it had a little bell on it. That way he'd get a signal. It was a dollar for a "Mickey," that's what they called a half-pint. You usually had to bring your bottle with you and you'd put it in the cup with your dollar, pull the string and ring the bell. He'd pull it up, take the money, fill your bottle and let it back down.

During Prohibition we'd do anything to buy some liquor. You had a lot of guys bootlegging. Most of them lived out in the country. A guy, I think I'll call him Jim, had this big farm where they used to make moonshine and we'd go out there in an old open Ford, usually at night. It had to be at least three guys if you was going to buy a couple of gallons at one time. They used to have the "Revenue-ers," as they called them, Government men that was trying to catch you with liquor and put you in jail. But they had to catch you with the evidence. When this bootlegger got through with cornmeal mash that he'd used to make the whiskey itself, he'd feed it to his livestock. It made those chickens and goats drunker than hell, and after drinking this damn stuff you'd see them staggering about. Real funny: I got the biggest kick out of that. We would get back in the car, and, in order to be sure that the Revenue-ers wouldn't catch us with the evidence if they stopped us, one of us would be sitting each side of the car with a gallon jug suspended outside and a hammer in our hands. The minute you'd see a suspicious light you wouldn't take a chance, you'd just hit the jug and break it, so if the Government men stopped you they couldn't do anything because they didn't have any evidence. For this to work you had to have a dirt road. I seen guys do all this on a cement road and the Revenue-ers would have a sponge in their pockets. There'd be some liquid left on the cement and they'd stick the sponge down there and squeeze into a jar they had. All they needed was a couple of teaspoonfuls and they'd arrest you.

One of the funniest guys I ever seen in my life was called Bilo; his right name was Sam Russell. I knew him real well when he worked here in Los Angeles at the Follies Theater. I remember during Prohibition we would go around these bootlegging joints together. One night the police was about to take us to jail, but Bilo got them laughing so much they decided to turn us loose. If he was living today he'd be making a million dollars.

Hell, we had a lot of fun on the medicine show, especially when we dated another show and met the other musicians. Sometimes we'd find ourselves in a town where we'd run into Sugarfoot Green or Silas Green from New Orleans. All of them had good musicians and we'd have ourselves a session. I remember Sweet Papa Snowball, and Strawberry Russell that played a music box that he made shaped like a cello with one string on it. This guy was an artist, he'd sound like Stuff Smith or one of the great violinists.

I had some time off from Doc Moon because he had some intervals down there. That way I could get on these other shows, like the Rogers's Sunshine deal, and not have to stay too long. I'd join 'em, get off, and then get back on any time I wanted. One time like that I was on the Snap Brothers' Carnival. See, we played all these little towns on the outskirts of St Louis, one week in every location, so we did the rounds every three or four weeks. That way I'd go and work with different groups or do anything I wanted, just having a ball. I met Les Hite while the medicine show was playing in Champaign, Illinois, and we happened to go to a little club where Les was playing. He was with a piano player and a bass man, and another guy named Leon Birdsong playing a tenor sax, which was terrific. What struck me with Les was that he was playing a C-melody saxophone and he could play so well. I never seen Les no more until I run into him here in Los Angeles. Les was a gentleman, one of the nicest guys you ever want to meet.

Around about this time I had a chance to work with Fate Marable on three or four of his excursion things. These were just afternoon deals where you got on the boat at St Louis and played an excursion across to Lovejoy, Illinois, and back again. This was on the *St Paul*. We'd have a picnic over there while we played. I guess the whole excursion would last five or six hours. This would be on Sundays, on my day off from the medicine show. Fate just used to pick up guys and hire them, change them around all the time. He'd come into a place and say, "You wanna play an excursion with me, go to Lovejoy or go across the river?" Then we'd get the boat and go to Alton, Illinois, or one of those other river towns. The charge would be 25 cents with a picnic or lunch. When you worked these towns invariably someone would say, "Hey, we'd like to hear you guys play." So they'd give a party just to hire the band and give you five dollars apiece, which is like 50 dollars now. They didn't have no chance to get good musicians in these little old places. We wasn't that great, but we was better than anything they ever heard in person. Anyway, Fate Marable was a nice guy and a good piano player.

A funny incident happened when we was on the *St Paul* going across the Mississippi River one time. They had a guy played a baritone horn for Fate that had just got a set of false teeth. I think he was half-drunk, but then he got seasick and felt like he had to throw up, so he leaned against the rail of this boat, way out in the middle of the river, and those damn teeth flew out of his mouth at the same time. No sooner did his teeth fly out than he jumped over after them. Naturally, he couldn't swim. Everybody hollered, "Man overboard!" They threw him one of the lifebelts and he caught hold of it. That was the only way he didn't get drowned. And he got his teeth. See, he jumped over there so fast he got in the water the same time the teeth did and he was just lucky to grab them. The captain wanted to kill him. The Streckfus Line boats was pretty big, and this captain said, "I'm gonna see that they fire you for doing this, upsetting this whole ship just for a pair of teeth. You could have drowned." This musician says, "Hell, I just paid 60 dollars for these teeth. I wasn't fixing to lose 'em." I think they did wind up by firing the guy. It just broke people up to see things like that. Unbelievable, maybe, but this was on one of those excursions that I was playing.

Later on the medicine show moved on to Cairo, Illinois, and that's where I worked a couple of weeks with Jelly Roll Morton in a little pick-up band. What a character. He was a big gambler and a half-assed pimp, too. A bunch of broads would give him money and he'd pull that pistol on you in a minute. He had a kinda short fuse; he'd get mad quick.

Our show was playing in Cairo and I went round to listen to Jelly play. A guy said, "Hell, Jelly Roll is looking for a sax player." I can't remember who had been playing with him and I can't remember any guys in that band I played in. When Jelly went on the road he just picked up anybody, because he never paid that much. His groups in those days wasn't good at all, nothing like the Red Hot Peppers. He never believed in paying guys too much money to start with – I think I got 30 dollars for that two weeks. None of these people was good payers for that matter.

Jelly Roll had seven pieces at this time, just playing for dances at a little club over in East St Louis. He played a lot of tunes that I didn't really know, but I just faked it. I never seen any music and he wasn't playing his records. He did play some of his own tunes and things like *Ballin' the Jack*. My library wasn't too big at the time, but I know everybody played *Tiger Rag*, *Sweet Georgia Brown* and those tunes. We were supposed to have a record date but it fell through. One thing I wanted to do was to record with Morton. Jelly Roll was a helluva name in those days and he could play, yessir. At least I thought he could. He was way ahead of his time. If he'd been living today he'd be making a lot of money.

The next time I run into Jelly was in California, where I played with him a couple of times, and then in Seattle when he came there. He stayed around Seattle and Vancouver, British Columbia, quite a while. He came up there with Bill Hoy, a drummer that I knew, and Oscar Holden, a piano player. I knew Oscar, too. Jelly was doing a lot of singing and Oscar doubled on bass fiddle. Oscar says Jelly Roll would get up and do a lot of talking, then sit at the piano and play. Jelly just had three pieces and I worked with the trio sometimes. Bill Hoy says Jelly Roll had a great big old straw suitcase and a beat-up old car they traveled in. Jelly would never let that suitcase out of his sight, so they was always trying to figure what he had in it; they thought he had some liquor and didn't want to give them none. Every time they stopped he'd take the case with him out of the car. One day he happened to leave it in the car. No sooner did Jelly leave but they got it open, and Bill says all he had in there was a great big old .45 pistol and two sets of dirty drawers. That's all they found. Jelly always had a pistol with him. He did some of the weirdest things. A lot of musicians wouldn't even play with him because they were afraid they wouldn't get their money. And he died flat broke.

After he died, though, money started popping up from every place. They was looking for his heirs to pay them the money. Several times people called me to see if I knew if Jelly Roll had any heirs. I know there was a woman around here used to say she was his wife, and some guy said he was Jelly Roll's son, but I don't know what happened about that.

I got one of the last programs that Jelly did, taken off the air around 1939. They had a program in the States called "We, the People" and Johnny Wittwer knew Jelly was gonna be on and he recorded the show. He cut a disc of it and he gave me a copy. I listened to the broadcast. Jelly died not long after that in Los Angeles, and that's where he's buried. Of course, I was still in Seattle then.

The medicine show moved on to Harrisburg, Illinois, and that's where I first got acquainted with Charlie Berger. He was the leader of a bunch of gangsters called the Berger–Sheldon Gang. Like I said before, we had a lot of spare time on the medicine show and some guys was talking about a terrific piano player and banjo player they had out at the Shady Rest. This was Charlie Berger's place, a road-house about ten miles from Harrisburg, and naturally you could get liquor there. So the whole outfit from the medicine show went around there and listened. They had a combo which had this banjo/guitar player named Baker, that was on the order of Eddie Peabody, the great banjo man. Then there was a drummer called Jack Popper, and Eddie Miller the piano man was great, too. We told Charlie who we was and he said he'd like to hear us play. So we sat in and had ourselves a jam session. I said to Miller, "You sound just like a piano roll." He says, "So I should. I make 'em. I go to Chicago and I record piano rolls every once in a while."

Anyway, when we got through playing Charlie wanted to know if we'd be interested in a job working for him. It seemed like his piano player was leaving, which he did after a couple of weeks. I don't know what happened to him after that. We said, yes, and right then and there I said, "I didn't pay for this saxophone." So when I went back that night I told Doc Moon we was gonna quit the medicine show. You were supposed to give notice and I think we did give two or three days' notice. So Doc said, "You haven't paid for that saxophone." I was supposed to pay him something every week. I went back to the Shady Rest that night and told Charlie that I owed 90 dollars, and Charlie told the cashier to give me the money, just like that. I practically didn't play clarinet at all then, just alto saxophone, and it was a sax player that Charlie wanted.

So I quit the medicine show and started working at the Shady Rest. We started out with a piano player, banjo, bass and myself; four pieces. They never had any big groups in these road-houses. We played for dancing. We had a kitty where people put money in. Road-houses, that was a popular thing to do in those days. They was set up with booths and they had a little piano that you could wheel round and play at the booths. Each booth had a curtain, so that a guy could go in there with his girl and be drinking. Some of these places was pretty elaborate, like Sebastian's Cotton Club in Los Angeles, which was one of the big road-houses and had big floorshows where Louis eventually played. The Shady Rest was on a smaller scale, wasn't nearly so fancy. But they all had little combos, bands, with a bar and a dance floor. The road-houses outside of the big cities usually had shows, too.

Although it was Prohibition, they was all associated with the law and paying protection to be able to operate. They had a lot of organized gangs then that controlled prostitution and liquor traffic, dope and every other thing. Charlie's gang was located there, right outside of Harrisburg, in what they called "bloody" Williamson County. Some of the biggest gangsters in America used to come out to the Shady Rest to gamble on rooster fights and pet bulldog fights. They had gangs such as the Egan Rats out of St Louis, the Purple Gang out of Detroit and Buggsy Moran's gang from Chicago. Machine Gun Jack McGurk and all of those guys would come out there. It's where I first seen Al Capone and his brother Ralph. I was just a young kid and I didn't realize the danger that we was in. We was having a ball, working at night and helping these guys make bootleg liquor during the day. They used to make whiskey and what they call "needle" beer, which was made as a home brew then fortified with alcohol to make it stronger. Between that and making music, and the tips we made in the road-house at nights, we was making like 75 dollars a week, with room and board, which for a kid of 18 years old is a helluva salary.

The gangsters didn't usually bother anybody unless you interfered with them. You had to make an enemy of them in some kinda way. You could say that Charlie Berger was one of the nicest guys in the world and one of the most cold-blooded killers you ever seen in your life. They eventually hung him for arranging the killing of the mayor of Johnson City, Tennessee, and they pinned some other murders on him also. He was a pretty rough guy but he was always good to musicians. He was wonderful to me and I never did pay him back for that saxophone.

Then we had one of the biggest gang wars in southern Illinois. Charlie was affiliated with another gang called the Sheldon Gang which was four brothers. They had slot machines. Their joints was just like a little Las Vegas. They had a string of road-houses in Du Quoin, Carbondale and West Frankfurt, Illinois, and they always had music playing in them, along with the slot machines. So then they had this dispute over the money split on the slot machines, and, without the Sheldon brothers knowing it, Charlie sent his gang out and they took the machines out of every one of the road-houses and brought them back to his club. Maybe a hundred of them. And that's when the gang war started.

Eventually we entertainers got mixed up in this damn thing and the Sheldons took it out on us, too. The Sheldons used an airplane in a gang war for the first time. They dropped a bomb on the kitchen of the Shady Rest but luckily it only hit the back part. One time the Sheldon brothers got control of a couple of road-houses themselves and put their own gang in there. They were always on the lookout for Charlie's guys coming in, so his men dug a big trench at night, took a tanker truck full of gasoline, opened the faucets on the truck, set it on fire and let it drive down the track. They almost burned the place up, could have killed a hundred people in there.

At the time we had this nutty piano player that was telling people that he was part of Charlie's gang, until the word got out that the music was just a front and we was actually part of the gang. One night we was coming back from another of Charlie's places where we'd been working and we stopped at another road-house, at Marion, about ten miles from the Shady Rest. A white girl named Ruby, a fine entertainer round there, was singing, and we stopped off to hear her. This was when this song *Go back where you stayed last night* had just come out. Ruby moved around all the road-houses singing. The next thing you know the Sheldon Gang was out, really looking out for Charlie. Sometimes we'd ride with Charlie, and if he'd been with us they'd have killed all of us.

So when we stopped at the road-house the Sheldon guys was laying in wait for us. They actually didn't mean to kill us, just wanted to scare the hell out of us, which they did. First of all they pistol-whipped me and creased my skull with a bullet, shot me in the arm and leg and then left me for dead. They killed two of the other guys. I was just able to crawl to the car and go over to Charlie's house in Harrisburg. Charlie took me to hospital and when I got there Charlie told the doctor, "This man's been in an automobile accident," and one of the doctors – I guess he didn't know Charlie – said, "No, this man's been shot." So Charlie said, "Listen, I'm Charlie Berger and I'm telling you this man has been in an automobile accident. OK?" After that the doctor put in a report that I was in an accident. And that's how it came out in the papers.

Charlie wanted to know what had happened, although I think somebody called him anyway. He asked, did I recognize them. I said, "Yeah, I know who did most of the damage, a guy named Bill." I knew this guy, and if it wasn't for one of the Sheldons he'd have killed me. He didn't like me on account of some gal he had that I was fooling around with. Still, Blackie Sheldon used to fool around with the saxophone and I'd show him a few things, so in a way I think he liked me. It was him that said, "Don't hit the guy no more or shoot him no more, I think he's already dead." I just lay there.

Charlie asked me, did I want to get even, because he was gonna set up a trap to kill some of them. I just told Charlie, no. I wanted to get the hell away from there and forget all about it. Charlie did kill some of them afterwards. Charlie went from one extreme to another. He was kind-hearted in some ways and he loved animals. He had pet bulldogs that would fight and fighting roosters, too, but his favorite was a little pet monkey called Jacko.

In front of the road-house they had a hamburger and a hot-dog stand set up among a whole lotta trees. Jacko was kept on a long chain so that he could go up in a tree and sleep there at nights. Anyway, we found that Jacko liked home-brew, which we made ourselves, so one day we gave him a little taste and Jacko lapped this stuff up. Finally we gave him too much and we got him drunk. One of the guys had a little rubber snake in his pocket and, just for the hell of it, he threw it on the monkey. That's one thing, a monkey is deathly afraid of snakes, and poor little Jacko tried to run up a tree, but he was so damn drunk he got only halfway up before he fell back down. When he saw the snake on the ground he went into hysterics, until finally he got exhausted and passed out. We thought he was dead.

In the meantime Charlie drove up and seen what was happening. He picked up this poor little monkey like it was a little kid. The look he gave us, it made chills go through us. It took a couple of guys to keep him from killing us all; he was on the verge of giving us a pistol-whipping. It was cruel what we did to poor little Jacko. Charlie rushed him to the hospital – not a veterinary place, a real hospital. Charlie told them to take care of the monkey, and, finally, after some arguments, they took him just like they would a person and straightened Jacko out. One of Charlie's men said, "I'm telling you guys, you in trouble. You better stay here and take care of that monkey and pray that he lives. If he don't, you better go join your circus now." See, I was always talking about leaving to join the circus.

Charlie came back and said, "Goddam, how could you do this?" We tried to explain. We didn't mean any harm; Charlie used to give Jacko a little home-brew himself. So Charlie says, "If that monkey dies, I better see none of you guys. I'm gonna kill every one of you." Thank God Jacko got all right.

Another thing happened during that time at the Shady Rest which stayed with me for the rest of my life. I met a real good-looking girl and I used to go to her house once in a while. One day she invited me to dinner, and I brought my clarinet and sax case because I wanted to impress her as to what a good musician I was. So before dinner she was playing the piano and I was playing my clarinet. She asked, did I want to hear her little brother Harry play. So here comes Harry with a violin, so I told her, "Hell, I used to be a violin player, I don't care about violin." Then she said, "Would you like to hear him play clarinet? He can do something on a clarinet that not many people can do, although he's only 12." I said, OK, as I figured this little guy couldn't play a damn thing anyway. So he picks up the clarinet, starts playing a tune, and he's doing the slap-tongue. I had heard slap-tonguing done before but I had never tried to do it. I was flabbergasted and fascinated by little Harry's playing. But I was kinda embarrassed too. Anyway, when he gets through playing this girl Bessie said, "Joe, can you do that on a clarinet?" I says, "Oh, sure." She says, "Well, let's see you do it." So right away I had to make some kind of an excuse. I think I told her I had a toothache. Really I felt like breaking the clarinet over this little dude's head. I wound up walking out of the house, mad, breaking up with the girl; and, on top of that, I didn't get my dinner. But from then on I vowed that I would learn how to do the slap-tongue, although up to that time I didn't know the technique of it. I tried and tried for a year and by trial and error it finally came to me, thank the Lord.

I recuperated in the hospital for about two weeks after the shooting. I was determined to get away from the Shady Rest. I had been there about three or four months. Charlie came to the hospital and he gave me a couple of hundred dollars. Life didn't mean nothing to these guys. If you got in their way they killed you, that's all. That was a way of life with them. The thing was, nothing would ever happen to them. Charlie was a deputy sheriff and he paid out a lot of protection money.

Right there I got me a *Billboard* magazine to see the different jobs. In those days, if you could play and wanted a job, all you'd do was get *Billboard*. There was pages of jobs: medicine-show jobs, circus jobs, even boat jobs, minstrel shows, stock-company shows that played under canvas, regular road-house jobs, and bands organizing that wanted musicians. They would put the itineraries of circuses in there and I seen right way that the Al G. Barnes Circus was in Cincinnati and they was traveling on down to southern Illinois, through Arkansas and Louisiana, back up into Texas, then on to California, where they would wind up in Los Angeles sometime in October. They laid off at their winter quarters in Culver City, not far from the Cotton Club. This was where they rested the animals, repaired the wagons and trained new acts.

This was around the August of '25 and I says, that's for me. The circus was my goal in the first place but I was detoured slightly by the glamor of all that gangster money. I was going to join the circus sooner or later, but after this came up I joined it sooner. And it just happened that Louisiana was on the itinerary and the circus was due in Baton Rouge in September. Right then I wanted to go home. Anyway, I wired ahead as I seen that Al G. Barnes wanted musicians. As luck would have it, there was two guys that was playing on the circus that knew me. One was Jug Everley, who played trombone, and his nephew, also named Everley. Right away they said, "Sure, there's a place for you, Joe." But even if I didn't know them, they would hire you if you could play at all. The Everleys just went and talked to the sideshow boss and he said it was OK. Circus paid 21 dollars, room and board. For those days it was all right. Jug led the band for the sideshow, a mixed band – seems to me like we had an Indian guy playing a mellophone. Jug himself was colored. It was a lousy band, I know that.

When I joined, the circus was in Cincinnati for two days. Usually they played for one day or night in a town. Always paraded in every town.

The circus is a miracle of organization, how they move all that stuff. Ours was a big show, about 35 cars. The only bigger show was the Ringling Brothers, which had 90 cars. They had to have a three-section train. Al G. Barnes traveled in one section but they had to have two locomotives to pull it.

We'd usually arrive about daybreak. A circus could load and unload all that equipment inside of three hours. The routine was that you'd play in the parade, but we didn't literally march, we just got on the wagon. The big circus band played in the big top on a regular stage, but they also had what they called a sideshow where they had all the unusual freaks and acts. They always carried a little minstrel show, almost like the medicine show. In the Al G. Barnes circus the sideshow band was about eight or nine pieces, while the big show band would be like 20 pieces.

I wasn't with the show that long but some guys would play year in and year out. I didn't know any big-time musicians that did it but I know that people like Punch Miller played with the circus for a while. I could have probably played in the big top but those jobs wasn't always available. In the sideshow band all we had to do was play for the show. Always had a singer and a comedian, maybe two girls that would sing and dance. There'd be a master of ceremonies. After the tickets was sold the band would go out front on the stage and ballyhoo to bring the people around. Then they might bring one of the freaks out, like the three-legged man, the armless girl, the fat lady or maybe a midget. In fact I hooked up with one midget act that was in the big show. One of them fell in love with me and this other midget wanted to kill me. The little rascal challenged me to a duel. Them midgets are the worst thing in the world that you can fool with.

You start fighting a midget and let him bite you, you likely to be in trouble. They'll bite you in the wrong place, put you out of commission. That's the way they get a guy.

Then I had a row with the fat lady. I was romancing her because the fat lady made good money on the circus. She always had a lot of goodies to lay on you. They also had a beautiful armless girl on the circus, did everything with her feet. She always had a little bootleg liquor around and I saved money that way, helping her drink up her liquor.

Damn right, they was good days – being young and traveling like that! So we played on down to New Orleans, where my brother Frank and one of my sisters was living at the time. And then we went on to Baton Rouge. The circus got into town around 5 a.m. I went home first and woke them up. I had written and told them I was on the circus. I had been away two years.

It was my lifelong ambition to play on a circus parade in my home town. I used to tell my friends, "One day, I'll be on that parade." So there I was playing on a circus and parading in that beautiful circus wagon. I forgot about southern Illinois when I got back there playing for my home folks. Naturally, all the kids were watching me. They always said, "You're too dumb, you'll never be a good enough musician to play on the circus." I couldn't have been that dumb, 'cause there must have been around 50 kids trying to play music down there and I'm the only one out of the whole bunch that ever amounted to anything.

Anyway, I was playing on that circus, coming down the street there, and them kids were saying, "There's old Joe. Look at old Dody." Dody was just a nickname and a lot of people in Baton Rouge only knew me as Dody. Everybody was watching me and was I nervous. I was so excited I couldn't hardly play but I'm hamming it up and waving. I was so happy and I was getting my revenge, too. See, I wanted to make those cats eat their words. A guy named Cook was the bandleader and he said, "You'd better put that horn up there and start playing or I'll drop you off here and you'll be home for good."

Nothing compares to the thrill that I got when I joined the circus and the double-barreled thrill that I got when I was up on that wagon parading through Baton Rouge. It was cloud nine. I played with Louis, I played Carnegie Hall, in Orchestra Hall, Chicago, played at Disneyland, played in the movies, met all kinds of celebrities, but nothing will ever come close to the thrill of that circus wagon. If I'd had any sense I'd have joined the circus in the first place instead of fooling with that damn Doc Moon. That way I wouldn't have got in all that trouble.

After that we didn't have too many stops to get back to the winter quarters in Los Angeles. I would have quit right then and there in Baton Rouge, but in those days the circus would always hold back two weeks' salary in order to ensure you finished the tour. A lot of guys just get on the circus and stay a week, then they get off. That way they have to hire somebody else. So I came back to the winter quarters, quit, got paid off and went back down to Baton Rouge. That's when I played some parties. I had a friend, his name was Leonard Esanault, and he was a kinda half-assed musician. He told me that my second cousin Henry Myers, which lived in Maringouin, had a daughter that was getting married and they could use some music there. He loaned me some money 'cause I was flat broke, and him and I picked up some guys. We went and played this thing, picked up some money and then came back to Baton Rouge.

Then Tody Harris hired me to play with his band. It seemed to me that he had the best band around Baton Rouge at the time. He had a bunch of new guys then. I think he had a trumpet player named Jareau and another guy named Verrett. I'm sure Toots Johnson was dead by then but I can't remember none of his old guys working in that band, although Booster may have been with us. I recall Guy Kelly was still in town. In those days I used to drink quite a bit and I was always looking for a little nip, so I can't remember too much about all this. I'd get high with these guys, I do know that.

Looking back now, I wasn't really good enough to cut it on the circus, to read circus music. You've got to be an excellent musician. I got by, just like when I played the Pollock Brothers Circus later on in Seattle or when I played the Ice Follies. That was because I played under leaders that ignored the clinkers. They could hear them but they liked me. A guy like Tommy Thomas, who was a helluva good musician, got to hear me in the Pollock Brothers and he said that people didn't know the difference with all those animals jumping and whooping around. But I found I didn't want that type of music. I didn't like it to start with; if I had, I would have practiced more. Actually the most important thing was to be playing as a jazz musician. Doing what you want to do – that spells happiness to me.

THREE

Los Angeles was really jumping

People talk about a Creole clarinet style but I never put it that way. To me it's more a matter of feeling. The first influences I had were from clarinet players that were not classed as Creoles, although I guess my teacher Manuel Roque did have some French blood in him. One of your first jazz clarinet players, if you're thinking about Creoles, would be Picou, although as a matter of fact Louisiana was so mixed up that almost everybody called themselves Creole. No place in the world mixed up more than Louisiana as far as the races is concerned. The true Creoles was a different class of people altogether because they had their own culture and society. For instance, Creoles had dance halls like the Sans Souci Hall or the Francs Amis Hall, where everything was by invitation. Of course, I'm talking about New Orleans. A lot of those so-called Creole people couldn't stand a black person. They used to have special dances for a certain class, where all of them was of a light skin. If you showed up there without an invitation you couldn't get in that dance. But if you talking about musicians on the type of Louis, Freddie Keppard or Sam Morgan, then they played at Economy Hall and that was a different deal altogether. Anybody could get in there.

The definition of a true Creole was a mixture of French and Spanish, but how many pure mixtures there was is anybody's guess. I've seen some guys two shades blacker than your shoes call themselves Creole. Looking at my family it wasn't any different; you couldn't tell whether we had any negro blood or not. I know there's some Spanish blood in there. The mixture of white and black is the standard belief now, but the people of Louisiana was too class-conscious to go along with that then. They had so many classes that thought they was better than each other. Like those octoroons that was supposed to be one-eighth black but had blonde hair and blue eyes – prettiest people in the world. You always had a little friction between the real dark race and the light-skinned Creoles. Like in Lulu White's whorehouse, where she wasn't supposed to have nothing but pure white, yet she always had a lot of light-skinned broads working for her.

It got so that anybody that could talk that Creole stuff could call himself a Creole. The color didn't make no difference. There was a famous story about Wellman Braud and Sonny Greer when they was with Duke Ellington. Now, Braud had nice hair and he could pass for an Indian or a dark-skinned Italian, anything like that. Sonny had nappy, conked hair and it was obvious what he was. Anyway, they was in Birmingham, Alabama, and that was a hot-bed of segregation then. Braud told me the story. He says, "Hell, I'd go any place, any of them white restaurants. They didn't know what the hell I was." That was true about the whole of the South. They might have doubts about you, but they wouldn't bring it up because they might be wrong and then they'd be in a helluva fix. Never accuse a white man of having negro blood unless you want him to sue you, or make sure he ain't gonna say a damn. So Braud goes in this restaurant and he starts eating. Then he sees Sonny in the street outside looking through the plate-glass window. Sonny couldn't pass for nothing, but he comes in and sits down next to Braud, who whispers to him to get out otherwise he's gonna get lynched. But Sonny says, "If you can eat in here, I can eat in here." In the meantime, even though there wasn't hardly anybody in there, the waitresses kept passing him by, not attempting to serve him. Finally Sonny says, "Say miss, can I get a little service here?" The waitress comes over and says, "You ain't got no business in here. We don't serve colored people. You gotta go round the back to the kitchen and eat there." Sonny says, "I beg your pardon. Did you say colored? I'm not colored. I want you to know I'm Creole." The girl says, "What did you say?" Sonny repeats, "I'm Creole. Cr-e-ole." So she says, "I don't give a goddam how *old* you are, you better get the hell out of here before I call the owner." Many years later I was standing on the corner at 49th Street and Seventh Avenue in New York City with Billy Kyle and here comes Sonny, so I asked him about this story and he said, no, it was the opposite way around, that Braud got into trouble, but I knew better than that.

My oldest sister was married to a Creole guy who was a kind of loan shark in New Orleans and he'd be loaning these guys money. They wouldn't pay him back and he'd get mad and say, "Everybody in Louisiana is dumb. I've come to the conclusion that it ain't their fault because it's this damn hot weather and humidity that slows their vibrations down."

During the time when Huey Long was Governor of Louisiana, some of the so-called lily-white state legislators wanted to pass a law where they would trace everybody's family tree to find out every pure white person and classify them that way. Long gets up and he says, "Look, you better stop right now, 'cause I believe you could actually count every pure white family on your two hands. If you start digging around you gonna find a lot of them boys in the woodpile. You're gonna dig up something you don't want to hear and you don't want to see. You'll be sorry." And they forgot that idea, right off the reel. They never tried to do it.

A lot of people don't know that a colored woman could legally marry a white man back then. I knew some families that way and some guys even had two families, one with a colored wife and the other with a white woman. It wasn't legitimate to have two at the same time but they did. That's why Louisiana has so many mixtures.

The only two free people in the South was the white man and the colored woman. If a white man liked a colored woman, she could do anything she wanted to do, more so than a white woman. You wouldn't dream of a white woman fooling with a colored man. Not on the surface anyway, although a lot of shenanigans went on under the table.

When I was a kid, and even after I was grown up, nothing like this ever worried me. Some of my people had actually owned slaves but my father taught us always to be nice to everybody. I went both ways and I had a lot of cousins that never associated with me for that reason. They knew I was liable to come round there with anybody. They'd see me coming along the sidewalk and cross the street. I didn't care who it was, I'd go play with them. Race didn't mean nothing to me. Even today I know people that are on the "other side," and they say there must be six million people in America "passing" on the other side.

I went with a girl when I was in Opelousas when I was working there. Her name was Mabel Estolet and her father was one of the big judges in Opelousas. He had two families. She was a beautiful girl and you couldn't tell her from white or colored. Her mother was a fine looking woman, too. I was over at the house one day and I run into him. He would come over there and stay about two or three days with this family. He also had some children by his other wife and they'd pass on the street and not know each other. I would be in there and he'd say, "I know you, you play music around here. You be sure and be nice to Mabel."

The judge had a son named Lincoln. That sonofabitch was the worst bastard you ever seen in your life, always getting into trouble; he'd beat up on white guys and the cops would arrest him and take him before his father. The judge would say, "Send him home." Isn't that ridiculous? One of the most dangerous things any colored guy could do was to fool with certain colored girls that was going with a sheriff or some high police official. Sometimes the girl wouldn't tell you and you'd be walking down the street and the cops would come and beat up on you, put you in jail, anything. All this because the important guy that was going with this girl would tell the cops to get you. And they would do it. Now if a colored guy was going to fool with a white girl he'd know what would happen, so they gonna duck around in the dark. They'd make sure that nobody caught them.

I almost got caught in a few of these things myself. When I was with one of the minstrel shows I was in a house in Greenville, Mississippi, and it turns out this woman was going with a sheriff. I should have known better but I'd had a few drinks. Anyway, I'm sitting there and we hear all this noise outside. In comes this sheriff with four or five other drunks. Lucky we wasn't in bed, 'cause otherwise I wouldn't have been here to tell the story. The woman says, "I can handle it. I'm just gonna tell him, you my cousin from Memphis." This guy looked at me and said, "Who the hell is this?" She told him I was her cousin and I had a drink with them. When they left this girl wanted to go to bed. I said, "Not me." I got the hell out of that house. I felt like killing her myself for almost getting me killed.

Another time I was sitting in a house with a couple of fairly nice girls and here comes the goddam sheriff again. He says, "We need someone to pick cotton today so you girls gotta come out and pick cotton." The sheriff asked me what I was doing and I said I was from out of town. These girls was turning some tricks and they thought I was white. That's the thing about me. I could go either way I wanted.

It's nice to be able to see both sides. I could see the injustice of the race thing. I had guys saying I was crazy to be fooling around with these colored guys, that I could be making more money working with white bands, which was true. But I enjoyed what I was doing. I'd much rather play with these fellows 'cause the colored guys just had it. It's not like now. The white class of musicians can play every bit as good as anybody, but in those days they couldn't. Sure, they had a few white musicians in New Orleans like Larry Shields and the Original Dixieland guys, they could play. But they was very much a minority. I just got a kick being around colored guys, meeting musicians like King Oliver and Buddy Petit. I liked it from when I was a kid, so that's the way I went.

It came about that I left Baton Rouge for good to go with a band called Hill and Vesthon's Original Dixieland, a ten-piece outfit trying to play dixieland. A drummer named Toby Mitchell was sent from Oakland, California, to come down to Louisiana to pick musicians for this band. Vesthon was a Jewish fellow who owned a cigar-making factory and Hill was a colored guy that had a restaurant on 7th and Willow in Oakland. They didn't know nothing about organizing a band, so that's why Toby came through town. He wanted a couple of sax players. He just asked around who was any good and who was available, which in Baton Rouge didn't mean a whole bunch of guys. Somebody told him about me just coming off the circus and being able to play pretty good, so Toby picked me for the band. He says, "I'm going to give you 75 dollars a week. We have a job in San Francisco but we have to go to Houston first." 75 dollars a week was a whole lot of money in those days. Toby, who was from Houston himself, picked a couple of other guys from New Orleans, plus Victor Spencer, a left-hand trumpet player out of New Iberia that had been playing with the Banner Band. Victor played real good and he looked just like a white boy. Later on he went back to New Orleans and he opened some kind of a gambling joint there. I think he got killed. Anyway, he was a helluva nice guy.

So I got on the train with Toby Mitchell to come to Houston, where we would be picking up the rest of the band and rehearsing. In the meantime Tody Harris was looking for me to come to rehearsal with his band and somebody says, "The last I seen of Joe, he was leaving to go to California, getting on the Santa Fe train." Next thing I seen Tody on the train. "Goddam, Joe, where's my sax parts?" I told him I didn't know and he says, "Look in your saxophone case. I don't think you trying to steal 'em but you don't need them, and I do. I'm not blaming you. I know you was excited, going to California. I hated for you to go but I want my music." I had forgotten all about these saxophone parts but I had them all right, there in my alto case.

Toby got the musicians he wanted but it was a pretty lousy band all the same. They made the trombone player the leader of the band. This was a Portuguese guy named Gus DeLuce. When we picked him up in Houston he was playing a trumpet with his left hand. Gus was a half-assed hustling pimp as well as a musician, and he had gotten in some kind of a fight with a gal he was staying with and she shot him through his right elbow so he couldn't play trombone. He always played both trumpet and trombone so he just switched to playing trumpet. Gus had been playing in the pit band at a little vaudeville house in Houston called the Key Theater. Gus could play with anybody's band. He was a good musician and quite a character too.

Just about this time they took his arm out of the cast, so he started playing trombone again. He was always the one that was late for rehearsal and his standard excuse was that his mute was broken and he had to get a new one. One of the organizers of the band was down there with us for a while and he was supposed to be a sophisticated guy who knew all about musicians. For the first couple of times the story about the mute worked but finally this guy got fed up and he says, "Goddam, Gus, every time you're late you tell me about your mute. What the hell is a mute anyway?"

We must have stayed for two weeks in Houston rehearsing the band, getting it together, and that's where we joined the union. None of us had belonged to it before. They didn't have any union on the circus or on the medicine show. In St Louis they never questioned it, nor when I played with Jelly Roll in Cairo.

They had two good bands around Houston then, Alphonso Trent and Troy Floyd, and I knew some of their guys. We used to go to a place where they'd have jam sessions, and I was talking to one of the musicians and he says, "How you guys getting on with Scanley?" This fellow Scanley was our piano player and a nicer guy you never met. I said that Scanley was fine as far as I was concerned, so then he says, "If Scanley ever starts taking a drink and you see him, give him a lot of room and a lot of air. Don't even get close to him, 'cause he's a wild man when he gets drunk. Like you say, when he isn't drinking you couldn't find a nicer guy. He knows he can't handle it. Just hope to God he don't start, 'cause if he does you gonna have some trouble on your hands."

During that time we played a cotton-jammers park in Galveston, Texas, and I noticed that Scanley never took a drink, although everybody else was drinking. So that was all right. From there we played one-nighters going up to San Francisco. We played in San Antonio, and some towns in New Mexico, in Phoenix, and right on into Los Angeles. We had this agent up there and he booked us for a banquet in Huntington Park, which was an industrial section of Los Angeles. This banquet was organized in an iron foundry. They had the place cleared and tables set up in there. This was in Prohibition time but they had plenty of alcohol around all the same. They didn't have a piano so Scanley didn't have nothing to do. They said, "You can sing a little, so you just stick with the band." They had forgotten about his drinking, otherwise they'd have handcuffed him to somebody. So we was playing and finally they asked, where was Scanley. We didn't know, but just then a couple of people came running to the bandstand with half their clothes torn off and their hair standing up on their heads. They said, "That feller standing up there with you guys, was he part of your outfit?" Vesthon and Hill, the band managers, said, yes. These others said, "We think you better go back in the men's room there. That sonofabitch has got an iron bar and he's about to kill somebody." One of them says, "He hit me with that damn thing, almost broke my arm when we tried to take it away from him, he's going berserk." They had to call the police, put him in a strait-jacket, and that's the last I seen of him. We had to move on and the managers said we wasn't fixing to fool with him no more.

We picked up another piano player named Red Cayou. He didn't stay with us too long. He went back up to San Francisco. He was a nice little piano player but he was also a kind of alcoholic himself. Red came from Louisiana and he'd been working in Oakland for another fellow from Louisiana named Slim Jenkins who owned a joint that always had good food. I can't exactly remember what style Red had but I know he played very good.

A little later we got to Oakland and ran into trouble right away. The very first day these idiots Hill and Vesthon decided we'd parade down 7th Street to advertise a dance, but they didn't get a permit. We was on the corner and a great big ol' cop came and stopped us from playing. The Oakland people liked our music so well, they got mad with the policemen, and jumped on them and beat them up. We kept playing and somebody called the riot squad who arrested a whole bunch of people. They nearly put all of us in jail, too. That was the first date we had. That should have told me something.

Oakland was the best place on the Pacific Coast for eating seafood because so many people from Louisiana lived there. Clem Raymond the clarinet player had a band in Oakland then. Wade Whaley was there, too. They was both originally from New Orleans.

Then we went up to San Francisco to go to work in a Greek restaurant called the Apollo. This job was the whole reason for organizing the band. So we went over to the radio station to do some publicity for this restaurant deal. Just before we got to start playing, in comes the business agent from the musicians' union and he says, "How long you guys been in town? What's your names and where you from?" And so forth. We told him that we was out of the Houston local. He says, "Did you transfer here? Did you get your cards transferred?" We said, no. Then the official says, "You cannot work in this jurisdiction but we're gonna give you a break. We could take you and fine you or expel you." Instead he pulled us off the broadcast and we got blackballed right then and there, couldn't work for six months. So we had to go back to Oakland, where we laid around just playing a few casual jobs. The great actor and comedian Phil Harris was on the staff of that radio station, just starting out. Much later on I got to know Phil real well and worked with him. It turned out that these idiot managers of ours didn't even have enough sense to know that when union musicians go into another town they have to notify the local union and put in a transfer, as they call it, deposit your cards. You had to get permission to work. San Francisco was, and still is, one of the strongest union towns in the whole USA. We never did work there.

We played some dances in Oakland at Sweets Ballroom and at a restaurant called the Granada. Old Hill, the restaurant owner, made sure we didn't ever have to worry about something to eat, 'cause he gave us meal tickets worth ten dollars. Each ticket had little holes in it that you punched from a nickel up to a dollar. If you ate 40 cents-worth of food, they'd punch out 40 cents. So we was eating good, even though we wasn't getting much money. We had some rooms upstairs. We was supposed to get 75 dollars a week, which we might have if we hadn't screwed up.

I used to do a little singing with the band. In those days they didn't have microphones or PA systems, so I'd sing out of a megaphone, like Rudy Vallee used. I would try to copy Louis. I'd get out there, play a chorus on the saxophone, and then I'd sing *Got the heebie-jeebies*, but I went a step further. I'd crawl on the floor and play my saxophone down on the floor. Even then, I was thinking of Louis. I'd listen to that record and try to get all the sounds. As far as my part is concerned that's probably the only guy I really tried to copy.

We wound up in Los Angeles, played a few more dances, and then the band broke up. That band was a half-deal really, just reading and faking, no good at all. Most of the guys went back home. They wasn't good players anyway. Gus, Victor and I stayed around town and worked there for a while. It took quite a time for us to latch on to anything. We'd get jobs individually and then finally we got with another big band. It wasn't exactly an organized band. I forget its name, but Gus helped to put it together. Then we went to work at a big dance hall on 15th and Main. We put advertisements in the paper and picked up various musicians like Al Pierre, one of your good piano players, that later died up in Seattle and who I worked with in Portland and Seattle. We had a tenor saxophone player named Green and I think we used Red Cayou on piano sometimes. This had to be very early in 1927.

Al Pierre was originally from Tacoma, Washington, and he owned his own tuxedo. Every time we did a job we got hooked up with the Spikes Brothers' agency, and they often used to book us on different jobs, like in the movies, where you'd have to have a tuxedo. We never had the money to rent a tuxedo, so we used to hustle over to Al Pierre's house and borrow his. We used it so much the knees was stretched out of shape; look like they had a couple of footballs in there. It was all frayed to hell. Anybody would see us they'd say, "I see you got Al's tuxedo!" We worked quite a bit like that.

Vic was still with us, but later he went back to New Iberia and the Banner Band. Gus and I stayed together, although you couldn't really depend on him. If he put his mind to it he might have had a good band, 'cause he could read well, write and he could organize a band. He could talk Portuguese and Spanish like hell. He'd promote deals with these Spanish people – he was a real con man. He'd hustle and he'd drink too much. If he'd borrowed some money from you he'd give you the shirt off his back, but half the time he didn't have a shirt to give you so he'd have your shirt instead!

When Vic left Milton Ellsworth took his place. Our band played every Monday. It was more or less all dances. They had a promoter here named Bill Heflin; he was an uncle of Marvin Johnson, a good saxophone player. In fact I gave Marvin a few lessons when he was just a little kid starting out. We played at the 15th and Main dance hall off and on for maybe four or five months. This went on until I joined Mutt Carey later that year. Winnow and Country Allen played with us at times: Winslow Allen played trumpet (we called him Winnow), and his brother Country played trombone. They was from Houston and Gus knew them. I remember Winnow used to pilot his own plane and he would fly out to work with us. Country also worked with Papa Mutt Carey later on.

Tram, the great old trombone player that had been with Toots Johnson, was playing in Los Angeles with the Mathews Brothers Band at a place called the Humming Bird Cafe. The Mathews brothers originally came from Louisiana but they had left when they was real young. They had played mostly in Texas. Gus knew them. That was the very last time I heard Tram perform. This was when we came through with Hill and Vesthon's band, had to be late '26. Later on Tram came to Seattle and he was shining shoes on 12th and Jackson, right in the midst of all those cabaret places. He never played any more, although we went down and talked to him about it. He said he would play with us sometime but he didn't have a trombone. Nothing happened after that.

At this time Alton Redd was working in a taxi-dance hall with a trumpet player named Charlie Echols, along with Al Pierre and a violinist named Atwell Rose. This was at the Four-Eleven Dance Hall on North Broadway, which was a Mexican place in Los Angeles. I think they had Edward Barnett on sax at one

Henry Darensbourg's shoe shop, North Boulevard, Baton Rouge, *c*1911: (left to right) Joe's father, Henry Darensbourg; unknown family servant; Joe's mother, Alice Darensbourg (*Joe Darensbourg collection*)

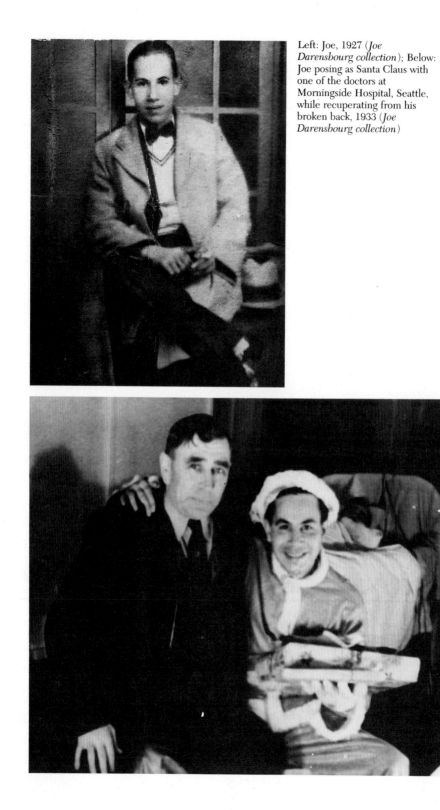

Left: Joe, 1927 (*Joe Darensbourg collection*); Below: Joe posing as Santa Claus with one of the doctors at Morningside Hospital, Seattle, while recuperating from his broken back, 1933 (*Joe Darensbourg collection*)

Johnny Wittwer's trio at the China Pheasant, Seattle, 1940s: (left to right) Keith Purvis, Joe, Wittwer (*Joe Darensbourg collection*)

The Gennessee Street Shufflers at Lyon's Music Hall, Seattle, 9 June 1936: (left to right) Jack Foy, Bill Rinaldi, Vic Sewell, Joe (*Joe Darensbourg collection*)

Kid Ory's Creole Jazz Band at the Jade Palace, Hollywood, 1945: (left to right) Ed Garland, Buster Wilson, Bud Scott, Minor Hall, Ory, Joe (*photo courtesy Floyd Levin*)

Kid Ory's Creole Jazz Band at the Jade Palace, Hollywood, 1945: (left to right) Bud Scott, Ory, Mutt Carey, Joe *(Joe Darensbourg collection)*

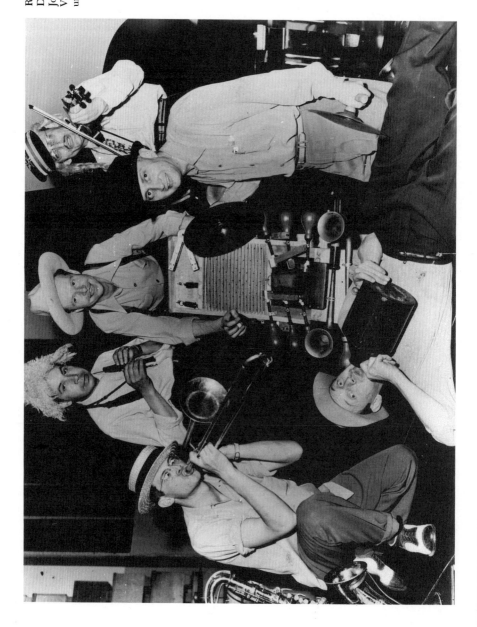

Red Fox and his Ding Dong Daddies, 1945: (left to right) Johnny Wittwer, Joe, Red Fox, Virgil Ireland, Abe Greenberg, unknown (at front)

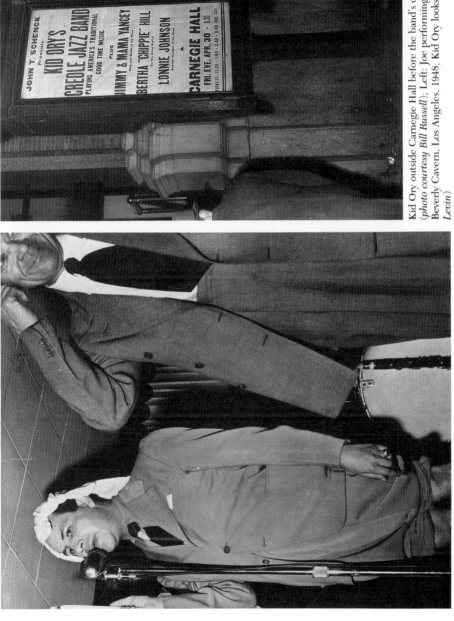

Kid Ory outside Carnegie Hall before the band's concert on 30 April 1948 (photo courtesy Bill Russell); Left: Joe performing *The Sheik of Araby* at the Beverly Cavern, Los Angeles, 1948; Kid Ory looks on (photo courtesy Floyd Levin)

Kid Ory's band at Carnegie Hall, 30 April 1948: (left to right) Little Brother Montgomery, Minor Hall, Bud Scott, Ory, Joe, Lee Collins (*photo courtesy Bill Russell*)
Below: Kid Ory's Creole Jazz Band at the Club Venus, San Francisco, 19 November 1948: (left to right) Bob Scobey, Joe, Ory, Minor Hall, Ed Garland, Frank Pasley, Gideon Honore (*photo courtesy Floyd Levin*).

Backstage at the first Dixieland Jubilee, Shrine Auditorium, Los Angeles, 7 October 1949: (left to right) Floyd Levin, Albert Nicholas, Joe, unknown, Zutty Singleton, Teddy Buckner (*photo courtesy Floyd Levin*)

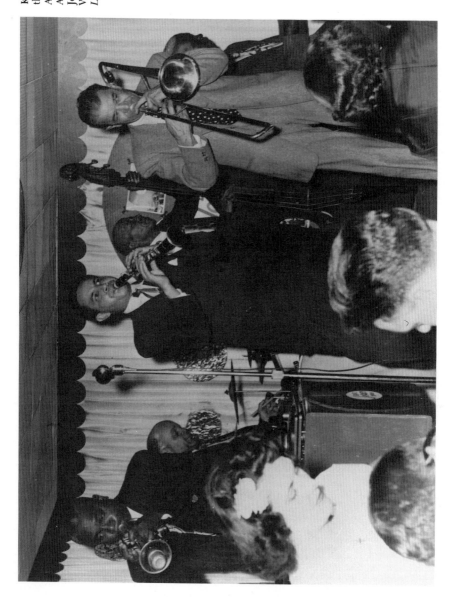

Kid Ory's Creole Jazz Band at the Beverly Cavern, Los Angeles, 1951: (left to right) Andy Blakeney, Minor Hall, Joe, Ed Garland, Ory, Buster Wilson (*photo courtesy Floyd Levin*)

A jam session at the Royal Room, 6700 Hollywood Boulevard, Los Angeles, 1952: musicians include Joe (clarinet), Zutty Singleton (cymbal), Johnny Lucas (trumpet), Pete Daily (trumpet), Pud Brown (clarinet) and the pianist Skippy Anderson (*Joe Darensbourg collection*)

Publicity still from *Mahogany Magic*, 1950: (left to right) Minor Hall, Kid Ory, Lloyd Glenn, Teddy Buckner, Joe, Ed Garland

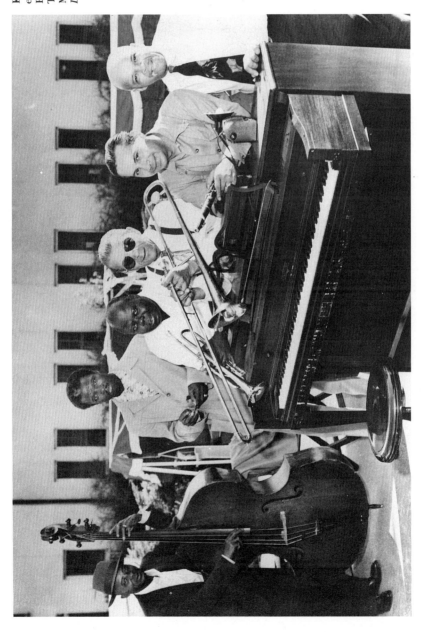

Kid Ory's Creole Jazz Band, early 1950s: (left to right) Ed Garland, Lloyd Glenn, Teddy Buckner, Ory, Joe, Minor Hall (*Joe Darensbourg collection*)

Backstage at the Beverly Cavern, Los Angeles, 1953: (left to right) Teddy Buckner, Ed Garland, Harvey Brooks, Joe, Minor Hall, Kid Ory

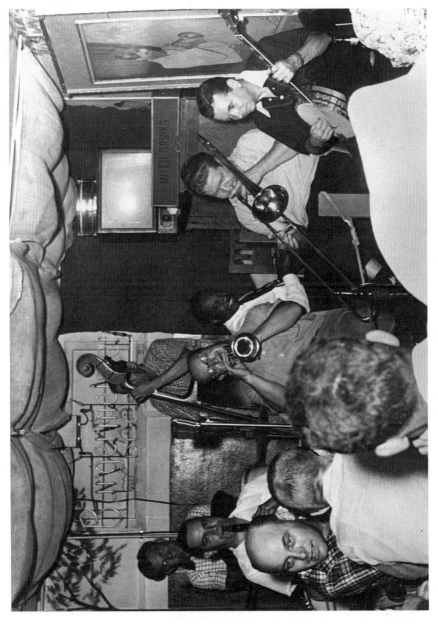

A jam session at the Blue Bird, Los Angeles, early 1950s: (left to right) unknown, Joe, unknown, Rico Valese, Lionel Reason, Bob Logan, Nappy Lamare (*Joe Darensbourg collection*)

Harvey and Daisy Brooks with Joe and Helen Darensbourg, early 1950s (*Joe Darensbourg collection*); Left: Brother Bones, 1950s

time. Anyway, Al, Gus and I worked jobs for various promoters and one that you was always running into was Ragtime Billy Tucker. Some of these guys didn't pay you your money and one of the most notorious was this Billy Tucker. He probably owed money to every musician in Los Angeles. The three of us worked a job for Billy and he disappeared without paying us. We didn't see him for about six months, so finally we ran into another musician and he says, "Hey, you seen Billy Tucker? Maybe you can get your money. Billy's round here at the Circus Museum on 5th and Main playing a wild man. They got him in a cage there, with a wig on and everything." The Circus Museum was another place where musicians used to work. They always had a band in there. It was like a sideshow in one of the circuses; they'd put on all the acts. So Gus and I went down and, sure enough, old Billy was in this great big cage. I guess he thought people wouldn't know him. He was real ferocious looking, with chains and a big long beard and a kind of leopard-skin outfit. They opened the cage door and threw a hambone in there and Billy started chomping on it, pretending he was eating, and growling. Gus goes up to the cage and says, "Billy, you ain't fooling us in there, we know who you are. How about that money you owe us?" He looked at us and growled. In the bottom of the cage they had a lot of dry hay, so Gus says, "OK, Billy, you won't talk to us, we gonna fix you." And he pulls out a box of matches. Billy sees Gus about to set light to this hay with the cage locked, so he says, "You dirty bastards, you gonna set a man on fire for 25 dollars apiece?" Gus says, "Hell, yes, we gonna burn up your rear end." Billy started hollering for help and the promoter ran over there, so Billy says, "You give these people their money before they set light to this damn hay. I owe them 25 dollars each." That's how we got our money from Billy Tucker.

Then I went with Papa Mutt. He had Edward Barnett with him, but Barnett left to go to Honolulu with a bandleader named Johnny Mitchell. Andy Blakeney went on that job, too. So I replaced Barnett for a one-nighter, an extra job on their day off, and started gigging around Los Angeles until Mutt got a steady job.

I never knew Mutt in New Orleans, I just met him in Los Angeles. We'd all meet on 12th and Central and, being from Louisiana, we'd talk about Baton Rouge. Old Mutt was always bullshitting about Toots Johnson. He'd say that they'd run Toots out of town when he came to New Orleans, but I'd remind him that Toots used to run Ory's band out of Baton Rouge. You know, just kidding each other.

The first thing Mutt wanted me to do was to come to his house and learn how to play the blues. He lived on Cheeseboro' Lane, in Boyle Heights, that's where all the Mexicans lived. That was way out in those days. Ram Hall used to live with Mutt, rented a room from him. Mutt was married to a beautiful Spanish woman and he told me, "Be sure and bring your lunch, home boy." Sonofabitch! "I ain't got nobody to cook, so you can bring me something to eat, too, if you want." Mutt was the nerviest, the cheekiest guy you ever seen in your life. So I went out there and he wanted to charge me money for lessons, no kidding. I told him I didn't want this damn job that bad and he says, "OK, home boy, you know I'm just kidding around with you." Ram says, "Bullshit, if you'd gave him 50 cents he'd have took it." I didn't learn anything from him; it turned out I could play the blues better than him, anyway.

Mutt was a pretty good trumpet player but he didn't have much power, he wasn't a high-note man. He was fairly good with the wa-wa mute but he didn't have a strong enough lip. When I first joined, Mutt was always calling rehearsals, but we never learned a goddam thing. We played all the same tunes, anyway. This was before we was working steady, while we was just gigging around Los Angeles. We'd rehearse at his house and afterwards he would always talk up a card game. He was ready to start a poker game no matter where you was, but you had to use his cards. We'd lose every time; Mutt would win all the money. We found out later that all the cards was marked. He always carried a couple of decks of marked cards in his trumpet case. Mutt was crookeder than a barrelful of snakes and the biggest bullshitter in the world.

I'd never seen a guy that could put a pack of cigarettes in his pocket, unopened, and then open it with one hand and take out a single cigarette. That's what Mutt could do. Every cigarette was his last, so you didn't ask him for no cigarette. He'd likely bum one off you with a pocketful of cigarettes of his own. That's how cheap he was.

Even so, Mutt was rated as one of your good bandleaders. He got a job for the band at the Liberty Dance Hall, which was a taxi-dance hall on East 3rd Street. They called the band Papa Mutt's Liberty Syncopators, and the job paid 45 dollars a week. In the band we had Minor Hall on drums; we called him Ram. Elzie Cooper was the piano player, Frank Pasley was on banjo and guitar, Leon White played trombone and Leonard "Big Boy" Davidson played tenor saxophone, while I played alto and soprano saxes. Leon also doubled piano and later on I got a baritone. Like a fool I never picked up my clarinet. I used to like to play saxophone for some reason but I was a good clarinet player really. A lot of people didn't even know I played clarinet. I just dropped it.

I think it was Frank that recommended me to Mutt. Frank and I stayed together, he had an apartment. We remained good friends for years and worked together with Joe Liggins in the forties.

They had a lot of taxi-dances then. Los Angeles had a whole slew of them when I first came around here. Solomon's was one of the biggest and the nicest of all of them, more like a jitney dance. Paul Howard's Quality Serenaders worked there. Tudi (Ed Garland) was round at the One-Eleven Dance Hall, upstairs at 111 West 3rd Street, a block across Main Street where East divides from West. He was the leader on his job and he had Everett Walsh on drums, Freddie Washington playing piano and a guy named Bonner on tenor. None of his men was top musicians. I think Edward Barnett also played with Tudi. I remember they had a Salvation Army band used to play at 3rd and Main, right around the corner from us, and I joined up with this band just to try to make it with this pretty little blond chick, but nothing happened. I found out I would have to marry her and join up steady with the Salvation Army, so that ended my career with them. Yes, taxi-dances was big in Los Angeles in those days.

Some people don't know what a taxi-dance is. This is where you have 30 or 40 girls working and they get a percentage on the tickets. The customers would go buy a roll of tickets to dance and give the girl a ticket. The customer paid a dime for each dance and the girl made a nickel. Every time she danced around she had to throw one ticket in the box and keep the other half; that's the way she made her money. That was the origin of the movie *Ten Cents a Dance*. Jitney dance is something else; you would bring your own girl and pay a nickel to dance. I played on carnivals where they had a tent and a little old band and you had to pay to go inside the tent if you wanted to dance.

In the taxi-dance each tune lasts for about a minute, then you change tunes so the girl can get a new ticket. Hell, on a Saturday night you played maybe half a minute and every third number was a waltz. We needed a violin to play for a waltz. We had a Filipino owned this dance hall, so your clientele was Filipinos and white girls. He had a cousin, or perhaps it was his wife's brother, that played a violin; he was Filipino and we fired Atwell Rose for this guy, whose name was Aspirin. The first night after we got through playing Mutt told him, "Look, now I know why they call you Aspirin, I get a headache every time you play a tune on that damn violin, so forget it. I'm gonna tell the owner to get Atwell Rose back or we ain't gonna use no violin." So the owner says, "I ain't gonna fire him, my wife would leave me. Either you use Aspirin on that violin or you get another job." That's the way it was. We never did fire Aspirin. But he did quit after two or three weeks and they decided not to have a violin any more. They just cut down on the band.

Mutt moved from Cheeseboro' Lane to a home in Los Angeles and in the meantime we sent out for Pops Foster, who was in New Orleans, and we added old Pops doubling on tuba and bass violin. Papa Mutt used to call him Fireman George. Elzie Cooper left the band – this was just after we opened at the taxi-dance – and he was replaced by the great piano player and arranger Alex Hill, who later on went to Chicago, and with Louis wrote a couple of tunes including *Beau Koo Jack*. Alex came to Los Angeles with a band named Speed Webb. He had originally been playing back East. Webb came out of some place in Ohio with that band. It was a big band, about 12 to 15 pieces. He had a great banjo player named Bob Robinson, and Parker Berry was on trombone – lot of good musicians. Alex was really outstanding: a good musician and a terrific guy. He originally came from Argenia, Arkansas, near South Little Rock. Alex was a helluva good writer and arranger but there wasn't any arranging in our band; we didn't play anything but choruses, all from stocks. Once in a while we'd have a chance to play a solo. I remember one time *Singing the Blues* had come out, and I wanted to play that Trumbauer solo on the alto, so Alex Hill says, "I'll take it off the record for you." We put it on and he took out his manuscript paper and got it down. He was that good.

Big Boy and I worked as a team. The brass would play a chorus and then we'd play our chorus. We had music to everything we played. We read all those alto and tenor duets. We had them all in rotation. We'd open the book at number one and go right down the line, the same thing every night. We probably had 150 tunes. Usually, if it was a quiet night, you might play for three minutes. But when the house got full of guys, like on Saturdays, we just played two choruses at most, so those girls could make some money. Leon White and Big Boy, they was adequate, never anything outstanding. Leon also used to play piano so we'd get another trombone player sometimes. Parker Berry came in for a while because he and Alex were good friends. Big Boy would play a chorus and then fall asleep; turn around and old Big Boy would be sleeping up a breeze. I never known him play any clarinet but he had a soprano. He could read well. Big Boy quit the band and Charlie Mosley, a saxophone player from Wilmington, Delaware, got in the band. He was a great musician and played all the saxes – alto, tenor, baritone – and some clarinet, too. He was part Indian, a nice-looking guy and a beautiful man. After he died Big Boy came back, but we also had Paul Howard with us for a short spell. I played again with Paul in the forties when he had a marching band.

At one time I had four or five instruments; I had me a tenor, a soprano, an alto, a C-melody and a baritone. In those days you got a dollar extra for every instrument you doubled on and a dollar extra for a tuxedo. Throw in all these things and you could make a little extra loot. The bandleaders didn't always do it, but the union said you were supposed to get that extra dollar. A dollar then was like five dollars now.

Saxophone is real easy. Clarinet is daddy of all the reeds: got so much more range, so many more octaves. A sax has got three octaves; clarinet has got about five. Sax has got keys and the clarinet has got holes. Your fingers have to cover these holes right, but with a sax, every time you hit the key, automatically the pad closes. There's no comparison. So I got my clarinet out and started playing it again. It made a good showing, having all these instruments down there. A lot of sax players would have 40 instruments in front of them, just for effect. Still, saxophone was a helluva popular instrument until Benny Goodman came into prominence.

The first time I ever got fired was with Mutt's band. I got drunk one night and overslept. I woke up at eight o'clock, pyjamas on and everything, and we were supposed to start work at eight. I was in such a hurry I put my clothes on over my pyjamas and made out a cock-and-bull story about the taxi having an accident. Mutt could see I had a hangover and, anyway, you could see the bottoms of my pyjamas. I finished the night but Mutt gave me two weeks' notice. What made it bad was I told him to go to hell. I bragged that I could get another job. I had been offered other jobs, like with Sonny Clay or Paul Howard, but I told Mutt I could go to work with Gus Arnheim, which was a lot of bullshit, and that made him mad. So Frank Pasley said he'd talk to Mutt about all this.

We had this whorehouse we'd go to, up on Central Avenue, run by this landlady, Ida Lewis, a wonderful woman. Every kind of broad would come there, and it just happened that a show had come to Los Angeles called, I think, Brownskin Models, and they got stranded. They must have had about 20 girls in this show. So they was hungry and decided to sell a little pussy. Ida hired them and I was going with one gal named Darlene Whaley and Charlie was going with another. They also had a beautiful dame there named Dorothy, and every time Papa Mutt seen this broad there he start frothing at the mouth. He really wanted to get some of that hide, but Dorothy never would have anything to do with him. Anyway, we used to go up there every night and drink, sit down and talk to the girls. If they got a trick, they'd go turn it, make a charge of two or three dollars and then come back. We'd drink some more, sitting and talking. Ida was surprised when Charlie said, "Joe ain't gonna be playing with us 'cause Mutt gave him his two weeks' notice." I told them why, so Dorothy says, "You want me to fix your job up for you? You get that sonofabitch to come up here. Tell him I want to see him." Naturally, if I'd told him he'd have smelled a rat, so next evening

Charlie says, "By the way, Mutt, I was up at Ida Lewis's last night and I seen Dorothy. She was asking about you and said she wanted to see you." Old Mutt's eyes start bugging out and he couldn't hardly play that night, he was so excited. So we went up there after work and Dorothy took him in a room. I still don't know what she told him or how she kept him from being suspicious. When he came out he said, "Hello, Creole, about that notice, we don't want you to leave the band. I just did that to teach you a little lesson, to make you be on time." Dorothy had laid some of that plunder on him, you see. That did it.

Our drummer Ram Hall was bald and he was always looking for a way to grow hair. He would do anything if he thought he could grow a couple of strands of hair on that bald head of his. A guy told Ram to try putting chicken crap on his head, make a poultice out of it. Ram promptly went out to Les Hite's chicken farm and got some fresh chicken droppings to make the poultice. This guy told him to keep it on for 24 hours at a stretch, so he marches up to the Liberty Dance Hall with this thing on his head. It was the summertime and all that stuff was pretty ripe. Pretty soon Mutt gets suspicious and says, "You guys must have stepped in some crap, got it on your shoes." Well, we all looked and finally Mutt spotted Ram with this thing on his head. Everybody started laughing and Mutt got mad. Anyway, he made Ram go to the bathroom and wash his head. Ram says, all hurt, "If that's the way you feel about it. You don't want me to grow any hair." Mutt says, "You'll get us all fired off the job. Clean it up." Ram would have lit a stick of dynamite on his head if he thought it would grow him hair. Still, it was a relief when he cleaned it off. Ram didn't try that any more.

Les Hite's chicken farm was in Alhambra. We used to go out there and have a lot of fun. It was a nice place. Les had run into some woman that was a multi-millionaire and she was crazy about him. She bought the chicken farm for him outright, paid for that, and then she bought him a couple of apartment houses. He was well fixed! She became a big shareholder in the Santa Ana racetrack and made all kinds of loot. She's the one that later bankrolled his big band.

Pops Foster was a funny guy and he told a whole lot of stories about his days in New Orleans. It seems he was working in the Irish Channel with a violin player, and that's a very notorious area. Pops was the leader and this big Irishman that owned the place wanted them to play a waltz. This was a very prejudiced place. Pops kept fooling around and hadn't played a waltz, so finally this guy got mad and came up on the bandstand and started shooting. Pops and them start running out of the back door. Bass players in those days used to have a strap on the bass where they could hang it on their backs and carry it. Pops says they had a big clothesline out back, and the bass neck got caught on this line. Pops ran from under the bass and he turns round to get it down and it was swinging. Then he sees this guy with his pistol who shot at him and missed. He shouts, "I missed you but I'm gonna get your bass." He shot the back of Pop's bass full of holes, shot it to smithereens.

One of the things I always wanted to do was to work in some kind of movie. Next to the circus and playing with Louis Armstrong, my biggest thrill was when Papa Mutt had the call to work in the studios. This was at the Paramount Studios, that's still here, right on Melrose Avenue, not far from the Musician's Union. It was a movie called *The Road to Ruin*, with Sally Eillers and Grant Withers. Of course, this was before the talkies came in. We're talking about 1927.

Our scene was a barn dance. We all had to wear overalls and straw hats like guys wear out in the cotton fields. We actually played music, for atmosphere. Naturally, it wasn't recorded. The work was easy; you just stood by, waiting to be called. That was the monotonous part, waiting all day for a five-minute scene. You might have all kinds of retakes so you had to be there. We got something like 40 dollars a day, which was almost a week's salary.

Los Angeles was awful prejudiced at that time. They didn't have a commissary in Paramount Studios or, if they did, we didn't use it. We had to go across the street to eat at a restaurant. This was Ram and me. They couldn't tell what Ram was, and, naturally, I ain't going to have any problems with prejudice, so we sit right down and put in our order. The girl took it and then here come Mutt and Elzie. Mutt couldn't pass for anything and Elzie sure couldn't, he was real dark. Me and Ram got our order and was eating but the waitress kept passing Mutt and Elzie by, until Mutt says, "Hey, young lady! We been waitin' and we gotta go back and get on the set. We movie actors." He wanted everybody to know he's a movie actor. In the meantime me and Ram got the drift, so Ram says, "You know one thing, I don't think they serve coons in here." Mutt says, "What did you say?" and Ram answered, "I'm telling you, I don't think they serve jigs in here. You better get up from here. You gonna get me and Joe in trouble." Mutt says, "To hell with you. If you can eat in here, I can, too." Then Ram tells him to go sit somewhere else as he's bothering us. Mutt says, "I'm gonna fire both of you bastards when I get outta here." Then he calls the girl and finally she comes over and she says, "I'm sorry we're not allowed to serve colored people in here. Didn't you see that sign up there?" The sign didn't say "We don't serve colored people" but it did say "We have the right to refuse service to anyone." Now at the time they did have a law, they didn't enforce it, but you could bring suit against any place that refused you service. Mutt starts hollering, "Give me a pencil," and he calls the manager, who won't serve him either. Then Elzie came over to us and he wanted a pencil. So Mutt turns around and tells Elzie, "You black sonofabitch, you get away from me, you causing all this trouble. They'd have served me but for you." Then the manager started looking at Ram but, by having that big old straw hat and being so light and bald-headed, you couldn't tell anything about him. What the hell, Ram was through eating by then. The guy had no reason to question me but he did ask if we was all working together. When I said, yes, the guy just looked at us. Ram and me laughed so much. This was one of the funniest incidents that ever happened to me.

After that we had a lot of extra gigs and I did quite a bit of movie work. There was plenty of that kind of work around. Satchel McVea, that's Jack McVea's father, often got these jobs and I did several movies with him. Satchel was just a little guy, remind you of Tudi, and he played a five-string banjo. He was a personality guy, very entertaining. His movie deals was always in the daytime, so I was able to continue working with Papa Mutt every night at the Liberty. Satchel never really had a band so he'd hire individual musicians. Maybe he would hire Mutt's whole band or pick out some of the guys. I used to enjoy talking to him so much that he'd get jobs and just say, "I want you to come and play for me." I carried one of his cards around for the longest time and all it said was "Satchel McVea and his Howdy Band." I never knew why he used that. We played in a picture with Gary Cooper called *Legion of the Condemned*. I think Satchel got that one. His son Jack was a little boy, and I never even knew him then. I got to know Jack after he wrote *Open the door, Richard* and he really blossomed out. I guess he was always a pretty good musician. When I left Los Angeles in '28 he wasn't playing much.

I also did some movie work with Rex Ingrams the actor, and some other stuff with George Olsen, and one job with some white guys that worked in Gus Arnheim's band. That's the advantage I had, either way, that's what made it so good for me. I worked with some Mexicans and they'd get a little deal in the movies. I used to go with a Mexican gal and I played with some Mexican bands. They had some pretty good Mexican players; some of them played good dixieland. That trombone player Jake Flores, he was Mexican. He had some beautiful cousins, they lived in Boyle Heights.

One of our favorite places to work was at Fatty Arbuckle's house. Playing for a great comedian like Fatty was a fun deal. He had a big house on Adams Boulevard right in Los Angeles proper, not in Hollywood. Old Fatty would get drunk and insist on all his guests and the musicians taking their clothes off. That's one thing, you'd always take a bath and put on clean underwear before you played for Fatty Arbuckle. We'd play in our shorts. I was in a couple of his films, can't remember the names now.

Another thing we musicians used to do in Los Angeles then was to play for real-estate promotion deals. They had all this fine property out in Burbank, Glendale, Pasadena and Beverley Hills. The real-estate office would get a bus and feed the prospective customers a box lunch. We'd get paid eight or ten dollars and our lunch to furnish a little music. You could buy great big lots as cheap as 150 or 200 dollars that now would be worth 100,000 dollars. I never bought any of them – if I had I probably wouldn't be writing this story now. I could kick myself over that.

While I was with Mutt I put in some time with George Teak, learning how to repair instruments. I mostly went up there because they always had something to drink. This was the top place for all musicians to get their instruments fixed and you'd see all the fellows out of Gus Arnheim's and George Olsen's bands or from the California Ramblers. George, who was of German descent, knew all of them. This particular day I was in the back, probably polishing a horn or washing it with ammonia, and George says, "Hey, we in for a treat today. Guess who I got out here, just brought his clarinet in to get it fixed? Larry Shields!" He had come to work in the movies, although it was still silent pictures at that time. Of course, I knew of him. George had met him before. "Look at that case he's got. We probably gonna see a couple of fine old clarinets in there." Larry had this beautiful alligator case and I think he did say that somebody in Europe gave it to him. I shook hands with him and I'm goggle-eyed, just wanting to see these two clarinets or whatever he had in there. Well, Larry's clarinet had more damn rubber bands and chewing gum on it than anything else and all kinds of funny old tape. George just looked at him. The case was big enough and I think Larry had some pyjamas or underwear in there or an old shirt. I was so brought down, man, it wasn't even funny. And the thing about it, although the clarinet was fouled up every kind of way, Larry just told George to fix the A key. Just that one key, I'll never forget that.

I told Larry I was playing with Mutt, so he says, "Oh yeah, I know that goddam Papa Mutt's brother in New Orleans, that Jack Carey that had the song wrote about him." And he start going: "Jack Carey, got your daughter/Has a whorehouse on the water/Selling hot pussy for a quarter." It was a takeoff, a parody to *Tiger Rag*. They call it "Jack Carey's Chorus" and they claim he's the one started it. It turns out Larry knew Tudi and Joe Oliver, all those guys. That's where they, the ODJB, picked up a lot of their shit, from those musicians down there.

Sure, I heard Larry Shields play. They had a place in Los Angeles used to have a function for musicians, very popular. Me and George went over there to hear him play. He was a good clarinet player; so was his brother Harry.

The twenties and thirties era in Los Angeles was the heyday of the music business in California. They had a terrific bunch of musicians then. In those days the musicians' hangout was at 12th and Central at a cafe called the Maybelle; that's where we would go to eat. The Maybelle Cafe was a New Orleans-type restaurant that served all the things we had at home: oysters, oyster-loaf, fried chicken, red beans and rice, gumbo. Every musician that amounted to anything in Los Angeles would be there. We used to go there and talk, after one o'clock. Reb Spikes, the guy that wrote *Someday Sweetheart*, had a music store and booking office at 12th and Central where the guys used to get work. Across the street they had a poolroom called Small Black's Pool Hall, where all the musicians used to go. That's where I first met Bojangles (Bill Robinson). He was a fine billiards and pool player, but he was pretty rugged and kinda belligerent, and evil on top of it. I seen him break a pool cue over a guy's head. And not only that, he once pulled out a pistol and shot up the joint.

That was the days of house-rent parties and it looked like they had a party every night. Chittlin'-switch, they call 'em. You could go there and eat a big plate of chittlin'. Hell, I never did like chittlin', but I remember the first time I ate it was with James Porter the trumpet player. I'm not saying I ran round with him, because he was a kinda lone wolf, a little antisocial really. I asked the cook, could he fry some chittlin', dip those things in some corn-meal and fry 'em like we did oysters down in Louisiana. The guy that was having the party was a tuba player named Brock. Every time you turned around he was having a house-rent party, so he fried me some chittlin' in cornmeal. That was the first and last time I ate that stuff. The guys used to kid old Brock and say with all these parties he should have enough money to own half the block, let alone pay his house-rent and hustle money.

This James Porter was a helluva trumpet player, that was an acknowledged fact, but a hard guy to get along with. He had a super ego, probably thought he was better than Louis. Naturally, he wasn't and a lot of musicians here will tell you that he was unpopular. When I left Los Angeles he was in his prime. When I came back in '44 I went down to the Musicians' Union and Frank Pasley pointed out a guy who was hustling and begging. It was Porter; we called him Porter, never did call him James. He came up to us and I think we all gave him some money. The poor guy was helpless really; he had had a stroke. That was the way he lived, walking the street and begging for money. I think he died a couple of years later. I know he still had that ego even after he was sick. I run into him another time and I gave him a half-dollar. Porter says, "Is this all you gonna give me? Here, you can have it back." I thought, to hell with you, and I took it back. Then he says, "On second thought, I'll take it. OK, give it to me." Maybe I should have felt sorry for the guy, he was really hurtin', but up to the last he had that belligerent disposition.

We'd take our instruments to these parties but we didn't call it jamming then, we'd say we was going to ballyhoo. Another place we'd play would be the Crawfish Inn, and there was also Nap Moore's, a joint that stayed open 24 hours a day. Guys could always go there and get something to eat or drink. Nap's was a big two-story house on Hooper Avenue in Los Angeles where they had a piano and a non-stop jam session. You'd go there and ball it up whenever you felt like it or didn't have nothing else to do.

I met Lionel Hampton first at the Maybelle Cafe. Me and Hamp and Alex Hill would go to Nap Moore's and have jam sessions. That was the first time I heard Hamp play that one-finger piano. This was before he started vibes. A tune I remember playing with Hamp was *Chinatown*. He did that with two fingers going. This was when I was with Mutt.

On Sunday nights Hamp had a band. It wasn't really his band, it belonged to a guy named Johnny Mitchell that was working at a place called the Vernon Country Club. I used to go out there. In fact I played a couple of jobs with Hamp. I know I could have played with Hamp when he started his big band, but I left Los Angeles just when Hamp was getting well known. I used to bring my horn to the Vernon Country Club and sit in with them once in a while. We'd all have a lot of fun. One night I was fooling around and Hamp didn't come back to the stand when Mitchell's band started playing, so I got back on the drums. I was kinda high and I knocked the snare drum off the stand and busted a head. I offered to pay Hamp for it right then but he said forget it. Even to this day when I see Hamp he asks, "When you gonna pay for that head you broke on my snare drum?"

They had a terrific vocalist named Roberta Hyson, a beautiful girl, and Sam McDaniels the brother of the actress Hattie McDaniels that won an Academy Award was also a singer there.

The first big colored theater that was built in Los Angeles was the Lincoln Theater and Hamp was working in the pit. Curtis Mosby had had a club around Los Angeles and he put a band in the Lincoln. Mosby himself was playing drums but he was such a lousy drummer they took him out and put Hamp in his place. I think he was still working in the Lincoln Theater when I left Los Angeles. I know I worked with Curtis Mosby a couple of times, just on extra deals. He wasn't a very good musician – more of a promoter than anything else.

Frank Sebastian's Cotton Club, out in Culver City, was one of the top spots with the best paying jobs for musicians. In the band there they had one of your real great drummers named Tin Can Henry Allen that could do anything on drums. He did actually play on tin cans, that's why they gave him that name. I worked at the Cotton Club once in a while. Of course, top white bands like

George Olsen also played there. Later on Les Hite had the band and he had Hamp, George Orendorff the trumpet player, and Lawrence Brown, the great trombone player that was with Duke Ellington for so long. Lawrence was the son of a preacher and he came from Pasadena. He was one of the younger members of the band. Lawrence had a younger brother, Harold Brown, a fine organ player and pianist, that I worked with on the boats. Harvey Brooks the pianist was in Les's band and his gal was in the floor show. They had a beautiful dance revue in there and the star of the show was Caroline Snowden. She herself was a great dancer.

There was another after-hours joint at the Gotham Hotel where we would go. Right now it's all slums around there. They used the basement of the hotel and it was strictly after-hours. A trumpet player from New Orleans named Andrew Kimball had a quartet down there. Leo Davis was on alto saxophone and he played baritone, too. Kimball's wife Margaret played piano and they had a drummer. I think Alton Redd worked with them sometimes. There was another drummer that Gus DeLuce knew from Texas, I can't remember his name. That's the first time I met Leo. I was mostly playing alto saxophone then, so when I'd go down and sit in on alto Leo would switch to his baritone. I think he played tenor, too. Kimball was a typical New Orleans trumpet player. He played a nice straight lead, good tone; he played well, though he wasn't one of the real hot kind of guys. Leo was a very good saxophone player and he played clarinet, too. Kimball's wife used to sing. I could relate to them because I was from Louisiana. Gus would bring his trombone down and sit in. A lot of musicians sat in, like when some of the big bands came in. That was a showcase. They'd all play down there for free so people could go down and listen to 'em. A good trumpet player named Claude Kennedy brought a band from Houston, Texas, and Speed Webb first came there. Speed made a pretty good impression on the musicians in Los Angeles because he had a good band. He had guys like Earl Thompson the trumpet player, that I played with later on the boats.

Another good job for musicians was the Follies Theater, which was a non-union house at the time, here in Los Angeles. This was a big-paying job. That's where old Slocum (Adam Mitchell) the clarinet player worked. Man, he was murder. He could wail, looked something like Sidney Bechet except all he played was clarinet. He could stop a show with a clarinet. Reb Spikes was leader of that band. They had two brothers that owned the Follies and the Burbank theaters, both girlie or burlesque shows. They didn't like the union for some reason, so they only hired non-union musicians. They paid more to get good musicians, so a lot of guys ignored the union and went to work for them.

In that Follies band you had Ash Hardee, a trombone player, and Edward Barnett the saxophone player from Sturgis, Kentucky. There was about eight or ten musicians in all. Ash was a *very* good trombone man, capable of working with any band. He played with all those good bands, including Curtis Mosby. He was a good arranger, too, if he was able to keep himself sober. Ash was a guy that drank a lot. Him and Buster Wilson recorded an album of tunes for Bill Russell or somebody. This was just before Buster died. Buster and Ash was drunk as hell, so they never did release that album.

Like I said before, we used to have jam sessions whenever we had a chance.

Most of the time we'd be broke; musicians never made a helluva lot of money. What we had we used to spend as fast as we made it. There was a mailman named John Myers that had every saxophone that was ever made, but he couldn't play anything worth a damn. He had a little money and a nice house. We hated to play with him, but whenever we wanted a drink and something to eat we'd go to John's house and have a jam session. Of course, he'd have to sit in, that was the bad part of it, but since we got all we wanted to drink we'd put up with it.

I knew Sonny Clay slightly, never knew him too good. He had a band around here and when he got ready to go to Australia, Griff (William Griffin) the saxophone player said he may not be able to go to Australia. He thought he might not be able to get a physical on account of he had messed with some broad and got a little clap. He wanted me to go in his place and Sonny asked me, too. I was working with Mutt and the loot Sonny was paying was pretty good. I thought I would go, but Griff was able to pass the physical and he went. The band got deported from Australia because they caught them up in a room with a couple of 16-year-old girls. Sonny got into a lot of trouble with the union over that. That's the only time I knew Sonny. It seems to me that I heard somebody say about a year ago that he was still living. He probably got out of music.

A nice thing about our local was the celebration we'd have every year. The bands would get on wagons or floats and parade down Central Avenue. All the good bands and musicians, they'd end up at the Musicians' Union and have a lot of drinks. Right there at 12th and Central, by the Humming Bird Cafe, the top colored nightclub where all the best entertainers used to play.

That whorehouse landlady Ida Lewis had a club in Watts called Leake's Lake that we worked. Then there was the Southern California Music Store that used to have one of your top bands every month, like Gus Arnheim or George Olsen. Los Angeles was really jumping in those days.

Around the end of April 1928 a Lieutenant of Detectives named McDuff came along and asked Mutt about our band playing for an Elks Convention in Chicago. McDuff was some kind of an official in the Elks Lodge in Los Angeles. They wanted to send a band to Chicago along with their delegation. He asked Mutt about bringing the whole band along, augmenting it with some other musicians to make it a marching band. McDuff played a little trumpet himself. So the band, which at the time consisted of Alex Hill, Ram, Frank, Pops Foster, Big Boy, Leon White playing trombone, and me, was set to go. At first I said I would go, but then a job with Freda Shaw on the *HF Alexander* came up. Big Boy was offered that job but he didn't want it. I thought about it for a long time and I took the boat job. I had been with Mutt for about a year. In the parade I think Frank played cymbals or a snare drum and Alex did the same. I know him and Pops never came back; they stayed in Chicago. I'm pretty sure that Leon was playing trombone with us then, although Country Allen did play with us for a while. He also played a little trumpet. Country was a funny son of a gun himself, but he was a good trombone player, no doubt about that.

We wasn't working at the Liberty Dance Hall when I left Mutt's band; we had gone to work for a guy named Jack Goldberg who had a place they called the Red Mill. Things was getting rough around Los Angeles; money was getting real tough. The stock market crashed and the Depression started. Everything went bad. Los Angeles was one of the hardest hit towns in the whole USA. Musicians here felt the pinch, more so because you had so many of them. Wasn't no place to work. Competition was hard. Mutt never did too good; he went back to work on the railroad. Oh, he had it rough in the thirties. I came back here twice in the thirties and it was pretty sad. Still, those days at the taxi-dance with Mutt was fun, the most fun I ever had. See, Mutt himself was a funny guy.

The *HF Alexander*, that was the Admiral Line, was the fastest coastal steamer in the world at that time. It had been a transport ship in World War I and it held the record. To show you how fast it was, we'd leave Los Angeles at seven in the morning and at 5 p.m. we were in San Francisco for our first stop. That was pretty damn fast for a boat, about 32 knots. We used to run between San Diego, Los Angeles and Seattle. This was a seasonal deal, started sometime in early May and ended around the first of October. We stayed two days in Seattle each trip. This was a wonderful thing because Seattle was really a jumping town. I was crazy about Seattle and all of its night-life. This was during Prohibition and Seattle had so many after-hours joints serving bootleg liquor after the legitimate places had closed for the night. Musicians around there was making a fabulous amount of money and I was all for settling for a job in Seattle, although I stayed on the boat until the season closed.

The boat deal was fun. You met a lot of people. The *HF Alexander* was a pleasure boat and you got a lot of honeymoon couples on there. We used to go peep through the port-holes at them young newly-weds. We seen a lot of funny tricks like that. The things people do when they undress in front of each other!

Freda Shaw was the leader of the band and she also played some drums and did the vocals. She was the worst one in the band but she had organized and angled the job. Freda used to organize choruses for movies and she'd work in the movies herself once in a while. Earl Thompson, the fine trumpet player that was later with Andy Kirk, was with us, too. Then we had Wilmer Bratton on violin and drums, and our piano player was Harold Brown – that's Lawrence Brown's brother. In fact we had a pretty good little band.

We used to play for dancing and dinner music. Freda sang those high-powered deals like operettas, things like *Naughty Marietta*, *The Chocolate Soldier* and *The Desert Song*. We had to play her arrangements at dinner. Earl could play real soft and he did it using open trumpet. Not many guys could do that in a dining room. He didn't need a mute and never used one. He had perfect control; he could make high C with his trumpet hanging up on a string, no pressure at all. With Earl we'd go play in the state rooms, since he played so soft. You couldn't make any noise there. The violin player would play guitar and I'd play low-register clarinet. Sometimes Earl would play guitar, too. Later on I saw him again in Seattle and he was playing steel guitar; he had quit playing trumpet. He'd play vibes, too. He was killed changing a tire by the side of the road. Earl was a wonderful musician. Wilmer Bratton was a helluva fiddler but you never heard of him; he never played any place outside Los Angeles.

Harold Brown was only 17 years old and he'd hardly had a professional job before, certainly not a boat job, which was considered a good deal at that time. We had to get permission from his father for him to play with us. Harold was a gullible young guy. The first thing one of the fellows working on the boat did was to give him a bucket and to tell him to go out and fill it with fog. And Harold tried.

Everyone knows they call San Francisco "the city by the Golden Gate," and Harold was under the impression you really sailed through a gate made of gold. I couldn't believe it when he asked me, had I seen the gate. I told him, "Yeah, I've seen it several times, but we don't pass through there until four o'clock in the morning." He asked me what it was like and I said it was made out of solid gold and had pretty red lights on it, diamonds and rubies, all this kind of stuff. You might think this was ridiculous but he believed it. Anyway poor Harold stayed up all night watching out for the Golden Gate. Him and me shared a state room and he came in about five o'clock and he was tireder than hell. He woke me up and he says, "I don't know about that Golden Gate. I stayed up all night long and I ain't seen it yet. How can I have missed it?" He was so cold from sitting up there on deck. I says, "Well you probably fell asleep and didn't even notice it. Too bad." And he believed me.

Another thing I remember about Harold from those days on the boat was when he went into one of the whorehouses on Yesler Way in Seattle. This was one of the big streets in Seattle for prostitution. A guy from Seattle met us off the boat and took us up to this whorehouse. This was probably the first time Harold had ever been in a house of prostitution and he was just fascinated. The going price for turning a trick with a broad was two dollars. I think he broke a 20-dollar bill and he turned about ten tricks that night: ten different broads. Like I say, he was young.

When we first got on the boat the captain, whose name was Proctor, was loaded all the time; he'd drink like hell. You had to go through your fire drill and all your instructions. In case of an emergency, any kind of disaster at sea, the musicians were supposed to stand there and play the National Anthem to help calm people down. We went to rehearsal and said we understood this. Sure enough, we did have an emergency. Bells started ringing and I thought, "Let's get out of here." The goddam boat had hit a rock and run off course. The guy on the top bunk fell down on to Bratton, the violin player, and he shouted out the boat was sinking. I got my pyjamas and left my clarinet and everything. When we got on deck old Proctor was there. I was running behind him, so he grabbed me by the back of the pyjamas and he says, "Where in the hell is your horn? You know your instructions, you supposed to play." I says, "Not me, every man for himself." He says, "I'm going to have you guys for mutiny. I'm gonna put you in irons." He fired a pistol in the air and I dived into a lifeboat. Not only me – all the waiters, too. However, the rock didn't knock a hole in the outer hull. The boat listed a little but it wasn't as bad as we thought. Nothing happened about all that mutiny stuff, either. It was real funny. We told Proctor that we wouldn't play any music if the boat was sinking. As scared as that, what would we play? I asked him if the other musicians played. He said, no, so that was that.

I was bootlegging on that boat, me and the second cook, whose name was Boudreau. He was a half-assed hustler in Seattle and we got in with him. He says, "I can't hustle them state rooms, I'm here cooking. This will make it just right for you and me. I can get us that White Satin gin out of San Francisco for 24 dollars a case." A case was 12 bottles. They was fifths, nothing but bath-tub gin in them, but they had all these phony labels stuck on them. Boudreau says, "I'll keep the stuff in the kitchen, in among the food where the people won't see it." You couldn't buy liquor on the boats. You have to remember it was Prohibition then; it wasn't legal to sell liquor. They could put you in irons for bootlegging on the high seas. That would be a Federal offence: everything is Federal when you hit the ocean.

After we got through playing for dinner the waiters would hustle the passengers for us, asking them if they wanted a little entertainment in the state rooms. So almost every night they'd give us ten dollars apiece to play for an hour or so. Usually this was me and Bratton. The passengers would always have something to drink and they'd run out and ask us whether we knew where they could get some extra liquor. I'd say, "Well I do know someone who's got some, but I don't know if he would sell us some. It's private stuff." They'd always want some and we'd tell them it would cost 15 dollars, something like that. We'd never sell it lower than ten dollars. Only cost us two. I'd go up there to the kitchen pantry and some nights I'd sell four or five bottles of gin. If I seen a cat who was real drunk I'd give him two bottles for 40 dollars. A lot of these guys had real money. This bootlegging money was more than we made in a week. It was beautiful.

We made a hundred dollars a month salary, plus our room and board. Freda Shaw seen that we got first-class accommodations. We didn't eat in no galley with the waiters, we ate with the passengers, and we had our own waiter, just like the passengers; Freda seen to that.

Whenever I got to Seattle I always had a room with some broad, something like that. We'd get in, just for two nights, and meet some broads, and when we got through we'd go down to 12th and Jackson. They had a zillion bootlegging joints in Seattle and there was always broads looking for you. Not only that, a lot of whores was crazy about musicians. They'd give you a little money, so I did a little light pimping on the side. That was just a way of life then. Syphilis? I did that, too, but it was nothing the medication couldn't handle. You name me a musician that didn't. Your standard equipment was a Bull Durham cigarette bag with a drawstring. If you got a little clap, as they called it then, you just got your gun with that medicine in it, took your bag, put a little cotton in it and tied it up.

All these houses had peep-holes, people was peeping and seeing. In fact there was an extra charge in whorehouses if you wanted to peek in at somebody. I'm simply telling you the facts of a musician's life then.

It's a miracle that any musician that lived during Prohibition and drank, like me and a lot of guys did, is still living today. The bad liquor was enough to kill a mule, and we drank it every day. It's nothing to brag about but it's the truth. It did kill a helluva lot of them and it's still killing a lot of them. Still, Alphonse Picou drank like a fish and so did Kid Ory, for that matter, and both of them lived to be a hundred years old, so what you going to say? Look at the wrong things people do today. You live until you die, until your time comes. God knows, I did enough wrong things.

When I was in Los Angeles a lot of musicians would come back from Seattle and tell you how great it was, how much money you could make. When I was offered the job on the boat I had that in mind, too. I did two seasons on the *HF Alexander* and I liked working on that boat. The Admiral Line was a subsidiary of the Dollar Line that ran the big passenger liners out of Seattle to the Orient. There must have been a half dozen of them, all named after presidents. So that was on my mind as well. Once you got on a boat you could get on another one.

Of course I never seen much of the Los Angeles guys once I got on the boat, but I used to read about them. Word of mouth, too, guys talking. The big thing was in 1930 when Louis came out to work at the Cotton Club. Louis got busted and went to jail but they let him out. He didn't stay in there no time at all.

After the first of October I was offered a job, and from then I stayed in Seattle working on the side in nightclubs. The salary wasn't too terrific, about 45 dollars a week, but you'd make 200 to 300 dollars a week in tips. I liked Seattle.

FOUR

There's never been a town like Seattle

Word spread around among musicians that you could make money in Seattle. It was a money town. You went to work in a joint there and you always had 45 dollars a week guaranteed. The house usually had a kitty cast out of plaster of Paris and painted; it would have a big mouth and they put a light in it. You had a lot of silver dollars in those days and people would throw a dollar into the kitty and hit a little level inside and its eyes would light up. People got a kick out of that, seeing the goddam cat blink his eyes. That's the way you'd make your tips.

With all of this going on, it brought whores in from all over the USA. They had legitimate red-light districts there, which consisted of Jackson Street, King Street and Yesler Way. Seattle was a seaport, an open town, and at these after-hours clubs we had a lot of the sporting class of people used to come in, like pimps and prostitutes. Black pimps would even get hold of white whores. Seattle was the first place I seen a pimp out with a stable of hustling broads. Sunday night was, for some reason, their night out. They'd come to show off in these different joints and see who could outspend each other putting money in the kitty. Us musicians just loved that. The whores would request a song and, if they didn't give you a five-dollar tip, they got an awful short song or a pretty bad version of it. In a place like the Black and Tan we'd have several entertainers that would go to the tables and sing songs. We would wind up sometimes making 200 or 300 dollars apiece – once in a while even 400 dollars.

Pretty soon I had this little ol' gal used to give me a few dollars. Her name was Lily. Very few of those loose whores didn't have a pimp. Now, whores like to be kicked around a little, that's part of their life. I think they get their jollies off that way, by getting beat up. A lot of them want to test you. Lily and me was coming out of a joint; I don't know where we'd been but I do know we were walking alongside a picket fence. She says, "You don't love me, do you? You don't like me much." I says, "Sure I like you, you giving me money, ain't you," and then she says, "How come you don't beat me up a little? You afraid of me? You don't beat me up like Walter Green or Cookie or them other big pimps. You kinda small-time."

That made me mad, so I said to myself, this bitch is trying to start some shit with me and I'm gonna show her. I let her have it. I wound up and hit her in the jaw, knocking her up against this picket fence. As I remember, she was a little bit heavy – shaped good but weighing about 150 pounds. She was strong, as I found out. She come off that fence with a piece of picket in her hand and she said, "You dirty bastard, I'll show you about hitting me." She just about tipped me with the end of that picket, but that was enough. I probably set a few world records in sprinting that night. The way I run across that field they couldn't catch me with an automobile. I think that ended my pimping days, too. I said, "I'm gonna stick with my music from now on. To hell with these whores, this ain't no life for me."

You know, you try these things. You smoke a little weed, and when I was with the gangsters I even sniffed a little coke. You see them doing it, you want to try. I didn't do it but once. First place, I never cared for any of that stuff 'cause it interfered with my drinking. It counteracts the alcohol and I loved alcohol too much.

Gus DeLuce came up to Seattle and stayed around there. We worked together on a few jobs and then he began pimping seriously. He got him a couple of broads and went to Bend, Oregon, which was nothing but a whistle stop then, although it's a place where a lot of people are moving now. You'd have a lot of sheep-herders coming in there, so Gus opened a whorehouse. He made a lot of money but he was a guy that, fast as he made it, he drank it up, spent it, or gambled it away. Finally him and the sheriff got into a fight because Gus didn't pay the protection money he's supposed to pay, and they gave him a floater out of town. That's when the guy tells you to float on out of town and you gotta go, man.

I worked first with a piano player named Palmer Johnson, moving around various clubs. The ones I remember most was owned by Bill Bowman, a nightclub promoter. He had a place they called the Chateau, which was on Yesler Way where all the hookers, pimps and whores hung out. When the Chateau closed Bill moved down about six or seven blocks from there to Reindeer Avenue and Yesler, to a place called the Blue Rose, a pretty elaborate after-hours joint. We had a combo with Palmer on piano, a banjo player that also played guitar named Banjoski (never knew his real name, good vocalist, too) and Bill Hoy on drums.

Palmer was born in Texas but he went to Los Angeles when he was very young. I met him there when he was about 17 years old. He was an amateur fighter and he was pretty good. Palmer's mother had a soul-food restaurant on 33rd and Central Avenue. I only remember playing a few jobs with Palmer in Los Angeles because he left for Seattle before I did, probably around 1926. We joined up again as soon as I got off the boat. We played at the Blue Rose for about six or eight months. Then Palmer and I started working with a good banjo player from Newark, New Jersey, named Freddy Vaughn, at Herman Myers's taxi-dance hall at the foot of Yesler Way on First Avenue. It catered for soldiers, sailors and different guys from the services. We had five pieces, all black musicians. Freddy was the leader. He had played at the Follies Theater and worked with Paul Howard and all those good bands in Los Angeles. I had met him there before he came to Seattle. I ran into him again when I was with Joe Liggins around 1945 in Newark. He came to the show to see me. Freddy was working there as an elevator operator and he died in Newark.

At that time Palmer, Freddy and I was the only guys in the band from Los Angeles; Lee Phillips the trumpet player and a drummer was local. It was a typical taxi-dance, they all had the same formula. You had no admission to pay and you got a roll of ten tickets for a dollar. It was a four-hour deal, 8 p.m. to 12 p.m. Mutt Carey's job was much easier because we had two saxophones. For

Myers's we had only one. Freddy never took too many solos, so it was just up to me and Lee. Still, the taxi-dance wasn't really hard. On top of that I'd work little extra music jobs in the daytime and then play a job in an after-hours joint. I'd go down to 12th and Jackson. Maybe I wasn't hired but the guy would say, "Come on and sit in, Joe, and we give you part of the kitty." That's where the money was anyway. Some of the musicians was just working for the kitty alone or for a dollar a night beside the kitty. If the kitty didn't make you 45 dollars a week the house would make up the difference; that was the guarantee. Hell, you made that money every night.

We stayed at Myers's place for a long time, maybe a year and a half. Then I went to Vancouver with Freddy in 1929 and played three weeks at the Capeliano Canyon Hotel. After that Palmer and I worked at a big road-house called the Jungle Temple on Everett Highway for a guy named Fred Owens. A girl named Babe Hackett had the band and later I took over. This was the first time I really had the opportunity to have my own band. Babe got drunk and they asked me to take the band over. It was a house band and they called it the Jungle Temple Syncopators. This was around the back end of 1929.

Palmer only played with us for a while. Of course, I teamed up with him again, but we replaced him with Oscar Holden, a piano player out of Chicago who had played with Freddie Keppard and those guys. He was very good. One of Oscar's great friends was Ollie Powers, who worked a lot in Chicago with Jimmie Noone in the early days. Ollie had quite a voice and was an entertainer.

Around this time I got to know a kid who would probably have been the greatest of all tenor men if he'd lived. This was Dick Wilson. His father died when he was real young and he was raised by his mother, a nice iron-willed woman. So it was just him and his mother. They were living in an apartment house right nextdoor to my house in Seattle. When Dick was about 17 years old his mother asked me if I would teach him saxophone. I didn't really want to be bothered with pupils, rather like Picou, but I said if he came over to the house I'd give him some pointers, just as a favor. I didn't want a regular pupil because it took too much time. Still, Dick was a helluva nice kid and I could see he was loaded with talent, so I started giving him lessons on alto sax. When he started playing he kinda copied my style a little, but he had an individual sound even then. He was just a natural. A year after I taught him he was a better saxophone player than me.

A piano player friend from Portland, Oregon, named Don Anderson, came to my house and he wanted me to go back to Portland to play tenor with him. I never played much tenor but I had one. I had a good job at the Jungle Temple so I told him, no. He asked me, could I recommend anybody, and I thought about Dick. I said, "I gotta pupil nextdoor, maybe his mother would let him go. He don't have a tenor sax but I could loan him mine if he'd be interested. He hasn't too much experience but plenty of talent." I took Don over to Dick's apartment and he talked to Dick and his mother. Dick was a good boy and usually listened to his mother. She was awful strict on him. Dick was 18 and he wanted to go, so his mother said, "Joe, you know this guy and Dick wants to go. If you loan him your horn, I'll be responsible for it." That's how Dick Wilson started playing tenor, using my old Holton. So Dick went on to Portland and worked with Don

Anderson for a year. Before that he had worked in my band with me; we made a team playing altos. Dick never did fool with a tenor, although he'd play clarinet sometimes.

Then Dick came home and he brought my tenor back. He liked tenor and he bought him his own horn and stayed with it. He rejoined my band. I was still playing alto and we'd been out at the Jungle Temple all the time Dick had been away. We had the two saxophones and a trumpet player named Jimmy Adams. Jimmy and his brother Wayne, a sax player that wasn't in the band, was very good musicians. I had Babe Hackett back playing piano, and a drummer out of Detroit named Baby Borders was with us. We didn't have a bass. Dick was playing good then. We used to broadcast twice a week. We were playing stuff something in the John Kirby style. Not quite as technical as Kirby, perhaps, but definitely swing. It wasn't dixieland.

For a while we had Eddie Rucker, one of the world's greatest nightclub entertainers, working with us. People came from all over the Pacific Northwest to hear Eddie; he used to do a lot of X-rated off-color tunes. He made so much money. The Jungle Temple had little individual booths with a drawn curtain so you could have private entertainment. You had to pay Eddie a lot of money to come in and sing for you. He might keep the curtain open a little, push in a little roll-away piano which had four octaves, and we'd stand around outside and play. We would average 75 or a hundred dollars a night in that kitty! I remember we had another trumpet player during that time; might have been Herman Grimes.

Dick wasn't with us too long, maybe a month or two. He left Seattle with a band called Gene Coy and another good tenor player named Bumps Myers came into the band. Bumps was another of those Los Angeles musicians that came to Seattle on account there was so much more money around. I worked with Bumps at the Entertainers, also in Seattle, but never in Los Angeles.

Gene Coy was originally from Amarillo, Texas, and his nephew is Jesse Sailes the drummer. Gene had settled in Seattle and I played a few dates with him before Dick did. When he had his big band, which was a pretty good band in those days, they played a place called the Butler Hotel. He'd sometimes need a saxophone player for a couple of weeks. Later Gene's band broke up and the rest of his musicians went down to Los Angeles – including Jonesy (Reginald Jones) the bass man. Then Gene and his wife had a duo deal. She played piano and he played drums. Later on Dick joined Zack Whyte, and from there he went with Andy Kirk. He was with Andy Kirk when he died. Kirk had a fine band. Talk to the top guys about Dick and they'll tell you he'd have been ranked up there with Lester Young as the greatest on his instrument. Try listening to *Until the real thing comes along*. I talked to Don Byas in Paris when I was over there with Louis and he said he was influenced by Dick Wilson.

Dick fell in love and married a beautiful little 17-year-old Canadian chick from Vancouver. She gave him syphilis and he failed to take proper care. Just went to hell, started drinking and going down. Over the next four or five years he went blind. When he knew what she'd done to him, he just didn't seem to care. He was drunk all the time. I run across him a couple of times with Andy, and I used to talk to him like a father. I'd say, "Goddam, Dick, what the hell you trying to do, kill yourself?" He says, "I'm just havin' fun." One time at a jam session him and me were playing some duets and he was so good. I asked him why he didn't look after himself. He said he'd had some shots but hadn't continued with the treatment. He was so crazy about this kid he married, he just gave up. Didn't want to live. This was just before the end. He died very young. He was such a nice clean-cut kid when I used to teach him. I wasn't that great a musician myself but he did listen to me and really learned how to read music. We had little orchestrations for our band. I was a better musician as a reader in those days. Now we don't see music too often. Looking back, Dick was one of the guys I sincerely liked in this business.

During this time I went to Frank Weldon, a helluva good saxophone teacher, the best technician around the Pacific Northwest. Before this I had never had a lesson on the saxophone. I didn't copy anybody. I played like I do now, only with a little more technique. I was considered the best alto saxophone in Seattle at that time, which wasn't saying much. To start with, we didn't have a helluva lot of good alto men in Seattle. Frank had a trio in a Chinese restaurant with a piano player named Archie Jackson, who was out of St Louis, and a drummer named Ralph Gibbs; Ralph doubled on xylophone. Colored guys. I'd go up there and sit in. On top of that, we always got a free meal.

As to sax players, it was Frankie Trumbauer, when those Bix records came out, that was the greatest thing to hit the music scene. Trumbauer's solo on *Singing the Blues* was one of the few tunes I ever copied off anybody. I loved Frankie's C-melody saxophone and I liked Rudy Wiedoft. I hadn't heard too much of Hodges and Carter at that time. I never listened to many records; those by Bix and Frankie were the only ones that made a big impression. Those guys could really play. Aside from them, I heard stuff like *Heebie Jeebies* that Louis did, where he's doing the scat singing, but really the first time I listened to the Hot Five was when I started with Ory in the forties. Hell, music never really bothered me too much, it was only a means of making a living. I couldn't really care less about who was good or who was in which band. I didn't try to copy anybody, just played my music. I drank so much liquor then I wasn't going to listen to any records unless they were extra special.

I left the Jungle Temple and started playing with a band led by a guy named Gerald Wells. He played saxophone and piccolo. Gerald was a prominent bandleader in Seattle and always had a pretty good little band. It was a mixed band: we had about seven pieces and some good arrangements, and we considered ourselves the top band in Seattle. Gerald was from the West Indies but I had first met him in Los Angeles when he used to work there. Originally he had been in San Diego working at Jack Johnson's club. Gerald told a story about some guy coming in the club, all fired up and looking to start a fight. Jack was the former heavyweight champion and came up to the guy to try to talk to him, quiet him down, when the guy swung and knocked Jack cold. The guy says, "I don't allow no one to pull on me, I'm the baddest cat down here." One of the others says, "I just wanted to tell you, in case you didn't know, you just hit Jack Johnson, the former heavyweight champion." When they told him that, the guy damn near tore the building down running out of there.

This had to be about 1918 or 1919 and before that Gerald was with the Spikes Brothers in a band called the So-Different Orchestra. Gerald used to talk about that band all the time. With them he only played flute and piccolo. Later, when I knew him, he played alto saxophone. He went to Seattle in the early twenties and he had a band around the Seattle road-houses for years. Gerald's band used to broadcast live from Station KOL, the biggest radio station in Seattle at the time, and the same station, incidentally, where I made the Johnny Wittwer Trio records in 1944.

Gerald and I worked together off and on for a long time. This would be from 1930. Sometimes I headed my own combos, sometimes I worked with him. He always had a good orchestra. Gerald was a fine musician, a good legitimate man, but he wasn't a jazzman by any stretch of the imagination. He'd play alto and double on flute and piccolo. I played alto and tenor. If a gig called for a tenor, I would play it: in fact I played any saxophone. We had another good saxophone player named Earl Whaley, a black guy, and my old friend Palmer Johnson on piano. Palmer was very good, played with the class of Billy Kyle and could work with anybody's band. Around 1932 Earl Whaley took a band to the Orient with Wayne Adams on sax, Palmer on piano, a drummer named Pumpkin Austin, and Jonesy on bass; Earl played tenor. There was a trumpet man as well. Earl approached me to go but I wanted to stay in Seattle. I think Earl had been over there before and somebody told me later that Earl got imprisoned by the Japanese. The last I heard of Palmer, he went up to Alaska in 1942 and never came back.

With Gerald we played in clubs like the High-Hatters and the Club Royale. Most of our stuff was for dances and we had singing entertainers in there with us, like Lillian Goode. We'd play for the vocalists and sometimes for shows, where you had to do a lot of reading. Some shows would have their own music. If we had some tap dancers or a little line, we would just get tunes like *Moonlight on the Ganges*, which was a great tune for dancers to use, and make up a little arrangement. We didn't play no dixieland because, in the first place, Gerald never knew anybody in that style or anything about the music.

We got a job out at McNeil Island, Washington, a little island in Puget Sound, right near Tacoma, that was a Federal prison for mild offenders. Every 4th of July the prisoners were allowed to bring in outside entertainment. They could do this on Labor Day and other holidays, too. The prisoners had it fairly easy. It was kinda agricultural there, almost a prison without walls; they went in for a lot of gardening and plenty of fresh air.

So we was hired to play for the 4th of July for pretty good money. We got there and they had all kinds of sporting events going on for the prisoners, like relay races, hundred-yard dash, wrestling matches, baseball. A great big colored guy called Iron Man was the favorite in the prison. The prisoners would bet on him to win anything and he won the 800-meter race, the 100-yard dash, the shot putt and the wrestling contest. Then he was up for the heavyweight boxing title of McNeil. That was his last event. Everybody was saying, "You gotta see him box, he's the next champion." He was a big, nice-looking guy, something like Jack Johnson. I didn't see how he could make it, after all he had been running and jumping all day. He's fighting a big Irishman named Willie Kelly and Willie had his rooting section, too. The guy next to me, one of the prisoners, says, "Maybe we could make a bet, 'cause I gotta hunch that Iron Man is about winded and this

Willie guy is kinda fresh. I know a little about fighters!" Iron Man had his seconds with big buckets of water to cool him off. Anyway, no sooner did the bell ring for the first round than Iron Man drew back a punch right from the floor and swung at Willie. If he'd hit him that would've been goodnight for Willie; but he missed by about half an inch. He hit at him so hard he tumbled over and hit his head on the ringpost. My prisoner friend, who had 50 dollars on Iron Man, went and poured a bucket of water on him but he was gone. He stayed out for five minutes, so Willie won the match without landing a punch. I'll never forget that.

Then it was time for us to play. They had a little auditorium for the prisoners and they had a band in there. Something should have told me ahead that it had to be a good band: you had a lot of musicians in there caught for smoking or selling tea – all mild offenders. They had a musician out of Chicago, a little white guy that had been a prominent musician and arranger at one time, and that was the leader of the band. It was a 15-piece orchestra. I remember there was three or four Indians in the band. Anything an Indian did at that time was considered as a Federal offence, so they would send them to McNeil Island. They had one Indian guy, a tenor saxophone player that I had talked to before; he was in there for selling marijuana. He had played with some good bands.

We played and we fancied ourselves a helluva good band, hoping we wouldn't show the prison band up. This was one of the biggest mistakes we ever made in our lives. The warden got up and announced, "Thank you very much, Gerald, and the men in your band. You did a wonderful job and I sincerely hope we can entertain you with our little offering." So we sit down and here come these guys on stage with all these instruments: five saxophones, three trombones and a section of four trumpets. I think the first goddam thing they started playing was *Rhapsody in Blue* and then they went into some hell-fired arrangements; sounded like one of these concert big bands. You talking about guys feeling embarrassed. This band must have played for about an hour. We felt so lousy we didn't want to applaud, but then we started admiring what these guys was doing 'cause they was much better musicians than us. They was pros, and whoever wrote those arrangements arranged like Benny Carter. That experience taught me never to underestimate anybody.

Ralph Capone was in McNeil at this time. He was never considered violent and they got him for tax evasion just as they got his brother Al. That's why they didn't send Ralph to Alcatraz where all the hardened criminals went; he never went in for all that violence like his brother. Al had so much notoriety behind him. A guy in Seattle named Benny Silver, who was a gangster, asked me to take Ralph some cigarettes. I bought them and said I wanted to leave them there for Ralph. Then I happened to see Ralph and we talked for a minute and I shook hands with him. He knew Charlie Berger and he pretended that he remembered me. We reminisced about Charlie and then Ralph says to tell Benny thanks for the cigarettes. Just when I got ready to leave another guy stops me and says, "I've gotta little something here for you that Ralph wanted you to have. Thanks for the cigarettes." It was a 50-dollar bill.

The last time I seen Gerald Wells he was out of the music business. He went into real estate and did very well, had a beautiful home. He died in the Seattle area.

It was around this time that I first met Barney Bigard. Duke Ellington came to Seattle with his band in 1931. I was working then for Noodles Smith, and Earl Whaley said, "Hey, you guys, you want to go down to the train and meet Duke?" Duke had a special car that he traveled in and they stayed right in this railroad car, for the special reason that they played a lot of towns where they couldn't get accommodation in hotels. They must have got into Seattle about five o'clock in the morning and we went down there at six. We'd been working late ourselves. Some of the Ellington guys was already up. First one I ran into was Wellman Braud. I didn't know him but I introduced myself, told him who I was, and he says, "Yeah, I know about you, Joe." Some bullshit like that. Then Barney came out and they introduced me to Barney. I had met his brother Alex when I worked with the Martels in Opelousas. Then I talked to Sonny Greer and Freddie Jenkins.

Noodles Smith owned the Black and Tan at 12th and Jackson, which was one of the top nightclubs in Seattle. He had another smaller club right nextdoor, an upstairs place that used to take the overflow from the Black and Tan downstairs. This little joint was called the Entertainers and the piano player there was Phil Moore. His dad, George Moore, was the manager. Phil was just getting started then. I worked with Phil and Lee Caldwell on drums. I seen Phil later in New York when I was working with Louis and he turned out to be some kind of top drama coach for big stars like Lena Horne and Pearl Bailey – any number of them. Another one who got their start with Noodles Smith was Evelyn Williamson, that later married Marshall Royal. She was a beautiful entertainer. All the big bands that came through Seattle would work at the Black and Tan – bands like Lucky Millinder.

There would always be big-name entertainers around Seattle in those days. Bricktop had been there for a while, although I never knew her. Glover Compton the piano player was a guy that played in these little nightclubs as a single. He never did work with any bands in Seattle that I knew. He had a great reputation as an accompanist and as a soloist, too. Piano players made a lot of money in those different clubs. They had some pretty good gal singers in Seattle then. I'd go in the clubs and sit in and sometimes Glover would be working there. As I remember, Glover was very good. The guy that wrote *I never knew I could love anybody*, a fellow named Tom Pitts, was another man I remember. I played with him. He wrote that tune and sold it to Leo Feist the music publisher for 25 dollars. Later he wrote another tune that Bill Robinson used to feature in his act, called *It's wrong to hit me with a brick*, which is the understatement of the year, isn't it?

I've already told you about Eddie Rucker and how he was one of the greatest-ever entertainers. Well, one time in the Black and Tan, Harold Roberts (the guy that wrote *Hindustan*) came in and asked Eddie if he knew his song – this was before it was published. Eddie prided himself he could sing any song you could name; for songs he didn't know he would make up the words. So he said, "Why, sure I know that song." He started singing *Hindustan* and he told the band, which included Oscar Holden and me, to make an introduction, although we had never played it or heard it before. Then Eddie sang some funny words and Harold let him finish. Eddie asked Harold how did he like his version of the song and Harold says, "I like it fine but it ain't the one I wrote, it ain't my *Hindustan!*"

Another guy that we'd see, especially when a circus was in town, was P. G. Lowery the cornet player, who was a good friend of Oscar's. He always wanted me to come to Cincinnati and work with him; he had a little teaching deal there.

There was a craze for marathon dances during the thirties. That was a damn hard job. We played them in Seattle and you blew your head off. Some of them used bands for a while; then they put on records and played them through a damn horn.

Diamond Lil was a real character and she came down to Seattle. She could sing a little and she sat in with us. Sang a lot of tunes and spent a lot of money – we used to love that. She had a diamond in her tooth like old Jelly Roll did. She had lived up in Alaska. She always said that *Frankie and Johnny* was a true story and I think she sued somebody about that. In later years she lived in Portland and had a shoe-shine stand. We'd go there and get our shoes shined all the time, bring her a little drink or something. She often talked about the incidents in *Frankie and Johnny*. Lil was in Portland for years.

After the stock market crash in '29 Seattle started going down, and after 1930 you couldn't come close to making big money any more. It fell off like hell. Things didn't improve until clear into the thirties. See, the twenties was the glory years and Seattle never did come back to the boom days. I had to look for some side jobs. I used to go out of town to different places. Sometimes we'd take a combo to Montana, other times to Wyoming, and even to Alaska once in a while. In 1929 I boarded the *Yukon Queen* and played on trips between Seattle and Alaska. They had a lot of places to play in Alaska; the tips was terrific. They had all these fishing villages and mining camps with no place else to spend their money. I played up there with Eskimo bands in Sitka, Juneau, Nome. A lot of money in Alaska at one time. Cost you a lot to live in Alaska. I could probably have married an Eskimo princess, but I didn't like fish and walrus meat, so I said that ain't for me. Forget it. I figured it was too damn cold anyway. Still, I'd probably have been a big man in the Eskimo tribe now.

We had a good guitar and banjo player named Ceele Burke from Los Angeles that was in Seattle, and I played with him. His first name was Cecil and his middle name was Louis. If you know Louis Armstrong's record of *I'm confessing*, it's Ceele that makes the introduction of steel guitar. Ceele would say, "I'd work with a snake if they'd pay me." That was my idea, too, which is why I'd play all kinds of music: Mexican bands, Eskimo bands and schottische bands up in Seattle, playing nothing but schottisches for the Swedes, just to keep making some money.

Around this time I took a trio to Green River, Wyoming, and worked for Cat Eye. His place was another kinda bootlegging joint; they had gambling and a lot of sporting women working there. But we didn't want to stay up in Green River for the winter, because in Wyoming you get snow six feet deep. Before we got ready to leave Cat Eye said he'd make a deal with us that we could stay there the winter and he'd put everything on the tab until the joint reopened the next spring. He wouldn't charge us much to stay there and he'd feed us. Then he would take it out of our salary for the next year.

During the winter we got a few customers, but not many, and we still had three or four prostitutes staying there. I liked one of them but the standard going-price in Cat Eye's place was four dollars. But then he gave us a special rate of two dollars for going with a gal; he put that on the tab as well. Cat Eye was another guy like Papa Mutt. He'd have poker games and his damn cards was marked. The thing about it was we knew it and just went along with it. We never figured on paying him in the first place. We'd start a card game and Cat Eye says, "How many chips you want?" I says, "Oh hell, let's go first class, give me 500-dollars-worth of chips." Cat Eye had a book where he kept tabs: like when we'd go to bed with one of the broads he'd put down two dollars, and meals at 25 cents. All the gambling debts would go in, and some nights I'd lose as much as 1000 or 2000 dollars – on credit, of course. Cat Eye would say, "I ain't worried about you guys. I trust you. Besides you better not try to run away from here." He had two great police dogs!

We figured we was going to have to run away sooner or later, 'cause by Christmas we owed Cat Eye about 10,000 dollars apiece. I started making friends with these police dogs, 'cause I knew there was no way in the world we could get away without making friends with these dogs. Cat Eye had a lot of good eats round there, steaks and pork chops, and we started saving part of our meat to feed it to the dogs. Pretty soon we was better friends with those dogs than Cat Eye 'cause we fed 'em better. Just about springtime, when the joint was fixing to reopen, we all slipped out of there one night and took the dogs with us. An old drunk that we'd met took us to the bus-stop and the dogs kept him quiet.

We got to Seattle and before we were settled back in our rooms the union called us. Cat Eye had called the union and told them we'd run off owing him this money. The union guy was flabbergasted. "How in hell can you guys owe this man up in Green River so much money? Joe, you owes 18,000 dollars and Jack Henshaw the piano player owes him 15,000 dollars and Al Riley the drummer owes 16,000 dollars." We explained what had happened and the union guy about fell over laughing. Cat Eye kept on calling and writing until everybody forgot all about the whole damn thing. Still, I never did go back to Green River no more!

I went out on the road with a white pick-up band led by Vic Sewell, part of a group called the Gennessee Street Shufflers. It was just a bunch of us musicians hired by an agent out of Seattle. We traveled in automobiles. This particular night we was coming out of Billings, Montana, and going down this old country road. A guitar player named Bill Rinaldi had been drinking that night and he was driving when this truck just came out and hit us. They didn't have any stop signs on that class of road. This threw me out of the car and then the truck ran over me and broke my back. It turned out a rib had punctured my lung, and later I developed tuberculosis. I was in pretty bad shape. They put me in the hospital in Helena, but they only kept me there a week or so before they brought me back to Seattle. They hadn't put me in a cast then. I don't know if they even knew I had a broken back, but they did know I couldn't walk. They brought me back on the train. I was in a cast for damn near a year. Who says a musician's life is easy?

It was my left lung that was punctured and I developed tuberculosis in that side. They had to give me this operation where they partially collapse the lung. Six doctors told me I wouldn't live six months. They're all dead now! They also told me never to go back to blowing my horn again. After they took the cast off I got so I could maneuver and move around. I had been bedridden for a whole year. They knew I had TB, but if you had a negative sputum, as they call it, your TB was kinda inactive and it was safe for you to be around people. The first thing I did was to take my clarinet and blow a little. They gave you a day off every week for so-called town leave, and every time I got into town I'd go in one of the joints and sit and play. Of course, the doctors didn't know I had my clarinet with me in the hospital.

It was out in the country and they had a lot of wild blackberries and cherries around there. We used to pick the berries all the time. I decided to brew some wine. Naturally, I didn't let the doctors or nurses know about it. Some friends brought me in a box of grapes. I couldn't eat them all so I took a sock, filled it with the grapes, and I squeezed their juice into a couple of gallon jugs. The orderly gave me all the sugar I wanted. I had a little cabinet by my bed which you could close, and I put these jugs in there to ferment. I rigged up an extension with a light bulb to keep it at a steady temperature, and inside 30 days the wine was ready. You put a little olive oil on top of the liquid to keep the air from going in. This stops it from blowing when you cork it. You drank that oil off the top; it didn't hurt you. That liquor was real potent. Every one of those guys in that ward was drunk, plus a couple of the nurses. The doctors never could figure where we got that booze. It was just a gag really.

Usually when you got TB in those days the first thing a person would do was to go to Arizona, on account of the mild climate. It was known for it. I was recommended to a doctor in Phoenix named Dr Merryman. My friend Al Pierre had a band in Portland, and the musicians in Seattle had raised a little money for me. Al said to stop in Portland and he'd have something for me. He had been working at a road-house called Burke's Chalet for quite a time. I stayed there with Al for a couple of days and came on to Los Angeles. This was 1932, right at the time when they was having the Olympics in Los Angeles. I stopped off to see some of my cousins. In fact my older brother Henry had a shoe shop and was living here, so he gave me some money, but things was rough in Los Angeles then.

I headed for Phoenix and found Dr Merryman, who turned out to be a really nice guy. I had met a doctor through Al and he said, "I know you don't have much money. Go and see Dr Merryman if you need any medicine and tell him as a favor to me to do whatever he can for you." This Doc Merryman said, "There ain't much I can do for you. You just have to have the proper diet and rest. I won't charge you anything." The only treatment then for TB was bedrest; now they cure it in a couple of months.

The doctors in Seattle had told me to quit playing when I got out of the hospital and left for Arizona. Don't fool with that horn, they said. I said, to hell with it; if I'm going to die, I'll die playing that horn.

I came down to Phoenix just with my clarinet. I sold my saxophone after the accident. I went to the Musicians' Union and I happened to run across some musicians. I was a pretty good musician and they recognized it. I needed money so I started playing with Terry Danzler's band at a place called the Cinderella Roof, and thinking about it, I started getting better right away. This was a dance band, all white guys. I was just playing clarinet then but there wasn't no dixieland out there. The money wasn't too good as we was only working two days a week. I got some other jobs and I stayed around there for a while until somebody told me the best climate was way up in the mountains. So I went on up to Flagstaff and I started working with a Mexican band – good band, too. We didn't just play Mexican music, no sir, we played a lot of pop music. They had a helluva beat and I taught them how to play some of the dixieland tunes. They was all good players. I got so by just being around them; I learned how to talk Mexican damn good, too. You could have a lot more fun when you met one of those Mexican chicks if you could explain what you wanted! By then I was back playing alto saxophone. One of the guys loaned me a saxophone. Later on this Mexican band went to work in Nogales at a place called the International Club. I didn't want to go and it was about then that somebody recommended me to a bandleader in Flagstaff named Gordon Moore.

This guy wasn't a full-time musician; in fact he worked on a newspaper. This was another all-white dance band and it was pretty bad really. Still, I met some nice guys there and they helped me out. We used to go to work and sometimes I didn't feel too good, and they'd say for me to sit there and not play. The piano player in the band was a woman named Mrs Ruffner. She was an undertaker, owned her own parlor – Ruffner's Undertaking – and I used to make a little side money helping to embalm people. Back in Seattle I had worked with another fellow that was an undertaker and a musician. His name was Ham Jenkins and he always had something to drink around there, so, naturally, I'd hang out with him. He'd be embalming a stiff and eating a sandwich at the same time. The things you do when you're young!

I never made much money around there. Wasn't that much money to be made. Everybody in the band had a day job but I never worked regularly at any place in the daytime. In fact I had a broad on the side used to take care of me and give me money, bring me food, so I stayed with her.

I didn't stay too long with any of these bands. I left Gordon's band and went on to Prescott. Somebody told me it would be cooler and much better for me. I was in a bad state and a doctor was saying that I had only six months to live. I just wanted to get back to Seattle, that was still my home. I was pretty broke and I was looking for ways to make some money. They had an old colored woman named Mrs Alexander that had a restaurant in the town. She didn't serve colored people there, only white. I used to go in there when I had some money to eat. She had a player piano in there and people would get up, put on a piano roll and play that piano. Back in Baton Rouge I had some friends that had a player piano and I used to put rolls on, pump the thing myself, take my clarinet and play old tunes like *Margie, Charmaine, Let me call you sweetheart* and *Over the Waves* – have a one-man band. So I went and told Mrs Alexander, "I'm expecting a wire from some guy about a job and, until I get it, how about you feeding me and I'll entertain the people?" In fact I was expecting a wire from Vic Sewell. She says, "What do you mean? You a piano player? Let me hear you play." I put some rolls on and showed her what I could do. She had tunes like *Angry, Margie* and *Sweet Georgia Brown*. I started pumping and playing the clarinet at the same time. She thought that was the greatest thing in the world. I was staying in a little old rat-trap joint then and paying a dollar a week for it. I told her all about my life story and how I was sick. Mrs Alexander says, "I got some rooms upstairs, nice rooms, and I'll give you your meals and a dollar a night. You don't even have to play if you don't feel like it. I'll put you a little kitty up on the piano so people can put money in there." Shoot, I started playing my low-register clarinet and pumping, and pretty soon I was a big attraction around there. People was amazed, coming round and telling me how nice it sounded. A guy came from the radio station and give me a little plug, and they wrote me up in the paper. I stayed around there for about two weeks until finally I got this wire from Vic Sewell to come and join the band. Mrs Alexander literally cried when I told her I was leaving. This was deep in Depression times, around '33. Things was bad, and with that dollar, room rent and meals, plus a dollar and a half or two dollars in tips, I'd be making maybe 20 or 25 dollars a week, which was a fortune in those days. I often think of that little town, Prescott, Arizona, and Mrs Alexander, that wonderful old lady, and how she looked after me.

I worked my way back to Seattle with Vic Sewell's band. Al Pierre wanted me to come back and work with him, but I didn't go to work with Al, not right away. I started working with Oscar Holden again, this time at Bill Bowman's Blue Rose. Bill was a helluva nice fellow. He wasn't a pimp but a businessman, and he married a Frenchwoman that had a whorehouse, made a lot of money. He had a nightclub, no special name, on 18th and Madison, where we used to play. We had a terrific singer with us named Velma Winslow, beautiful girl. Then he opened the Blue Rose, a fabulous nightclub, on the edge of the red-light district – after-hours and bootlegging, of course. In Oscar's band we had Bill Hoy on drums, a guitar player named Bill Page, and Bill Trent, a guy that sang tenor. He was from Chicago, sang beautifully. We also had Oscar Low, a terrific bass singer, and that gave us a quartet: I sang baritone, Trent tenor and the two Oscars sang bass. Low and Trent didn't play instruments and we had no trumpet player in the band. We played the popular tunes of the day; during that time *After you've gone* came out, and McKinney's Cotton Pickers made a terrific record of *If I could be with you one hour tonight*. In those days all the music publishers had a list of bands and active nightclubs, and they'd send you a lead sheet or little orchestration *free* 'cause they wanted their tunes played. That's the way we came by a lot of our music.

We didn't have any special arrangements, we just read the stocks. A lot of times we only had the piano part, and if somebody didn't write the lead, we would just listen while the piano player played it through. We got a lot of songs from the entertainers because they had to know the current pop tunes in order to make money. You probably had one new pop song a month in those days.

I could read well and I did a lot of solos, too. Hell, I was often working by myself. I would pick up my clarinet and play but I played more saxophone for the simple reason a lot of people wanted saxophone then. Up until Benny Goodman started coming along on records they didn't want a clarinet; after that they started looking back to the clarinet, and gradually I played more. Our group was a jazz band; we didn't call it dixieland. I didn't play any dixieland in Seattle until I met Doc Exner in the forties.

While I was working at the Blue Rose in 1934, I remember the Dionne quintuplets was born and John Dillinger was killed. One of our best customers was one of the Seagrams that owned Seagram's Distillery in Canada. He'd come down just to hear Eddie Rucker. Other prominent people that came in included Gypsy Rose Lee – she's from Seattle – Johnny Dore, the Mayor of Seattle, who was a good friend of mine and liked a nip, and Joe Gottstein that had a couple of whorehouses for both men and women.

Another guy who came by all the time was Judge Bell; they called him the hanging judge in Seattle. If he caught you in one of these illegal bootlegging joints or he caught you speeding, he'd give you the limit of what he could give you. He was an old guy, a Southerner from Virginia, and he used to like to sing quartets with the band. We asked him, "What if this place gets raided, what's gonna happen if they catch you here?" Judge Bell says, "Don't worry, they ain't gonna catch me in a raid but they gonna catch you guys, though." We thought we was friends with the Judge but he says, "We friends as far as the nightclub is concerned but please don't come before me in court." Sure enough, they raided the place and for some reason they threw us in the drunk tank. Bill Bowman bailed us out right away, so three or four days later the place opened up again and we went back to work. Judge Bell had fined us all a hundred dollars for a first offence and here he comes back into the Blue Rose. We said, "Judge, you ought to be ashamed of yourself. You knew us, we thought we was friends, and you fine us a hundred dollars." He starts laughing and he says, "Well, I tell you, Joe, don't do as I do, do as I *tell* you to do, and bring a round of drinks." Kinda funny.

Actually, the damn place was always getting raided and we was jumping out of the windows, out of back doors, stupid things like that, to get away from the Federal agents or the sheriff. This was during Prohibition days. Even after President Roosevelt got elected and the Federal Government decided to abolish Prohibition, they left it up to the individual states to make their own laws. In California they started having beer parlors and open bars, but Washington and Oregon voted to have the state handle liquor sales through state stores. You had to have a permit to buy liquor. You didn't have any open bars in Seattle; that's why they had bootlegging joints up until I left in 1944 to come back down to Los Angeles to play with Kid Ory. We'd stay in those joints all night and all the next day sometimes. We'd go to work about one o'clock in the morning and never leave as long as we had some paying customers. Once in a while you'd get some guys that would stay drinking ten or 12 hours, guys with a lot of money, keeping the musicians there. We played songs like *Dream House, Ballin' the Jack, Margie, If ever I had my way* and *My Man*, one of the great, great favorites where we made a lot of money.

I was on the WPA (Works Progress Administration) during the Depression. I thought I wanted to teach and I had a bunch of kids that was the dumbest you ever seen in your life. They hurt my ear drums and I had a hangover one morning, just went out of my mind. I had one kid called Johnny, squeakin' and squallin' on his clarinet, and I knew he wasn't practicing; 20 kids blowing their horns and my head was hurtin'. I got the axe I kept in the broom closet to split kindling for our big old wood-burning stove. I wanted to impress that kid, so I says, "If you don't learn, I'm gonna crease your skull with this axe." He started howling and then all of them started howling and I went berserk. I almost got into a lot of trouble; they was going to put me into a strait-jacket. I says, "I better get out of this business. Will you guys take these damn kids, do something with them? I'm gonna quit." In fact they fired me anyway. I quit drinking heavy after that.

Thinking back to my drinking days, you'd find that bootleggers had all kinds of ways to attract customers. We had a great big old colored guy called Doorbelly (he had a belly as big as a door), who had a bootlegging joint where we'd go when we got off work at six or seven in the morning. You'd go there and get a "deep moon" – that's moonshine. Doorbelly always gave you the first drink for free, otherwise it was half a water-glass of moonshine for 25 cents. You'd find all the musicians drank liquor at Doorbelly's just because the first one was on the house. He was a nice guy and we'd hang around there. I don't think the law ever did catch him bootlegging. The cops never found out that Doorbelly had his vats of liquor up in the loft of the house with some pipes leading down to the faucet, just like water. Naturally, you had to pay protection to the city police to keep them from raiding the joint; you couldn't pay any protection to the Federal agents or G-Men. Seattle was a racket town where you could open any kind of joint if you paid off the right people. They had a colored go-between named Felix Crane that went between the law in Seattle and the operators; he was what you call a bag man. He handled the protection money paid by the bootleggers, the whore houses, the hop joints where you could smoke opium, or anything else illegal. If you wanted to open an after-hours joint or if you had a house of prostitution, you'd see Felix and pay the going rate. This all lasted until they voted in a woman mayor. An old preacher named Mathews got her into it and after that they closed up the joints for a couple of years. Then they put in Johnny Dore and he opened everything up again.

We musicians would often wind up at these whorehouses just to be drinking and talking to the broads. We didn't necessarily go there to turn a trick or go to bed with them. Fancy Johnson was a friend of ours that had a whorehouse, and we was sitting there one time when they ran out of liquor. This was in the summertime so they sent this little Japanese guy out to get supplies. We look out and here he comes with a big overcoat on, looking to be the same size as Meade "Lux" Lewis. It turns out that he had about 15 douche bags, we used to call them hot water bottles, full of moonshine under his coat. He went in the kitchen and poured them into a big container – came to about three gallons. I never seen nothing like that before. Another thing, a lot of these places had colored fags. I worked with a lot of gay piano players, too, like Jack Henshaw. What I wanted to say about gay people was that I never had any problems with them. I really liked them all.

I started running on the ocean liners again, going to Alaska and different places. Boat music was a lot of fun and you made money a lot of ways. Al Riley the drummer offered me a job on the President boats going to the Orient. We had a piano player named Ronnie Bowers, and Frank Bufaro, an accordion player. We was making a hundred dollars a month but we also made a lot of tips and we did a little bootlegging on the side. We could buy a lot of stuff. We took the head off the bass drum and put a whole lot of cymbals in there, bought them for practically nothing. When we sold them we made more than our pay for the trip.

The boat left from Seattle and went to Tokyo, Yokohama, Hong Kong, Manila, sometimes to Honolulu, each trip lasting 21 days. When we hit these ports we always went to the dance halls, just like the taxi-dances back home. We'd go pick up a couple of broads and go home with them. One time Al Riley, who was the bandleader, and I went out on the *President McKinley* and when we docked in Manlai, which was one of our favourite places, we picked up two beautiful Filipino girls. They had long silky black hair and we bought them lot of drinks and food; wound up going to their room and, naturally, we was looking to have a little romance with them. We came to find out they wasn't girls at all, more like gay people, and we got as mad as hell. Al says, "Look, you guys or gals, whatever you are, we spent 10 or 15 dollars apiece on you and we want our damn money back. If we don't get it back I'm gonna cut your goddam hair right off." Al went and found a pair of scissors but these guys didn't want that beautiful long hair cut off so they gave us our money back.

We'd just have four or five pieces with Jack Henshaw on piano, or sometimes Vic Sewell, then Arnie Sewell, his brother, with Jack Foy or Al on drums. Jack Foy and I worked together for a long time in Seattle. Later on Jack was President of the Las Vegas Musicians' Union for 20 years.

Most of these liners had colored waiters and we had a waiter called Sheffield who fell into the ocean when we was docking at Hong Kong. A Chinaman with a sampan came along and got him half out of the water. He asked Sheffield, "You gimme cumshaw?" – "cumshaw" meaning money. Sheffield says, "I don't know what the hell you mean," so the Chinaman drops him back in the ocean and he damn near drowned. This had to be in 1934. I made half a dozen trips on these ocean liners, and when the boats docked back in Seattle we'd be in port for a month or more before we'd go out again, so we'd go right back to work in the clubs.

I also ran on excursion boats out of Portland, Oregon. One time there was a guy that had gotten into an argument with some broad. The guy was drunk and the girl stuck a knife in his back; he didn't even feel it. She ran off. I was just standing there looking on and somebody said, "Hey, do you know what that girl did to you? She stuck a knife in your back." It's a wonder it didn't puncture his lung. The fellow reached round, pulled the knife out and told the bartender to put a little rye on the wound.

Al and I used to go out on the crabbing boats, too. They had fleets of them, way out in Puget Sound. The boats had a little galley on board and they needed a guy to cook. You didn't need to be a good cook to go out there and I didn't really want to go but Al said, "For the hell of it, come on and we'll get drunk." We bought some flour and I had mixed some biscuits, plus stuff like spaghetti and meat balls. We was out for three weeks. This was between music jobs.

About this time I went back to the Black and Tan and I had a chance to work with Eubie Blake. He had come to Seattle with a show which had ended its run there, so he decided to stay around and he worked down at the Black and Tan with us for a couple of weeks. What a nice guy he was. My good friends Floyd and Lucille Levin always doubted my veracity when I told them about Eubie being in Seattle in 1934. In April 1980 I played a concert with Bob Higgins's band at Barnsdall Park in Hollywood and Eubie was there as a guest of Floyd and

Lucille. I went over and started talking to Eubie about the different things that had happened in Seattle, about us getting drunk together and working at the Black and Tan. Finally Eubie says, "Hey, Joe, something's been bothering me for 15 years. I'm sure glad to see you and maybe you can put my mind at ease. What was the name of the owner of the Black and Tan? You remember the guy, he used to sleep all the time. He'd ask you a question, and before you could answer he would fall asleep." I says, "Oh yeah, I remember. His name was Noodles Smith. He was so busy making money, he never got any rest." Eubie just howled with laughter and he says, "That's been worrying me for years trying to think of that guy's name. I ain't never run into anybody like that." Floyd thought I was telling one of my stories but Eubie said it was all true. We had a real good reunion.

Another story from those days concerns a guy named Rooster Jenkins that had a trained rooster called Sonny Boy. I first met Rooster when I was in the minstrel show down South. He was a genius when it came to training birds and had a quality act. He was on the Pantages and Orpheum circuits with Sonny Boy, and came to Seattle on the Pantages circuit. His contract ran out there so he decided to stay around and book his act locally. We was all working at a place called the Chinese Garden where they had a floorshow, and in the band was Earl Whaley on tenor and a trombone player out of Chicago called Lafayette "Fate" Williams that died in Seattle.

Rooster had a big carrying box for Sonny Boy which he never let out of his sight, even kept it in his hotel room. The act consisted of doing a parody on the tune *Sonny Boy* in blackface with the rooster standing up in the palm of his hand, following the words of the song and looking at Rooster. The finale of the act had the bird making chicken noises and Rooster saying . . . "the world knows and I do, you taste better than beef stew. You've chased your last hen, Sonny Boy," and with that, he'd take Sonny Boy, put him in a big gunny sack and sling him over his shoulder as he went off stage. You had to see the whole act; it was kinda funny. Rooster never drank too much, but this particular night at the Chinese Garden we had a few drinks and Rooster left Sonny Boy in the kitchen. A Chinaman named Charlie Louis owned the place. The head chef didn't show up so they put another guy on. He mistook Sonny Boy for a live chicken and butchered him. We didn't know nothing about this when we came back to work that night. Rooster didn't come on for his part of the show for an hour and he arrived late. He says, "I'll go on back there and get Sonny Boy and you can hit my introduction." We hit it. No Rooster. So we hit again. Pretty soon all hell let loose in the kitchen with Chinamen flying out in all directions. Here comes Rooster with this cleaver chasing one of them, and, believe me, the place cleared except for one guy sitting at a table eating chop suey. Rooster wanted to kill this poor guy and went over, picked up the bowl of chop suey and dumped it on top of his head. "You know what you doing? You eating my act, you eating Sonny Boy." They had to put him in a strait-jacket and lock him up. Rooster had plumb black hair before all this, but when he got out of jail the next day he was white-haired. He had turned gray overnight. A booking agent in New York sent him a telegram three or four days later offering him 500 dollars for his act and Rooster replied, "Sorry, Chinaman eat my act." That was the end of that deal.

Talking about the heart of the Depression, things was pretty tough. I was married at that time to Margaret and we had a nice home but I had to look for some side jobs. They had big warehouses where people on welfare that wasn't working could come with vouchers and get coal and all kinds of groceries. I knew some people there so I got me a job at the commissary. It was just like a supermarket today, full of hams, sides of bacon, big bags of beans, potatoes, so consequently I'd take stuff home every night. My apartment looked like a supermarket. Everybody else was stealing and I'd sell the food on the side, like a 15-pound ham for three or four dollars, making money that way, too. Welfare couldn't give you cash to buy anything; you had to take your vouchers to the commissary. You had a slip showing how many you had in your family and they had your record right there. I got something like 30 dollars a month, my groceries and whatever I could steal!

In another way, I was lucky. I got a job working in a club over at the Bremerton Navy Yard across in Bremerton, Washington. It was a club called Houghton's, later known as the Shellback Inn. I was also able to work at the Officers' Club there. They always had some kind of money. The navy always managed to pay off their men, no question of going broke. I didn't make a lot of money, we worked as cheap as 14 or 15 dollars a week, but the tips, that's what carried you.

The Shellback Inn was right on a lake, kinda like a resort, called Kitsap Lake. You had to take the ferry between Seattle and Bremerton, about an hour's ride. You'd always have time to play cards and have drinks. Eventually we started staying over at the club. We had an entertainer with that band, a gal named Flo, who was so damn fat she could hardly stand up. She used to drink a lot, and even when she was singing a song she'd always be leaning up against a post or the piano just to keep from falling over.

Sometimes the band was white guys, sometimes it was black guys, sometimes it was mixed. I met a guitar player named Virgil Ireland – called him Irish – and we got to be friends and started working together. He had come to Seattle from Kansas City with a guy named Joe Callantyne to work on the ocean liners. Later on we played with a band led by Red Fox.

Big Foot Smitty was a piano player that I knew from Seattle that was living in Bremerton. Him, me and Irish worked together at times at the Shellback Inn. They had little cabins there where we used to stay sometimes. Liquor was legal then but you couldn't buy it over the bar, so bootleg liquor was always on sale. Old Roy Houghton, the owner, was a character and he'd say, "I guess you boys want a little oil, don't you? Let's get oiled up." He never called it liquor, always oil. That was his expression. So we used to stay "oiled up" quite a lot.

Anyway, this particular night it was just Smitty, me and a drummer. It was colder than hell and a week night; wasn't anybody in the place. We got a small salary plus the kitty, which on weekends was terrific. These officers would come in there from a torpedo base called Keepwater. Torpedoes have a little motor that's run by alcohol; for some reason they used pure-grain wood alcohol and it's the strongest you can get, like 200 proof. The officers would bring it into the club in gallon cans. You had to cut it, like eight-for-one, with Coca-Cola, or mix it with something. Smitty wanted a drink that night, but Houghton wasn't there so he couldn't get anything. He was mad. We continued playing until this officer comes in with a gal and a gallon of alcohol. His favorite tune was *Paradise*, a waltz, so he came to the piano to ask Smitty to sing it for him. Smitty could sing nicely, he did a single a lot. I knew we was gonna make a little money and he was gonna tip us something plus a drink, but Smitty wanted a drink so goddam bad he was nearly frothing at the mouth. He says, "I'll play it but I won't sing it. I don't feel like singing." The officer was really disappointed. He says, "I'm a good customer." Then he starts thinking of ways to make Smitty sing 'cause his girl wanted to hear that song. Smitty says, "If I had a drink I might change my mind," so the officer says, "I'll tell you what I'll do. I won't only give you a drink, I'll give you five dollars on the side." That was pretty good. Then he says, "I'll pour you out a whole glass of this torpedo juice. See if you can drink it down straight and then play and sing *Paradise*." I don't know why he wanted to do that to Smitty except to get even with him for not doing the tune. Smitty agreed, although I tried to stop him. I wanted that five dollars and a drink myself, but not at that price. Smitty took that glass and he downed it straight. He hit the piano to start the tune and fell off the piano stool backwards. I thought he was dead. Honest to God, he was barely breathing. I run into the kitchen and got Roy to come out with a bucket of water and I doused Smitty with it. He woke up and said, "Where am I, what happened, who hit me?"

The Chief of Police in Bremerton, a guy named Jamie Rondo, had a little boy that fancied himself as a singer. Smitty was teaching the kid how to sing and at that time I had a little radio program on Station KXA in Seattle, so we gave the kid a break and let him sing with us on the radio. It was pretty bad but his dad was a nice guy and he appreciated it. He would let us do anything in Bremerton, even if it was against the law. Bremerton was an open town and if you paid protection you could do what you wanted. You had to buy Jamie. Smitty figured he'd open a whorehouse right by the navy yard gate where all the sailors came out. He had made-to-order customers right there so he got this place and outfitted it like a small hotel. He opened up and on the very first night he got drunk. After the place closed the whores rolled him and robbed him, took all his money. There he was, that was his first and last deal as a landlord in a whorehouse. We laughed like hell. Jamie asked him if he wanted to try again but Smitty said he wasn't cut out to be a landlord. Jamie said, "No, you like gashing whiskey too damn much. Plus you too much of a gash hound." A couple of the whores had made Smitty turn a trick with them and pay off. He didn't like that either, him being the landlord and having to pay the whores.

Things continued like that at Bremerton for quite a few years. It seemed like I more or less settled down. From there, I went back to working in Seattle at a place called Doc Hamilton's along with Palmer Johnson, Bill Page and Pumpkin Austin on drums. Later Oscar Holden worked there as well, along with Bill Hoy. We also had a saxophone player named Tootie Boyd, different musicians all the time. Doc was a big, jolly-looking colored guy, had gold teeth, looked like Jack Johnson. He was probably the greatest barbecue man in the world and invented a secret sauce, had it registered. He put it out for sale in the stores. Doc had all individual rooms in his place and he painted them different colors. He'd say that in the red room there was always fighting breaking out, five to one compared with any other room; purple was next to red, and no fighting in the pale ivory room. Doc kept track of all this, and when he painted all the rooms pale ivory the fights went down one hundred percent. Doc's was a good job; we made good money and tips, got all our food. Our cook used to play as well and I was still working at the commissary off and on, bringing that food home. This was 1936.

I was working there when Kate Smith came to Seattle with her show. Her managers used to come into the club once in a while and I got to be good friends with her drummer. When their saxophone quit he wanted me to go with the show, but I didn't want to go, I was making too much money. I met Jimmie Lunceford for the first time at Pop's place. I remember Jimmie had been playing at Tacoma, about 30 miles from Seattle, and they came in early. I met Jimmie and we went to breakfast. We was friends for a long time after that. The next night, after the band got through playing, Willie Smith and Trummy Young came in and sat in with us. Willie brought his saxophone and his clarinet down there. His clarinet was metal and Willie was the first big-time musician I ever met that played a metal clarinet.

Eddie Swanson, a good piano player, worked with me at this time and we used to go to an Italian restaurant owned by a guy named Joe Romana. Business got so bad he decided to quit. He took a liking to Eddie and me so he just up and gave us the restaurant. Eddie had another deal outside music, he was a supervisor in a state-owned liquor store, but we went in there and did all right. We could have made money, but every broken-down, hungry musician that came to Seattle would head straight for us. It went out all over the States that Joe and Eddie had this restaurant in Seattle. These guys never had any money so we fed them and gave them all the drinks they wanted; we never could turn a hard-luck story down. We had a ball but it was a losing proposition, never made a nickel. A lot of good musicians used to come and sit in, people like Billy Stewart, a fine trumpet player that used to be with Vic Myers, Monty Sewell, my old friend Jack Foy, Bill Trent the vocalist. We probably stayed in there eight or nine months, until the place went broke. Like I said, it didn't cost anything. You'd come, too, wouldn't you?

This was about the time I joined up again with Vic Sewell and his brother Monty in their band the Gennessee Street Shufflers. Vic played piano and Monty was a trumpeter. We started working in a regular beer joint on First Avenue called Lyon's Music Hall. You could serve beer and wine legally in Seattle but you couldn't sell hard liquor. It was Vic, Monty, a bass player named Bill Rinaldi that also played guitar, and Jack Foy on drums. Sometimes Tommy Foy, who played tenor, was with us. We also worked a place called the Spinning Wheel and another one called the Chinese Castle, where I first met Johnny Wittwer's father and mother. The Chinese Castle was a road-house right across from where the big Boeing factory is now. It was a just a cow-pasture then. We was making 200 or 300 dollars a week, tips like nothing, and, fast as we made it, we drank it up or gambled it away. Easy come, easy go.

Sometimes we'd go out fishing in Puget Sound after work. We'd go rent a boat, half-drunk a lot of times, and once in a while we'd catch some salmon. One time it was in the winter and it was colder than hell. The boat turned over and we all damn near got drowned. Lucky we was right near the boat-house and the guy was able to fish us out of the water!

In 1938 I went down to Bakersfield, California, with a pick-up group. We had a six-week engagement at a road-house called Mother Brown's. Al Riley had some connections there, as did Duke Ellefson, a pretty good tenor player, so they got us the job. These were white musicians. We just had four pieces, with Duke and me on saxophones, Jack Henshaw, the gay piano player who was very good, and Al on drums. After a while, we got Monty Sewell down from Seattle to make it a quintet. We got 35 dollars a week with room and board. Played for tips, which was pretty good. We had a girl vocalist and played for dancing. I was on alto and tenor.

We stayed out at the bartender's house. The night we got there the guy says, make yourselves at home. He had a little cabin in the back. Al wanted something to eat and he seen a dozen eggs set out so we made an omelet. When the guy came back he asked us if we'd eaten and we said we'd made an omelet. He says, "Where did you get the eggs?" and Al says, "Well, you had fresh eggs sitting over there." It turns out the guy raised fighting cocks and these happened to be prize eggs for fighting cocks that was just gonna hatch out. We ate those eggs. He about wanted to kill Al. The eggs had cost him ten dollars each and we damn near got fired on our first night.

After that engagement was over I came down to Los Angeles for my first visit there since 1932. Prohibition had gone out and beer joints had sprang up all over LA. They also had open liquor places where you could buy whiskey and mixed drinks. But you still couldn't make money in Los Angeles then, even with tips. The competition was so great musicians would go to work in these joints for nothing, no salary, and a lot of them would pass a hat around or get a little soup bowl and pass it round to get some tips. Things were tough all right.

I turned around and came back to Seattle. I went to work out at the Officers' Club and then I started back with Vic Sewell, still with the Gennessee Street Shufflers. This time they had a bunch of new guys, including someone called Aldrey on guitar, with Vic on piano, Monty and Jack Foy. We used to work with that band at the Follies Theater. We played for dancers but considered ourselves as jazz players, yessir. During that time, ours was just as good a band as they had around there.

Bill Rinaldi the guitar player got a job out where they were building the Grand Coulee Dam near Spokane, Washington. We worked at a place called the Silver Dollar and we had my good friend Irish (Virgil Ireland), Jack Henshaw and Bill, of course. Bill was an ex-fighter and he had just married a chorus girl. Her name was Lorna and she used to be a kind of B-girl in the Silver Dollar, just hustling drinks off the customers. Bill was a jealous guy, and, if he'd see Lorna getting too close to a guy or the guy holding her too close, he would jump off the bandstand and hit the guy in the mouth. He'd start a big fight like that. It was a lot of fun. Any time you work around a place where you have construction workers, fights break all the time. Nothing is rougher.

Irish was a guitar and violin player, and quite a hustler himself. A con man, too: he opened a race-track book and took bets. He'd get the results by wire from all over the country. He had one of these Okies, a white fellow from Oklahoma, to post the winners. We was in there playing but Irish wouldn't come in!

We worked in the Silver Dollar from about 9 p.m. to 1 a.m., and when they closed we'd go play at an after-hours joint owned by a colored guy named Moses Johnson. Mose made a lot of money. Right across from the Silver Dollar they had a Piggly-Wiggly store, forerunners of the supermarkets. One day, it was summertime, we was standing outside around noon and we saw old Mose go in this Piggly-Wiggly store. It was a nice sunny day but Mose had this big raincoat on. He goes in and buys a pack of cigarettes or something like that and everybody is wondering what Mose is doing with this raincoat on. The night before this particular incident happened Mose and his wife had had a fight and he beat his wife up, gave her a black eye. Anyway, the store is right on a corner, and when he came out his wife is waiting for him round the corner, and she shot him in the leg. Old Mose hit the sidewalk, whoopin' and hollerin', calling for a doctor and an ambulance. The manager of the store came out, wanting to know what all the trouble was, and he saw Mose laying on the sidewalk, when suddenly his raincoat flew open and about seven cabbages fell out. So instead of calling the ambulance the manager starts telling Mose what a dirty black sonofabitch he was and how he's a wicked crook. Mose is howling, "Help me. I'm dying," and the manager shouts back, "Goddam you, Mose, I ain't calling no doctor until you pay me 15 cents for all them cabbages you stole. They can shoot you again." Can you imagine, 15 cents for about half a dozen heads of cabbage? Things was cheap in those days. Mose had a whorehouse and you could turn a trick there for a dollar and a half. That's real cheap, too.

At the beginning of the war, around 1941, I started playing with Tommy Thomas. This was the top big band in the Pacific Northwest at that time. Tommy was a piano player and bandleader, originally from Philadelphia. This was an all-white band. No prominent musicians, but it was a good band and a good-paying job. Tommy had a radio program sponsored by Ben Tipp, the biggest jeweller in Seattle. This went up and down the Coast and Tommy had another broadcast for the Armed Forces. See, when the war started, the money started. People got working again. We'd go play army camps, and the USO sent us to the Pacific Northwest, way up to Fairbanks and Anchorage in Alaska. Tommy never did record.

I did play with a band that recorded before I was with them and that was the Vic Myers band. The Chesterfield program ran a contest for big bands, a national contest, and Vic won it. He had four saxes, three trumpets, three trombones, drums, piano, bass and guitar. I used to play third alto, doubling clarinet, 'cause third had the clarinet parts. Lead alto strictly played lead. This was an all-white band, too. You didn't find too many integrated bands in Seattle. Vic was a drummer and eventually became the Lieutenant Governor of the State of Washington. He had a big club called Club Victor and, when he was running for office, he used to hire musicians to ballyhoo for him. We toured with Vic, like with Tommy, and broadcast, too. Nothing ever really happened with his band but it was pretty good. It worked like this. If I could make more money with Vic or Tommy, I'd work with them. If not, I'd go back to Palmer Johnson, who would call me when he got a job. He never traveled.

Later on, the Katherine Dunham Dancers came to Seattle and with them they had a band, including Bobby Hackett, Brad Gowans on clarinet, and Tony Spargo, the guy that played drums with the Original Dixieland Jazz Band. Bobby

Hackett got drunk one night and they fired him, so they was left without a trumpet player. We had Evan Humphrey playing trumpet with us, a little fat guy, only about 20 years old. They got Evan to sit in for Bobby. He worked with them in the afternoons and I think they got another trumpet player for the nights, 'cause we was working at night. Anyway, they liked Evan so he put in his notice and left Seattle with them. I know that left us without a trumpet player and we brought in some Italian kid to play with us. That was the first time I had met Brad or Bobby or any of those guys. Bobby went on back to New York after that. This was at the end of 1943.

Like I said, there's never been a town like Seattle to my idea. Seattle and New Orleans is the two distinct towns in the USA, so different from any others. But now it's all gone. Nothing happens in Seattle any more. Not much happens in Los Angeles, either.

Quite a lot of good musicians came out of Seattle. Quincy Jones is from Seattle and I knew all of his people, but I never knew him then. I think he majored in music at the University of Washington and then went to Juilliard in New York. Of course, I've seen him since then and talked to him. The bass player Buddy Catlett that was with Louis Armstrong in Reno, he's from Seattle. I knew his whole family. Ray Charles played in a small nightclub in Seattle, way before he got big. Then there was a New Zealand Maori girl piano player, they called her Princess, I worked with her in Seattle in a road-house. She was wonderful. Lee Caldwell was on drums. Princess was Curtis Mosby's girlfriend when he was at the Humming Bird.

One of the best musicians was a guitar player named Rudy Goldberg, who was, like Buster Wilson used to say, so goddam black that a piece of charcoal would make a white mark on him. There was two amazing guitar players in Seattle, Rudy and Bill Page, and neither could read a note. I remember one time we was playing some place with Page and a guy came in with the score of *Rhapsody in Blue* in a special arrangement. On the part which old Pingatore did on banjo with Paul Whiteman, he had it written out for guitar. Now, Bill had fooled us all that he could read. He had such a good ear but when we got to the guitar solo he didn't know what to do. Finally Gerald Wells says, "That's a guitar solo. I thought you could read. Why don't you play it?" Bill admitted he couldn't read at all but he says, "One of you guys play that thing and let me listen to it once!" Old Gerald was a good musician and he took his piccolo and played it for Bill. After that Bill just played it like nothing happened, the whole thing. A natural musician, the way Bix was.

Another musician I worked with in Seattle was a black saxophone player named Jim Juicy. He told me that he had this gal with him in some southern town and it had been raining: everywhere was wet through. They was walking down the railroad, going home, and he says, "Both of us got hot pants and we decided we was gonna get a little piece right then." The gal was ready so they lay down and they start wailing. Pretty soon they heard this little old southern train-whistle and they seen the light coming round. It's lucky the engineer seen them, 'cause it was really getting to them, both of them was howling. The engineer stopped the train and gets out. "Can't you quit and find another place to screw? If I run you over, you be sueing the railroad. What the hell you doin'?" Old Jim looked at him, "Mister, I'm sorry about that, but it just happened when you come round the bend. She was coming and I was coming and you the only one that had any brakes!" We always kidded him about that.

Wilbert Baranco was a helluva good piano player that worked with me in Seattle, and one time I took him over to Bremerton, too. I knew him from when I was a kid in Baton Rouge. My brother had a shoe shop right across the street from where Wilbert lived in Baton Rouge. He had brothers named Lester and Vernon but I don't think they played music. Wilbert went to public school but he took piano lessons from Mother Rosary, one of the nuns at my Catholic school. We used to kid him, tease him, call him a sissy, get into fights over that. I had a bicycle and every time I see him now he says, "I learned how to ride a bicycle because Joe loaned me his bicycle." He had a band later on in Oakland, called it Baranco's Band. This was about the time I went up there with Hill and Vesthon's band but I never connected the two names until way later. I never played with him in California – only when he came to Washington. He teaches now at the University of California and works in clubs around there two or three nights a week.

FIVE

I never did lose my touch for dixieland

I knew Johnny Wittwer's father way before I knew Johnny. This was when Johnny was just a little kid. His dad was known as J. J., and he used to come round the places we played on 12th and Jackson. He was a big music fan. In fact I sold him a saxophone one time. I lost track of Johnny until he came in with his dad to a club called the 908 Club at 908 12th Avenue, where I was working with Al Pierre. This was about ten or 12 blocks from the Black and Tan. All the musicians would come and sit in, that is, if they could play. Johnny was there to sit in. He bought me a drink and we got to talking about the old days. He was kinda surprised at the way I played. I was playing alto and clarinet then. He said, "You sound like you could be from Louisiana." From the first we took a liking to each other. Johnny came from a very wealthy family. His grandfather and great-grandfather owned a factory where they made Golden Glint shampoo. I remember his grandmother used to live in an exclusive part of Seattle. She had a little Pekinese dog that was 14 years old. The poor dog lost all its teeth so she had dentures made for it. First time I seen a dog wear dentures. When you got money you can do anything.

Pretty soon Johnny started telling me about Doc Exner, who used to have jam sessions at his house. Doc was a top radiologist in Seattle, had a big office down-town and a beautiful house out at a place called Sand Point. He was a great jazz fan and had a phenomenal collection of records, all indexed like nobody's business; you ask him for any record and he had them all labeled. Doc was nice and he had plenty of loot. I went out the following Sunday to his home and had a session. A lot of the guys would go there, like Vic Sewell, Monty Sewell, Jack Foy, and Johnny, of course. We'd have these sessions every Sunday. Doc and I became friends.

Johnny was always wanting me to go to work with him. He was crazy about dixieland. By then I was back with Tommy Thomas. This must have been about the beginning of the war, out at Bremerton working the swing-shift from midnight to four in the morning. I think I did work at the 908 sometimes while I was with Tommy because of the shortage of musicians. They took all the young guys for the service but I was just automatically exempt from the draft on account of my back having been broken, so that wasn't any problem at all. My back still bothers me now, especially in damp weather, plus I have a touch of emphysema which makes me pretty short-winded. I never did lose my touch for dixieland. I had played real dixieland in Seattle; we played a lot. Hell, when I was with Tommy he used to feature me on a lot of dixie tunes. Sometimes Tommy would get a small combo to go in a place. In other words, I always had that style. The thing about it, I never tried to copy Jimmie Noone, never tried to copy anybody. I would listen to them play but I couldn't do like some guys and listen to their notes to help me play their way.

Right after that Johnny approached me to go to work at a place called the China Pheasant, a big Chinese restaurant where they had gambling. The job paid good so I accepted. The China Pheasant was located between Seattle and Tacoma, Washington. We couldn't find a bass player so we called the union in Seattle. The only available bass player was a kid called Tommy Kelly, nicknamed Red Kelly. We held the rehearsal and this big red-headed, freckle-faced kid came out there. He was probably 18 years old; had a nice smile and plenty of enthusiasm. Johnny said, "Now we got a bass player, we gonna start our rehearsal. Are you tuned up, fellers?"

Keith Purvis was on drums; he was a young kid, too, and we had another youngster named Marlon Klein on accordion. I can't remember who else was in the band. So Red says, "Tuned up? What do you mean, tuned up?" So Johnny says, "Oh Lord, here's another sonofabitch that can't play a goddam thing. You mean you got enough nerve to come out here to play with us and you can't even tune your damn bass?" Red looks at him and says, "Do I have to tune it? I can still pick it." Johnny could play bass himself, so he showed Red how to tune the thing. Really this kid couldn't play at all at the time, but Johnny says, "I'm gonna try to teach you something, we gotta have a bass player." Red was taking lessons, I don't know who from, but he didn't know how to tune that bass! Anyway, he could slap well enough to get by. We nicknamed him Jimmy Blanton, after the greatest bass player in the world. He got the biggest kick out of that, and still does, up to this day. A few years ago I was playing in Seattle and I went to see him. Red owns a fine club in Olympia, Washington, and he says, "Yeah, I can play as good as Blanton now, can't I?" I had bumped into Red one time down at the union in Los Angeles when he was with Woody Herman. Then when I was with Louis, he was with Harry James, and we ran into him up at Lake Tahoe. He must have stayed with Harry James ten or 12 years, and turned out to be a terrific bass player.

Johnny and I went out to Red's club and sat in with him. When we left to go to the club Johnny had two cardboard boxes with him. I wondered what he was doing with these empty boxes. Johnny says, "Wait until we get to Blanton's place, then I'll show you." Johnny sees Red and he says, "Red, I bought you a present." Red had a big smile and asked what it is, so Johnny hands him the two cardboard cartons and he says, "This is a set of Polish luggage I bought you for a present!" Red laughed like hell. His club was nice and he had a good combo in there. Corky Corcoran was playing with Red when he died. Red wanted me to go back and do a couple of weeks with him, but I never did.

These days Johnny does a single sometimes or he plays with singers, but he's mostly into teaching. His parents died and he lives in a beautiful home on Lake Washington in Seattle; he's got the whole house to himself. He's always wanting me to come up there. Johnny's a beautiful guy, a fine piano player and a good musician. He worked with Jack Teagarden, that's how he got to playing the trombone himself, with Doc Evans, and a whole lot of bands.

Bob Scobey the trumpet player was in the army and they stationed him at Fort

Lewis, about six miles from Tacoma and about 20 miles from the China Pheasant. Fort Lewis was one of the big training camps during that time. Bob found out we was at the China Pheasant and he wanted somewhere to jam. He was playing with a military band up at the base and he could get a furlough almost any time he wanted. He'd come down and work weekends with us. Damn right, he was good. He was playing then just like he played later on with Turk Murphy and them. Next time I run into him was when Bob took Blakeney's place with Ory in San Francisco for a couple of weeks. He fit well.

We all used to smoke, especially Scobey and Johnny. They didn't only *smoke* tea, they would practically eat it. On our days off we'd drive into the country, break off all kinds of plants, dry 'em up and try to discover a new way to get high. We had a lot of sore chops, I'm telling you. We never did find anything and it could have killed us.

This leads me to a story about Marlon Klein, our accordion player. Marlon had never played a job around professional musicians before, but the owner of the China Pheasant liked the accordion to play for dances. We played a lot of rhumbas, waltzes, and all that shit, so we hired Marlon especially for that. He was only about 17 or 18 years old and he was kinda like a mama's boy, but he wanted to act sophisticated, like he's been around musicians all his life. Like I said, I would smoke tea once in a while but I used to drink quite a bit, and tea and liquor together didn't agree with me. One night Marlon came over to me and asked, could I get him some tea. I was dumbfounded when he asked me that, him being a kid, only 17 years old. I says, "You gotta be kidding." He says, "No sir, I know all about that Montana grass picked by the light of the moon. That stuff will set you free." I told him to get the hell away from me, as I didn't want his father and mother to get mad at me. Anyway, he begged for about a week for me to get him some tea, until finally I told Scobey and Johnny about it and we figured we'd teach him a lesson. We went to work and got some brown cigarette paper like we always used and got a handful of Chinese tea that they brewed for drinking. We rolled up a couple of cigarettes and I put them in my pocket. The next time Marlon mentioned it to me he said, "I know you guys are smoking that shit, I want some so I can take my gal out on Green Lake." So I told him, "Since you told me you smoked and know all about it, I gotta couple of joints in my pocket. They'll cost you two dollars 50 apiece." He says, "Hell, that's all right, I been paying more than that." This Green Lake was in a swank neighborhood where Marlon lived and a lot of guys would go out with their gals and paddle around in canoes.

It so happened the next night was our night off, so we had to wait until the following night to see what Marlon was going to say. We was all standing in front of the bandstand watching for him when he comes in the door. We figured he was gonna raise hell but he came up there beaming. He starts shaking hands with all of us and he says, "Thanks a lot, fellers, that was some of the greatest shit I ever tasted. Me and my gal got in that canoe and we blowed that shit all night long in the moonlight." Johnny looked at Scobey and then he looked at me. "You thinking what I'm thinking?" The three of us had the same thing in mind. We just made a bee-line for the kitchen and grabbed a handful of that tea out of the box. We still had some of them brown cigarette papers left so we ran out the back and started rolling like crazy. We figured Marlon had stumbled on something. We lit up and Johnny was looking over to me, "You feel anything yet?" All I could feel was my mouth burning. We all felt the same and finally it dawned on us this tea wasn't gonna do nothing for us. All we had was some sore chops. Johnny says, "I'm going right in that place and fire that damn Marlon." So he calls Marlon over and he says, "You crazier than hell, you can't get high on this stuff, here's your goddam money back." Marlon didn't want his money but finally he did take it back, although he never would admit he hadn't got high. "Maybe you guys can't get high off it but I sure in hell can," he said. I thought that was real funny.

That whole deal at the China Pheasant was fun. We was up there a long time, a year or more. It was during that time that Doc Exner decided that he wanted us to do some trio recordings. They had a small recording studio in Seattle, out at Radio Station KOL, and those Wittwer Trio recordings was made like on the spur of the moment. We figured out the tunes the night before and the next morning we went down to KOL and made those records. Our drummer Keith Purvis was about 17 years old at the time. I used to sing the blues, so we included my *Joe's Blues*, and when the record came out Louis Jordan claimed some of my lines was his. Doc Exner says, "Let him sue, then we'll be famous." Doc released the records on his own label and they sold. He did pretty good on them, but Doc was like a lot of guys, he gave a lot of them away, too. He really didn't get a distributor as you should. I think the records could have done better.

After this Doc asked me, did I know Ory and Papa Mutt and those guys? I said I didn't know Ory too well but I knew most of the others. This was during the time they had started some of the early broadcasts from Los Angeles on the "Orson Welles Show." This was with Ory, Jimmie Noone, Zutty, Tudi and Papa Mutt. I had met Kid Ory when I first went to Los Angeles and he was just leaving to go to Chicago to make those Hot Five and Hot Seven records with Louis. The first clarinet player on the "Orson Welles Show" was Wade Whaley, who I knew from Oakland. They also had a piano player in Oakland named S. F. Donkin, called him Stompin' Fess. The guy played so loud he brought a little flat cushion with him which he'd put under his right foot, 'cause people down below couldn't sleep. Fess could play pretty good and we'd often jam together in joints. Of course, I knew Papa Mutt and Ram real good.

Doc wanted Ory to do some recording for him. He was a great fan of Ory's and he says to me, "I wonder, would you consider going down to Los Angeles and talking to Ory?" I was figuring on coming down to Los Angeles anyway. I had met Gladys in the meantime and she had a lot of loot – she was almost a millionaire. So between Doc Exner and her, they bankrolled my trip to Los Angeles. That's how I happened to come down here. I had me a lot of new threads and plenty of money, so I flew down. I called up Mutt first and went out to his house. I hadn't seen Mutt since '28. I knew Mutt a lot better than I knew Ory, from working with him in the taxi-dance, so I asked Mutt about it and he said, "We ain't doing much around here. I would sure like to record some. I'll call Red right now." Mutt always called him Red for some reason, never did call him Kid. So Mutt says, "Hey, Red, Joe Darensbourg's over here, he want to talk to you 'bout some records."

Ory was tickled to death to get a recording session, so then we had to go to the union to get a permit. Ed Bailey was the president of the colored local (767) then, and he wanted us to put a deposit down as Doc Exner was from out of town; in other words, he wanted to make some money for himself. Bailey wasn't too popular. He threw all kinds of stumbling blocks in the way of getting a permit for Doc 'cause I wasn't in the local at the time. They didn't want to reinstate me. They had two locals then and I knew some of the guys in the other local (47). Spike Wallace was the president of 47 so I says, "Let's get down and talk to Spike." We went to see him and he said, "Since we're the oldest local we have jurisdiction over 767. Hell, Doc, go ahead, I'll give you a permit, make the record, pay no attention to what they saying down there." Originally I was a member of both locals, then I fell out of it. I was fortunate enough to go both ways. That's what made it good, I always had a choice.

The Ory records was made at C. P. McGregor's, one of the big studios, out on Western Avenue in Los Angeles. In fact it was the same studio where I made some V-discs later on with Red Fox. (Victory discs, they called them, strictly for the armed services.) We rehearsed the tunes quite a bit 'cause I hadn't played with the full Ory band, only with the quartet. We recorded the tunes we played real good, which I still think wasn't too great, but Doc Exner was thrilled and satisfied. He had come down for the session, although I had already been down a month or so. On a recording session or on a stage, Ory was a very excitable guy, look like he always would get stage fright. He had to have a big glass of water next to him.

Doc Exner's Ory records never made a big splash. He did not have a distributor and he admitted afterwards he didn't know what to do. He sold a lot of them to stores which didn't pay him, so he never got his money out of it. A lot of people had those records, but so far as being a financial success for Doc, well they wasn't. He didn't particularly care too much about that. The satisfaction for him was making 'em. They wasn't the greatest records in the world but they are all collectors' items now.

During that time Ory's full band would work maybe one or two gigs a week. Ory was working four nights a week with a quartet out at the Tip Toe Inn on Whittier Boulevard in Los Angeles. This was with Buster Wilson on piano, Alton Redd on drums and a trumpet player that doubled on saxophone. Ory was playing bass and trombone. Anyway, the trumpet player had to leave, I think he got in some trouble with the law and they came for him, so Ory asked me to replace him. I went out to work at the Tip Toe Inn playing saxophone and clarinet. That's when I first started with him, before the Exner record session.

After Jimmie Noone died Ory was looking for a clarinet player for the "Orson Welles Show." He had Wade back in there. Wade had retired from music and been working in the shipyard. Mutt and them had been working some deal around Los Angeles with Wade. Then Barney Bigard came in to do some of the shows but he had something else to do, so Ory asked me to come on the show. I think I only played a couple of times. This was right at the end of the run of that show.

The Tip Toe Inn was tough, you better believe it. It was a hangout for Mexican ex-fighters. It was more or less exclusively Mexican; if anyone outside of a Mexican came in, even a Spanish guy, you could expect trouble. Look like there wouldn't be an hour pass without a fight would break out in the damn place.

Orson Welles came out to the Tip Toe Inn, as did Nesuhi Ertegun and Marili Morden, that owned the Jazzman Record Shop, all of them came out there. One night a funny incident happened at the Tip Toe Inn. We was all standing around before work and here comes a guy with a sheet of blank paper on a clipboard and he asks Ory to give him an autograph. He tells him to sign at the bottom of the page so Ory just took the clipboard and signed it. They guy walks out the door and, as soon as he goes, Alton Redd goes to Ed and says, "Kid, you signed that autograph on a blank piece of paper, that guy could have written a contract saying you bought an automobile or you owed him money and it's your name signed on the bottom." Ory got all excited and he said, "Goddam, I'm gonna catch that sonofabitch." So he ran out and got this guy who was half a block away by this time. Ory took the sheet of paper and tore it up. "Give me that piece of paper. You trying to pull a deal on me." The guy was dumbfounded. He didn't know what was happening. We all laughed like hell.

Ory played pretty good bass; he knew the right notes to hit. Barney had used him on some things and Ory had used Barney after he left Duke. Barney had a little deal around Los Angeles but I don't think he used Ory too much. He had a six-piece dixie-type combo and he let me photostat his library. Barney mostly used white musicians and he played with Freddie Slack for a while. I ran into him one time in Seattle when he came up there with Freddie.

Another guy that came down to the Tip Toe Inn was Bunk Johnson. He came out there to sit in, but he was pretty feeble then and couldn't play very good. He wasn't like Louis; he didn't have any chops. Still, up in San Francisco he was a legend, he could do no wrong. They had this concert in San Francisco on a Sunday afternoon, a thousand people waiting there, and Bunk shows up about half an hour late and he's pretty well loaded, oiled up, didn't have his teeth or his horn. He says, "If you want me to play, you gotta get my teeth and horn out of hock," and he hands them the pawn ticket. The owner of the hock shop lived way over in Sausalito and they had to go wake him up and get him to come to San Francisco and open up his shop. This took every bit of three hours but the people waited for old Bunk to play. But that sucker was so loaded he couldn't hardly play anyway. Still, they enjoyed it.

They had an after-hours joint on Central Avenue where Alton Redd used to play; I think Frank Pasley played there sometimes and maybe Ory once in a while. I never played there but I was down there with Frank, and here comes Bunk drunker than hell and he's one of these loudmouth guys always trying to show off, saying, "I taught that gatemouth sonofabitch Louis Armstrong how to play," and all that stuff. According to him, all the trumpet players tried to play like Bunk. Ory and Bunk always got into big arguments about this. This one night Bunk comes in and it's about 20 minutes before closing time. Finally he says, "I'll show you about me being one of those New Iberia sports," and Frank says, "Goddam, Bunk, spend some of that money you made making that tabasco sauce down there in New Iberia, that's all you good for, making that hot sauce." Bunk says, "I'll show you, give everybody a drink." Good thing there was only about ten people in there, 'cause drinks in this bootlegging joint cost like a dollar and a half, so Bunk's drinks come to about 18 or 20 dollars. Bunk pulls out three dollars and he says, "Here you are, I go first class," and the bartender says, "What's that, is that all the money you got? You buy the house a drink, you nothing but a signifying sonofabitch. Where's the rest of my money?" Bunk says, "Well I have the money here someplace," and he pulls off his shoe. "I think I got some money in this shoe," he says. Frank tells him to put his shoe back on and picks up the three dollars and gives it back to Bunk. "Here, you damn fool, put that in your pocket. Three dollars is a lot of money in New Orleans but not up here. We'll pay for the drinks." Then the owner says, "I don't know if this guy is a friend of yours but I'm gonna lock you in here until you pay me the money. If I have to keep you in here all day and all night, you gonna stay until you pay me." Bunk didn't have his horn, otherwise the guy would have taken it. Bunk didn't have nothing, not a watch or a ring. The guy says, "What kind of a musician are you?" We was just laughin', 'cause Bunk was such a damn fool.

Most of these older musicians drank like hell but it seemed to me they could still play. It wasn't like the younger class of musicians that drank and then fell off the stand. I seen Jim Robinson get drunk at the Beverly Cavern a couple of times, but he could manage to play pretty good. Then one time down at the Green Room Big Sid Catlett was so drunk they had to take cold towels with ice in them to put on his head to get him awake. They kept hold of him and set him back on the drums and he still played the set. Ory could drink when he was young, but as he got older he couldn't handle it all. He would get lap-legged, lap-tongued, and the slide would fly out of his hand.

Then Ory got in an argument with the owner of the Tip Toe Inn. He fired Ory and gave him his two weeks' notice. I kinda suspected that Alton Redd and this guy got together to get Ory fired so Alton could put a combo in there; he took the job himself – cheaper I guess. We found this out afterwards. That's true, Redd undermined Ory out of the Tip Toe Inn. I didn't stay there with Redd, no way. I wouldn't have stayed with him even if he'd offered me more money, 'cause I didn't like his playing. With Ram Hall, he'd always be speeding up, but Alton Redd was just the opposite, look like his feet was tired all the time. You'd start a tempo off at 80 miles an hour and when you got through the tune he was going about 20. Alton was a kinda gash hound, everybody knew that; he liked a lot of broads. The only thing was, all his broads was ugly, every one. Out of 20 you'd think one would be good-looking, but not him, this cat would go looking for these ugly broads. One time we was going crawfishing and Alton says, "Hey, I'm gonna bring a chick along for you." I should have known better but I happened to get a glimpse of her about half a block away when he was driving over there. I seen this broad and I was long gone. He ain't found me yet! When we was kids, Alton lived right around the corner from my house in Baton Rouge. He was a little older than me but I remember him well. He wasn't playing music then.

We came out of the Tip Toe and we started getting jobs for the bigger band. I'm talking about the regular Creole Band with the seven pieces. Bud Scott and Tudi didn't work at the Tip Toe Inn, but they came in the band when we took other jobs. After Redd, Zutty worked with us for a while and then Ram joined the band. Ram had been in the army. I knew he was a sergeant in World War I and I couldn't figure what the hell Ram was doing in World War II at his age. I came to find out that Ram had put his age back so much he got caught for both wars. A lot of New Orleans musicians is good for that, always trying to act like they're younger than they are. Anyway, Ram came by and told Ory he was just fixing to get out of the service. I think they'd found out his real age and kicked him out.

I was ready to go back to Seattle but Ory asked me to stay. You could hardly get a room or an apartment in Los Angeles at that time due to the war, so Ory said he had a spare room in his house. I moved in with him. He had a small house on 33rd Street and Central which is now a very rough part of Los Angeles. He had quit playing for a long time, having worked with all kinds of different bands – everybody in fact. Ory more or less was always some kind of leader, mostly had his own groups. Then him and his brother went to work on the Santa Fe railroad; first thing was doing janitor work and then Kid started cooking. He was a real good cook. They had a little chicken farm at one time, raised chickens to make money. Up until the time they went on the "Orson Welles Show" and the jazz revival started they was having it pretty rough. Mrs Ory, name of Dorothy – they called her Dort for short – she used to go out and work at the studios in the wardrobe department. She did sewing and altering costumes, any kind of thing to make a buck. She'd work anyplace, sometime do janitor work.

We had a beautiful life there. We got along real well. Ory had a nice house. Then a few months later he started prospering a little and bought a beautiful home over on the West Side on Arlington Avenue; this was a much nicer and bigger house. Ram was in the army then and he helped us to move from 33rd Street. That was the first time I had run across old Ram in years. In the thirties he was in a band with Winnow Allen and I think he did a couple of day jobs, too. You couldn't make it playing music then, no way. Very few could make a living, and that included white musicians, the black ones and everybody else. The only lucky guys was those that was set in the movie studios, guys like Martin Peppi, that later played with Ory. That class of musician always managed to do well; there was a certain call for them.

I had like a small apartment up above the house. There was a big garage and we used it to raise chickens to eat and to sell. Ory had a little brooder there to hatch the eggs and we got a helluva kick out of seeing those chicks grow. We'd sell the little chicks around Easter, and the rest we ate or gave away. We had a lot of time on our hands so we'd often go crawfishing, too. We used to go just about ten miles out of Los Angeles on Balboa Boulevard. Behind the Birmingham Hospital they had a little stream with a lot of crawfish – "crawdads" is what we called them – and we'd go out there and catch crawfish. Look like a small lobster. Zutty would go with us, Barney would be there and different musicians. We'd have a ball catching those crawfish. We'd take them home, boil 'em up and have our beer. This was when we was at the Tip Toe Inn and later. We had a lot of fun. That was one of the good parts.

It was always so hot out there. There was nothing but farms where they raised corn, potatoes and pumpkins and, in fact, we used to go through some farmer's fence to get to this creek where we caught the crawfish. Sometimes Mrs Ory used to go with us; Tudi, Floyd Levin, maybe Marili sometimes. A few years later Eddie Miller and Matty Matlock used to come out and crawfish, too. This was around the time that Nappy Lamare and Doc Rando had a place on Ventura Boulevard called Club 47, where a lot of musicians used to go to jam. Eddie and

Matty were always out there. Good times.

We played a few more broadcasts after the "Orson Welles Show" finished. These were called Standard Schools Broadcasts. We had one or two different guys in the band then. The trumpeter Jake Porter played a couple of the school broadcasts with us. I think he worked with Ory before that, too, but he wasn't there too much when I was in the band. Although he played in small combos, Jake was primarily a big-band man; he was the first one to admit he wasn't really a dixieland man. Jake's a good musician, a good guy and a helluva cook.

We also used Charlie Blackwell at times. In fact we made a Decca record session with Charlie on drums. Bill Colburn set it up. Something happened on that session and Ory blamed it on Charlie's drums, but Charlie was a pretty good drummer. That particular day we couldn't play one tune properly. They ruined so many acetates the guys said, "Forget this." Ory was so nervous, he kept having to drink water and his throat would get dry and he'd cut more hogs than a butcher. Ory was the most nervous guy you ever seen on any kind of deal like that. We got hooked up on *Muskrat Ramble* and we just couldn't make it. For three hours we couldn't do a damn thing right. Anyway, we got paid for the session and we did it again two weeks later with Ram on drums.

Charlie plays around here in Los Angeles now. He's originally from Seattle and I played with him up there. He had a brother named Bumps Blackwell, who used to be the manager of Sam Cooke the singer. Bumps called me up once about a show they was gonna have for Della Reese, that collapsed on the set in a show with Scat Man. I couldn't consider it as I was recovering from the heart attack.

After the Tip Toe we worked a lot of places around Los Angeles. We went out to Huntington Beach, played a few gigs in Pasadena at the Elks and other clubs around there – all short jobs. We played the Santa Monica Civic Theater and we went to Phoenix, Arizona, a couple of times to work in Bud Brown's Barn, a terrific old Western place on the outskirts of Phoenix. They had barn dances there, supposed to have been the best barbecue this side of Texas. Bud Brown himself used to own a cement factory in Phoenix. He liked us and we was big favorites there. That was the start of the good days for the Ory band. We went up to San Francisco for the first time, soon after we made the Exner records, just doing one-nighters and working a lot of little places. Then they had a big old place on Western Avenue in Los Angeles, Ace Cain's was the name of it. They'd have jam sessions on Sunday afternoons and bring us in. We played there all the time. A lot of people wanted our kind of music. Nobody had any money to buy it in the thirties, so you couldn't hardly find anybody playing any kind of traditional music in the whole state of California. It was happy music – something they didn't have for a long time. A lot of kids round here had read about it but they had never heard it. Billy Berg's and Ace Cain's would bring in someone like Erskine Hawkins and the kids had heard his records, so they'd see he was in town and line up to see him. This would be on a Sunday. You didn't have to pay anything to get in but there was a two-drinks minimum. The kids would try and stay for two sets, when they'd make you get out because there were so many people waiting to get in. The kids would sip their drinks, listen to the music and go crazy. Billy Berg's started all this first with the big-name saxophone players like Illinois Jacquet.

I also worked with Red Fox before we went into the Jade Palace and I guess I had more fun with Red than with any other band. Red was funnier than hell and I knew some of the guys real well, even better than Ory and them. Of course, I had known Irish (Virgil Ireland) and Johnny Wittwer in Seattle and they was in the band. I had met Red in Seattle when he came through with Freddie "Schnickelfritz" Fisher as his drummer, but it was Irish that got me in the band. Irish and Red had worked together in Kansas City; they was always into some kind of shady deal to make money. You see the ads where they'll publish a tune if you send in a poem and then make a recording of it, all this for a certain amount of dollars. Naturally, every poem or verse that you sent them was the greatest according to their idea. That was their racket. They'd write back and tell you, "Why you probably have a national hit on your hands." I hadn't seen Irish since the Grand Coulee Dam days. Irish had gone back to Bremerton and was working for some hustlers there in a syndicate gambling joint. Well, they raided the joint and Irish jumped out of the place and hid in a chicken coop. The law came out looking for him but they didn't find him so he made his way to Los Angeles. Meantime Red had quit Freddie Fisher and started his own group down here. He called it Red Fox and his Ding Dong Daddies, and then Red Fox and his Pack of Hungry Hounds. In that band at the time was Jackie Coon on trumpet and the great comedian Stan Freberg on banjo and bass. This was strictly a novelty band. Red had been with Spike Jones as an arranger and he was a naturally funny guy with great ideas for comedy. He was a good arranger, too. I did a few little comedy things. I'm not funny-looking but I can do comedy. Sometimes I'm funny.

We worked at Ken Murray's Blackouts in Hollywood. Naturally, Ken was the big star of the show. We worked all around town and down at the beach at a couple of places and took a few out-of-town gigs. One time we went out to this motel where we was gonna stay and Red knocked on the door and said, "Well, here I am, I'm Red Fox. Are you ready for us?" The woman says, "Come on in, Mr Fox, I got some kennels round the back for your hungry hounds." Red says, "The pooches is waiting out there in the car," and he came out there and calls, "Come in, you pooches." The guys wanted to kill him but the woman was serious, she didn't know any better.

Irish played violin and guitar but he wasn't too much of a musician really. Johnny Wittwer played trombone and piano in the band. He'd have his trombone on the piano but he had no chops. He never played enough but he could wail like hell. He was like a prizefighter, good for one round and then his chops was gone, couldn't play nothing.

While I was with Red we made some V-disc recordings for the Government out at McGregor's. Joe Venuti came in there with his fiddle and decided to do a couple of things with us. He was that crazy. "Let me get a piece of this," he says. Joe was on his way to another studio to do something so that's the way it happened. Red knew him and we enjoyed being around Joe. The records were darn good, I got some of the dubs, but they were never released. This was right after I came down from Seattle and made the Exner records with Ory. See, I didn't start working with Ory straightaway. Anyway, Red paid pretty good. He has an advertising business now; he does all right.

In 1945 the Jade Palace job came up in Hollywood and that's when we had the original Ory band with Ram on drums. That was one of the first regular jobs he worked with us. I think Ram played a couple of things while he was on leave from the army. Anyway, he came into the Jade with us and stayed with the band from then on.

At first Wade Whaley worked in my place a couple of times. I remember I had a hard time finding a clarinet player to take my place. I know Ory was awful unhappy with him because he couldn't play very well as he was out of practice. Wade was horrible really. Turk Murphy and them started bringing dixieland in even before Ory. They had a band with two trumpets, a clarinet player named Ellis Horne, Burt Bales on piano, two banjos and a tuba. I got to hear some of their records when I was up in Seattle and I thought they had a better sound than Ory, especially when he had guys like Wade playing. Turk and Scobey really went into it.

The Jade was a beautiful club, owned by some kind of syndicate. They had wonderful original paintings up on the walls, naked women and that sort of thing, all by James Montgomery Flagg. We used to get a lot of movie stars who would come in and listen to the band. It was a great success. That's when the band really got going. I think we worked a few studio jobs during that time and different extra things. To me it was a pretty good band and we had all the work we could do. A lot of musicians would come into the Jade to listen. The Ory thing was something new. Of course, Jimmie Noone had been here a while before us but he never did use a band around Los Angeles too much, 'cause you couldn't get work for a full band. He had a trio or a quartet; people like Gideon Honore or my old drummer George Vann worked for him. I guess they had a few other small combos but it wasn't any full dixieland bands working except Wingy's – he had a little thing going around here. Red Nichols still had a big band; he hadn't started his small band yet.

I was still living with Ory at his house. I had bought a place of my own for six thousand dollars and inside of three or four months I had sold it for ten. It was a nice house, on Slauson Avenue and Van Nessen, that was in Los Angeles proper. Then I bought another, sold it, and made several thousand dollars more. That should have told me: right then and there, if I'd had any brains, I should have thrown that clarinet away and gone into the real-estate business. I was young and Gladys had a lot of money. I figured it would never run out. I wasn't interested in that stuff. I stayed at the Jade until the day Japan surrendered. I was there about five months, I guess.

I used to like Ory, I really did, but when he got drunk you couldn't get through to him. He was an awful evil guy and suspicious of everybody. I remember I tried to talk Ory into getting an agent, so finally we went around and talked to some of the agents. When the guy gets through talking and starts telling Ory about the percentage, he always thought the agent was trying to screw him up, so he'd talk himself right out of anything. One time Joe Glaser came to see us and offered Ory a helluva good deal, booking him right behind Louis. They got in a big argument and Joe turned around and said, "What's the matter with that sonofabitch? He's crazy, you can't talk to him. The hell with him." And he walked off.

This is how I happened to leave the Jade Palace. The usual quitting time was one o'clock. Ory was half-drunk one night and so was I. Instead of quitting at one o'clock, Ory would play 15 or 20 minutes over time, and I didn't like that. We was playing and here come 1.15 a.m., and I'm saying, "Jesus Christ, it's time to quit." I had told Ory, the very next time he played after one o'clock I was going to walk off the stand. So Ory turned round and told me, "I'm the leader of the band. If you don't like the way I'm running the band you can quit." So I says, "To hell with you, I do quit. You can have my two weeks' notice." Then he says, "You gotta find yourself another place to stay." So I said, "I'm going back to Seattle anyway." I didn't really have to work, 'cause Gladys was giving me all the money I needed. All the guys in the band was flabbergasted, but they should have known. Mrs Ory got real mad and felt bad about it, so I says, " Don't feel too bad about it. Hell, I want to go back to Seattle."

Like I said, Ory wasn't the easiest guy in the world to get along with, especially when the sonofagun was drinking, which was mostly all of the time. He wasn't too bright when he was sober, either. The rest of the guys was all right. You had a lot of harmless arguments in the band, that's all. Buster Wilson and Bud Scott never had nothing to say, they could get along with a jackass or a tiger. They was nice, easy-going guys, and Tudi was OK, too. Mutt was kinda argumentative and there was always a little undercurrent in the band; I think Mutt figured that it should have been his band, even when Jimmie Noone had it. Later on he and Ory fell out and Mutt went back to being a railroad porter. Southern Pacific had a train that was called the *Argonaut* but it was so slow they called it Sad Sam: it made all the little stops and took 12 hours to get to San Francisco. Mutt never came back to the band.

I put in my two weeks' notice and moved out of Ory's house. During that time gasoline was rationed and you had to use gasoline coupons. You could never get enough gas to do any real traveling, so I had bought a hundred dollars' worth of bootleg coupons when here comes Armistice Day with the Japanese. The minute the Japanese surrendered they took all the rationing off, so there I was stuck with all these goddam coupons I couldn't use. That was the time I left the Jade Palace, the very next day after Japan surrendered. In the meantime Ory had sent for Darnell Howard, who was living in San Francisco. He wanted to kinda change things afterwards, but I said, no, and went back to Seattle. Gladys was up there. I just got in the car and picked me up three rides that paid. You always had guys looking for transportation and they paid you ten dollars. Seattle is 1200 miles from Los Angeles, so I had three service guys which was going back to Fort Lewis riding with me for company.

I went back to work with different groups around Seattle. I took a few gigs whenever I wanted to work; if not, I didn't. I worked again with Tommy Thomas on his radio show and on the special broadcasts for the armed services. We played for dances, still with the 15-piece band. I was on third E flat saxophone and clarinet, just like before. Tommy had some nice stock arrangements and special arrangements. Sometimes we'd work at the Fifth Avenue Theater and we'd still play swing-shift dances for the navy yard workers over at Bremerton.

Seattle didn't have the after-hours joints like they had before. Things was kinda bad for the nightclub business, so I came back down to Los Angeles. My good friend Frank Pasley was playing with Joe Liggins and the Honeydrippers, which was the top rhythm-and-blues deal at the time. I also knew Peppy Prince, the drummer in the band. Peppy had a nephew, Wesley Prince, that was an original member of the Nat "King" Cole Trio. Joe Liggins had started playing this old club on San Pedro Street in Los Angeles, and whenever he played his tune *The Honeydripper* he got a terrific hand. One of the René brothers, Leon René, happened to go in there one night and he heard the tune. Leon René is the guy that wrote *Sleepy Time Down South*; him and Clarence Muse, the movie actor. Anyway, René recorded that tune and he made a zillion dollars. That recording made Joe Liggins, too.

The original *Honeydripper* was made with five pieces. Let's see, two saxophones, piano, bass and drums. Joe was using Little Willie Jackson on alto, James Jackson on tenor, Frank on guitar, Peppy on drums and, naturally, himself on piano. Joe had two hit tunes going at the same time, *The Honeydripper* and *I gotta right to cry*, which is very unusual. Later they decided to add the clarinet and Frank called me to ask if I was interested. Joe heard me playing someplace and he wanted me to record a new tune he wrote, called *Sugar Lump*, which never did do anything. So we had a recording session. I remember we did *Caravan, Stardust, Sugar Lump* and some other tunes. None of them was a hit. This was for Otis and Leon René's company that recorded *The Honeydripper*.

Right after the session I went on the road with the band. Nothing much else was happening. I stayed with the Honeydrippers about three months. This was rhythm-and-blues – but not like these guys do now, just blowing up a lot of crazy notes. Every one of Joe's things had a nice pattern of music and some of his stuff was pretty; you not talking about any flat out rock-and-roll with Joe. We'd play a pretty B flat blues just like you'd play in dixieland. Clarinet, that's all I played, because of Willie; I didn't play any sax. It was very enjoyable and I fit in fine. I really didn't have but one solo on that *Sugar Lump* but it was a solo that Joe had written out. I improvised on it, but all of that stuff was down pat. I did have a lot of fun.

The first job I played with Joe was a club here called Shepp's Playhouse in down-town Los Angeles. After that we took a train to New York. This was in late 1945. We stayed in New York but we opened in Newark, New Jersey. We was going to play the Apollo Theater later. It was colder than hell. We got a cab to go over to Jersey and when we got within a block of the Addams Theater we seen a line-up. Me, Frank and Peppy was in this cab and we didn't even connect this line-up with the Honeydrippers. Peppy says, "What the hell are these people doing lining up, they on welfare or something?" The cab driver says, "No, they're a bunch of goddam fools staying out in the rain to see some shit 'n' ass outfit from California, call themselves the Honeydrippers. I wouldn't be caught doing that!" Frank says, "Yeah, do you know who we are?" It dawns on the cab driver and he says, "You don't mean to tell me . . . ." Frank says, "Yeah, you sonofabitch, we the Honeydrippers and you ain't getting no tip, low-ratin' us like that!" The guy started apologizing all over the place but we didn't give him a tip, no sir!

Joe was big. You couldn't have got any bigger. When we did stage shows Joe was the top attraction, but we always had some other act with us. When we opened at the Addams Theater Billy Eckstine's band was with us on the bill; he was just getting started at the time, after singing with Earl Hines. We did one-nighters, a few clubs, but more or less theaters, like the Apollo in New York, the Regal in Chicago, the Paradise in Detroit, and the Howard in Washington – all on the same circuit. The Howard, that's where I met Cleanhead Vinson. He was bald-headed and that's where he got that name Cleanhead. He was known as a great blues singer and that's what he featured; he was a terrific alto saxophone player, too. I seen him once or twice at the Musicians' Union here in Los Angeles where he lives.

We had some pretty tunes, like my *Sugar Lump*, and Little Willie Jackson had *Tanya*, where he played a beautiful alto solo. He's here now in Los Angeles, still playing. Of course, Willie's blind, you know. The only thing with that band was we had to play that goddam *Honeydripper* about 900 times a night. We was playing this dance hall in Wilmington, Delaware, and this big old gal walked in and came up to the piano. Joe had just got through singing *Honeydripper*. She says, "I come 50 miles across the river just to hear you and I wanta hear that *Honeydripper*. Play it for me, Joe!" In the meantime we was playing *I gotta right to cry* and Joe was singing. When he got through he said, "Madam, we just played *Honeydripper* and we gotta finish this one. I'll play it for you after a while." Then he start to sing again and this old broad is getting madder every minute. Finally she goes down to her stocking and pulls out this switch blade. You heard that little click and that blade flew open. Old Joe was looking and singing *I gotta right*, and she struck that knife right up to his throat and she says, "Joe Liggins, you big juicy-mouthed mother, I wanta hear *Honeydripper* and I wanta hear it right now!"

I gotta right turned into *Honeydripper* there and then and Joe didn't miss a note. Talk about a guy singing and sweating. Joe sang it like he never sang it before and this old gal sat up popping her fingers and shakin' her big ass. When he got through Joe says, under his breath, "The goddam bitch," and she says, "What did you say, Joe?" So he says something about doing it without a hitch. She says, "Joe, that was great. I come 50 miles to hear that. I'm going home now." She just walked out of the place. I think Peppy fell off the drums laughing so damn much. Joe is a nice guy so I hope I don't embarrass him with this story.

Joe Liggins:
Joe Darensbourg was a very welcome entity of my band the Honeydrippers. He recorded a couple of sides with me also: "Going back to New Orleans" and "Sugar Lump" are the ones that stick out in my mind. Joe was quite a musician. He could play anything you wrote and could improvise on the spot. I loved that. Joe kept us laughing all the time out on the road while doing one-nighters and the theater dates. One incident stands out in my mind. Joe was asleep in the back of the car when it pulled into a southern US gas station. The owner didn't want to pump gas for a black customer. Joe woke up, got out and told the man that "These are my boys and I'm Mr Darensbourg. You get to pumping that gas." The station owner apologized and started pumpin'. You see, Joe Darensbourg looks like a white man.

During the time I was with Joe's band I shared an apartment with Frank Pasley. He was my number one friend in the music business, along with Ram and Pops Foster. Naturally we used to have them broads up to his two-bedroom apartment all the time. I wasn't married then. It was Frank's idea to see Charlie Parker's opening night at Billy Berg's. Frank knew Dizzy Gillespie from playing with Les Hite when Dizzy was in the band. Maybe he knew Charlie, too. We went by there, had a drink and listened to them. I didn't think much of that type of music then, and I don't think much of it now for that matter, but it was the going stuff. I couldn't understand what Dizzy was playing, just like Cab Calloway, who fired Dizzy, saying, "I don't want nobody in my band playing something I don't understand."

After a few months on the road with the Honeydrippers I got tired; I left Joe's band and came back home. I stayed around Los Angeles for a while and then decided to go back to Seattle again. Gladys and I had a house here but we closed it up, jumped on a plane, and flew back to Seattle. Gladys still had her business to run, although her brother really took care of it for her. She had two trucking companies and then she had a pinball route, pinball machines set up in places to play with a partner, so she had a good income and a beautiful home.

Then I got in an automobile accident. I was playing around Seattle, nothing steady, and I had been to play a gig with the Rainy City Jazz Band. I was coming back from the concert in my Ford with Doc Exner and a radio, now TV, announcer named Lynn Beardsley, when a bakery truck made an illegal left turn in front of me. I was going down 4th Street and I'd had a few drinks. Anyway, I hit the rear of the truck, the lights of the others blinded me, the steering wheel broke off, and I busted my lip. They took me to hospital and somebody stitched my mouth. I had to take about 25 stitches in there; it was busted right open. Doc was the first guy to come and see me. My own lawyer was out of town, and, instead of putting my horn down and waiting for him, I got hold of another lawyer and he says they wanted to settle for 5000 dollars. He agreed to do it for 30 percent of the five grand and I didn't care. I could have probably got 100,000 dollars out of that, busting my lip and being a musician. I was in the right. Still, I wanted to come back to Los Angeles and go back to work.

What made me do things quicker was that Kid Ory called me just as I was recuperating and said he wanted me back with the band to go into Billy Berg's, along with the Mills Brothers and the Teddy Bunn Trio. The money was good and he says, "Hell, I'm not mad at you any more, I don't want you to be mad at me. We forget about everything and we'll get along." I says, "I'm not mad at you either. I'll come on down." I was ready to play and I had got tired of Seattle. In the meantime Ory had had a few other things, and that's when he used Archie Rosate.

I came down but I didn't go to work right away with Ory. I played a few deals with Red Fox again and some other things with Red Nichols and Jack Teagarden; different gigs with people like Pete Daily, nothing too exciting. This was after the time that Louis was here to make the film *New Orleans*. I know I was out of town for that. I also worked some with Wingy Manone – all short spells. Wingy just happened to have little club jobs and I played them. Just some places in Hollywood, including the Hangover, that was like a house converted into a nightclub. Pete Daily worked there for years. I was with Red Nichols for a while and then I worked with Jack Teagarden at a club called Astor's; just a pick-up affair. Funnily enough, I had a chance to work with Jack when he had his big band, playing alto saxophone, up in Seattle. I was with Johnny Wittwer then. Jack wanted to change saxophone players, so I went up and sat in with him at a rehearsal. Then I seen how Jack was drinking and I said, to hell with it. Anyway, the band was about to break up and Johnny was the one who talked me out of it. I stayed in Seattle. Funny thing, when I had a chance to record with Ory, Johnny was all for it. He said, "Now's your big opportunity. You gone long enough without getting any recognition for your playing." Left to him, I was the greatest clarinet player in the world. With Jack, you just went in there and played the tunes, just like Louis. He never had any library. Jack was on a four-week thing but I didn't stay that long, I was just subbing for somebody.

I had so much money I didn't give a damn. I worked if I felt like it. I had all the bread I needed from Gladys. At one time we came right out to Woodland Hills. They had a lot of ground here; you could get a plot for 10,000 dollars which would cost half a million dollars today. There was a place past Calabasas called Thousand Oaks, where they had a circus-animal compound where circuses used to bring their animals during the winter. I ran across my old friend Mabel Spark, who used to be the famous animal trainer with the Al G. Barnes Circus; she was the first lady trainer that trained tigers. I came across a lot of guys I'd worked for on different circuses. It was an interesting place to go and I loved to see all the circus wagons. I said to Gladys, "It would be nice to open a motel and have a little theater or pavilion or restaurant where musicians could come, a place where musicians could stay and the price would be right. If the musician had money, he would pay and we'd have continuous jam sessions. I would cook and I'd train guys to cook, always have a big pot on the stove like those places in Kansas City or St Louis in the early days." In other words, musicians would always be welcome and it would be one continuous jam session. We came out and looked at a 40-acre spread. Had we bought that and held on to it we'd have been billionaires, because all of that area is built up now and worth a fabulous amount of money. It could have been a mistake but I guess it worked out all right; you can't go back. We talked about it and I started to thinking, "Do I want to be pinned down with Gladys the rest of my life?" She was a beautiful woman in a way of speaking, nice and everything, but she was a little possessive. I really didn't love her and money didn't mean that much to me in those days. I always could make enough to get by. I never jumped up and bought a Cadillac, which Gladys wanted me to a lot of times. Big cars and things like that didn't impress me.

My old friend Ceele Burke was another guy who I worked with in those days. I had known Ceele in Los Angeles before I went to Seattle. I played some with him then. Frank Pasley would play sometimes on banjo, and Ceele was a very good guitar player. He picked up the steel guitar when he went to Honolulu on a deal with a guy named Johnny Mitchell. Sometimes he'd pose as a Hawaiian, call himself Joe Panouii. A guy would come up to him and say, "Hey, Ceele," and he'd look at him and say, "Me no savvy, me Hawaiian." We used to laugh about that all the time. I think Blake (Andy Blakeney) was in the band, along with Barnett, the saxophone player.

Ceele and I used to play out at Boyle Heights for the Mexicans and after the war I played a couple of gigs with him at the Bal Tabarin. This was a big place on Western Avenue, quite a way out, where they bought in a lot of big bands. When I first came back, in 1944, Jack Teagarden was there, and Louis worked there as late as 1949 or 1950. Anyway, I had a lot of time on my hands and I wanted to see the different guys. Ceele asked me if I would work for him when his saxophone player didn't show up so I run out there and played alto saxophone for him. He had three saxophones, including Griff (William Griffin) and a guy named Bonner; George Orendorff was on trumpet, plus some other musicians from the Cotton Club days.

Billy Berg's was on Vine Street in Hollywood. All the top musicians and entertainers worked in there. Originally Billy had a place down-town on Main Street called the Waldorf Cellar but Ory never worked for him there. I think Wingy took a band into the Cellar and Billy came to Hollywood a little later. Pretty soon Billy Berg's on Vine Street was *the* place to go. Every Sunday they would have concerts where different up-and-coming singers would come out and sing, people like Kay Starr and Frankie Laine. Los Angeles was a jumping town then. There still wasn't too much money around, but everything was relative and you could live cheap. You had a lot of good bands and joints was springing up everywhere.

Can you imagine Berg's never charged admission? They opened at two o'clock in the afternoon on Sundays and people would line up clear down Vine Street, from Hollywood and Vine to Sunset and Vine. Later Louis played there, Harry "the Hipster" Gibson, Billie Holiday, all the big names; a variety of musicians – not only dixieland. When I went in with Ory's band we had the Teddy Bunn Trio and the Mills Brothers on the same bill. Teddy was one of the top guitar players at one time and he had a great big old guy named Gilmore on bass. The trio was pretty good. This was the first time I got acquainted with the Mills Brothers and we became very good friends from then on. They had Norman Brown playing guitar.

As far as I can remember, we had Jack LaRue on piano at Billy Berg's. He had been hanging around Los Angeles playing with different groups. I don't think he had ever played any dixieland, but, by him being from New Orleans, that's how he got in the band. I don't know who recommended him. He could play, damn right, but he's one of those guys where you don't know which way he's going to jump. He wasn't dependable. Buster was sick but he came back after we left Berg's. We stayed in there four weeks.

Around this time there was some changes in the band. That original Ory band was pretty good but I always felt it could have been a helluva lot better with certain other people in it. Ory played some tunes that I liked. One thing about Ory, he let everybody select tunes. He gave you a chance to play your tunes, because it seemed to me that he had a very limited knowledge himself about a lot of these things he wanted to do. For all that, we had a very good library. We played a lot of traditional tunes like *Bill Bailey*, *Indiana*, *Maryland*, *1919 March*, and a tune that Bechet made famous, *The Gypsy*; there was also *Memphis Blues* and a tune that you never hear now, *Farewell to Storyville*. Ory knocked off the tunes sometimes or he'd let Mutt knock them off. Once in a while he would let

Mutt do a tune and he would be the leader on that particular number. We played sometimes on the order of the old New Orleans bands, where we would get on an ensemble deal, play eight or ten ensemble choruses and then the leader would hit his foot; that means on the next chorus you going out. That was always the signal, so everybody stops at the same time. A lot of those old bands didn't have particular endings for their tunes. Ory always used to say, it's not the tune you play, it's the way you play it. You had to see Ory's band. Tudi bowed his bass and we had a lot of specialties. Ory's band never did record as good as it sounded in person; that band didn't tell the truth on records.

Each guy in the band had his own special personality. I told you before that Papa Mutt was so cheap. We had a job coming up in San Francisco. A prizefighter had a club on Filmore Street and we was traveling up in my car to play there. Mutt always used to go round with a big old thermos filled with coffee when he was going on the road. He liked a lot of cream, but he never put any in: he'd wait until you stopped to get a drink or to eat, and then he'd use the sugar and cream, get it free. We stopped at this little lunch counter outside Bakersfield. Buster and I wanted a sandwich and some chili but Mutt seen a bakery across the street where it said "Day-old Do'nuts – Three for 5c." In other words, stale donuts, damn cheap. So Mutt went and got a paper bag of these donuts. There was half a dozen in there and he starts using the guy's sugar and cream. He had a top on his thermos to use for a cup and he's chomping on these donuts. He wouldn't even give us one. He says, "That's the way to save money." Then the owner of the counter seen him and says, "Where did you get those donuts?" Mutt gives him a smart answer and says, "What's it to you?" The guy says, "I'll tell you, you cheap sonofabitch. You using my cream and sugar, you about the nerviest bastard I ever seen. Is he with you?" Buster said, "Hell, no, we don't know the bastard." The guy told Mutt to get the hell out of there and he says, "I seen a lot of cheap bastards in my life but you take the cake." Finally Mutt tells him, "I don't like your attitude. I think I'll take my business some other place." If the guy had one of them bush knives or a cleaver he would have killed Mutt.

I think this might have been the trip where we met Lu Watters out at his club. They called it the Dawn Club. I can't remember the street it was on but it had a low ceiling, the acoustics wasn't good and the band was loud. As I remember, this was the first time the Ory band had gone to San Francisco to play, and they considered it quite an honor to have us there. Mama Watters had all this food cooked up: red beans and rice, fried chicken, the whole bit. We start eating and old Buster was laughing, "Bud, you really gonna have a ball with all of this food laid out here, you ain't never gonna finish." Bud got mad and said, "See you starting already. Shut up, Buster," but finally he says, "I've ate all the beans here, you better pass me some more so I can make the chicken and rice come out even." When he gets through this he says, "Now I'm out of chicken so you gotta pass me more chicken to make the other stuff come out even." We was through eating, I don't know how long, and Bud was still making things come out even. He liked to eat; he could eat aplenty, probably three or four times as much as anybody in the band. His trick was not to take a whole plate of food and then he'd start this constant merry-go-round of making things even. It was so subtle, nobody hardly picked up on it.

I first knew Bud in Los Angeles around the time I left. He came here about the time Ory returned after making those Hot Five records with Louis. I don't remember him before that. Bud was a sport and he always dressed like a fashion plate, wore spats and a nice Stetson hat, shoes always shined, smoking that cigar with a little cigar-holder that he had. Bud was a gentleman, always smiling. He was a kinda gash hound, too, and had a few broads on the side. He was very sensitive about his color. Bud was real dark and Buster could get his goat better than anybody I ever knew. Like, if anyone was taking a picture, he'd tell Bud, "Don't stand next to me, you go over and stand next to Tudi. Let Joe stand next to me and lighten me. You too black." Bud would say, "Buster, you no gentleman." Bud loved to sing, you know, and like Buster he was a good reader.

I remember Buster slightly from the early days but I never worked with him then. He told me he learned a lot from Jelly Roll. Both of them liked to heist a few, drink a little, have fun like that. I wasn't around here when Jelly Roll died but he and Buster was living together then. If you'd hear him play, you'd think it was Jelly Roll playing. Buster was a terrific rhythm man and had a cute way of playing. Once in a while he caught himself singing a song. He never could really sing but he would kinda talk a song along.

Buster's wife Carmelita was nice and she was with Buster all the way. All the good musicians that wanted a drink would go out to Buster's house because he always had a drink. It was like a continuous jam session. He lived on 51st and Central, which is the roughest part of Los Angeles now. You couldn't do now what we did then; you didn't have any muggings in those days. Musicians would bring liquor if they had it, and if they didn't they'd come and hustle up some. A bunch of them would be sitting around and one would say, "I gotta quarter," and another would have 50 cents, and that's how we'd get enough to go out and buy a bottle. I just liked Buster because he was a nice man; he could play and he was a gentleman. He had broads crazy about him because he was a nice-looking black man with fine features. Some guy told Buster, "If you had white skin, you'd look like Rudolph Valentino." In fact Buster looked like a black Hindu or a white man doing blackface. He didn't have the features of a black man; the only thing was his hair wasn't silky smooth.

Ram was most sensitive about his bald head. He was another gash hound. He liked his broads and he had some, too. On top of it, although he was a nice guy, he could handle himself pretty good. One time at the Liberty Dance Hall a couple of big wrestlers came in and did something wrong, so Ram threw them both out of the joint. He got his nickname from fighting; he'd butt a guy and that was it. He could hurt you with his head. As a drummer, he was good and steady but he always seemed to be speeding up.

When I left the Ory band, Ram was still there. Ory went to Europe and Ram got sick over there and had to come home. Ory wouldn't even pay his return transportation. Ram had enough money to get home, plus Ory owed him some money anyway. When you take a man out of the country, if the man gets sick the union requires the leader to pay that man's transportation back home and see he gets home. If a guy was worth a damn or if he had any kind of principles, the union wouldn't have to make a leader do that. Anyway, Ram got back. I used to know Ram's wife real well and I knew Ram's father-in-law, who was an ex-trumpet player from New Orleans. He never was a "name" guy. They had a little house on Compton Avenue, over in South Los Angeles, so I used to go over and see Ram. By that time he was in a wheelchair. He had started getting kidney trouble and had got into an automobile accident, him and Tudi, I believe, and hurt his leg. He was havin' it rough, so I thought we should raise some money for him. He could use it. His father-in-law had a little grocery store nearby where they was living, and I think he helped to take care of Ram. See, there was no Medicare then. Ram's wife was kinda alcoholic so she had her own problems. I came away and talked to several other musicians, like Gordon Mitchell, and we gave this benefit for Ram. He's one of the first we did that for but he died before the concert. The idea was to wheel him up there in his wheelchair. Instead we took his drums and set them up. Somebody else played his drums and we raised 1200 dollars.

His wife gave me Ram's cymbal, his snare drum and a stand. Actually Ram wanted me to have all of his kit but I didn't want to argue with her, so she took the bass drum and sold it. I had the snare drum for the longest time until Lucille Levin says, "I want to give Floyd something unusual for his birthday and there's nothing he'd like better than Ram's snare drum. Would you sell it to me?" I says, "How can you put a price on something like that." Still and all, I had the drum and it was just gathering dust. Floyd collected instruments and different things from musicians so I gave the drum to Lucille. As to Ram's cymbal, it was a Zildjian which he worked over, made it into a sizzler, and I sold that to another drummer, a good friend of mine, for 35 dollars. Finally this guy called me and said, "Joe, I'm gonna quit playing drums. I'm going deaf. Would you sell that cymbal for me?" In the meantime I had given Floyd the snare-drum rack, so I called him up and said, "Stan wants to sell the cymbal." Now Floyd has the cymbal to go with the snare drum.

After Billy Berg's we went on some other jobs, including the Rendezvous Ballroom out at Huntington Beach. There wasn't much other work then and we was kinda hurtin'. By this time Andy Blakeney had taken over from Papa Mutt. He fell in a helluva lot better than Mutt, course he did. He was a lot stronger than he is now and he knew the tunes. He had been playing some dixieland before. I have been knowing Blake for many years, since 1926, in fact, right after I came through Los Angeles with Vesthon and Hill's Original Dixieland. We was on our way to San Francisco and we met Blake, Ceele, and Johnny Mitchell at a party; they had just come back from Honolulu. When I came back later to Los Angeles I gigged around with Blake on different jobs, long before the Ory band. Naturally, after I left in '28 and went on the ocean liners I didn't see Blake again until I joined the Ory band. He was a guy that wasn't too particular about a steady job, 'cause he held a good job with the Los Angeles School Board as a maintenance man or something. The reason he wanted to hold on to that school job is because he gets a pension from it right now. He could take time off so he would go with us on out-of-town jobs, like he went up to San Francisco a few times. Blakeney was no different then to how he is now; he's a helluva good musician, better than a lot of those well-known trumpet players. He's very soulful, very dependable. When he starts out on a lead you know it's there and that's what trumpet playing is about, isn't it? Blake's been on a couple of minstrel shows and he's the one that first brought Hamp to Chicago. He showed me a picture of Hamp that was taken in 1922 or 1923 when he got Hamp out of Alabama, I believe. Hamp was only about 14 or 15 years old. Blake spent a lot of time round Chicago. That's when he took Louis's place in the King Oliver band. He can sit in anywhere. Right now he plays in the park here in Los Angeles with some big brass band that the union sends out. Blake can do it all and he's a very nice guy as well.

I took time out in 1947 to go back to Baton Rouge. I walked into Jim Bernard's restaurant and the guys couldn't figure out who I was, but an old punch-drunk fighter named Kid Archey looked up and said, "There's old Dody. Where you been? Somebody told me you been travelin'. Dody, you a big musician now. I'm so glad to see you. When you leave here, Dody, take me with you." In his young days the Kid was a contender and he used to take me to his fights. He was a helluva fighter then. I said, "I can't take you, Kid, but give me your address, and when I get back to California I'll write to you." I gave him a card and he scribbled something on there I never could read. Poor old punch-drunk Archey was the only one that recognized me.

In the meantime Louis Armstrong came into Billy Berg's for two or three weeks and didn't get paid. Billy owed him 1400 dollars and this caused a helluva big humbug. By not paying Louis, Billy Berg was put on the union's "Unfair" list and no musician was supposed to do any business with him. In other words, they blackballed Billy. He had paid Louis some of the salary but he owed the balance, so the union made him close his club.

Billy was always after Ory to open a club with him. He put up the bankroll and the place opened under the name Kid Ory's Club. It was in a great big building on Vine Street and the guy that had charge of the kitchen was Sidney Desvigne, the old trumpet player from New Orleans. He had stopped playing by then. He was serving gumbo, red beans and rice, that sort of thing, but it was pretty lousy 'cause he tried to make it with lesser ingredients. I remember one time me and Ram went in there to eat and there was only one shrimp in a big bowl of gumbo. Ram cussed him out. Afterwards Sidney opened a joint on Jefferson and guys used to go over once in a while and have sessions. Anyway, Kid Ory's Club didn't do much business; it was going broke when the union got wind of it and found out it was being bankrolled by Billy Berg. They summoned all the band, sent us letters and brought us before the trial board and suspended us; kicked us out of the union. They put *us* on the "Unfair" list! We said, "How in hell you gonna kick us out? We don't know anything. Billy Berg doesn't pay us," which he didn't. We had nothing to do with the business arrangements so, after thinking it over, the union dropped the charges, but they kept Ory suspended for a longer period. I think they kept him from playing until Billy paid Louis. It's a mystery why he didn't pay him in the first place. In the meantime the union closed Kid Ory's Club, and they never attempted to open it up again 'cause business wasn't any good. It was open maybe a month but they lost money from the first. You didn't have any of the big dixieland crowds like later on.

After that we all got pretty mad at Ory and I left the band again because he wasn't doing too much after the club closed. Then Ory was booked for a two-week concert tour by Gene Williams where we was to play Orchestra Hall in Chicago and Carnegie Hall in New York City. Andy was with the band, but Gene wanted Lee Collins on trumpet and he's the one that said Little Brother Montgomery was going to play piano. Ory didn't have any say about that. We had LaRue at that time but Little Brother was a bigger name. Gene was the one that set up the show, along with John Schenk in Chicago. When the plane stopped in Chicago on the way to New York, Lee, Chippie Hill, Little Brother, Lonnie Johnson, and Mama and Jimmy Yancey joined us. From the Ory band we had Ram, Tudi, Bud, Kid and me.

None of the concerts was really a success. Gene had given the advance man money to go ahead and advertise the concerts, but it turned out the guy had never paid for any publicity and never even booked the places for us to play, so consequently the only dates we made was New York City, Chicago and Providence. That was it: no publicity and no money, so Gene went under.

Little Brother fit real good, but Lee Collins had a helluva time because Ory had all of these tunes written out and Lee couldn't read nothing – even tunes like *Bill Bailey*, because he had never played them before. We settled for tunes that he really could play, like *Cornet Chop Suey*, and I don't think I ever seen anybody play them much better. Lee was a real nice guy.

As to Carnegie Hall, I didn't think too much about it; to me it was just another job. Wellman Braud had a poolroom in New York and he came to see us and said, "You guys gotta come up and eat dinner with me. I'm gonna fix you a special dinner." Talk about a good cook – he fixed the goddamnedest dinner you ever did see. Braud lived in what you called a cold-water flat, six flights up and no elevator. Me, Ram, Tudi and Bud were the ones he invited. Braud was crazy about Bud. As we walked up a flight of stairs, we'd have to wait for old Bud. He had terrifically bad feet and it took him five minutes to walk up each flight of stairs. Tudi said, "We can't wait for him, let him come up by himself." We was up there and sitting down for five minutes before old Bud got to the top of the stairs. He was madder than hell. "You dirty bastards, leaving me downstairs to walk up all by myself," he says. Tudi kidded him along and then we sat down to fried chicken, gumbo, red beans and rice – just about the best deal we ever had on the road.

We had quite a time on that tour. Little Brother did quite a lot of drinking and so did Chippie Hill and both the Yanceys. Every night they used to get Papa Yancey a bottle of Old Grandad, and we'd have a couple of nips and then go out there and play. They had a lot of people on the show so we didn't have too much to do. First Lonnie Johnson did his bit – good blues singing – then Mama and Papa Yancey, then Chippie Hill, and then it was our turn. Still, the drinking didn't stop any one of them from doing their part.

The tour ended at Orchestra Hall in Chicago and that's where Chippie Hill and Little Brother had this humbug. I think they had been going together and Chippie got mad with him on stage. She pulled a knife and threatened to cut him. The concert just went on. We stayed around Chicago for two or three days, and on the Sunday we found out where Sidney Bechet was playing and me and Tudi went over to see him and talk to him. It was some kind of jam session. Bechet always could play, although I thought he played a little out of tune. He was one of the guys that would come over to Perseverance Hall in New Orleans when I was a kid. I never saw Bechet again.

After the tour we went back to Huntington Beach and then we went into the Beverly Cavern, which was the first big club we worked after Billy Berg's. The Cavern had opened with a dixieland band led by Ted Veseley, one of your best trombonists. He had Bob Higgins on trumpet and a drummer named Smoky Stover that we worked with later on up at the Hangover. Veseley was a great trombone player, up there in the class of Tommy Dorsey. We went in behind him. Blake was back in the band and in the meantime Buster had got better and he was able to play with us. Bud Scott did not come in with us. He must have stayed sick with his heart condition for a couple of years. I used to go round to his house and see him. Buster was sick, too, and I seem to recall that he died while we was playing the Cavern.

Once in a while we used another guitar player, a white guy named Ralph Peters, and he got us the job in the Beverly Cavern. He was never a great guitarist; he mostly worked in the studios as a movie extra. He would come and listen to the band and sit in sometimes, usually when we played the jam sessions at Ace Cain's. Ralph said he could get us into the Beverly Cavern and asked Ory to use him on guitar. Ory agreed. The owners of the Cavern, Sam Rittenberg and Rose Stanman, said it was OK, and we went in. Ralph played with us for about two weeks, then for some reason him and Ory fell out. Ory fired him.

Sam Rittenberg liked the band because we started packing the place, and he kept us there for several weeks. Sam and I got to be good friends and he asked me if I knew a band that could play for him on Mondays, our night off. That was the way I got Ward Kimball and the Firehouse Five their first pro job. I said to Ward, "Why don't you guys go in the Cavern? I think you could do pretty good." They went in and they packed the joint. They brought in more people than we did. They wore these fire hats and set sirens off. After their first night we went to work and Sam said, "Yeah, we had a lot of people here and that band was all right. It was pretty good until that trombone player set that si-rene off and made all that goddam noise." "Siren, Sam, siren," we said. "Siren or si-rene, whatever you call it, it's a noisy sonofabitch. Still, I don't care, they made a lot of money for me. They can set that si-rene off any time they like."

It was always a hobby really but Ward wanted to sell that band. MCA used to book them and make money with them. Ward never had an exclusive contract with MCA and he had to approve anything they got first. If they got a good job for one night Ward would take it. He was damn near second-in-charge at the Disney Studios. He was a very clever man, a director, and Disney's right-hand man; him and Walt practically came up together. Anyway, he would get these jobs and sometimes George Probert wasn't available, so I would play with him. When the band first started Johnny Lucas, a crippled trumpet player, worked with them. This was out at the Walt Disney Studios. They played every Tuesday and Friday, like they do now, during the lunch hour. Everybody that could play any music would get together for an informal session for about an hour. They would come where we was playing and invite us over to the studios for lunch and to play. That's how I met Ward, when me and Ram gave them some pointers.

Ward is the one who introduced me to Walt Disney himself. We was walking one day out at the studio and there's Walt over there, wearing an old sweater with the sleeves all torn out and looking like any of the laborers or handymen. Ward says, "Walt, I want you to meet Joe Darensbourg." "Hi, Mr Disney." "Call me Walt." Then Ward says, "This is about the cheapest guy on the lot. Walt'll spend all the money if his brother don't catch him." Walt laughed. He was a nice guy to talk to, no doubt about that.

This was close to New Year and Ward said, "I'm gonna have a party out at the house and I want all you guys from the band to come out there." I think this was shortly after the time that Teddy Buckner had started playing trumpet with us, 'cause I remember he was at a lot of the parties. He'd invite a lot of movie people, too. Ward had a huge place in Santa Gabriel with five acres of land. He's about the foremost collector of miniature trains and full-size, old-time trains. In his yard he has a locomotive, a chair-car, a caboose, a roundhouse and a railway station, all full-size. He acquired the track and everything from some abandoned railroad and set them up in his yard, circling the five acres. He'd fire it all up and we'd ride around. He had a fortune tied up in those trains. He set up a couple of railway museums, one out in Sacramento and another someplace in Pennsylvania. He's such an interesting guy, they had a whole movie just about him. Naturally enough, he collected fire-engines as well. One time Ory got bursitis and Ward Kimball took over from him for a week. He played good. I led the band for that period and, as usual, Tudi and I got in a lot of hassles over me being the leader. That's just typical of Louisiana musicians.

At the back end of 1948 we went up to San Francisco again, this time to the Venus Club, which is one of the worst dives in San Francisco. We'd have to move the drunks out of the way to get in and out of the place. This was down in the Mission district, which was a rough part of town and still is: nothing but winos hanging round. We had worked the Blackshears and a lot of other joints in San Francisco and Ory was a big favorite there. There was a better audience for traditional jazz than in Los Angeles. A Greek woman owned the Venus and she liked the band. The money was right and we worked there about six weeks, which was long enough. They had worse liquor than anywhere, you had to hold your nose before you could take a drink. Gideon Honore was on piano and Bob Scobey came in on trumpet because Blake couldn't travel. The first time we worked in San Francisco Blake did go but his wife got sick and he had to bring her back here. That's how Scobey came to be working with us.

I remember another place we worked in Frisco. This was a beautiful club, shaped like an opera house, with a restaurant. At the front by the cash register the guy had two little canaries named Tom and Jerry. The cashier told me, "Every time you guys play St Louis Blues these birds break out singing, but not on other tunes." I told Ory about it and we played a couple of tunes with Tom and Jerry doing nothing. Then the guy gave us the signal for St Louis Blues and Ory started laughing and laughing. Sure enough them canaries was wailing duets! Ory said, "I'll be goddamned, you ever seen anything like that?"

Another crazy thing that happened in San Francisco involved a friend of mine, a big fan of Ory's. He was a policeman up there named Bill Rogers, and one time he says, "Come on up to my house, I gotta parakeet I want you guys to hear. Joe, you bring your clarinet." Bill had a wire recorder and he says to me, "I want to record Bing." Bing is what he called the parakeet. I had some eyeglasses then that had a metal frame, and this sonofagun would come light on the frames; the glitter of the gold metal just fascinated him. It would say, "My name is Bing, what's yours? I can sing like Bing." Then he'd whistle *Blues in the Night*. Bill recorded me playing clarinet in a duet with this parakeet. Kinda cute, too. I wish to hell I'd had a copy. That was some bird. The first thing Bill taught it was its name, address and phone number in case it got lost. Bing did get free one day but he told the people his name and asked them to call "his daddy." This fellow couldn't believe it, but Bill says, "Hold him there, I'll come right over and get him."

SIX

Ory was a very suspicious character

I recommended Lloyd Glenn to Ory and he joined us later in 1949. I think they may have had some other piano players in there before Lloyd came along. How I come to know Lloyd was because he used to rehearse and play out at a nightclub called the Hawaiian Village right next door to my cousin's shoe shop on Western Avenue. Just to keep in touch with the shoemaking trade, I would go in and help my cousin to repair shoes or take care of his joint sometimes. I heard Lloyd and his band play and right away I seen he had possibilities: he could be converted to playing dixieland. Lloyd worked out pretty good and he stayed with our band a few years. He had a sort of hit record called *Sh-boom* which was a beautiful tune, and he wrote several other things. He had been with Barney Bigard's cousin Don Albert down in San Antonio, Texas. That's where Lloyd is from.

Then it was Blake's turn to leave the band. He couldn't work all the time otherwise he would have probably stayed with us. He never did entirely stop playing or go into retirement. After Blake we had several different trumpet players, including Winnow Allen and others like Martin Peppi. See, dumb as Ory was, he always had scores to these tunes we played. He'd have a trumpet lead sheet and a piano sheet with the chords. So if you got a good trumpet player, everybody else fell in. Martin Peppi was primarily a studio musician in the class of Manny Klein and Cappy Lewis. Him and Barney was great friends and he went to play with Barney when he organized his band. Then he decided to quit playing and the last time I seen him he said, "I just don't want to play no more."

Teddy Buckner was Blake's steady replacement and he fit in real good. I first got to know Teddy when the Ory band was in San Francisco playing the Blackshears, a club on Fillmore Street owned by an ex-prizefighter. Benny Carter was up there and he had Teddy with him, along with Jesse Price on drums. I knew Teddy wasn't exactly a dixieland man, but I could see he had possibilities just like Lloyd. There's no doubt his inspiration was Louis, he always says that. I told Ory about him, so when Teddy came back to Los Angeles with Benny, they didn't work all the time and Ory tried Teddy out. The first job he worked with us was at the Beverly Cavern. Teddy kinda changed the character of the band. For instance, he started playing a few different tunes. We got a request for *Just a closer walk with thee* and that became one of his featured numbers, just played with a little wa-wa mute. We did a few other things, which we discontinued but which were really good, where the instruments would have a conversation, like between the trumpet and the trombone; we'd be playing a beautiful slow blues and the trumpet and the trombone would answer each other. Then Teddy and Ory got to arguing about who should play what, so they stopped it.

Teddy had been with Hamp and he had worked with Fats Waller. I met Fats when Teddy was playing with him at some of the clubs in Los Angeles. He had this clarinet player, Gene Sedric, with him and they came out here a couple of times. Fats is the only man who used to buy cases of half-pints of liquor. They called them "Mickeys," and whenever Fats would uncork a half that was one drink for him; when he put that bottle to his lips it never came down until it was finished. That bottle was gone. If you wanted a drink, he'd hand you a fresh bottle.

Teddy's very nice. Him and I got along fine and we became real friends. He has a beautiful wife, Minnie is her name, and they used to come out to the house in North Hollywood when me and Helen moved there. All of the guys used to come over and swim. I'm the first of them that had a house with a swimming pool. Lloyd and his wife came, along with Harvey Brooks and his wife Daisy. Daisy was real nice and she and I collaborated on a couple of tunes where she helped out with the lyrics. Harvey was well known from the stuff he did with Mae West. He wrote *Dallas Man* and his big tune was *A little bird told me*. He made a lot of money out of it.

Some time later on Ory was trying to act bigger than he was, telling everybody about his 75,000-dollar home and swimming pool. Old Wellman Braud said, "What the hell is that, a swimming pool? Joe here was just a sideman and he's got a pool in North Hollywood." Still, pools didn't impress me; I didn't buy the house for the pool. It was nice for Helen and we enjoyed it, but by the same token you got a lot of unwelcome visitors. Guys that wouldn't even think about coming to visit me came just to spend time by my pool. For example, Stan Storey, the clarinet player with Pete Daily, who in a way was a nice guy, came by the house one day. Usually when you go to a person's house where they have a pool you bring your own towels and, out of common courtesy, a six-pack or a bottle. So here he comes with two six-packs and he drinks one six-pack and half of all my drinks, then takes the other six-pack home with him. That's pretty cheeky. I put a six-foot fence around my house with a lock on the gate and I'd still come back to find that guys had jumped the fence to go swimming!

I enjoyed working at the Cavern. We had a nice, presentable band. We was making a little more than scale, but it wasn't no big deal – there wasn't that much big money around. Our pay was flat salary, something like a hundred dollars a week. Ory was just as big time as any of the rest of us really. We got along but he was not a good business man. Ory was a very suspicious character – he always figured somebody was trying to pull a deal on him, trying to beat him out of some money or trying to take his band away from him or run his business. He was a hard man to get through to, to make him understand things. You'd tell him one thing and he'd take it to mean another. You know the old saying, "You can get a sonofabitch out of the country but you can't get the country out of that sonofabitch." That describes Ory about right.

We had a lot of fun at times and we had some funny incidents, too. After we was at the Cavern a while we decided to bring Papa Celestin in as a guest. Papa used to have a broadcast program in New Orleans and that was one thing that helped him to become known. People out in Los Angeles wanted to hear him. I remember listening to one broadcast and the bass man in Celestin's band says, "Hey, Papa, let's play *Jazz me Blues*," and right away Papa Celestin says, "You can't say that on the radio, you get us in trouble. Don't you know what it means when you say 'Jazz *me* Blues?' You gotta say 'Jazz *it* Blues.' Remember that." I never forgot that. We'd play that tune a lot of times and Ory would says, "Well, we'll play *Jazz me Blues* now," and I'd say, "Wait a minute, Kid, don't say that." Ory would say, "Why, what the hell you talking about?" I'd explain, "You heard what Papa Celestin said, didn't you? You say 'Jazz it . . . .'." Kid would say, "To hell with Papa Celestin, we gonna play *Jazz me Blues*. OK?"

From the very first night Papa Celestin got up with us he took the band over, lock, stock and barrel. It wasn't right and I remember Ram saying at intermission, "We are in for a helluva two weeks, Lord have mercy, with these two bastards up here, specially with that goddam Tudi sticking his nose in, too!" Sure enough, Papa started his big tune *L'il Liza Jane* and Ory wanted to play something else, but no, Papa wanted his tune. He called the tunes, it look like he wouldn't let Ory off. We'd be playing a tune and Ory would try to get a word in or he might start taking a chorus, then Papa would say, "Take it down, Kid, let Joe take a chorus." He'd make Ory stop playing, in other words. Ory would get so goddam mad, you could see smoke coming from that slide. He put up with all that shit for the whole two weeks but he was fuming. He was so mad he couldn't hardly drink. This goes on until Papa's closing night, and Ory was a happy soul to see this cat leaving. He was really celebrating, heisting a few and bending his elbow all night long. We figured there was going to be trouble. Then everybody started breathing a little easier that the night had come to a close and Papa was going back to New Orleans in one piece. We was standing around talking and having a drink when we heard a helluva big racket. They had a lunch room right next door to the Cavern which was owned by the Cavern but leased as a concession to a very good clarinet player named Johnny Costello, who used to have a spaghetti joint there. For some reason it wasn't open, although the doors to the restaurant was open. I don't know whether Ory invited Papa into the kitchen or vice versa, but suddenly all hell broke loose, pots and pans flying around, until somebody come running out and says, "You guys better go in there, Celestin and Ory's gonna kill each other!" We all rushed to the door and Celestin was stood one side of the big meat chopping block holding a butcher's knife and a cleaver, with Ory on the other side with a knife in one hand and a hatchet in the other. They was taking cuts at each other and I never seen two old men that could jump so high and so fast, ducking like that. They was swinging at each other but they was missing. Whether they wanted to kill each other I don't know. The argument was about Papa Celestin taking the band over. "You come here and took my band away from me, next thing you be taking them back to New Orleans. No goddam way," and then Papa says, "Take 'em back? I wouldn't have 'em. Hell, those guys can't play nothin!" We all got mad at him then and I was ready to get me a cleaver and go after him.

The people enjoyed Celestin but he wasn't any big deal with me. He reminded me of Mutt with that trumpet; he couldn't play anything. Celestin was never one of your powerhouse trumpet players. He was a promoter who would book eight jobs in one night in New Orleans. He had a big car with a chauffeur and he'd run from one job to another, collecting money from all of them. He had all these bands under his name. Celestin was slicker than hot axle grease and that's pretty hot!

Ory was sweating like hell that night and he says, "Phew, that's the last sonofabitch that ever gonna sit in this band so long as I'm the leader. I got rid of the bastard and there'll be no more." He told Sam Rittenberg, the owner, "Don't come bitching that nobody will come here and be a guest with my band. If you do, you gonna have to get a new band." There was no more guests after that – I should say not!

You know, these New Orleans musicians can always find a reason to fight. In the Ory band if it wasn't Tudi it was Ram. One time they got in a big fight in the Cavern over nothing. It just shows you how crazy they was, especially when you think Ram was built like a bull and Tudi was so small. When I first met him he was like 5 ft 10 in tall, then he shrunk to 5 ft 5 in; he's proof that as you get older you get smaller! Anyway, some guy came in the Cavern and started talking about delivering mail and what a "scheme" was. So Tudi says to Ram, "I'll bet you a dollar you don't know what a scheme is." Ram says, it's when you go to be a mail carrier and you gotta learn the location of all the streets, the numbers and everything. Tudi says in reply that a scheme is to do with sorting letters at the Post Office. Of course, Ram was right and whoever was holding the dollar said to give it to Ram. Tudi says, "Gimme my dollar back," but Ram says, "To hell with you, I won it." Some guy that knew about the mail confirmed what Ram had said and, before you knew it, Tudi had hit Ram in the eye. During that time they was building an addition to the Cavern and they had all kinds of lumber and bricks laying in a pile and, like Teddy says, the waltzing started. Ram grabbed Tudi and he started hollering, "Wait a minute, Ram, I got glasses on, don't hit me." Ram replies, "I don't care if you got glasses on," and he took Tudi's glasses off and hit him. Little as Tudi was, he was strong. He was a guy that knew everything – you would say something and he'd contradict you, especially he'd contradict Ram. Look like they'd argue all the time. They'd get mad about who played the right rhythm, little things like that. But that's typical of New Orleans musicians, they'll fight like dogs one minute and then they'll kiss each other the next.

We used to make quite a bit with tips at times: people would give us money for tunes and we would split it every month. We made Tudi the treasurer; when we got money we gave it to him and he'd fold it up and put it in one corner of his wallet. Ram would write it down in a notebook, 'cause we knew when Tudi got off work he always gambled. We needed to keep track of how much money Tudi had at all times. They had a gambling joint on the South Side, on Central Avenue close to Tudi's house. He'd make a bee-line for that joint and a lot of time he'd run out of money and borrow from the kitty. Ram always used to kid him about it. "I seen you over there gambling and I watched you take some of that kitty money. You better have our money at the end of the month." Tudi would say, "That's all right, you sonofabitch, I got enough money to buy and sell you. You know how much you got coming and I got it for you. Don't worry 'bout me spending any of your damn money." Which was right, he always had the money when it was time to split.

During this time Lucky Strike cigarettes used to give out little coupons that you could redeem for cash or more cigarettes at a discount. These coupons almost looked like green dollar-bills and Blakeney and me got hold of some of them and handed them to Tudi one night. "Here's ten dollars, put this with the kitty money." We knew Tudi was using our money for gambling but we shouldn't have done what we did, 'cause we almost got Tudi killed. This night in particular Tudi had run out of money and he went to a barbecue stand and bought some barbecue. He pulled out these coupons so the guy says, "What the hell is this?" Tudi wasn't paying no attention but then the guy accused him of passing counterfeit money, so Tudi told him that he got the money from where he'd been working. Tudi's eyesight wasn't too good, besides it was kinda dark, so the man says, "I'm gonna have you arrested or else cut you with this cleaver." Tudi pulled his knife (he always carried a knife and sometimes a pistol) and they was about to kill each other when Ram stopped them. He told Tudi the story about the Lucky Strike bills, so Tudi says, "Wait until I catch up with those guys." The only thing that saved us, he couldn't figure which one of us gave him that funny money. "What I ought to do is to cut both of you, then I'll know which one of you bastards did this." Right to this day we talk about that. Otherwise Tudi and I were good friends. Hell, I was good friends with all the guys in the band. I was the youngest one there but I got along OK.

Tudi used to like to tell stories from his early days in New Orleans, like when he was a grand marshall on a parade where they had a horse-drawn hearse which tipped over. The casket flew out, the lid flipped open and the guy sits up. He hadn't been embalmed and everybody just took off. I says to Tudi, "Do you mean to tell me you fellows didn't stay and help this poor guy?" Tudi says, "Are you kidding? I was over in Algiers across the river when they picked that cat up." They come to find he wasn't dead, he was just in a trance, which happened with a lot of people.

Tudi told another true story about King Oliver when he was leaving New Orleans to come to Chicago. He had a big lunch basket and he wanted to find a place to put this basket. All them trains got brake cords for emergencies and King Oliver took this basket and hung it on the brake cord – near wrecked the train. Then they come trying to find out who did it, but they never did find out, otherwise they'd have thrown them all off the train.

Tudi says they had a Chinese restaurant near where they worked in Chicago and all of them would eat in there, pork and noodles, that sort of thing. Old Joe Oliver was so goddam cheap all he would do was order a glass of iced tea, and he'd bring a great big loaf of French bread in there with him. You could get a day-old loaf for a nickel then, plus he'd pay a nickel for that glass of tea. They had a water cooler by the table, and when he got through with his tea he'd use this Chinaman's sugar all night long to make sweetening water. He'd take about 50-cents-worth of sugar after buying just that one glass of tea. So the Chinese guy says, "No good, you go outside, black boy, get out of here."

There was another story about New Orleans that both Tudi and Ory told. It concerns a fellow named Rabbit who was a very popular drummer. When a well-liked musician died they had a wake: an occasion to have drinks, have a ball, get drunk and gamble. So the word went out when Rabbit died they was gonna wake him. Everybody came to pay their respects, play cards and shoot a little dice. After the third night more people was coming in and there was so many guys there, they didn't hardly have any place to shoot dice. Now they had old Rabbit laying out on the cooling board. He wasn't embalmed and it was summertime. Some guy says, "Say, why don't we move old Rabbit off that cooling board and stand him up in the corner. Hell, he's stiff anyway and we can use that table to play cards." Sure enough, they did this and then another guy, who hadn't seen Rabbit or heard he was dead, he comes in there. Old Rabbit, dressed in his tuxedo, was standing up in his corner. This guy walks over and looks at him, "I thought you was dead when here you are just standing up here asleep. Have a drink, Rabbit. Man, you look in pretty good shape, nice tuxedo." Then he pulled Rabbit's mouth open and poured this moonshine down his throat and says, "I've got a couple of good gigs coming up next week over in Algiers. I'll call you and see you there." The same day the police came round and said Rabbit is getting pretty ripe, start smelling up the whole neighborhood. All this is true!

Tudi and Ory always had their differences, their little arguments. They had a helluva fight in San Francisco after I left the band (Phil Gomez had taken my place). This was right up on the stand. It seems that Doc Dougherty, the owner of the Hangover, had given Ory some extra money to give to the musicians. Ory didn't do it and Tudi found out. At that time Ory had a special-made big old brass mute that he used. I'm the one that started him to using it again. When I first went to work with him, he had a kinda junk pile in this yard and this mute was there. It was sure unusual, made of brass and full of holes. Ory explained that somebody made it for him so I asked him why he didn't try it. He picked it up and that got to be one of his favorite mutes. Anyway, it was pretty heavy. The bandstand at the Hangover was directly in the back of the bar on a raised platform. If you sat at the bar you could gaze right up at the musicians. In other words, it was a one-sided place, one big flat wall with the bar and the band. The brass section would stand on one side and the rhythm section would stand on the other. Tudi had found out that day about the money. Him and Ory started the argument over this before they got on the stand and they continued arguing up on the stand. Ory was a kinda quick-tempered guy and he picked up the brass mute and hit Tudi with it. Tudi would fight at the drop of a hat and he hit Ory. Ory had his back to the bar and, had Doc not caught Ory, he might have been killed. As it was, the way he fell his back was hurt, I think on the right side, and he broke three or four ribs. He might have broke his back had Doc not been tending bar and caught him. Kid was in the hospital for a good few weeks. Naturally, Tudi left the band.

On Sundays, which was our day off from the Cavern, I had a band at Sardi's, another popular jazz spot on Hollywood Boulevard. We'd usually have two bands in there, and for several Sunday afternoons it was Benny Carter's band up there with mine. Ben Webster played saxophone with Carter and he was kinda evil. He used to drink quite a bit and sometimes he'd be half-drunk sitting there playing the piano. Freddie Slack, the piano player that made *Cow Cow Boogie* famous, came by one time to sit in with my band. For no reason, Ben said to Freddie, "Get up there, let me show you how to play." Freddie didn't want to get up so they got in an argument. Ben pulled out a knife and cut Freddie on the arm right there on the stand; if it wasn't for Benny Carter, who pulled Ben away, he might have cut Freddie more than that. There's never a dull moment in music with all these little entertaining things!

At Sardi's I used to have musicians with me like Cappy Lewis, a tremendous high-note trumpet player, Tommy Rundell or Nick Pelico (who is in charge of recordings for the union now) on drums and a part-Indian saxophone player named Billy Myles. He was another fine musician but he was kinda unusual. Billy was always after me to go in business with him, peddling tea. He was a great one for peote, a plant. He'd say, "That's what made Jim Thorpe the great Indian athlete so good." Billy would take the peote plant, boil it up, make a tea out of it and drink it. I met Billy first in the 331 Club when he had just come here from Denver, this would be around 1950. A real character.

All the movie stars used to come into Sardi's, guys like Raymond Burr and Bruce Cabot. Monette Moore, the vocalist that later worked with us at Disneyland, would come in and sing. Not only her, but other top singers like Anita O'Day as well.

Johnny Lucas, the crippled trumpet player, Zutty and Bud Hatch, different guys in the band, would go in the back store-room at Sardi's and smoke tea. One time I made a miracle happen when I walked in there and hollered, "This is the FBI. Freeze!" Little Johnny got up and walked right out of that chair. He'd never done that before but I scared the hell out of him. He still doesn't walk!

Sometime in late 1948 the Ory band played the first Dixieland Jubilee concert out at the Pan-Pacific Auditorium, a great big place. Zutty was the grand marshall and Red Nichols was there. It was the first time I had seen Louis and the All Stars and I remember I brought Picou, my old clarinet teacher, and his daughter Olga out there as my guests. Picou was living in Los Angeles then. Louis had Bob Stone on bass, a white guy that plays with the Symphony now; in fact I played with Bob at McArthur Park recently. Dick Cary was on piano and Barney and Jack Teagarden was in the band, too. Zutty at the time was working with Nappy Lamare and Ray Bauduc around here; in fact he went on tour with them. Nappy and them had opened Club 47 and Zutty played there. I used to see Zutty all the time when we'd go crawfishing, buy beers and go to Ory's house, have a good time; but so far as playing together – him and Ory didn't get along. Zutty had his certain ways. I never really worked on a steady job with Zutty, only a few casuals and sessions. He'd play all the jam sessions and he'd play as good as he wanted to play. He might not like the piano player that was sitting in so he'd slow the tempo, stop beating the bass drum altogether, just let the rhythm drop out, 'cause he was mad about something. Zutty did a little pimping on the side; he had an old broad that used to hustle and get a little money.

The Pan-Pacific must have held 10 to 15 thousand people. This was the first time we had a big thing like that in Los Angeles. It was the beginning of the Dixieland Jubilees which was held every year at the Shrine for maybe eight or ten years after that. The finale of this first one had all the musicians playing *The Saints* together, with old Zutty leading the parade. Ben Pollack had his band on the show and him and Zutty played a duet. They must have had half a dozen good clarinet players there. It was a very, very impressive thing when all the different musicians, about 60 of them, lined up on that huge stage.

Picou's daughter lived over on Jefferson near Western; that was a popular part of town, and he came to stay with her 'cause she wanted him to do some tile-work for her. Picou was a tile-setter, terrific with mosaic and things like that, like an artist really. He said his people originally did that type of work in France. They had a lot of New Orleans people living in that part of Los Angeles and Picou got them to help him build a little restaurant called the New Orleans Kitchen, which was situated right on Adams near Western. Olga had a big house in the back and that's where we would congregate every night and have jam sessions. If we wasn't at Buster's, we was over at Picou's – more so 'cause they'd always have a lot to eat from the restaurant. Frank Pasley was a good friend of Picou and Reb Spikes used to come over all the time. Buddy Burns the bass player and Picou's brother called Little Pic, that played a guitar, they'd be there. My brother-in-law Warren that was married to my sister Rose was a distant relative of Picou; their mothers was first cousins. We'd all go round there and have a ball.

Picou would come over to Sardi's and sit in. Him and I would play clarinet duets and then maybe he'd play one with Barney. Another guy that would come in was Pete Fountain. He was real young then but we'd let him sit in. He came here to visit long before he started working with Lawrence Welk. Then he lived right close to me in North Hollywood. Eddie Miller brought him to Sardi's. Really Sardi's was best known for Red Nichols. In fact I think he played there more than any other spot in Los Angeles.

While we was in the Beverly Cavern we'd go out to Arizona once in a while on a weekend or get a few extra party dates. We drew a lot of movie people and we'd stay in these different places at least six or eight weeks. Other times we'd go to San Francisco and work different clubs, but we always managed to come back to the Beverly Cavern; we was in there on and off for years. Another place we played was Mike Lyman's on Vine Street near Hollywood Boulevard, which was primarily one of your top restaurants. Ory's was the first band of any kind to appear at Mike Lyman's, even though Mike and his brother Abe had a club down-town where Abe played with his big band – fairly well-known band, too. I remember Mickey Cohen hanging around Mike's place, gambling in a room upstairs. That's just a very little part of the scene. Cohen was notorious for being a racketeer. When we left the Cavern we went into the Royal Room located on Hollywood Boulevard and Las Palmas, which was a fairly small place until they enlarged it.

We stayed in the Royal Room about 12 weeks and then we went into Mike Lyman's. After us he had the top bands of the time like Nichols, Pete Daily and Joe Yukl. We were in Mike's place a long time, six months at least. Hollywood was the center of the entertainment business then. At one time you might hear six or seven dixieland bands, all in Hollywood. The heyday for all this was the early 1950s.

As a matter of fact, black people didn't support the music then and they still don't. It was their music but the black kids seen it wasn't their kind of mood; besides they didn't like it, even in New Orleans. If you had to depend on black audiences, forget it.

The Royal Room had the biggest jam sessions I ever seen. I've counted 30 musicians playing at a time. The owner, Abe Bush, was a good friend of mine and he put me in charge of some of the Sunday afternoon sessions. All sorts of different famous people used to come and sit in with us. Ory never would play, but Harry James's dad, that used to be the leader of the band on the Christie Brothers Circus out of Galveston, Texas, he'd come by with his horn. Then there'd be Phil Harris, Johnny Lucas, Zutty, and Sal Franzella, the great clarinet player from New Orleans that used to be with Paul Whiteman. After the Ory band finished at the Royal Room Pete Daily moved in and that's when the jam sessions took off. They had another club on Vine Street called the Hangover that Pete worked for about five or six years, right down from Billy Berg's. That's where I first met Pete.

Pete drew good crowds. He was just as big a name as Ory in Los Angeles and a bigger name than Jack Teagarden; he'd also draw more people than Red Nichols, but he fouled up his money. Fast as he made it, he spent it, and yet he had a wife and a big family. His wife was an alcoholic, too. Pete is the only musician I ever seen that people enjoyed going to see even when he was drunk. For instance, we'd be playing someplace like Mike Lyman's and the crowd would go down to the Hangover and see Pete. And here they come back saying Pete's in good form. "He's drunker than a sonofabitch." For some reason, the guy had a magic personality and he had a helluva following. Pete made so much money for Abe Bush. He had made a tune, *When the war breaks out in Mexico, I'm going to Montreal*, and another tune that he used as a theme song, called *I want to linger*, which was a big number. Pud Brown had a feature, a great tenor solo, on another of Pete's tune, called *Johnson Rag*. Pete had a helluva good contract with Capitol to make ten albums a year.

One time Louis Armstrong was in town playing at the Crescendo and I called him up and asked if he would do me a favor and be the guest at the Royal Room Sunday jam session. We started at seven o'clock on a Sunday morning. All the clubs here closed at two o'clock in the morning and, as you can imagine, half the musicians were hung over from Saturday night. Still, there'd be people lined up clear down Hollywood Boulevard waiting to get in to hear these musicians play. Anyway, I got Louis to appear. We all went to his apartment at the Knickerbocker Hotel for a party after he finished playing and before the jam session. Lucille told Louis it was time for his pills. Naturally, Louis was the center of attraction and Lucille brought him this little alligator case full of his vitamin pills – all different colors, looked like jelly beans. Louis had his hand out and Lucille gave him about nine of these pills and then went to get him some water. Louis said, "The directions say you take the different colors at different times but, hell, I get tired going through all of that so I take 'em all at once and let each one find their own way." Meade "Lux" Lewis laughed so much at that he almost fell out of the window.

After we had drinks and everything we went on to the jam session. When it was over we went to have breakfast, and that's when Louis insisted on everybody having ice-cream after the ham and eggs. The waitress came over and Louis asked her what kind of ice-cream they had. She said all the flavors and Louis said, "Good, give me a ball of each." The waitress looked flabbergasted. "What do you mean, a ball of each, Mr Armstrong?" Louis says, "I mean a ball of each, a ball. Can't you understand English? A scoop!" So we all had a big dish of ice-cream and sherbet. Everything Louis did was funny to me.

Like another time when we was up in San Francisco with the Ory band and Louis was working there. We'd go see him after we got off work at the Hangover. We was staying at a house where we could cook, so Ory said he would cook some stewed chicken and red beans and rice. Louis and some of his band came over for that dinner and we all had a great time. I had my car up there and Louis asked me if I could take him next day to the dentist before work. Now I had a battery in that car that was kinda weak, so I always made it a point to park on the side of the hill where I could get a start. In front of this dentist's office it was more or less flat. Louis was in his tuxedo and when he came out the car wouldn't start. I told Louis, "Pops, you gotta get out and push." He says, "That's all right, home boy, I'll push you." In the meantime some people had recognized him and Louis says, "That's OK, gates, open it up." But it was hard to get started and old Louis was sweating until some guy came up to help him. Then Louis says, "Goddam, home boy, from now on you get a Cadillac or a Rolls, 'cause if *Down Beat* get a hold that I'm pushing your old Ford, my reputation will be ruined." And he just laughed like hell. I thought it was kinda funny, too. Finally we got the car started and he jumped in.

Did you know I could have been part of the book *From Here to Eternity* that James Jones wrote? He used to come in the Royal Room along with Lowny Handy, the woman that was sponsoring him. She came up to me and she says, "Jim here is writing a book about the army. In a chapter of the book, it's about some soldiers in the guard-house, they sing a blues song called *The Re-enlistment Blues*. I have the words of this blues and if I send you some of the chapters of the book, would you write the music to it?" This James Jones was a real screwy-acting guy, had a funny little smile and all he would drink was Cokes, although they bought me drinks. I'm not a writer but I could have done what she asked as easy as nothing. She said, "Who knows, if the book ever happens, you'll come into a little part of it. We won't forget you." Sure enough, they sent me photostat copies of this thing, but I wouldn't even answer their letters; drove me mad, but I thought they were a couple of nuts. Helen read the outline and they used all these cuss words so she wouldn't read any more of it. I just didn't want to be bothered and I ignored those chapters. Every other person writes a song or something. Musicians go through a lot of stuff like that.

Jones was an orphan kid, he really didn't have any people, but this Lowny Handy seen something in him, thinking he had a talent for writing. Jones went to the army but they kicked him out, gave him a Section Eight discharge, and he came back to Robbins, Illinois. She wanted to get him out of there so she went in hock to borrow money and bought a jeep and a house trailer. He had the outline of the book and he thought he could write the story if he could just go round the country. They lived in the trailer and traveled all over while he was writing the book. Anyway, one night we picked up *Life* magazine and on the front cover was James Jones with his best-seller *From Here to Eternity*. We sent him a wire saying congratulations, and he sent me an autographed copy of the book with a nice little inscription which said, "To the world's greatest clarinet player – better luck next time." Meantime he came to Los Angeles when we was back working at the Beverly Cavern and came over to see me. He was the technical adviser on the movie of the book they was making. He bought me a drink and told me he was sorry things turned out the way they did, but he was writing another book and he would probably have something in it for me. I never heard from him again, for which I don't blame him; that's just one of the opportunities I missed. In the back of the book is all the words to *The Re-enlistment Blues*, but no music. In the film they had some guy playing a guitar. I know I'd have got to record the music in the film, plus he'd probably have slipped me a few bucks on the side. I found out afterwards that's the type of people they were. So I really fluffed on that deal. It was a great movie, too. It turns out they took the money from the book and the movie, which was a tremendous amount, and organized a colony for artists someplace in Florida.

The thing about this business, if you pay attention to every screwball that's writing a song or something, you'd waste half your life. Like now, people write from all over wanting a picture or a reed from my clarinet. Helen will write them a letter and we never hear from them again. It's expensive, too.

The Royal Room, that's where Helen and I started going out. What made me like her, she bought me a couple of drinks the night we met. That really did it. Of course, we did a little fooling around and then we got married.

Helen Darensbourg:
 I saw Joe at the Jade Palace but I didn't pay any attention to him. I loved the music and I used to go to Billy Berg's every Sunday to see what bands they had. Later on I was going with another fellow and he asked me if I liked dixieland. I said, yes, so he said, "There's a great band playing at Beverly Cavern." This was around 1949. We went over to see Kid Ory and naturally I liked the music right away. When the band finished playing Joe came down and, like he does every place he goes, he sat down with us and started talking. He visits with everybody in the audience and he says he used to get a lot of free drinks that way. The fellow I was with introduced me to Joe. I liked him because of the clarinet. We went back several times to hear the band, and every time we'd come in Joe would sit at our table and talk to us. One night at the Cavern I was going to the rest room, which was in the back of the big room where they played, and Joe was standing there. They were getting ready to go on stage. Joe stopped me and he said, "Say, why don't you ever come in by yourself?" So I said, "Well, I don't go in bars by myself," and Joe said, "This is a nice place. I know everybody here and it would be safe for you to come in." I kinda liked Joe, so after I'd gone home I kept thinking about it, but I wouldn't go over there by myself. In the meantime the band left the Beverly Cavern and went into the Royal Room. This was around 1950. So the same fellow took me over there one night to see the band. Of course, Joe was happy to see us; in fact everybody was happy to see us. We used to talk to Kid Ory, Ram, Tudi, everybody in the band between sets.
 Joe had mentioned that Louis Armstrong was to appear at the Bal Tabarin in Gardena for a week, and he says, "Why don't you go?" I had met a couple of waitresses at the Royal Room and I had a car, so I asked them what night they had off, and they told me, Tuesday night. That was Joe's night off, too. I said, "Why don't we go down to hear Louis? Gee, I'd love to see him." I'd never seen

him and I'd always loved him so much. We didn't know that Joe was going to be there that night. Anyway, we went. The place was jam-packed. There were ropes on both sides of the stage, sectioning it off. We're sitting there having a drink and here comes Joe. He was there with his woman friend Gladys, also with Kid Ory and his girl friend Barbara. Joe spotted us and naturally I spotted Joe. He leaves Gladys and walks clear round the whole room to the other side where we were sitting. He wanted to buy us a drink so we let him buy us a drink. He kept talking and saying, why didn't I go out with him some night. He suggested taking me to dinner the next Tuesday, and I said, OK. That's how we started going together. We went together for two and a half years.

Talking about the jam session days, Nappy Lamare's Club 47 was always very popular, especially with musicians. Every jazz musician that came to Los Angeles would be there. Sharkey Bonano came to town to work at the Tiffany Club, down from the 400 Club on 8th Street, and he came over. Look like a jam session was going on most of the time. Phil Harris was another regular, as was Dan Dailey. Club 47 was out at Studio City, so a lot of movie people came in. Nappy and his partner Doc Rando would tend bar and then they'd come and play. Often they'd have a party, send out little invitations to all the musicians, just for a get-together on their night off. Being from New Orleans, they'd have gumbo, red beans and rice, and always keep a pot on the stove. Zutty was funny then. I remember he used to get full of gin and he'd go up to Nappy at the bar and say, "Goddam, Nappy, give me another shot of that good old J-I-N." Club 47 never had big jam sessions like the Royal Room; their deals was more like musicians' get-togethers.

Nappy is a helluva nice guy. I first met him in Seattle in the thirties when he was with the Bob Crosby band at the Trianon Ballroom. They wanted a place to jam, but they was only in Seattle for the one afternoon, so they didn't have a chance. I was working in one of the clubs and I wanted Nappy to come down there. I never did see Nappy too much after that because he was always on tour, that is until the Club 47 days. Like a lot of guys in New Orleans, Nappy is just a quality person. If everybody was like Nappy this would be an awful nice world, that's all I got to say. He knows everything, he sings good, has a great sense of humor and he's a funny guy.

Nappy had his own radio show called "Dixie Showboat," which was a terrific success. I remember he had Scat Man Crothers singing with his band. I met Scat Man first when the Ory band was working at the New Orleans Swing Club in San Francisco in 1949. The owner, Lou Landry, was from New Orleans and he knew Ory from way back. He was a typical hustling pimp, dealt in narcotics, everything. Lou told Ory he had a piece of property near Fillmore and asked him to work there if he opened a place. Ory said, OK, so long as the money was right. So Landry opened this place and it went terrific. He felt he wanted an MC so he got Scat Man up from Los Angeles through a booking agency. See, they had different little acts in there to make a floor-show alongside Ory. When we was leaving, Ted Veseley, which was a white band, was due to come in, so Scat Man says, "We gonna have a distinct novelty in a colored club, a white dixieland band is coming in here." That's the first time I met Ted and his drummer, Smoky Stover.

Scat Man plays a four-string guitar and sings. He worked with Slim Gaillard a long time, playing drums and singing. He was always working with a trio or a quartet. He also had a piano player named Sylvester Stewart who was a friend of mine. Every chance I'd get when I wasn't working and felt like having a little fun, I'd have a few drinks with old Scat.

One time when I was with Louis, years later, we was playing in San Jose, probably in '62 or '63, at a big auditorium there and we looked across the street and there's a big sign advertising "Scat Man Crothers and his Hollywood Revue." Louis knew the Scat Man and he says, "That goddam Scat Man is fooling the public again. I wonder what kind of revue he got over there." So I went over to see him. We was in San Jose on a one-night stand but Scat Man was there for two weeks. He says, "Hey, Joe, I'm glad to see you, I was just coming over to see old Louis. I wanted to invite you and Louis to come and catch the show and have a drink on the house." Big deal, this was just some little chicken-shit club. Anyway, Louis and the whole band went over there. We had a table set up and here come old Scat Man and his revue. All it was, he had a trio with him singing and some gal dancers; that was the Hollywood Revue. Louis just cracked up laughing and said, "Call that a revue? That old sonofabitch is game and nervous, ain't he? How cheeky can you get?" The thing that got us, he had a guy keep on bringing us drinks and then he brought Louis the bill. I think Scat Man had cut out after he got through. Louis laughed like hell, it didn't make him mad. He said, "That's a nervy cat, ain't it? Stuck me with a bill for 30 dollars!"

Scat Man is big now. He was in that picture I made called *The Great White Hope* and he was in *Roots*. I see him on the "Merv Griffin Show." He's got a helluva good agent, keep him busy all the time. He's filming right now.

Another place where they had great jam sessions was the Blue Bird, a club out on Vermont Avenue. Among the people that came in there was Jack Teagarden's mother. Mama Teagarden was a piano player herself and she'd come to sit in with us. She's the one that taught the whole family their music, and during those days she was pretty spry. I had a band later on at Morgan Hall, out by Long Beach, when she lived out there. She would come and play every Sunday afternoon with us. Boy, she could *play*! I think she was about 75 years old, had beautiful white hair – wonderful lady.

The Blue Bird was owned by three brothers. One of them is Russ Bissett and he's doing a little promoting now. He does things at the Elks in Saugus, California, which started off just as a beer-joint. Russ used to work in the studios: he was a propman on "I Love Lucy" for the whole series and then he worked with Dean Martin. Dean calls him right now if he has to go on location, 'cause Russ is such a terrific organizer. See, when you go on location, you gotta have a portable dressing room and all the equipment, and that's what Russ had covered. His brother Bus Bisset was a crane operator, he built roads and drove those big cats, and the other brother Jack did the same thing. Russ and them all had a little money in the club, but it was more or less for their own pleasure and for musicians really. They'd start early in the morning, maybe ten o'clock, on any given Sunday and all the musicians would come out there. We didn't go out for any money, it was fun. They had a sort of club, called it the Stein Club, and Pete

Daily was the vice-chairman. In other words, he was in charge of all the vice that went on! It was just a beer-joint at first but finally they got mixed drinks. We had musicians from every place. Wingy Manone lived here then, so you'd see him once in a while. Desi Arnaz and Russ was both supposed to have a lot of tapes from those sessions but I never listened to them.

One time when I was in Seattle, Wingy wanted me to come down and work with him. I didn't make it then but I did work a few short jobs with him during the Red Fox days. He was always after me to open a restaurant with him. He was gonna cook the Italian food and I was gonna do the New Orleans style; it was going to be a combination Italian and New Orleans restaurant. We never followed up on that idea, thank God. Wingy went to live in Vegas way before any of the big casinos was built on the Strip, stayed there, off and on, for a long time.

When I was with Louis, Wingy and I did a recording session for Louis Prima in Vegas. Prima had a terrific set-up in Vegas with 40 acres of land by the airport, which was worth a lot of money, even at that time. He liked crawfish so much he built a little lake and brought in crayfish to stock it. Prima had his own record label and he had a helluva nice studio in the house. Wingy used Prima's whole band, except for Prima himself, and added me. This had to be '62 or '63. From the first it seemed to me that Prima and Wingy didn't get along, cussin' each other out – typical of New Orleans musicians. Wingy would be at the mike, testing it or singing into it, and Prima would come out of the booth and say, "Goddam, you dago, keep your nose and mouth out of that microphone. That cost me more than that trumpet you playing." I know Wingy had two or three tunes he wanted to do so he brought the music out and set up the music racks. Prima came out again and says, "What the hell is this?" Wingy says it's his music and Prima replies, "You fool, who the hell you trying to kid? You can't read a goddam note."

The Prima records never was released, I don't know why. I seen Prima a lot of times afterwards but he had so many things going I guess he couldn't be bothered with our records. Prima had one of the best shows in Las Vegas. His band was terrific, a very entertaining band. Every time I would see him he'd say, "I'm gonna get those records out, they all right," but he never released them.

Wingy was with Jack Teagarden's band in Chicago. Jack had a big band then and you had to read some, so poor Wingy had to go 'cause he couldn't read. He went to New York, and about two months later Jack got a letter from Wingy saying he'd been taking lessons and could read anything. So Jack, who liked Wingy, sent him a ticket to come out to Chicago. When Wingy got there Jack called a rehearsal and stuck that music up in front of Wingy, who couldn't read any better than he did in the first place. Jack said, "You gotta lot of nerve, man, making me send you money to come here and take up all my time." So Wingy says, "I don't see what you getting so excited about, you don't realize how rusty a guy can get on them long train rides." In those days the train ride from New York to Chicago was a matter of seven or eight hours!

I remember I went around a place where Wingy was working out at Newport Beach. He had a guy playing the trombone that was very good, so when they got off the stand I asked Wingy what the trombone player's name was. Wingy thought a minute. "Name?" he says. "I can't remember his name. Go over there and ask him his name so I know how to make the payroll out."

Here's another story about Wingy. It seems he was auditioning acts to go out with him on the road in a show, when here comes a guy with a little Boston bulldog. Wingy says, "What the hell can this dog do?" and the guy said, "This dog can do a helluva lot. He can sing, dance and play the piano." Wingy said, "I'd like to see that. I'll interview him and if he can do them things he's got a job." So the dog danced the charleston, the black bottom and different steps, and Wingy says, "So far, so good. Now I wanta hear him play the piano and sing." The dog jumped up on the piano stool and played tunes like *Rhapsody in Blue* and *Canadian Capers*, and he sang *Basin Street Blues*. When he got through the guy says, "What do you think, Wingy. Are you gonna book him?" Wingy says he can't use him and the guy asks, why not. Wingy says, "He's damn good on the piano but that sonofabitch sings out of tune. I can't use him."

You sure get some funny cats in this business. Like one time, I was at the Hangover with Ory and Rico Valese on trumpet, when Nappy came by to see us, along with his piano player Fidgey McGrath. Fidgey was an alcoholic and when he took one drink that was it, but he'd been on the wagon for two years. Tremendous piano player. Nappy and them was opening the next night at a place called the Italian Village. It was intermission time at the Hangover and somebody offered to buy us a drink. Fidgey says, "Just bring me a Coke," but Rico opens his big mouth and says, "Fidgey, have a beer." Nappy says, "Goddam, Rico, you know Fidgey ain't supposed to drink. He don't want a beer." Rico says, "One ain't gonna hurt him," but Fidgey says, "No, I don't want any." Anyway, Rico kept on and he talked Fidgey into taking that beer, and from then on, all night long, Fidgey continued drinking. When they left the club I told Nappy I would see him next day at his hotel and when I got there, about noon, Nappy was walking round like a crazy man. No Fidgey, and he was opening that night and they had to have a rehearsal. Fidgey hadn't been seen since the night before but then Nappy says, "Lord have mercy, here he come." Here's poor Fidgey staggering in the door, couldn't hardly walk, just fell in the foyer. He never did open that night and Nappy had a helluva time getting a piano player in time. You had to see the picture of dejection on Nappy's face. I felt so sorry for him.

After we closed at the Hangover in San Francisco in 1949 I was driving back down to Los Angeles by myself. It was always in my mind to write a tune or something about Baton Rouge or Louisiana, preferably Baton Rouge, but what the hell rhymes with Baton Rouge? Well, I'm riding along and during that time the road wasn't as good as it is now so this is about a seven- or eight-hour drive. I started to thinking, maybe I can write something by spelling it out, and gradually it came . . . *Lou-easy-an-ia*. In fact I'd heard that expression before. That's the way it happened and it all seemed to be very easy. The words just came and as soon as I got back home I wrote 'em down and took my horn and made up a little melody. I got a piece of manuscript paper and sketched a lead, but I hadn't wrote the verse at that time – that came later. I don't really write too much but I can do enough to get a lead down so as not to forget it. Even at the time when Pete Daily made the first record of *Lou-easy-an-ia* in 1950 for Capitol, I hadn't wrote the verse. So we didn't use a verse on that. Red Fox wrote the lead sheet out with the chords and everything. I have that original copy on the wall at home here. Pete picked the tune just from making the jam session. He said, "Joe, how about us recording this tune of yours?" He had this session coming along so we up and seen Dave Dexter, and he said, OK. It was on the back of *Johnson Rag*, which sold good. I was on the session, too. This was while I was working for Ory. He probably didn't like it too much.

After Pete recorded it a lot of bands here and in Europe followed on. I would say the first real good recording of it was by George Lewis; on the flip side was Monette Moore doing *Burgundy Street Blues*, which was more or less a recitation behind George's solo. From what I understand, that record went pretty well in Europe and that's how a lot of the English and French musicians picked up my tune. Acker Bilk recorded it right after that. He really helped it along. I never made a great deal of money from it. If you put it all together, I'll average maybe 500 dollars a year now. My big mistake was not getting into ASCAP to start with, that's where your big royalties come from. The only way Capitol would record it was for me to put it in a subsidiary publishing company called Beechwood, which was affiliated with BMI. They gave me the impression that, if I didn't put my tune in BMI, they wouldn't record it, so I said, "Hell, put it in any company you want." It didn't matter; BMI's all right but ASCAP's better. Scat Man Crothers was the first to do my tune, on Nappy's "Dixie Showboat" radio show. *Lou-easy-an-ia* is one of the tunes that is still a favorite with Scat Man right up to today.

Like I said, I made some mistakes with *Lou-easy-an-ia*. For instance, when I recorded *Yellow Dog Blues* and had a big hit with that, I should have put my tune on the back of it. I would have made a helluva lot of money from that; instead I made the De Paris brothers rich by putting *Martinique* on the flip side.

Brother Bones, whose real name was Freeman Davis, was a carpenter by trade and did this bones and whistling routine as a novelty in clubs. He had been with the Harlem Globetrotters and he made that version of *Sweet Georgia Brown* which they use for their warm-up. It was only done with about four pieces and it wasn't a very good band, but it just happened they hit on something. The whistling and the sound of the bones, the novelty part, is what sold the record. The sax player was lousy but they had a girl played a piano with a celeste attachment to give it that unusual sound.

We was working at the 331 Club on 8th Street in 1951, that's the same club where Nat "King" Cole got started, and Brother Bones wanted to do some recording. He asked Ory to record with him, but Ory told him, no. He didn't want to make any records with bones, plus he would want it under his own name. So I start talking to old Bones and I agreed to record with him. I didn't give a damn whose name they used; I was the leader and I made the money. It was just that simple. On the label it says "Brother Bones featuring Joe Darensbourg."

We set it up for two sessions of four sides each. I did the routines and Gerry Wiggins helped. Brother Bones was no musician; he did what we told him to do. All he wanted was to get in there and beat those bones. I didn't use a trombone player and Ory didn't have anything to say about it. I didn't have any kind of contract with Ory, but I decided I didn't want to cause any confusion with him by using the guys from the band – not too many of them anyway. We had Teddy

Buckner, Gerry Wiggins, Frank Pasley and Billy Hadnott on bass. Teddy was with Ory then and so was Lloyd Glenn, but for some reason we didn't use Lloyd. Frank said, "Hell, don't use Tudi," so that's why we had Billy. There was no drums. On the second session we used the same line-up, except Billy was out of town and we had Dave Bryant in his place.

On those dates we did *Lou-easy-an-ia* of course, plus *Bye Bye Blues*, *Me and my Shadow* and a tune that Harvey Brooks and I wrote, a little novelty called *Monkey Snoots and Dumplings*. It was originally called *Monkey Hips*, and in fact Deacon Jones, the bass player that used to be with Louis, did a vocal on it with Darlene Devenny, who used to sing with Horace Heidt. We got her to sing on the record but nothing happened. Those Bones records was good but they was never distributed right.

Bones himself was a very nice fellow. He worked later on at Disneyland for a little while with Nellie Lutcher. She had a deal there in the Blue Bayou and they figured they'd put in some kind of variety show. It was a tryout really, but it didn't go; they came out after two weeks. That was around 1965 and that's the last time I seen Brother Bones. He died in the seventies.

In 1952 I met a fellow named Bob Peterson and we got to be friends. He had just started a magazine for hot-rodders called *Hot Rod Magazine*, which was fabulously successful. Him and his partner had started the company with 500 dollars apiece, and Bob had just bought his partner out for a quarter of a million dollars. Bob was an awfully nice guy. We all used to go round together. Now he's a multi-millionaire with big offices and puts out about 20 magazines. One of the guys that worked in Bob's office, named Tom Medley, fancied himself as some kind of a songwriter. Him and Bob was good friends, so they decided to do a promotional thing on some special records as a publicity deal for the magazine. Bob asked me to do them and said, "You and Tom can collaborate on some of the tunes and we'll record them." The idea was, he'd give you one of the records whenever you took out a subscription to one of his magazines.

Scat Man helped me with the routines and, naturally, he did the vocals. We tried to make them like jump tunes, except they all had something to do with hot-rod cars to tie in with the magazine promotion. Outside of Scat Man, it was a kinda pick-up band with Teddy Buckner, Gerry Wiggins, Frank Pasley and Dave Bryant – just one of those quickie deals. We would have had a good session out of this, but, when we was up there recording, Bob (the owner) come up there with Tom Medley; they got so carried away with the first record we cut that they sent out for a bunch of liquor, and we started drinking before we finished the session. It was the merriest shit, it really was. I told Bob, "Go ahead and press 'em. They'll be all right." I got money for arranging the tunes, money for being leader and then money for playing. I would average 500 dollars for a session like that, which was a helluva lot of money in those days. Those Hot Rod records was only a moderate success, but then again they never was sold in music stores. I had a spread in *Teen* magazine and in *Time* over this – a real success story!

Around this time things went wrong between me and Ory. He started going with this gal Barbara and right from the first she began interfering with the band, telling Ory about changes he should make. Ory liked her and he eventually left his wife for her; Barbara's husband was a major in the army and he was transferred to Japan, so she and Ory practically started living together. That's what started all the shit – she caused so much trouble. On top of it she had two kids. Her husband left a lot of civilian clothes behind when he went to Japan. He was the same size as Ory so this fool starts wearing his clothes, seersucker suits with blue and white stripes from when her husband had been stationed down South. Barbara had red hair and she had Ory's hair dyed red, too, so here they come to the Beverly Cavern, both with red hair and him with that seersucker suit. We start calling them "the Gold-Dust Twins." Tudi says, "Goddam, Red, with that suit, you look like the ice-cream man." Ory got so mad he wanted to fire all of us. He had beautiful gray hair before this.

Barbara followed Ory when we came back down to Los Angeles. We went back to work at Mike Lyman's and she kept interfering with the band until all of us told Ory we was quitting. He made her the manager, took out papers and everything. She made me doubly mad 'cause she knew I was going with Gladys then, and she told Gladys a lot of shit about me fooling with gals in San Francisco and drinking, staying out all night with different broads. This got me in a lot of trouble, so I told her one day in front of Ory, "Don't you ever tell Gladys anything about me, bitch." Ory didn't say anything to me right off but I could see he didn't like it. She said, "You gonna let him talk to me like that, Kid?" and Ory said something like, "Well, I'll talk to him later." He didn't really want to start anything 'cause we had been after him about her anyway. Finally the band had a meeting and we told Ory we'd all quit unless he got rid of her, and he seen he was gonna lose his band. In the meantime he got mad with her himself, so he agreed to get rid of her and she went back to Japan to her husband. The band got together and continued. Ory didn't want nothing to do with her – he just wanted the band going along good. Then here she come back again. She had called him long-distance from Japan and they started living together, off and on; I guess he was stuck with her.

Barbara always had a lot of goddam pills. Sometimes Tudi would go and gamble all night and he'd be literally standing asleep playing the bass. Ory had these pills from Barbara and he didn't know it was dangerous, so he says, "Wake up Nap" – he used to call him Nap – and Tudi said he had a headache, wasn't feeling good, so Ory gave him a pill. I wasn't paying too much attention but it was a ten-milligram bennie. Tudi took it and for four nights he couldn't sleep. He was in misery and finally it dawned on me and I told him about the bennie. Tudi went and lit into Ory, "Goddam you, Red, you give me dope and now I can't sleep. You gonna get in a lot of trouble passing them fucking pills around." See, Ory didn't know what these pills was himself. He says, "You know, I ain't been able to sleep either." Tudi says, "No wonder, you fool with that Barbara and she gives you dope. You crazy enough as it is."

I was always after Ory to use *Muskrat Ramble* as his theme song. If you wrote a song like that, wouldn't you use it? This Barbara talked him into using a song by Freddie "Schnickelfritz" Fisher, a pretty tune made for dancing called *Without you for an Inspiration*. On top of that he would try to sing it. Right then and there we really started falling out. I told him, "You must be crazy. Every time we play *Without you* we make money for Freddie Fisher." We did it on the radio but because of Barbara he wouldn't change it. To cap it all, he started mistreating

Dort, giving her a helluva time. Then *Life* magazine came out with a story about the old southern mansions owned by slave owners and plantation owners in Louisiana. They showed all these different mansions, some in Baton Rouge, some elsewhere in Louisiana, and one of the big ones was the Ory Plantation in LaPlace. We was standing up at the bar at the Beverly Cavern and Barbara has the magazine and she's showing it round to people and she says, "I told you about how Kid Ory came from a great family. This is where the Kid was born." A guy turns to me and says, "Isn't that great, Joe?" and I says, "Are you kidding? The Kid was born on that plantation all right, but not in that house. He was born back there in the slave quarters." I shouldn't have said that. Barbara told Ory and that did it. Still, even then he didn't say too much about it, but he never quite forgave me. This happened during the time when Helen and I decided to get married. I took a week off, which Ory didn't like too much, and put Bob McCracken in my place. We got married in September 1952. I came back and carried right on with the band, although the atmosphere between me and Ory wasn't too hot. Things came to a head when I told him I wanted a vacation. This was in June 1953. Helen was working at the *Hollywood Citizen News* and she had three weeks' vacation due to her, so I asked for a leave of absence and again put Bob McCracken in my place. We wanted to go east to see Helen's folks and also to go down to New Orleans. Ory told me to try and talk to Alvin Alcorn the New Orleans trumpet player about coming with the band.

Anyway, we took this trip to Ohio and that was the first time I met Helen's folks. She was born in North Carolina but her folks lived in a suburb of Akron, a place called Barberton. I met Bill, her dad, her mother Sue, her brother Hugh and all the family. Helen had a couple of little nephews and I started giving them lessons. One played clarinet and the other played trumpet. That was one of the nicest times of my life. Then we drove to Asheville, North Carolina. Helen's grandmother lived in Candler, which is a suburb of Asheville, and I really got a kick out of meeting her and all of Helen's aunts and uncles. I used to kid her uncles about how we could make a lot of money by bootlegging, but they told me, "Up in these hills we got more people making mountain dew, moonshine and jackass than forever." Helen's grandmother was 90 years old and you never seen a woman get around so fast. The reason she lived so long, it seemed to me, was because she liked to have a little nip once in a while. Anyway, we had a lot of fun in North Carolina, stayed there for four or five days, and then went back to Barberton before heading down to New Orleans. This was 26th June 1953 and I had told Helen I didn't think we should go to New Orleans at that time of year. They was having a heat-wave down there and it got so hot that all the mosquitoes left town. Even so, we decided to go. The first night Helen came out with me and seen as much as she could see. We ran into Pete Fountain, who was playing with George Girard at the Famous Door. He was real young then, like 22 or something. Then Helen got sick with the heat; she started swelling up like a bullfrog. I talked to Doc Souchon and he came over and told me to get her back to Los Angeles as quick as possible as she was going to die in that hot climate. Everything was swelled up; her arms, neck, even her eyes was swollen. Doc gave her some pills. It was hot, man. Meantime I had the chance to go to a jazz club meeting with Al van Court the promoter. He was a kinda manager for Brother

Bones and we happened to meet him in New Orleans. At the New Orleans Jazz Society meeting I met the Assunto Brothers and Papa Jac Assunto, and some other musicians I hadn't seen in a long time, like Johnny Wiggs and Joe Mares (that used to own Southland Records) – all of them was there. We had a ball that night.

Helen Darensbourg:
We went into the Famous Door and when they finished playing, naturally, Pete and George Girard recognized Joe and they came and sat with us in the booth. Joe bought them a drink and Pete said, "Man, you've been my idol ever since I was a little kid. I just hope some day I can play as good as you."

The very first night I came back on the job after my trip Ory handed me my two weeks' notice. Barbara had talked to Ory and he made up his mind to fire me. That was the first and only job I was fired off, and the end of my career with Ory; I never worked with him again, except at Disneyland much later when I was with the Young Men from New Orleans.

I always thought Ory was an idiot. Just to be frank with you, he was a very ignorant man. As a traditional bandleader, he wasn't too good really. I thought the George Lewis band was much better. Ory had some sly tricks, like his tune *Eh là bas*, which was a version of *Over There*, no question about it; hell, the name means "over there." Irving Berlin wrote that melody, Ory admitted that. He just put Creole words to it and some of them didn't mean a damn thing. On *Do what Ory say*, he has a phrase "Tino fino ah," which didn't mean nothing, but when people asked him about it, Ory would say, "That means 'Kiss my loving lips'." If I'd be there I'd say, "You lying. It means 'Kiss my fucking ass.' Shame on you, Kid." After that I started working around different places with different bands. I did some things with the Firehouse Five Plus Two. Bob McCracken went with Louis for a while, replacing Barney, and eventually Pud Brown took my place with Ory's band. Buckner was still with Ory but Lloyd had gone and Harvey Brooks came in for him. Tudi and Ram was still there.

Then Gene Mayl came to Los Angeles looking for somebody to play clarinet with his band. He got my address from the Musicians' Union, called me up and came out to our apartment in Hollywood one Saturday night along with Vastine, his banjo player. He found out I wasn't doing anything much and he offered me a job to come back to Dayton and work with him. He had a band called the Dixieland Rhythm Kings but I had never heard them at that time. I didn't know what kind of band Gene had, but Helen and I figured it would be something different and new. Dayton was close to Helen's home, for one thing.

So I went to Dayton to play with Gene at a place called the Turf Club. This was owned by a Greek named George Anagnos. One time I called the place long distance and said I wanted to talk to George Anagnos, and the operator said, "George and Agnes who?" He had a restaurant called the Hitching Post and Gene and them talked him into building an annexe on the building to give us a place to play. This was around November 1953; I remember all that damn snow and ice. I got along fine with Gene but it was a pretty lousy band, if you ask me. He tried to copy Turk Murphy, and they believed you could cut a couple of clinkers if you was making a record and they belonged in there. Wasn't no such thing as a perfect record according to them. They used to say that all the old New Orleans musicians did that. I'd say, "I don't want to be on a record with a lot of clinkers. We gotta make this thing over."

I recorded quite a few albums with Gene's band. Ed Nunn brought a great big sound truck to Dayton with all of that nice recording equipment. They didn't have any big recording studios in Dayton so Nunn recorded us in the Van Cleve Hotel. This was for Audiophile. Just before that we made some records for Davey Jones of Empirical. This was out at Yellow Springs, which is a suburb of Dayton. I remember that well because Jones, who was a sound engineer, had his studio on Polecat Lane in Yellow Springs! The personnel was the same on all the albums. On cornet was Bob Hodes, trombone was Charles Sonnanstine, piano was Robin Wetterau, banjo was Jack Vastine – we called him "Kentucky Sour Mash" because he used to drink a lot, and Gene was on tuba. I played clarinet.

We would play some jobs that wasn't far away, just a few nice gigs in the vicinity; we never went out of the state. I don't remember anyone sitting in, although Snooky Young was living around there. I always thought he was Trummy Young's brother; I found out later they wasn't no relation, even though Trummy always used to say, "That's my brother." A big portion of McKinney's Cotton Pickers had come out of Springfield, Ohio, which was only 35 miles away from Dayton. They used to talk about that all the time, but I never knew any of those fellows.

In January 1954 I called Helen to say that I'd signed for six more months and that she should quit her job at the *Citizen News* and come back to Ohio with me. I flew to Los Angeles and we put all our stuff in store, but we kept the apartment because they were so hard to find then. Then we drove back to Dayton. They had a housing shortage there then, too, with apartments going for 90 dollars a week, so George and his wife Tony said to come stay with them. They had a big fancy home in a real exclusive neighborhood, so we moved in. They fixed a nice apartment for us in their house. Helen took care of their two little girls, who was aged about five and eight. They stayed with her and she would be there when they came home from school. They were crazy about Helen.

George and I got to be good friends. I always liked cooking, that was my hobby, so I used to go in the kitchen and I guess I cooked a few things around there. An old friend of Helen's mother in Barberton gave me a recipe for what I think is the best apple pie you've ever tasted, so I told George I could make apple pies. He really didn't believe me, but one day I got a bunch of apples and made half a dozen pies in our kitchen. The restaurant opened at six in the morning and George took the pies down and he calls up about an hour later and sets us to making more pies. He said, "I've sold all those pies in an hour. Everyone bought them for breakfast and they were raving about who was the baker and where did we get them." So then we start peeling apples and I start making more pies.

Business at the Turf Club got lousy. On Fridays and Saturdays you couldn't hardly get in that club it was so jammed, but it wasn't good during the week at all. They charged an admission to get in and Helen would sell tickets at the door, but the club just wasn't making it. Gene wanted to go to another club on a percentage deal but George persuaded me to stay. He thought I should put a trio in, but I hadn't been in the union long enough. He gave Gene notice and brought a drummer in to lead a trio. Gene picked up another clarinet player and I stayed at the Hitching Post with this trio called the Parlays. We had a great piano player and sounded pretty good, but we didn't do too well either. Dayton just wasn't a nightclub town then, which probably it still isn't.

George was paying me to stay there but I wasn't earning my money. He said he would give me a partnership in the restaurant, especially after the incident with the apple pies. "Look, if you want to open a music studio and teach, I'll build it for you. If you want to go in the restaurant business with me, I'll make you a partner. You could teach and you could play once in a while. You could be part of the business in any way you want and you've got a home here for as long as you live. You'd have a good life here." I told him, "George, there's no way I can stay here. In the first place, I don't like the cold weather. I've got things I want to do in the music business and I can't do 'em in Ohio. California is where I should be, where the action is." No sir, Ohio wasn't for me. George was a helluva nice guy and I liked him, along with his whole family. He's dead now but we got a letter from his wife recently and she sent us pictures of the girls and her grandchildren. When we got ready to leave, they actually broke down and cried. It was kinda sad 'cause they was such nice people. We packed up and came back to Los Angeles in June 1954. I run into Gene again in 1960 and he had a job as manager of a chain of laundromats, though he was playing music two nights a week.

Around this time Eddie Miller asked me if I had an Albert system clarinet because Brad Gowans wanted one. Brad was staying here in Los Angeles and he got sick. I don't think he knew he'd got cancer then. I had changed to a Boehm clarinet in 1950 while I was with Ory because I thought I wanted to teach. A guy had offered me a good deal to go with him in his music school. Hell, I should have known better. That's why I had a spare Buffet Albert system clarinet. Brad called me up and asked, did I want to sell it. He said, "The reason why I'm doing this is my stomach has been hurting and every time I pick up my trombone it hurts me to blow, so I thought I'd go back to playing clarinet." I said I didn't know he'd been a clarinet player and he said, "Oh yeah, I used to play and I prefer Albert system. I'll have Eddie do a couple of adjustments to your horn if you decide to loan it to me. To tell you the truth, I don't have the 35 dollars you want, but I'll trade you my trombone 'cause I don't want to play it no more." I told him, "No, I don't want your trombone but, so far as the clarinet is concerned, take it and use it as long as you want." If I'd had any sense I'd have taken up his offer. They say that Brad invented that particular horn where you could use the slide or valve, either one. That trombone today would be worth a lot. I gave the clarinet to Eddie to take to Brad. He lived out in the Valley and so did Eddie. Eddie made the adjustments but I don't know whether Brad ever played it 'cause he died about two weeks afterwards. Eddie got the clarinet back for me.

George Lewis was in town in late 1954 and he got sick, so I played for him for two weeks at the Royal Room. I also had to front his band for him at the Dixieland Jubilee. This was when I was freelancing.

Back home things was kinda jumping with Teddy Buckner, who was just starting his own band. He was doing jam sessions at the Beverly Cavern and, naturally, I went to hear them. Teddy had an offer to go in the 400 Club in Los

Angeles, which was owned by a real screw-ball named Happy Koomer, and he asked me if I would like to play with his band. Pud Brown had been playing clarinet with him before that. Teddy had Harvey Brooks on piano, old man Woody Woodman on trombone, Jesse Sailes on drums and Art Edwards, the same guy he has now, on bass.

Teddy's band rehearsed and soon we had a pretty good little outfit. We went into the 400 Club in October 1954 and I guess we must have stayed there for nearly a year. It was a steady job, six nights a week, and the place was packed every night. This Happy Koomer was some kind of half-assed ex-gangster and it seemed to me that he was the last guy in the world who ought to be known as Happy. His club was where I first got to know the notorious gangster Mickey Cohen. Later on, when I quit Teddy to start my own band, Happy tried to put out a contract on me but Mickey wouldn't do it, even though they was good friends. Happy wanted to keep me at the club but Cohen said, "The hell with you, I know Joe. Why would I want to do anything to him?" In fact he turned around and made Happy Koomer a counter-offer. He said he wanted to borrow 15,000 dollars and if Happy couldn't come up with the money he'd put a contract out on him. That's true.

I never really knew some of the guys in Teddy's band until I played with them but I really enjoyed working there. The only guys I knew were Teddy himself and Harvey Brooks. Woody Woodman had three sons that was all good musicians. One was Britt Woodman the great trombonist that went with Duke for a long time. I did a couple of things with Britt here in Los Angeles, overdubbing on a record date for John Fahey. Then there was a piano player and a sax player they called Woody, Jr. We called the old man Woody, too. He was a band man really; never played too much dixieland. Before he went to work with Teddy he used to play in the pit at the Follies Theater. He was a barber, had two shops, and he sold barber's supplies. In fact while he was with Teddy he still had his barber business, and consequently he'd fall asleep on the bandstand at times. He'd come to work at seven o'clock, park his car in front of the place, and when we got ready to play we'd have to go out to the car and wake him up to come to work. Woody was making a lot of money and he was a wonderful gentleman. He fitted in good and did his job adequately, I'd say.

Of course, Art Edwards was a terrific bass player, which he is still. Had Louis been able to contact him at one time he would have used Art in his band. That's just one of those things. Art had played with the Walter Barnes band out of Chicago, which was caught up in the fire at the Rhythm Club in Natchez. I think about 200 people died in that fire. *Life* magazine had pictures of it and it was horrible; bodies was stacked up like logs. Art told me he's the only one who got out of there. He said there was a little opening in the back of the men's toilet and what really saved his life was guys just pushing him through. The rest of the band, including Walter Barnes, burned up. The funny thing, I played that very same place when I was about 17 with the Martels. We played all over parts of Mississippi and Arkansas and every one of these old dance halls, all over the South, had the same format. Usually made of wood, some of them literally was big old cabins. If they had any back doors, they boarded them up, and they boarded up the windows as well. They had a reason for that: a guy would come in and buy one ticket, open a window and let in half a dozen others, all for free. The tragic part of it was that they had a couple of big doors which swung open from the inside. Had they been able to swing them open from the outside, the people could have got out, but when this fire broke out they hit the door and forced it closed. These doors was heavy and the people panicked and piled on top of each other. See, all these places would have a lot of tissue paper and old Spanish moss for decoration that over a period had got so dry it would literally explode in a fire. That Natchez fire was one of the big disasters.

Harvey was our piano player and the first time I met him was at the Cotton Club with Les Hite. He came out of Philadelphia with Mamie Smith and a show called *Struttin' Along*. He told me they came here in 1923 and he decided to stay.

Teddy did a lot of nice solos, never got too far out. He had a lot of technique and he did all right. The difficult part about getting a trumpet player to do dixieland is to keep him on that straight melody. Louis said one of the hardest things is to play a straight melody and to play it pretty and good. A lot of guys can't do it, but Teddy was very versatile and he fell right into it. He'd pace himself and he'd sing a little, like Louis. Louis was his idol. We recorded three or four albums and we was halfway through another when I left the band. Teddy's records went over fine. He had an excellent record company, Crescendo, which was run by Frank Bull and Gene Norman. Frank had a publicity agent's business and he helped with the publicity. Gene was a radio announcer. The records were big sellers in Europe and we had a lot of offers to go over there, but the money was never right. I know I wanted to go.

One of the recordings was taken off a concert we played with Louis at the Pasadena Civic Auditorium in June 1956. I think it was probably the first time I had played slap-tongue in front of such a big audience. They must have applauded for ten minutes. I think they made a whole album out of that show. That was the first time Louis mentioned to me that he'd like me to come with the band when he had an opening. He had Trummy, Ed Hall, Barrett Deems on drums, Billy Kyle and Arvell Shaw.

Teddy got a lot of film work. I remember when Jack Webb wanted him for *Pete Kelly's Blues*. Jack came in the Beverly Cavern and talked to all of us. At first they thought of taking the whole band down to New Orleans but they found it cost too much money, so they wound up just taking Teddy and Matty Matlock to arrange a little music. When they got to New Orleans they had a big hassle because the union said they had local musicians that was capable, let them make the money. But since they had brought Teddy down they compromised and used him. Matty did all the arranging.

Teddy and I worked some film dates together. We made *Mahogany Magic* when I was still with Kid Ory, along with Sarah Vaughan, the Treniers and Herb Jeffries. It took two or three days to make. Herb was the MC on this thing and it took him a day and half to do his lines. He'd always flub them for some reason, he was kinda nervous. We used to deliberately hope that guys would do that, because the longer you worked on a movie the more money you made. So we said, "Let him cut hogs all day long, it's all right with us." That was the first chance I got to know the Treniers real well. I had known their saxophone player Donald Hill; they called him "Duck," from when he played with Luis Russell's band while Louis worked with them.

I remember Teddy and I working on *Imitation of Life*, which starred Lana Turner. Making a film is one of the most monotonous things you can ever do, so we was wandering around the studio between scenes and Teddy had walked down to another set where they was filming some kind of Tarzan jungle picture. Suddenly old Teddy comes racing back, whooping and hollering about taking cover. All hell broke loose on this set and we was wondering what had happened. It turns out they needed black leopards for this particular scene but they couldn't get 'em, so they said they was gonna take a couple of mountain lions and dye 'em black. All these animals was real harmless, and when you seen them in a fight they was playing really. That's the training coming in there. But after the make-up men put this black stuff on them, the other animals rejected them. Fights broke out in earnest when they confronted each other; all of them animals started going crazy. The lions smelled different on account of the dye. They had to get hoses and the set was smashed to smithereens. They just busted the whole thing.

I had a nice feature on a tune called *The Martinique* which the De Paris brothers brought out during that time. We liked that record, and, although Harvey Brooks wasn't a great arranger, he could copy music, so he took down the solo off the record. I just listened to the clarinet solo and played it. Harvey wrote the chords out for the whole thing, and there's a kind of little modulation that changes key which was a big favorite. Another thing with Teddy was that he liked the soprano, which suited me. Now, with Ory it was altogether different. Ory didn't care much for me playing the soprano. I've had my soprano since the thirties and I kept it with me all the time, even though I didn't use it much.

Helen and I moved into our new house in February 1955 and right after that, in June 1955, the band went up to San Francisco for a 12-week engagement at the Hangover. That was a jumping joint, a class place, the top dixieland club in the country to me. It was kinda exclusive, too; you had to have a coat on and a necktie to get in there. If you came in there with a coat but without a necktie, Doc would furnish you with a necktie from a bunch he had there before he would let you in. It was a pleasant place to work in, probably one of the best run clubs that I ever played in. The Hangover had a lot of people all the time and we made a lot of friends. It didn't open until eight o'clock and the hours was like from nine to one. It didn't serve food or nothing; there was just music.

We used to broadcast from the Hangover every Saturday. We had two announcers and one of them was Jimmy Lyons, who now promotes the Monterey Jazz Festival. During that time I imagine they must have recorded or taped all of these shows we broadcast, that's why a lot of them is coming out on LP now. We tried, but we never got paid for that stuff. Still, it was a fun job and Teddy's band was very good.

The Hangover had Joe Sullivan on piano, playing intermission, with Smoky Stover on drums. Now both Joe and Harvey was half lit up all the time. I think Harvey stayed drunk the whole 12 weeks we was at the Hangover, and so did Joe. Once in a while they would pass each other in the passage and Harvey would say to me, "Do you see that Joe Sullivan, how can he play, drunk as he is?" and Harvey would be drunker than hell himself. Then I'd meet Joe and he'd say, "I like your piano player but he's drunk all the time." Talk about the blind leading the blind.

They wouldn't serve Joe any drinks but he had bottles stashed all over the Hangover. Doc knew it, but Joe could still play fairly well and he had a following, so Doc never fired him. Doc would find the bottles and water them down. Then one night Joe was real hungover, couldn't hardly play, so Doc came up to me and said, "What the hell can I do with this goddam Joe Sullivan? He's so drunk he won't be able to finish the night." I told Doc to get hold of some bennies, crush them, put them in a bottle and shake them up. We did that and, sure enough, old Joe came around and took a couple of swigs and he was jumping. He got up there and played better than you ever heard him play in his life. He sounded like three piano players – played his ass off. You know how bennies work on you. That was all right until the next night. What a let down. He couldn't hardly move after all that liquor and the bennies, let alone play. It almost killed the gig. He had used up all his energy the night before. Doc wanted to fire me for my suggestion. He said, "We'll take Joe like he is. If he gets sleepy, whatever, no more bennies." We enjoyed that.

After the Hangover we came down to Los Angeles and went right back into the 400 Club, stayed there a long time – at least another six or eight months. Eventually I decided to get my own band. Harvey left the band before I did. In fact Teddy let him go after the Hangover incident and he brought in Gideon Honore. Then Chester Lane joined the band in Honore's place. He was with the famous Jeter–Pillars Orchestra out of St Louis and had been with Louis Jordan's band. Chester is a real nice guy and a fine piano player.

SEVEN

Yes, the Lord picked out Louis

We knew some people that was good friends of the owners of The Lark on 3rd Street near Vermont in Los Angeles. They wanted to put a dixieland band in there and they particularly wanted me to be the leader. The Lark was a new place as far as music was concerned. It was primarily a top restaurant where they had a big room and a lot of space to put in a bandstand. I never did really want my own band, but these friends talked me into going over to see George Sanders, the owner, and it turns out the price was right, way over scale, which was unusual for Los Angeles. They kept saying it was time for me to get some recognition and they convinced me that I should get a band. Besides, I was getting very unhappy with this Happy Koomer because, in order to work for him, you had to make yourself a B-boy. You heard of B-girls? They was girls that had to mingle with the customers and hustle drinks. Happy literally wanted the musicians to do that, too. Him and I got in a few arguments because I wouldn't do what he wanted, so I said to myself it would be a good time to quit Teddy and go. This was in 1957.

Right away I started thinking about who I would use. On trumpet I picked Mike DeLay. I had worked with Mike, but not on any jobs, just at jazz club meetings. Mike recommended Georgie Vann the drummer to me. I hadn't worked with him before, but I knew what he could do. Then I had Warren Smith on trombone – we called him Smitty – who I knew from when we worked together with Red Nichols and Wingy. Smitty was one of the guys that had been around a long time. Meanwhile Frank Pasley had introduced me to Al Morgan, who hadn't long been in Los Angeles; I think Al was a distant relative of Frank's, anyway he knew him well. Up to that time I hadn't worked with Al but I decided on him as my bass man. That left Harvey Brooks for the piano chair and, of course, I had worked with Harvey in the Ory band and with Teddy. That completed the band.

From the beginning it was a very good band. My idea was for it to be a little different from the average run of the mill dixieland combo. The musical policy came from the guys in the band. We would talk about what would be good, and we worked out the routines more or less all together. Riffs came from me or from Mike, then some of them was Smitty's ideas. Like with the piano intro on *Dreamboat*, that was my idea, just for the hell of it; *Careless Love* was another one, a lot of disc jockeys liked that. *Winin' Boy* was another favorite. That's the way I wanted it, different ideas. It was very subtle. In other words, we was always trying to say something, tell a little story; keeping things tight, not just letting it go wild.

Smitty did quite a bit all round and he wrote *Dixie Flyer March* for us. Harvey and I wrote the tune *Rockin' in Dixie*. I had one thing that helped, and that was the whole Lu Watters library that I had gotten from Bob Scobey when I played with him.

We rehearsed at The Lark and opened there on July 19th, when we got a nice telegram from Pops Foster wishing us well. The very first night that goddam Harvey Brooks fell off the stand. He got drunk after the first set – that part I'll always remember. The whole place was packed with people and we nearly had the contract canceled. We had to make a hurry call and we was just lucky enough to get Alton Purnell to come in for the second act. Aside from that, we had a terrific opening and really drew the people, damn near bankrupted the 400 Club. That's when Happy Koomer wanted to put out a contract on me. The next night Harvey was all right. Our first contract was for 12 weeks and they renewed it. We stayed in there for a total of 16 weeks.

I didn't call the band the Dixie Flyers at first. We thought up that name when we recorded. They researched a lot of names and found out that the Dixie Flyer was the name of a famous old train down South. We named the band after that about the time we picked out the Lark name for the record label.

As for recording the band, it all started with a fellow named Hubie Jensen, who we called Swede. Him and his wife used to come in the 400 Club and they loved to hear me play *Yellow Dog Blues* when I slap-tongued it, so they'd request it all the time. Swede had a machine shop business and he suggested that we get together and make a recording of that tune. I had told him that when I was with Ory I wanted to record it, but Ory wouldn't listen. We agreed to record right after we got the band in shape, out at the Capitol Studios, where they had the finest engineers. This was after we had opened at The Lark, and initially it was going to be just a hobby for Swede. He named it the Lark label not necessarily because of the club, but because he had thought of the little bird design for the label. One of the first tunes we recorded was *Yellow Dog* and it was my idea to do it with the slap-tongue clarinet.

With slap-tongue, what you are actually doing is just the opposite of what you say you're doing: you create a suction with your tongue right against the reed. You make a stiff staccato and pull your tongue back from the reed at the same time. Not too many guys can do it now. After that incident with the kid I told you about, it took me about a year to get it right. I twisted my tongue and tried to bite the mouthpiece, anything to make it work. I guess I wore out a couple of mouthpieces that way. I just liked it as something different. In those days, with the medicine show or the minstrels, there wasn't no amplifiers, so you could get a really full sound with the slap-tongue. After that I didn't do it any more until I was with Kid Ory. I don't know what made me do it then. We was playing a concert at an auditorium in Santa Barbara and old Dink Johnson was backstage. He had a sister living in that town and had some kind of bootlegging joint there, too. He had his clarinet out but Ory wouldn't let him sit in because he was half-drunk. I was fooling around there and gave the clarinet a couple of slaps. I would still slap-tongue once in a while but I never did it in front of an audience. Dink says, "I could never do that. Why don't you do that on stage, see what Ory says?" I was half-high myself, so I thought I'd try it. We was playing *Sugar Blues*, on which Papa Mutt would get his mute and play like Clyde McCoy, then I had a low-register clarinet solo with a break. I was playing into a mike, so instead of playing the break straight I slap-tongued the whole thing. It brought the house down and right then and there I knew I had a gimmick. Ory says, "What the hell you doing?" but the guys said to do it again, so I took two choruses. Ory got mad as hell. I says, "Well, it went over good, didn't it?" I started thnking what the hell else I could do this on. Every time we played *Sugar Blues* I'd use slap-tongue on the break and people would be clapping, so when we played *Yellow Dog Blues* I could see it would fit there as well. This was low-register, too, with that low E, the lowest note on the clarinet. I started using it on the band but Ory wouldn't let me record it. He says, "They don't do that stuff no more." So I says, if I ever get a chance of a recording session of my own, I'm gonna record *Yellow Dog*, because every time I played it, it got a helluva hand. Ory should have been able to see it. It's nothing but a gimmick but a pleasing one. It had its place and it paid off. Naturally, I wouldn't try to saturate the people with it. Anyway, that's when the slap-tongue started.

Incidentally, old Dink had had a cafe in Los Angeles where we used to go after hours. He used to bootleg and we'd buy liquor from him. He'd put some of his records on the jukebox and play piano along with them, then he'd pick up his clarinet and play along with that. Dink died in Santa Barbara.

When the record of *Yellow Dog* came out Swede sent copies to each radio station all over the USA, and in Cleveland, Ohio, the record just took off. That's where it first became a hit; it was number one on their hit-song list for five straight weeks. In all that record sold over a million copies. See, everybody liked it and in the studio they just flipped. They figured it was so unusual. They had never heard anything like that. Swede decided to get a list of disc jockeys and distributors and he sent them each a copy of the single, maybe 200 complimentary copies in all. He was putting out the money to do this, just to see the reaction. Then we started to get letters from these different DJs about how great it was and some guy who had a big distribution company in Cleveland got it on the air there. Oh God, it was an avalanche, one helluva big hit there. That's where it started, then Chicago, St Louis, New Orleans – terrific sales. It was less of a hit in California than in any other state, ain't that funny! That's what really established the Dixie Flyers. Swede and I went on a personal appearance tour to Ohio, just him and me. The single had broken while we was at The Lark, so I put Johnny Lane in my place there and stayed out about four days. We played Shaker Heights, Youngstown, then did some TV and radio in Cleveland. This gave me a chance to have a reunion with Helen's folks.

Helen Darensbourg:
I was on a trip to Ohio to see my mother and father when the record broke. You could turn on any station in Akron, Cleveland or Columbus and "Yellow Dog Blues" was playing day and night. Every hour it was played and I was just going into hysterics. It was so fabulous and then Joe took a tour back there.

Originally, we just cut *Yellow Dog* for a single. A lot of DJs will not play a single at all if the time isn't right – that's in order to get their commercials in for them to make money. We just cut the time down for the single. We edited it like they wanted. *Martinique* was taking off, too, and that was a helluva big favorite. The two tunes should have been on separate singles. *Yellow Dog* was the first single that was sent out and then later we did singles on *Snag it* and things like that with the slap-tongue on the soprano sax. That was a mild hit but nothing close to *Yellow Dog*. Later on we put all these tunes out on an album. We went into the studio and re-recorded them and we added guitar just for the session, never did have one with the band otherwise.

Johnny Maddox covered *Yellow Dog*, made a copy of it, using my arrangement note for note. I don't know where he found a clarinet player to do it. Some people said it was Matty Matlock, but he always denied it. Pete Fountain also made a version but he didn't do slap-tongue on it. I met Pete in North Hollywood at the Post Office right after he made his record, and he apologized to me. "I want to apologize for coming right behind you and making your *Yellow Dog*, but it wasn't my idea. The record company wanted it," he said. I told Pete there was nothing wrong about that.

I had a letter from W. C. Handy himself and he said, "I listened to your record of *Yellow Dog Blues* and it warmed the cockles of my heart because I wasn't sure the way I wanted it played, but since hearing your record I know now that's exactly the way it should be played. What a thrill I got out of listening to the record. I'd like to meet you sometime." So I went to New York and met him. He died shortly after that. I met his son Bill and daughter Katherine and one of his grandsons who had all taken over the publishing company. I seen Mr Handy's desk there with all the paraphernalia on it and the chair with all the papers, and nobody would ever sit at it. One time, without thinking, I sat at the desk and Katherine came over and said, "Joe, I know Dad wouldn't have minded, but we made it a policy after he died that nobody would ever sit at this desk any more." So I just politely moved. As far as I know, the desk sits in their office just like the day he died right uᵢ 'il now.

So we had an overnight success: the first time we recorded it was a hit. Swede could have sold the record outright but he wanted to keep it. Then he really got the bug and that was mistake number one. He wanted to start a big company of his own, but he was told by a lot of people in the trade that you could go broke with a hit record if you didn't know what to do. Anyway, he decided to go ahead with the idea that he should start recording different people and get big in the music business. Now we was partners in the publishing company but we wasn't on the record side. I should have insisted that we was partners in the recording company, then I would have had something to say. That's what really ruined the whole thing. I should have taken my royalties myself as they came along. *Yellow Dog* made a lot of money and the worst mistake I ever made was to listen to Swede. I agreed to let him put the royalty money back into other records. I was supposed to get three cents a record and I never saw that money. It was my fault. You learn as you go along but it was an unfortunate thing.

We recorded the Two Hot Coles, that's Nat "King" Cole's brother Eddie Cole and his wife Betty. We did one good tune with them, *Sweet Someone*. They had a piano duo. Eddie was the oldest of the Cole brothers and he's the one that taught the rest of his brothers to play – that's what he told me. Streamline Ewing came to us and we recorded him. That cost about 5000 dollars; we spent a huge lot of money. These things was released but they didn't do anything. We didn't have the right distributor and the distributors Swede did have didn't pay him. If you go into this business you gotta know what you're doing. Of course, our band recorded more, including the EP, and I know Swede still has some tapes. I tried to buy them but he wouldn't give them up.

We stayed at The Lark but we started getting all kinds of offers to go out. Joe Glaser of ABC wanted to book us for a tour, but I wasn't particular about going on the road 'cause I couldn't get the amount of money I wanted. Then the guys in the band wanted too much money and I didn't want to go through all that crap. It would have been better if I had just went by myself. Bob Scobey also sent me a letter and wanted me to tour with him, but I was making enough money around here. I just wanted to stay home, so I told Bob, no.

We did real fine at The Lark until George Sanders started watering the drinks and trying to overcharge the people. He was making money but he got greedy and screwed up the business. People started complaining. After that we worked various places in Los Angeles, like the Royal Room and the Beverly Cavern. The band continued to do very well and we also did some TV work. Bobby Troup had a TV show out here on the West Coast called "Stars of Jazz," where bands would play and talk about the music. We did the show four times, more than any other group. The first time we were on the show George Vann did a vocal on *Closer Walk* and he had everybody in the audience crying. He was a real black cat with a sorrowful face and he did that tune so soulful. They'd bring the camera close into his face and you literally could see tears coming out of his eyes, and that did it – they got thousands of letters and calls from all over. "Stars of Jazz" was a coast-to-coast national program and people seen George everywhere in the USA. That helped the band, brought my name out more. They wanted more Georgie Vann, too. Troup was probably on that show for over a year, and every four or five weeks he would call me about being on the show. It was the same thing, do *Closer Walk* or *Four or Five Times*. One time they had a whole scene set up like an old-time medicine show with a wagon saying "Doc Moon." When I went with Louis, it seemed to me almost every place we played people knew me from that show. They'd come up to me and start talking about George. People would say that they were so moved and so impressed, even Mahalia Jackson never moved them so much, and she could move a mountain with her singing, believe me. I just loved to hear him do those tunes. Georgie was a nice guy, real funny. He was a little, short, chubby fellow and his drumming was good. He was a show stopper.

The next big thing for us was when Turk Murphy got us up to his club in San Francisco. He had a nice place called Easy Street. Lizzie Miles was one of the attractions and Ralph Sutton was playing intermission piano. The Dixie Flyers worked with Lizzie and that was all right musically, but she was a typical New Orleans broad, just as evil as hell. What's that song? *Go to church all day Sunday and barrel-house all day Monday*. That was Lizzie. She was supposed to be a great church broad, went to church almost every day, yet she had a young-assed pimp on the side, taking all her money. We was there about three weeks.

By that time Smitty had left the band. I can't remember why he left but I know he went back with Bob Crosby some more. Smitty was an underrated trombone player. He could really play, just as good as any of them: I put him up there with Jack Teagarden and Georg Brunis. Smitty was a nice guy, he loved to drink a little at times, never too much. I had been knowing him for years. Later we worked together again down at Delmar with Nappy and Marvin Ash. Anyway, by the time we went up to Easy Street Tommy Gekler was on trombone. He's a very good musician and went with Pete Fountain later. Tommy had been playing with Pete Daily and others. He was born in Chicago and didn't have a name like Brunis 'cause he wasn't from New Orleans. Still, any time you play with Wingy, Red Nichols and Pete Fountain, you have to be capable. When Tommy left my band he went with Clyde McCoy. Then we had another very fine trombone man named Roy Brewer who works out at Disney Studios as a film editor.

Roy was with us when we went into Zucca's, an Italian restaurant over in Pasadena that had started a dixieland policy. We followed Rosy McHargue. It was a good little job. They used a lot of name bands there and had about the best meatballs and spaghetti in town. Ted Veseley had worked at Zucca's with various groups, steady and off and on, for quite a long time. In December 1959 we opened at Armantrout's, a nice nightclub on Ventura Boulevard in Sherman Oaks. The guy spent about 50,000 dollars renovating the place and remodeling it. He made it like a roaring twenties road-house on the style of New Orleans. I always thought the owner was a sucker to get himself into debt like that when, with our following, we'd have filled the club anyway. Some deal, he's still paying off the debts. We stayed in Armantrout's for about 12 weeks. By then George Vann had taken sick and died. I used to go see him before he died. I really liked old George. I replaced him with Lou Diamond, probably used some other drummers in the meantime. Lou was a wonderful drummer and had played with bands like Gus Arnheim. He came up to Easy Street with us and played some of the TV shows with the band.

I know that Roy Brewer and Lou was with us when we played the first of the "Dixieland at Disneyland" concerts. This was where they had different bands from all over the USA and, in itself, this was one of the finest productions of dixieland I've ever seen. They have this big river out at Disneyland where the riverboat *Mark Twain* used to go, and they would put bands on rafts and have a big searchlight out in the river. As the bands came down the river they would be playing, and there'd be a sound system on each raft. It was the most beautiful thing. I played it some years later with Louis and he said it was the greatest he'd ever seen. They would always have someone to be the king of the show and I remember one year it was Al Hirt. Going back to the time I played it with Louis, the Bob Crosby band was one of the features, and for the finale all the bands combined together and played on the *Mark Twain*. Everybody in the park was given little sparklers and there was a whole fireworks display. It's hard to describe how beautiful it was. They don't have it any more.

As for Mike DeLay, he was playing good then. He's another guy that could be a tremendous trumpet player, as good as he wanted to be in my opinion. He was a nervous fellow, but whenever he was right he was hard to beat. His sister told me that when he was little he was kinda shy 'cause he stuttered. When he got so he lost the stutter and found out he could talk, he never stopped. We nicknamed

Joe with George Lewis during a radio broadcast for Station **KFI**, Los Angeles, April 1951

Teddy Buckner's band at the 400 Club, Los Angeles: (left to right) Jesse Sailes, William Woodman, Sr, Buckner, Art Edwards, Joe, Harvey Brooks

Joe Darensbourg's Dixie Flyers at the Lark Restaurant, Los Angeles, July 1957: (left to right) Harvey Brooks, George Vann, Joe, Mike DeLay, Warren Smith, Al Morgan

Joe performing with Louis Armstrong on Ed Sullivan's television show, 1961 (*Joe Darensbourg collection*)

Joe with Duke Ellington during a broadcast of Ed Sullivan's television show, New York, 17 December 1961 (*Joe Darensbourg collection*)

At Kastrup Airport, Copenhagen, August 1962: (left to right) Jewel Brown, Louis Armstrong, Joe, Trummy Young

Joe performing with Trummy Young and Louis Armstrong at the Murat Theatre, Indianapolis, 5 May 1963 (*photo courtesy Duncan Schiedt*)

Louis Armstrong and his All Stars at the Fairmont Hotel, San Francisco, January 1962: (left to right) Billy Kyle, Trummy Young, Jewel Brown, Armstrong, Joe

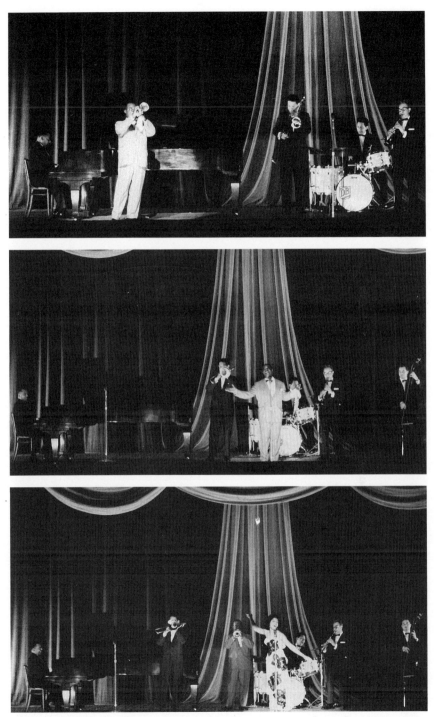

Louis Armstrong and his All Stars on stage at the Odeon, Hammersmith, London, 13 May 1962 (*photo courtesy Ian Powell*)

Joe with a native of Melbourne while on tour in Australia with the All Stars, March 1963 (*Joe Darensbourg collection*)

Joe with (left to right) Barney Bigard, Teddy Edwards, Al Reiman and Teddy Buckner, 1960s (*photo courtesy Floyd Levin*)

The All Stars in Albuquerque, New Mexico, 1964: (left to right) Billy Kyle, Joe, Danny Barcelona, Big Chief Russell Moore

Joe with Pops Foster and Ed Garland at a celebration for the latter at the Southern California Hot Jazz Society, Los Angeles, 1969 (*photo courtesy Floyd Levin*)

Opposite, top: A jazz club meeting, Los Angeles, 1960s: musicians include Ed Garland (double bass), Andy Blakeney (trumpet), Joe (clarinet) and Johnny St Cyr (banjo) (*Joe Darensbourg collection*); below: The Young Men from New Orleans, Disneyland, c1967: (left to right) Harvey Brooks, Bernard Carriere, Alton Redd, Mike DeLay, Joe (*Joe Darensbourg collection*)

The Legends of Jazz, 1973: (left to right) Barry Martyn, Alton Purnell, Andy Blakeney, Joe, Louis Nelson, Ed Garland (*photo courtesy Floyd Levin*)

At the Burbank Elks Club, 16 September 1978: (left to right) Dick Cary, unknown, Joe, Nappy Lamare, Eddie Miller (*Joe Darensbourg collection*)

The best amateur cook in the world, Magnolia Boulevard, North Hollywood, July 1970 (*Joe Darensbourg collection*)

Joe with Nappy Lamare in front of the *Mark Twain* riverboat at Disneyland, 11 October 1979 (*Peter Vacher*)

Eddie Miller presenting Joe with a scroll from the State Governor of Louisiana at the Hacienda Hotel, Sepulveda, California, on the occasion of *Jazz Forum*'s "Jazzman of the Year," 1983 *(Joe Darensbourg collection)*

him L. P. – for long-play. I liked Mike but I still threatened to fire him a couple of times. We was playing a party up in Santa Barbara at an exclusive club one New Year's Eve and Mike was talking away, so I says, "Goddam, Mike, if you can't keep your mouth closed, you just get another job." He turned around and told me, "Hell, I don't want to keep working with your band. I can go to Los Angeles and draw my unemployment pay and get welfare, make more money than I do playing with you." I said, "You do that. When I call a tune I want you to be ready to play it." I'm announcing our next number and there's a tap on my shoulder, but I says, "You get another job," so he got off the stand. After that I'm up at the bar getting a drink, so finally he stuck out his hand and said, "I want to apologize, Joe, I know I was wrong." It takes a man to apologize, so I told him to forget it, but, hell, as soon as we got back on the stand the same shit started again. He laughed about it but I never held any animosity. I played with Mike all the time.

He had a nice wife, Olivette, a beautiful girl, and he was raising canaries at his house. God, he had about 300 canaries. He'd give everybody a canary. Mike had a peach tree with the most delicious peaches in the world. One year he never brought me no peaches and it turned out Olivette had cut the tree down. When I asked why, Mike said, "It was keeping the sun out of the window." Hell, I'd have paid 500 dollars to have that tree transplanted.

Al Morgan fitted in the band perfectly. He was very quiet, never drank, smoked or nothing. I first met him here through Frank but I knew he had played with Cab Calloway, and Sabby Lewis in Boston. He was a capable bass player and I respected him as a musician and as a man. He was just a nice fellow with a beautiful manner. I was flabbergasted when he died. I had had my first heart attack and he called me. He says, "Joe, you know we getting older. Now you be good and take care of yourself, man, I'm sure glad that you getting better. I had a nice thing happen to me not long ago . . . ." In fact I had seen his picture in the paper; he had won 5000 dollars when a gas station gave out some kind of game tag. He said we'd get together soon, but within the next couple of weeks he'd died. Al was a guy you would think could live to be a hundred years old, he was never overweight or anything.

After Armantrout's and some other things it seemed like the band was kinda fading out a little. To tell the truth, I had lost interest in being a leader. I never liked being a leader too much – I still don't. You have responsibility and you got headaches with your sidemen. A lot of times, if you're not careful, you wind up making less money than your sidemen, that's if you figure all your phone calls, the taxes you gotta pay and the aspirins you have to buy for your headaches. You make out the payrolls and there's a lot of hidden stuff that costs you money. Most of the headaches come from sidemen getting drunk or sleeping late. The leader's gotta to be figuring out where the band is gonna work next, hustling up jobs and fighting these damn club owners. When you a leader, you responsible for everything. If a sideman gets drunk and starts raising hell around the club, they come to the leader and never say nothing to the sideman. So I got tired of being a leader and I gave the band up. Anyway, the guys wanted their own groups.

From then I worked with different groups until Jimmy Rushing came through here. He was looking for a combo to go to San Francisco to play at the Hangover for four weeks. At that time Les Hite and Elmer Fain, another saxophone player, had an office here booking bands, and they called me and we arranged to work with Jimmy. This was 1960. Doc Dougherty had been trying to get in touch with me but I had been away someplace. The money was pretty good after I talked to them. I did most of the business direct with Doc and I got equal billing with Jimmy.

I had Mike DeLay on trumpet, George Washington, a good trombone player that used to play with Luis Russell's band, Alton Purnell on piano, Wellman Braud on bass and I can't think who played drums. I know Harvey was doing something else and he didn't want to travel. George I had first met when he was with Louis. He was a nice guy and a little gay, everybody knew it. We had a helluva good time with old Jimmy. He was fine so far as working was concerned. We had just one rehearsal and learned his tunes. I hadn't known Jimmy before, although I knew he played out here. He played piano, too. After the Hangover he wanted me to go back east with him – in fact he wanted me to go to Europe and bring a bunch behind him. But the money wasn't right and, anyway, I couldn't get the guys I needed. Jimmy wanted all the money himself, so I wouldn't go.

A couple of nutty things happened on that gig, like on all jobs. Jimmy used to do a tune called *New Orleans*, the Hoagy Carmichael thing, which had a real tricky bridge, and if you don't see the music it's hard to play the right chords, especially for a guy like Purnell. He ain't got a helluva good ear and he can't read good either. We was right up on stage, above the bar, when somebody asked for the tune, and Jimmy says to Purnell, "Can you play it?" Purnell says, "Well, I could play it if I had the music." Old Jimmy says, "I have the music to it back there in the dressing room. We'll have somebody get it and in the meantime we'll do something else." Jimmy had his valet with him and he got the music and set it up. Everything went fine until we got to the bridge and old Purnell's fingers got all hooked up in that piano. He couldn't play it and he started sweating. Jimmy was one of those loudmouth guys, typical Kansas City style, that'll turn around and embarrass you. He says, "What the hell's the matter with you. Didn't you tell me you could play the tune if you had the music? Now you got the goddam music up there and you can't play it. Play something else. Play *All of me*." That was one of his big tunes, he'd make a comedy routine out of it, on account of his size. Purnell got mad. "Goddam," he says, "this guy embarrassing me like that," and he came off the stand still arguing. Jimmy was waiting for him as he came out of the little entrance to the bandstand, so Purnell told him, "I don't appreciate you loud-talking me on the stand. You embarrassed me." So Jimmy says, "I embarrass you, you little no-piano-playing sonofabitch. I thought you told me you could play it if you had the music. Why didn't you keep your mouth closed? You embarrassed both of us. Another thing, I been playing and singing music for 50-some years and you the first goddam musician I ever seen that brought me some new chords. I never heard chords like that in my life. Don't you open your mouth to me about me embarrassing you 'cause I got a knife here and I'll cut your goddam throat." Of course, he was half-way kidding but Purnell didn't fool with him. Jimmy was right, too, Purnell should have kept his mouth shut. He would have two briefcases full of music and he's telling everybody how he used to be an arranger down in New Orleans for A. J. Piron. Anybody that arranged for Piron had to be a good musician, so I don't know who Purnell was trying to kid.

As far as I know, Piron's was the first band in New Orleans that started to use saxophone sections and he did the arranging himself. Still, that was the only hitch with the music.

All during this time I had been working with other different combos, including Ben Pollack and Mike Riley. Ben had a place on Sunset Strip and he decided to enlarge it and put a new bar in. He got to talking to Buddy Burns, the bass player who is also a good carpenter, about a price for the work, when it dawned on him that if he gave Buddy a job as bandleader he'd get the carpentry work for something less. See, Buddy was always around there asking Ben for a job and he would have given his right nut to get to play in a place like Ben's, especially if he was able to tell everybody it was his band. Ben was slick and he put two and two together. He says, "I could probably use you as a bandleader. I know you capable of it and I want to get this work done but I don't have too much loot." Buddy fell in that trap, so Pollack got all that carpentry work for nothing. Buddy had Barney playing clarinet, and I know he had a trombone player from New Iberia named Cajun Verret that used to be with Phil Harris. Sylvester Rice played drums sometimes and I think Ram Hall worked up there, too; of course Ben was a drummer himself. They didn't use the same guys all the time. For instance, Martin Peppi played there. He had a brother that had just got out of San Quentin that was a pizza cook. Ben served pizza, ribs and stuff like that – he called his restaurant The Pick-a-Rib. When Barney decided to go back with Louis in 1960 I went in there behind him. Buddy couldn't lead the band, so I had to be the leader; Buddy was just the leader in name only. I had to call the tunes, which was just like Barney used to do when he was in there. Cajun played with me, sometimes George Orendorff played, and once in a while, Andy Blakeney. One time Meade "Lux" Lewis played with me – that was when I was in Ben's place with the Dixie Flyers. Meade was the worst band piano player in the world; he couldn't play with a band at all, no rhythm. He was strictly a soloist. I only used him twice. I worked at Pollack's for a while, then I quit and went to work for Mike Riley – me and Nappy and Rico Valese – 'cause Ben wouldn't give us enough money.

I had known Mike a long time. He's a funny guy – only criticism I got with Mike is his bad timing. He'd get on that stand and didn't know when to stop. He'd try to do comedy instead of playing music. Mike had a lot of capable musicians and people came there to hear a little comedy, but they also wanted to hear music. We had guys like Jackie Coon on trumpet, Charlie Lodice, the drummer that's with Pete Fountain now, Moe Schneider on trombone, who is one of the great ones, yet Mike would get up and clown all night long. He wouldn't let us play, so people would walk out.

Mike's place was called the Mad House. His first place, which he had here in Hollywood during the war, was called Mike Riley's Mad House; that was after *The music goes 'round and around* was such a big hit and he made a zillion dollars. Then, when he had his joint in Pasadena, he opened up next to a church, kinda like a mission, where they had this old preacher. They was running in competition to each other, so Mike decided to put up a loudspeaker. You could do that to play records or beam your band out on to the street, so the preacher put one up next door to play hymns. They'd have battles of music! You'd go there and the church was blaring out hymns and Mike was blaring out dixieland. Then he opened another club on Western Avenue. We worked both places. He'd had two locations in Pasadena and he lost a fortune on each of them.

After we started working for him he was drinking quite a bit. Sometimes he'd pay us two or three times and forget he'd done it. We always gave him the money back; we didn't want to take his money like that. I'll tell you one thing about Mike, if he would really buckle down to it, he'd be one helluva trombone player. I seen Jimmy Dorsey come in several times just to watch him play. And how he played this old trombone he had, I'll never know: you couldn't hardly move the slide, it was so bent and crooked. When he got through playing he just threw that horn on top of the piano. I've heard guys play a trumpet and a trombone at the same time where they use their foot to operate the slide, but he could do it better than anybody. We would play *Tiger Rag* or *Muskrat Ramble* and you'd think it was two distinct musicians playing the horns, but it would be Mike doing both parts. And he played 'em good but he did them too long. Sometimes he'd stay on the stand nearly two hours. People would come and say they wanted to hear Jackie, Nappy or me play dixieland.

Mike had two sons, very nice guys. Mike, Jr, was a priest and Joe is an insurance man out here, and they the ones that put up the money. So I called them up and I said, "You guys is gonna go for broke in this joint, you hear what I'm telling you." They kinda resented me saying that and said their dad had been in the business a long time. I says, "I don't give a damn how long your dad's been in business. Can't you see what's happening in there? You get on the stand and the place is full of people Friday and Saturday nights, and before Mike is off the stand everybody's gone." Which was true. They said everything would work out fine but finally they had to close. Both of them called me to say they wished they'd taken my advice and listened to me. It happened exactly like I said.

I was with Mike for a short while and then I just got up and left without giving notice. I remember Mike got as mad as hell about that. I says, "I couldn't put up with your shit, Mike, I don't give a damn, you take me to the union." Anyway, we still friends. I played with him again later on and he still gets big royalties from *The music goes 'round and around.*

After that I went into the Gilded Rafters, a club out in the Valley, with three pieces. It was Marvin Ash the piano player, Nappy and me. From then on Nappy was involved in mostly all of my jobs. The thing with me and Nappy goes like this: if Nappy would get a job I would be on it, or he would be on mine. A lot of times Nappy would get a job as a single, but somehow he would talk them into using me, even if he'd have to split his money with me. He's just one of the nicest guys you want to know and a helluva good musician. We're friends. When his wife Alice was around we'd have dinner, do a lot of things together. Alice was a very nice person and had been in show business, too. She was from New York and her and her sisters had a song-and-dance act.

About this time Tommy Walker, who was the talent and music director for Disneyland, decided to put a regular band on the *Mark Twain* riverboat they have out there. Now I had worked out at Disneyland with a different group altogether when it opened in 1954. Some guy from the Santa Ana local called me to play with a white group, I can't think who it was. Later I was on those

"Dixieland at Disneyland" things with the Dixie Flyers. Anyway, they approached me early in 1961 and we all met over at Johnny St Cyr's house with some of the big wheels from Disneyland and tried to figure out the band. Gordon Mitchell helped to organize things and it was Gordon that called me. As a matter of fact, I wasn't exactly the type that Disneyland wanted. They wanted definitely all-black guys, looks and everything. The original guy they wanted was an old saxophone player from New Orleans named Mosley, so damn old he couldn't hardly walk or play. He dropped dead and that's why they decided to use me. It wasn't prejudice, they really wanted black musicians, close as they could get. They didn't want Mike DeLay for the same reason. That's why I wasn't chosen to be leader of the band. We had St Cyr, Mike, Harvey Brooks, myself and Alton Redd, along with Monette Moore, at the meeting. They had a vote as to who would be the leader and, as me or Mike was the last guys they would ever pick, they picked Harvey. He was the leader of the band from the very first, believe me. Now Alton Purnell goes round telling people that he's the one that thought up the name of the Young Men from New Orleans and give it to the band. That's a lot of bullshit. He says it was his band, but he wasn't even in the picture at the start. I know 'cause I was there. Disneyland had the name copyrighted and they the ones that started the band.

There was five pieces at first, no trombone or bass at that time. They decided to pattern it after some group one of these guys is supposed to have heard in New Orleans. The original line-up was Harvey, Johnny, Redd, Mike and me, with Monette on vocals. Of course we had worked with Monette on jam sessions, like with my band at the Royal Room. She'd show up at all the jam sessions and sing. She was a fairly well-known singer around Chicago in the twenties and she recorded quite a bit on some of the old labels. Monette was a very nice woman. She died while I was with Louis.

So we went out there in June of 1961. In the first place the bandstand was too small, but afterwards they changed the routine and it was OK. They had a couple of dancers, put on a little show. We'd go on the boat at five o'clock, make two trips which took roughly half an hour, and then we got an hour for dinner. We came back, made two more trips, had 45 minutes off, then made three trips, with one trip off, continuously until midnight, that's the way we worked it. We did that six days a week in the summertime. At first they had us wearing old-time tuxedos, button shoes and high wing-collars like you wore in 1905. That first week my neck was so goddam sore you couldn't hardly touch it, so finally we told them we ain't putting them things on no more and we changed to soft shirts and bow ties. Before that we looked like giraffes peering over a fence.

It was a seven-hour deal and every other regular musician in Disneyland worked the same hours. How they fixed that was by practically owning the Santa Ana musicians' local, which was way out of the jurisdiction of Local 47. Disney was smart enough to do that, otherwise we'd have been making three times the salary and working conditions would have been a lot better. Disney told the Santa Ana local what to do and they did just about what he wanted. They set the scale down way low, and it was a standing joke that we didn't get the same respect as the jackasses out at Disneyland. They was on a mule train and the Humane Society said they could only work four hours, but we had to do seven. We didn't even get the respect of a damn mule!

Still, it was a beautiful thing in many ways. It was nice to meet the people and, naturally, they came from all over the world. They would always come up and talk to you. It took roughly 14 minutes to make the round-trip along that little river, and people danced, plus they had a little bar that sold non-alcoholic drinks. You couldn't buy alcohol in that park, so if you wanted a drink you had to get on the monorail and go to the Disneyland Hotel.

The *Mark Twain* was strictly Disney's own brainchild, his favorite thing, his pet. Strangely enough, a lot of people thought that boat was brought up from New Orleans, but it was designed and built here at Disney Studios. The craftsmen and carpenters made it and they cut it in half in order to transport it to the park. The boat runs on tracks under the water so they can steer and control it. Looking at the river you would think it was a real riverboat on a small river, but they needed those tracks to help them handle the boat and dock it. Then they had to figure out a way to keep the river real muddy, like the Mississippi, so they put some sort of a dye in it; that way you can't see the tracks under the boat.

It was a real river for all that and Walt built it himself. Sometimes he'd stay in the park, where he had an apartment with a maid and a valet, so whenever he had a chance, which was maybe two or three times a week, he would come over to the *Mark Twain* and have a dance and talk to the people. When he was in the park it look like they sent word ahead about being on your toes but, hell, we didn't pay any attention to that 'cause to us he was a very friendly guy and easy to talk to. He'd come around in one of the earliest automobiles, one that didn't have a steering wheel but a long rod, and he'd say, "Hello, fellers, how you doing?" Sometimes he'd be dressed real nice, other times just like you and me after a night on the town. A real ordinary guy. He always wanted you to call him Walt; he didn't care about "Mr Disney." One time I asked him what he was going to do and he said, "I just decided to come up here to see you fellers and ride around on my boat on my river for a while." He looked at me and I thought for a while. This seemed real funny to me, so I says, "Walt, I been playing music for a lot of years and I've played on a lot of boats and rivers but you the first guy I ever seen that owned his own river." He laughed and he says, "By golly, you right. This is my river and this is my boat. Let's have some fun. Play me a waltz so we can dance." So we played him *Let me call you sweetheart*, and he bought us some of that steamboat punch that they sold on board. He got a kick out of that.

I was only on the *Mark Twain* about three weeks when Joe Glaser gave me a call out at Disneyland. They called me to the office to take it. Louis wanted me to join the All Stars because Barney was leaving. I had a contract at Disneyland for the season and when Joe called me I told him that. He said to talk it over with them and call him back. "Let me know if you can get out of your contract." So I spoke to them about it and Tommy Walker said, "Sure, we wouldn't want you to miss an opportunity to work with Louis." They was very fond of Louis out at Disneyland 'cause he often had worked there. They thought it was a great opportunity for me and so did I, but they had a helluva time getting a clarinet player to replace me. In the end they put in Sammy Lee. Sammy could hardly play any clarinet at all then, but they were forced to use him in a pinch. I flew to New York and joined Louis around July 15th.

Like I said before, I first remember hearing Louis Armstrong play when he came to Baton Rouge with the Tuxedo Band. All the marching bands from New Orleans would come to Baton Rouge and the Tuxedo Band was one of the best of them. We heard this cornet and everybody was hollerin', "Who's playing that horn?" Then some guy that had been to New Orleans and knew Papa Celestin said, "That's some little gatemouth-sonofagun called Louis Armstrong." Louis was wailing and he was outstanding even then, made all of those others guys in the band sound like beginners. I hadn't started fooling with the clarinet then, but I knew I wanted to play with that guy someday.

I didn't get to meet Louis until some time in 1938 or '39. He was on one of the Bremerton boats, going over there with his band to play a one-nighter and I was playing somewhere with Vic Sewell's Gennessee Street Shufflers. It just happened all of us was on that ferry boat together. Some guy passed me and I think I remarked to Vic that he looked just like Louis. He seemed like he was feeling no pain, pretty high. Sure enough, I ran into Fireman George – old Pops Foster – who was there drinking beer, so I says, "What the hell you doin' on this boat?" and he says, "Well, I'm here with Pops, with Louis." He seemed surprised to see me. He said, "I heard you was living in Seattle. Would you like to meet Pops?" I hadn't seen Fireman George since '28 and the days with Papa Mutt. He took me over to where Louis was eating and, right off from there, Louis started calling me "another home boy." We talked for a long time and I told him I was from Baton Rouge. I think we had a beer together. I remember asking Louis, would he like to come over to my house for some gumbo that I'd fix him, and he said he didn't have a chance this time as they was leaving the next day after playing this one-nighter. Then I talked some more with George and he introduced me to all the guys in the band, including George Washington the trombone player, Don Stovall, who was a helluva good sax player, and Joe Garland, the fellow who wrote *In the Mood*. Big Sid Catlett was around, too.

Louis took a liking to me and I liked him, too. We became friends right off. He was partial to people from Louisiana, he really was, and to young musicians starting out. He always did nice things for everybody. He wanted to know how long I'd been in Seattle, so I told him I'd been running on the boats and before that I'd been living in Los Angeles. So he asked me, did I know Ory and Tudi, so I said I'd been working with Pops Foster, Frank Pasley, Alex Hill, all these guys. And right then he figured it out. "Well, I know you can play something to be able to work with these musicians," he said.

I didn't run across him again until 1942 when he happened to come to Seattle to play a concert. I found out he was staying at a hotel on Jackson Street. I think it was the Golden Rest Hotel, and I went down there looking for him. They told me they thought he had run around the corner to the barber's shop to get a haircut. There he was, sitting in the chair, and Lucille was waiting for him. They had got married a short while before and he introduced me to her. We got to talking and I says, "How long you gonna be in town?" And I think they was going to be staying over for two or three days, so I said, "How about some red beans and rice, and some gumbo?" So Louis says, "You my man!" By this time I was working with Johnny Wittwer, so I had Johnny and Doc Exner over, too. They was thrilled at that. I was married then to this girl Margaret. I cooked some gumbo, we had fried chicken and rice, home-made ice-cream, and we started talking about Ory and the early days in New Orleans. He told me how Ory used to get permission to bring Louis out of the Waif's Home to play with Ory's band at Milneberg, a resort on the lake. They had dance halls and picnics there and, from what I could understand, Ory and them used to play there every Sunday. This was when Louis was about 14 years old. Ory told me later on that the first thing Louis started playing was *Sister Kate*. He also said Louis wrote the tune, made it up, then Clarence Williams or somebody got hold of it, but they had to change the words!

It seems the drummer Black Benny was about the toughest character in New Orleans in those days. He loved musicians and the musicians loved him back for the protection he gave them. He wouldn't let anything happen to a musician; nobody would walk over a musician when Benny was around. Benny himself was never a good musician, but he used to fool around with a bass drum. Ory said a couple of times he sent guys to get Louis and as soon as he got out of the gate he run off and they had to go find him. They told Benny and sent him after Louis. Benny took a piece of rope with him and no sooner did he get in there but he roped Louis to one of his arms and he drug Louis out. There wasn't no way Louis would get away from Benny. I asked Louis about that and he laughed and says, "Who told you that?" I said Ory told me. "Well," he says, "I guess he was right." He never would really admit it, but they say it was true. Ory was always talking to me about it. "Yeah, I gave him his start." Ory got Louis in to his band after he fired Mutt Carey, when Louis was about 18.

Louis was so nice. If he talked about musicians, he'd say nothing but good about them. If you'd bring the subject up, he always talked about Louisiana musicians. He asked me about Buddy Petit, and when I told him I played with Buddy in Toots Johnson's band he said, "I know old Toots Johnson, that banjo player in Baton Rouge. That cat could play. I remember we had battles of bands. I come there with Kid Ory one time and they run us out of town. He had my boy Buddy in his band." Louis never talked about Guy Kelly; the trumpet players he spoke about was older, cats like Wesley "Kid" Dimes and Kid Shots Madison.

When he came to my house Louis told me that his first wife, Lil Hardin, had a brother that lived in Seattle right around the corner from my house, and, although he was separated from Lil, he always stayed friends with her brothers. It turns out I knew his brother-in-law slightly. So every time Louis came to Seattle, which looked like every year, he'd come over and see him.

I didn't run into Louis too much again until I went down to Los Angeles and started playing with Kid Ory. Louis was in and out of Los Angeles all the time, so I'd see him often. Of course, when I first went down there to record for Doc Exner, the All Stars hadn't been organized. Barney had a group of his own for a while and him and Ory was very good friends. This was when I stayed over at Ory's house. Barney was like God, he was always over there. A couple of times when Louis was in town he came over to see us.

Another time, Louis was staying on Central Avenue at the Dunbar Hotel and I went down there for his show. It was raining like hell and it was just Louis and me in the hotel room. Lucille had went some place. He had just got a tape recorder and he wanted me to hear some stuff, plus somebody had just sent him some pralines and he wanted me to eat some of them. He had a lot of his tapes with him. All this was about one or two in the morning. It was still raining and I could have gone home if I'd had my car, but we was having a good time eating pralines and drinking beer. Finally Louis called Helen and said, "Helen, don't worry about Joe, him and me is having a ball eating this good old New Orleans candy."

I told you already about the time Louis played at one of my Royal Room jam sessions. He had a good time, the place was packed and Louis played as hard as any one would for money. Also, he played the tunes *we* wanted to play.

We'd meet up regularly in San Francisco, like when Ory's band was playing at the New Orleans Swing Club and Louis was working at the Golden Gate Theater. We had an apartment that me, Ory, Bud Scott and Ram Hall stayed in. We could use the kitchen in this rooming house and one night after work we made stewed chicken and rice and gumbo for Louis and some of his guys. Another time we was brought to San Francisco to play in the Green Room. The All Stars hadn't been organized long and we all lived at the Sullivan Hotel, both bands. Louis and I used to have a few nips together and he said, "If anything ever happens to Barney, maybe we can get together. Course I wouldn't take you from Ory's band, I know you a valuable part of the band. But if I ever have an opening and you not doing anything, the job is yours."

Nothing more was said until one time at the Hollywood Bowl when I was working with Teddy Buckner's band and Louis mentioned it again. Peanuts Hucko was playing clarinet with the All Stars then and he was talking about leaving, so Louis said, pointing to me, "This is the guy I want with the band." Joe Glaser called me and I was practically ready to leave, then for some reason Joe wanted Barney, who was working for Ben Pollack, back in the band. They changed the plan, I don't know why.

That Hollywood Bowl concert was kinda funny anyway. Louis had to say a little speech on the stage, "Hark, I hear an angel sing," and that was the cue for this chorus that was supposed to sing with him. For this, they were supposed to raise the curtain, make a production deal of it, but these guys must have fallen asleep because nothing happened. So Louis says it louder – still nothing. And finally he says, "Hell, I *think* I hear an angel singing. What's the matter with them cats back there?" With that, the curtain came up. I was backstage with Frenchie, the road manager for Louis, and that's the night Louis said I should come with the band.

In fact I played with Louis a couple of times when Barney wanted to take off. First, I made a TV commercial which Barney didn't want to do for some reason, I can't even remember its name, and then Doc Pugh called me to play a concert at the Swing Auditorium in San Bernardino. This was no problem to me as I had heard the band so many times and I knew the routines. I just walked in and started playing.

Barney wasn't back with the band more than five or six months when I received that call from Joe Glaser, out at Disneyland. I knew from the first time I talked with Louis that eventually I would be with the band. Doc Pugh said Louis wanted me there from way back. Finally it came true, and I was tickled to death about it.

I joined Louis in Buffalo, New York, where the band had a night off. Barney had already quit and I run into him at the airport in Albany as he was coming back to Los Angeles. Our opening day was in Bala, Ontario, where we played a concert at a place right on the lake, kinda like a resort. There was no rehearsal. Louis never had a library or any music. You had to get in there and play. Even if I hadn't worked with him before I could have played those routines pretty good, because I'd heard the All Stars so many times. One of the first things Louis said to me was, "Well, Joe, now you with the All Stars, so *you* a star. Let's see you shine."

The regular line-up of the band at that time was Trummy Young on trombone, Billy Kyle, piano, Irv Manning, bass, and Danny Barcelona on drums, with vocalist Jewel Brown. Jewel Brown hadn't been with the band too long and Irv Manning joined about the same time as me. Usually Louis never rehearsed, but Irv had a little skit on *The Rain in Spain* and he wanted to rehearse it with Louis. Also I needed to run over *Yellow Dog Blues* and *Sweet Georgia Brown*. This was just to get your solos worked out; it wasn't to get any new numbers for the band because they didn't change them. It was just for our benefit to get some idea of how we was gonna play our solo features. Up to then I had played *Rose Room*, and I had been using *How Long Blues* and *Bourbon Street Parade*. I hadn't played *Yellow Dog*, so we had to rehearse it and get a routine on it. People was asking about *Yellow Dog Blues* right along when they found out I was in the band: "When you gonna play your tune?" So that was a fixture in the show. Naturally, you had some background stuff behind Louis or behind some of Trummy's solos. Billy Kyle and Louis himself told me what to do. Sometimes Danny, the drummer, would give me some pointers. No problem.

About two weeks after I joined the band we was playing at Salisbury Beach, which is like a suburb of Boston, for two weeks, and that's when we had the rehearsal. Louis agreed to do this to accommodate Irv. Now Irv was a kinda short-tempered guy, had a short fuse, and Louis was about the same. Louis tried to do this *Rain in Spain* but nobody liked it and finally Louis got fed up and he says, "I don't know, Irv, I don't think it will fit." Irv says, "The only reason I was doing it was to get *you* a laugh." When he said that, Louis got as mad as hell. He said, "I been playing since before you was born. I don't need you to get a laugh for me." Irv called Louis a sonofabitch and said he was just trying to be nice to Louis, so Louis said, "I don't need you to be nice to me," and then Irv said, "I don't need this job anyway," so Louis told him to quit. The minute after that, Irv said he was sorry. He and I was good friends; essentially Irv was a nice guy. When we got back to the hotel we went for a drink and he says, "I'm sure sorry I said that to Louis. I don't want to leave the band. Do you think I was right?" Everybody liked Irv, so somebody said, "Why don't you go talk to Louis? You don't have to quit." We got in the bus and Irv started talking to Louis, who said, "Fine, you still stay with the band, it's OK with me, everything is forgotten." And it was.

As to *Yellow Dog*, Louis liked the slap-tonguing very much. When you got ready to play, Louis would say, "This is your solo, play whatever you want, long as your want, short as you want, just do it." Those were his very words. He never told anybody how to play. He wasn't one of them bandleaders that would tell you this or that. I'm not calling any names, but one of the guys was having a little problem and he wasn't really doing his job, so Louis came up to me and a couple of the others and he says, "I don't know what the trouble is with this guy. I guess you have noticed, but I'm afraid to say anything because he might get excited and play worse. I don't want to fire him so we'll just let it go for a few days. What do you think?" Eventually the guy straightened himself out without Louis saying anything to him. We always had a lot of fun and, certainly, I never worked for a better guy or a better bandleader.

As far as money was concerned, I made more with Louis than anyone else, and after three years I had enough to retire. By the same token, I earned my money: I stayed with Louis for those three years especially to get some kind of financial security. When I went with him, I told Louis I would go with the band for just one year. At the time Helen had a good job; she was a payroll clerk at the *Hollywood Citizen News* and we saved our loot. That's one thing Louis used to tell me all the time, "Don't do like the rest of the guys in this band. You save your money." I didn't end up a millionaire, but I could always pick my spots and that was entirely due to my years with Louis.

I think we all negotiated differently with Joe Glaser. As long as you stayed with the band, Joe took care of a raise every six months or so. I know every time I asked for a raise I got it. He never turned me down once and when I left, Joe was still offering me more money. The thing about old Joe was that he was a kinda rough-acting guy. Joe always kept his word with me. He had a funny way with him, sorta gruff, but he was a guy who had so much on his mind, always wanted to do everything himself. People say he was an ex-gangster, which I don't know about. In his office he would mostly be on two telephones at once, talking to two people at one time, hootin' and hollerin'. You never seen him relaxing. He was on the phone to Duke Ellington, always called him "Mr Ellington." "Now, Mr Ellington, I cannot send you more money," and when he got through, he was talking about all the money Duke owed him, that Joe had advanced him on royalties.

Joe seemed to like Helen and me. He knew how Helen loved baseball and he would give us box seats at the Yankee Stadium – did that four or five times. Joe had a couple of boxes at the Yankee Stadium and at the polo grounds, too. We'd take a cab out there and as soon as we got all set, here would come Joe. He would hardly sit down before he'd go get a whole mass of peanuts, stand at the end of the aisle, throw them to you and say, "Hey you guys, have some peanuts. Now make yourselves sick." That was one of his funny lines. If the Yankees was behind he would get so mad, but he'd scream and yell if they were winning. When it was time to leave he'd always bring us back in his Rolls Royce. Joe was really nice. A lot of people didn't know about that. Another thing, he raised poodles and he knew Helen had poodles. He was always saying, "Any time you want a poodle, you've got one." Every Christmas he'd send us a picture of his prize poodles on a card.

We most certainly had a good band. The whole thing was more like a family affair. One thing that helped to seal this was the deal between Louis and Joe. From what I can understand, Louis told Joe, "All I want to do is to get our business straight. I want to play my horn. I don't want to have any responsibilities with the guys, hiring and firing. Naturally, if I got somebody that bugs me too much, I would have something to say." Louis could hire and fire anybody but he wasn't that type of guy, wouldn't like to do it in the first place. That's why before we got a guy in the band they would know pretty much about him. All the guys was beautiful but Louis was the best of them. He was something special to me from the first time I seen him. One thing made him great. You know the hardships you have to cope with in New Orleans, especially if you're black: Louis never held any resentment against that. I think the Lord said when Louis was born, "I'm gonna take this little boy and make a genius out of him just to show the people they got a Supreme Being someplace." Otherwise where would all that talent have come from? Can you explain it?

Louis used to talk about Mayann, his mother, and his sister, tell us how his mother used to go out to work, how she could take 30 cents and feed six people. In one of his standard deals he'd tell us about when he was a kid and would visit his grandmother who was living out in the country in Boutte, Louisiana. They'd have to go down to the creek and haul their water up in buckets – didn't have faucets, nor even a well. One day his grandmother says, "Louis, take this bucket and go down to the creek and fill it up." Louis got down there and there's this big alligator in the water, so he lit out back to the house. His grandmother said to Louis he should fetch the water, and that the alligator was just as afraid of him as Louis was of the alligator. Louis said, "I looked at Grandma and told her, 'Grandma, if that alligator is as afraid of me as I am of him, that water ain't fit to drink anyway!'"

Louis could say something to a person and that person would laugh, but if *you* said the same thing to him he would probably be insulted. From Louis it was acceptable. Louis always had time for everybody and he used to like a lot of people around him. He loved attention, like when we was in Las Vegas, where one of the guys that stuck with him, like white on rice, was Wingy Manone. Every night Wingy would be there and Louis would give him money to play blackjack. In fact Louis would give money to anybody that came around, like when the Dukes of Dixieland, the Assunto Brothers, was in town, and Louis gave their mother and sister money to play the tables. Another guy he bankrolled was George Jenkins, who was a helluva good drummer in Los Angeles and had been married to Dinah Washington at one time. George was a died-in-the-wool gambler; he'd drink a little and smoke a little tea, never had any money, drums always in hock. He came to Vegas to play with Billy Williams from the Inkspots, who had a terrific singing act, along with Billy Mackel, the left-hand guitar player, who like George had worked with Hamp. No sooner did George get into town than he started gambling and lost all his money. He put his drums in hock for 150 dollars and he came up to Louis's room to tell him about it, so Louis gave him the money to get his drums back. George thanked Louis and went on downstairs; we forgot about it for the time being. Later we all went down, and who's there shooting dice? George's hair was all standing up on his head and he's sweating like hell 'cause he's down to his last five-dollar bill. We run upstairs and told Louis, who started laughing, and then, sure enough, here's George again. George was crying and fell down on his knees. Louis never could get mad at anybody so he says, "George, get off your knees. I'll give you some more money." I think he got the drums out of hock this time for sure!

Another time we was playing in Chicago, and here comes some guy that Louis knew from years back and he told Louis he was broke. It wound up Louis gave him a 50-dollar bill and this guy walked out of the door, then he turned right round and came back saying, "Hey, Pops, I don't care to break into this 50-dollar bill. Have you got an extra five-dollar bill for my fare?" Louis said, OK, and he gave him another five dollars. Can you believe that? A lot of people used to say Louis was gonna wind up broke because of his generosity. Louis told me himself that him and Joe didn't have any kind of written contract. People would say that nobody knew how Joe was splitting the money, but Louis wasn't as dumb as they thought. Once every six months him and Joe would have a meeting so he knew what was happening, or Lucille did. Anyway, when he died he'd wound up a millionaire and Lucille had all the money she needed. Lucille was a smart woman and she was well satisfied.

Louis tried to stay out of politics. He would talk about things but he never really made an issue out of them. Louis let his money do his talking for him. He spent a lot of money on people, orphanages, things that you never seen in the papers. Like when we went down to Tennessee, where they had the only all-colored medical school. Louis and Joe had donated thousands of dollars to help them build a new wing for heart research and we went down to play for them. I felt it was a beautiful thing to play for something like this and I enjoyed meeting some very prominent doctors. Louis never turned anybody down. I seen him give away cash money to all sorts of people that was having a hard time.

For all his popularity, Louis could be sitting in his dressing room and he looked like the saddest guy in the world. That always amazed me. He'd be sitting with his horn in his hand, just looking at it, turning it over, looking at the bell, picking it up and blowing a little, that's all. He appreciated any little thing; it was just the thought. When we played Las Vegas, a lot of times we didn't stay in the Riviera Hotel. I'd get my own apartment where they had a stove and I could do some cooking. That way Helen could be with me, too. I'd cook and one of my favorites was barbecued chicken wings, Chinese style, with rice, and Louis was crazy about them as well. So whenever I fixed them I would always make enough to bring him some. He would take the stuff up to his room and him and Lucille would have that for their supper instead of eating the hotel's food. Sometimes I cooked red beans and rice and he'd come over and eat with us. Louis didn't care for high-toned food. Give him the simple things.

Here's another thing he used to do. They got a kind of popcorn called Crackerjack, and it comes in little boxes with prizes in each box – whistles and noise-makers for your fingers. Louis was crazy about that popcorn, so every time I'd pass a place I'd pick up about half a dozen boxes for him. As soon as he opened that box he'd look for the prize. One time it was a little trumpet, made a whistling sound when he blew it, so he says, "I hope it's a Selmer." He played it all the time on the bus. He was just like a little kid that had found a diamond ring. What a guy!

We was always hoping to play somewhere where we had friends who might cook us a little feed, have some home-cooked food for once. We was in Chicago this one time, at the home of some people that knew Louis from New Orleans. They'd invited us there for this after-hours supper and they really had a spread with gumbo, fried chicken, potato salad, cabbage and red beans and rice. We was sitting down there eating and drinking, having a ball, and Louis was sitting over in a corner by himself. I see him motioning to me to come over so I went over and he says, "Hey, home boy, this woman got a few crabs and she stuffed them for me. She couldn't get many, only about a dozen. That's just enough for me but I'll give you a couple, so go get your plate but make it kinda quiet, don't let these other guys see. I wouldn't mind giving them some but I don't have enough to go round. Hell, if I start giving everybody some, I won't have none for myself. She just fixed them for me but I know you like this stuff and you always laying that good food on me, y'know, so pick out a couple of 'em." I wanted to be kinda nice, so I picked out a couple of medium-sized crabs. Louis looked and looked at the crabs and finally he says, "Take another one." Now in all this bunch of crabs they had this real big one, so I went to reach for it when Louis says, "Hold it, don't be greedy now. I've given you two already, now you want to take the biggest one. Put it back and take this skinny one here." I thought that was the funniest thing. I didn't laugh but I wanted to. He wasn't acting funny, he was just scolding me like a kid, shaming me, as if to say, "You lucky you got those two." Louis couldn't never be any more simple than he was, that's another reason he was so great.

Like all the cats from Louisiana, Louis loved that hot tabasco sauce, only he called it "Nancy White," after some real hot chick in New Orleans. She was a gal that worked in the District and the guys was all after her. She did more business than any broad in Storyville, so they named that hot sauce for her. I wouldn't doubt that Louis knew Nancy. I guess he went out and got a little taste once in a while!

We had various guys which traveled with the band and kept things on an even keel. First off there was Doc Pugh. He was a wonderful guy and we had been friends a long time. He was there for one purpose, to take care of Louis, act as his valet, see that Louis got whatever he wanted at all times. He had to be on call. Louis used to tell him, "Go on about your business, Pugh, I can take care of myself," but Joe Glaser wanted Doc there. He was very likeable and he had worked with Hamp and other bands before. Doc knew exactly what to do.

Doc died after I left the band. Somebody was asking Louis about him and they said they'd heard that Doc had died and asked Louis what was wrong with him. Louis looked at them with a kinda sad face and finally he says, "What was wrong with Doc? Man, when you die, *everything* is wrong with you." I told you Louis was funny even when he wasn't trying to be funny. That was just his way of talking.

Frenchie was the road manager for the band. He was really a wiggy guy, very prejudiced, didn't believe in any kind of mixing. In fact one time we was going through Kansas, looking out at the scenery, and Frenchie sees a bunch of white cows and black cows out eating in a big field. He looks at them and says, "Gee, I hate to see that. A black and a white cow, just like a white man and a colored woman." Billy Kyle says, "You prejudiced sonofabitch, I don't know how Louis puts up with you." Louis didn't do anything but look at it and laugh. He could have fired Frenchie but he never did. Louis figured Frenchie didn't have any sense to start with.

I remember we was in Mexico City, going through the airport, and Louis was half-drunk. Some Mexican guy had one of those souvenir stands selling hats and ponchos and he says, "Satchmo, I want you to come over here and help me sell this stuff." So Louis went back there and started helping him out. He bought Helen some tom-toms and autographed them; we still got 'em. Finally we was about to miss the plane and Frenchie was pleading with Louis to come on the plane. Louis looked at Frenchie and he says, "You say the plane's ready to leave?" and he took a great big bow, with everybody lookin' and laughin'.

This Frenchie was a miserable guy, evil, and nobody in the band liked him. Why Joe kept him as the road manager I don't know. Still, he cut out several years ago. Now, whenever we went to an airport or had to get in a cab we all went together and split the money. This one ride Frenchie had to borrow a dollar from Irv Manning. Later we was grounded in Kansas City Airport and Frenchie was paying us some money, so Irv says, "How about that dollar you owe me?" and Frenchie says, "Well, I don't owe you a dollar." Eventually one thing led to another, Irv got mad and he pushed Frenchie on to a stanchion or something. The floor had just been mopped and Frenchie slipped. Somebody told Louis that they had got into a fight and Frenchie was down on the floor. Right then and there Louis says, "That's one thing I won't have. Frenchie may be no good, but I don't want nobody to hit and hurt him. You're fired, Irv." That's when Billy Cronk came in the band.

Everybody was forever trying to change the tunes the band played, especially when Frenchie was with us. For that matter, Joe Glaser wanted them changed, but all of them was afraid to tell Louis. I'd go up to the office and Joe would say, "Why don't you guys play some different tunes? Do you want to talk to Louis about it?" I says, "Not me, why don't you get Frenchie to talk to him?" Frenchie was the one with the big mouth so I said, "I just want to hear you step up there and tell Louis." Hell, he'd rather stick his head in a Bengal tiger's mouth than do anything like that. Frenchie was afraid of Louis.

Dr Alexander Schiff was Louis's personal physician. He was a good friend of Joe Glaser's and originally he was the official doctor for the New York State Athletic Commission. The boxers had to take a physical before big championship fights and Doc Schiff was the man to say whether you could fight or not. He didn't travel with Louis all the time, at least not when the All Stars was first formed. Later on he came out with us more and more; that way we had a doctor to take care of us if we got sick, like the time he had to bring me to the hospital in England when I got something like kidney stones. Also Doc Schiff handled the finances on the road, leaving the road manager to take care of all the other business in the matter of the show and hotel accommodation. Then we also had a band boy, cat by the name of Leroy Smith, to take care of the instruments and the uniforms. We had three different uniforms, had to be cleaned every week.

It was Doc Schiff that insisted that Louis take a rest, that he was tired. I think this was after we'd been playing at the Riviera in Las Vegas. They told us that Louis was taking off for an eight-week Caribbean cruise with Lucille and that we was having a paid vacation. They paid us for the eight weeks, post-dated all the checks. Man, I started singing, I was so happy. Nobody in the band could believe it. A vacation with pay! I came on home and relaxed for about three weeks, just thinking about five more solid weeks, enjoying my swimming pool. I didn't take any jobs, just took my horn out and blew for fun, when here comes a call from the office saying to get ready to come back to New York 'cause Louis was itching to go back to work. He wasn't having any fun on that cruise. We kept the money, although it wouldn't have mattered about the money. Louis just loved playing that horn, he never really wanted to lay off. The guys once told me that Louis had the feeling that, if he ever had a long lay off, he was afraid he wouldn't be able to come back.

Every time I got close to home, Helen would try to come and see me. I just didn't have time to get home with playing so many one-nighters. Later on she quit her job and started traveling with me when she could. Coming back from San Francisco one time with the guy that owned Lark, Swede Jensen, she got in a snowstorm, couldn't get through the Grapevine – that's a place near Bakersfield, California, where you have a winding highway. You need chains if it snows, and she didn't get through there until six o'clock in the morning. She had to go to work – didn't want anyone to know that she'd been up to see me because she had taken too much time off previously, and they were hollering. She went right into the office and all day she was dead on her feet. Incidentally, my old friend Red Fox and his wife both got jobs at the *Citizen News* during that time when Red decided to quit the music business.

Helen would have traveled more with me but it was always hard for her getting on and off buses due to her having to wear a brace. Then we had some animals that had to be taken care of, cats and dogs. We love our animals and they'd probably die if you put 'em in a kennel. A girl that Helen knew at the newspaper used to come stay at the house, but a lot of times Helen would have to stay home herself. Louis would look at me, "Home boy, you look a little lonesome, you better send and get Helen."

One of the things I enjoyed most was when we would charter a Greyhound bus for some of the tour dates. We'd have this great big bus that could seat 60 people all to ourselves – just ten of us. We had a wonderful bus driver called Rupert Moore – we'd call him Rupe; he drove us every place. When we stayed in New York we'd go over to his house. They lived near the airport in Jamaica, and Rupe's wife Sarah was a great cook. She used to cook for one of the Father Divine restaurants in Brooklyn. They took us over one day, and that's where they had all that soul food: chittlin' and black-eyed peas, red beans and rice, collard greens, mustard greens, smothered pork chops. That was one of the best meals we ever ate in our life.

When I joined the band Louis was going strong, still playing well. It seemed to me after I had been there a couple of years his lip would get sore. He had quite a problem there. Louis was from the old-time school, like Freddie Keppard or some of those typical cornet or trumpet players from New Orleans that didn't use the non-pressure system like modern trumpet players. You blow from the lip, whereas Louis blew from the throat muscles and from his chest and his mouth. Even though they say he blew wrong and played wrong, in his time no one could even come close to Louis. The wonder of it was that his lip lasted that long. The man had so much strength and so much talent that the Lord himself must have picked him out. Yes, the Lord picked out Louis.

EIGHT

I know I'll be playing until I cut out

Playing dances, that's what I really enjoyed, and so did everybody else in the band. You had a chance to get away from the regular routine that we played on stage in auditoriums, schools, wherever, which was all set. Once in a while some important person would get to Louis backstage or holler out for a number and he might put it in. For instance, *Someday*, the tune that he wrote, wasn't on his regular program but anytime Helen was in the audience, like in Vegas or someplace, he would always play it 'cause he knew she liked it. He was very nice that way. Otherwise it was the same all the time. But when we played dances you could really go. Everybody could play whatever they wanted. Louis would say, "Now we gonna play a medley of tunes. You play any three tunes you want, Joe." So they might walk off the stage, everybody but me and the rhythm section, and I'd play my three tunes. Then Trummy would come and deal his choice, and then Billy Kyle would play, and so on. The band would play a lot of old dixieland tunes like *Muskrat Ramble*, *Fidgety Feet*, and *Dixieland One-step*, tunes that Louis liked – but not for concerts. The stage routine naturally had the hit records like *Mack the Knife* and *The Faithful Hussar*. People used to criticize Louis for sticking to these songs, but he knew if we didn't play them the audience would holler and demand them. At the dances sometimes we'd play a waltz, *Let me call you sweetheart* or *Alice Blue Gown*. To me, a dance was easier, 'cause you was right in contact with the audience.

We did this pretty often for private clubs, like in St Louis where they had an organization that always hired us for a dance. Women's clubs, too, often in pretty big dance halls. We played a dance for some civic group in Detroit at the Cobalt Hall, one of the biggest there is. Another dance we played was on the *Delta Queen*, a big boat still owned by the Streckfus Brothers. This was to raise money for the St Louis Symphony Orchestra. One of the Streckfus Brothers came on there just to see Louis and they had a helluva time drinking together. Streckfus bought box lunches for all of us, some of the best fried chicken you ever ate. They had 4000 people on that damn boat, which is probably one of the biggest riverboats ever built, had four decks on it. For that one day the city gave them permission to gamble, and I know they raised a lot of money that way. Then I remember a dance at the Beverley Hills Hilton given by an organization called the Rinkidinks that had a lot of movie people belonging to it. Also Louis played a lot of dances in smaller places, little towns, you can't even find them on a map. Then we played dances for that girls' school, Smith College in Massachusetts, and at MIT in Boston; also at Jet Propulsion (JPL) in Pasadena and at a little old school in Maryville, Missouri.

We'd go to all the out of the way places, and one that sticks in my mind was Grand Island, Nebraska, which is one of the coldest states in the USA. A lot of people don't realize the Middle West and the Far West, states like Missouri and Montana, is some of the coldest places in the world. For instance, Montana registers temperatures like 76 degrees below zero. I had an uncle that had a meat market in a little town named Havre, Montana, and one Christmas, when I was living in Seattle, I went there to see him. When I got there the market was deserted, but they had a sign on the deep freeze saying "Ring the bell for service." I rang the bell and my uncle stuck his head out of the door of the freezer and says, "What the hell you doing out there in the cold? Come in this freezer." And they was all in the deep freeze playing pinochle, trying to keep warm. It was about 20 below in there but about 90 below outside, so it was warmer in the deep freeze than outside!

We was on the bus in Grand Island and the heat went off. It was 30 below. I don't know why the office even booked Louis into cold places like that during the winter months. God knows, they didn't need the money. Louis could have been booked in a lot of warmer places than that. On second thoughts, they must have been paying pretty good money! Anyway, usually Louis could sleep all the time on the bus, but that's one time he didn't sleep. He was drinking that gin right and left but still he couldn't keep warm. He was pacing up and down the aisle, swearing. We were all damn near frozen. The heat stayed out for about five days with the Greyhound people saying they needed a part they couldn't get to fix the heating system. Meantime the office didn't know nothing about this and our dumb road manager never told anybody. We got to Iowa and all went to Montgomery Ward in Sioux City, bought great big thick Indian blankets to wrap up in, until finally Doc Pugh called Lucille in New York and she got Joe Glaser on the phone and raised hell, said she was gonna call Louis and make him come home. So then Joe got busy, made them get us a new bus and every other thing. The damage was done then, we was all damn near dead.

We got called to make a picture called *Winter Carnival in Sun Valley*, which was a nice deal, but it turns out Sun Valley, Idaho, was one of the coldest places I've ever been. In order to get there from New York, you had to fly into a small airport ten miles away and then finish the journey by bus. We flew into Salt Lake and had to change onto a private plane, because they grounded all the commercial airliners it was snowing so hard. They had a tight schedule for this movie with all the equipment they had to get to Sun Valley, so they found this private charter air company that would fly us in there. It was a small plane that held about 30 people and, man, I'll never forget that thing. It was pitch black in that plane and I never seen Louis so scared. Everybody started praying. I never felt such turbulence. We thought we was all gonna die, everything was shakin'. Finally when we did set down on this little airstrip, Louis got out and kissed the ground. Everybody else did, too.

This was in January 1962. Sheila and Gordon McRae and Jack Carter was in the movie with us. A well-known designer had to furnish us with ski jackets and this special thermal underwear; this was in the contract – you sure in hell needed it. It was beautiful, but so cold all the instruments froze up. This particular day we had to do an outside scene and it was 30 below. It was lucky we had recorded the actual music in New York before we left, because if you look real close you can see where we had gloves on and had cut the fingers out of them. They had this piano bench out in the open and Billy sat down. When he got ready to get up the whole seat of his tuxedo came off in the cold weather. Everywhere I had moisture in my clarinet keys they would freeze up, and the valves on Louis's trumpet froze up, as did Trummy's slide. The hotel where we stayed was right on the edge of this skating rink and had a big fireplace, so me and Trummy went in front of this fire to try and warm up our horns, thaw 'em out a little. We wasn't actually recording the music but your fingers had to be synchronized to look like you was playing it. Louis handed his horn to Doc Pugh and said, "Get them valves thawed out and keep them working. Come on out here and hand the trumpet to me and I'll keep the action going. That way, maybe we can do it." Sure enough we got everything working. Pugh never could see too good, had these big bifocal glasses, and he started hollering, "Pops, I got your horn working here," until he stepped in some loose snow near the edge of the bandstand and he start sliding. Believe me, all hell broke loose. Louis seen what was happening and shouts, "Hey, Doc, watch that horn, keep those valves working." Poor Pugh was sliding on the ice. Naturally, everybody was watching him and Louis was getting excited. "Don't bend that horn, work them valves." Pugh didn't know what the hell was going on and when they helped him on to his feet, half-crippled, almost broke a hip, the damn trumpet had froze up again. Louis says, "All this trouble for nothing," so Pugh replies, "Louis, if you want the valves to work, you take it in there yourself." Then the director runs over and says, "Hey, Doc, that's about the funniest scene I seen in my life. Can you do it again?"

After that we came to San Francisco for an engagement at the Fairmont Hotel for three weeks from January 18th. This was one of your top hotels, one of the better jobs Louis played. I was glad to get to San Francisco to get out of the cold in Sun Valley, and I knew I would get some home-cooked food 'cause I had two sisters living there at the time. One of them was married to a French Creole, and they had a big house where I used to stay. My sisters was glad to see me and would fix me anything I wanted to eat. In the morning we'd have sausage 'n' grits, Creole-style smothered potatoes, and for dinner it'd be gumbo. That's where I got plenty of red beans and rice and smothered pork chops. Naturally I put on a lot of weight.

To me, San Francisco and New Orleans are the two most interesting cities in the USA, and both have different types of food. San Francisco has a lot of Italian restaurants and then there's Fisherman's Wharf where you can get all your good seafood – crab, lobster, shrimp, anything. For fine soul food you just drove over to Oakland, where a lot of colored people live. A guy named Slim Jenkins had a joint there where you could get all the soul food you wanted. One of my favorite places was Chinatown; naturally, I liked Chinese food, and that's where I learned to cook a lot of my Chinese dishes. I would always have a ball in San Francisco. I'd been coming there off and on since the twenties, in the days when I was shipping out of Seattle.

The Fairmont Hotel had two bands alternating. Helen took time off work and came up to see me. Turk Murphy and Pops Foster came by to see us, too. In the meantime the Hangover, that jazz joint in San Francisco, had closed and some Japanese took it over and they called it Ginza West. Muggsy Spanier had just left there. We had quite a few celebrities in the audience, people like Ava Gardner, Pat Boone, Tennessee Ernie Ford and Gary Merrill, who was that drunk he came up and kissed us all, which was the first time I was ever kissed by a movie star – a male one anyway!

After that we spent some time in Las Vegas, which was one of our favorite places to play; it's also where we made the most money. Acts like Billy Williams played the lounge, but we'd always play the main show room. The first time we worked there it was on the same bill with Marlene Dietrich. I used to see her on the screen, and people say big stars is kinda high-hat, stuck-up, but her dressing room was right next to ours and I used to go talk to her. She was a wonderful person to talk to and in fact most of the big-time stars are nice and thoughtful.

Another time it was Kay Starr that was on the bill with us. What a wonderful person. She had a big party for the band one night after the show. She fried the chicken, made all the food and furnished all the liquor. We had fried chicken coming out of our ears and more liquor than you've ever seen. This was up in her suite, after the last show finished at a quarter to one; me and Helen, too. Kay is a very generous person and she was very fond of Jewel Brown, our vocalist. She'd wear a dress just one time and then give it to Jewel. Kay always wore gorgeous clothes. Later on we played at Vegas with Jane Russell, Connie Haines and the Burt Dale Trio. Jane's big number was *Mack the Knife*, and when he heard this, Ira Mangel, who was Louis's road manager then, hit the ceiling. He was a very uncouth guy and he went and told Jane she couldn't use that number, that it was one of Louis's hit numbers, and I think she almost broke down in tears. Louis seen what was going on and got into conversation with her. "Hell, I gotta lot of numbers I can do. Go ahead and do the number, Jane." She had a big party for us, too. Jane was a very nice person. Helen and I would sit down at the table and talk to her about her deal with Howard Hughes. She was signed up in 1947 for 1000 dollars a week and had a 20-year contract when they made that picture *The Outlaw*. Every week she got this money, even though she never worked for Hughes after that. She told us she was still getting it. Connie Haines we knew from the "Stars of Jazz" TV show, and we saw her again just before I had my heart attack, at the Sacramento Jazz Festival. She came up and kissed us. Now she sings spirituals and other things and carries a band with her.

In these Las Vegas shows they don't want you to go over time at all, on account of the gambling. They want the people to get the hell out of the show rooms and over to the tables. One night Louis went one minute over time, just one minute, and the manager raised hell. Ira started making excuses but they said, "We don't care if it's the Angel Gabriel himself, you don't play over time. We paying this big salary to get these people in here to entertain them but we want them back out on them tables. In that one minute we could have won half a million dollars."

We did the eight o'clock dinner show, only 45 minutes long, and then the midnight show. We'd eat at the Riviera and we were off at quarter to one. Louis liked to gamble after the last show and he always wanted someone to play with him. Helen was the one and they would sit and play blackjack until maybe three or four in the morning.

When we was walking through the casino Louis had a habit of taking a silver dollar and stuffing it in a slot machine, saying, "I'll try this one," and going for the 300-dollar jackpot. He'd walk on and pretty soon you heard dollars jingling all over and he didn't even know it – and didn't need it either!

Another time Clara Ward, who I knew very well, and her Gospel Singers was there and they happened to be living upstairs at the same motel as us – a place called the Desert Villa. They used to have a big party every night. They'd get drunker than hell. We had a maid that we liked a lot and I gathered she was kinda religious. One day we got to talking about Clara Ward and she asked, "Hey, do you know Clara Ward? I want to ask you something. Are these gospel singers supposed to drink liquor and do things like that? I went up there one morning and opened the door and Clara Ward fell out of bed, so drunk, and she had a fifth of liquor in her hand." This broad couldn't figure that out, she was flabbergasted. I thought it was kinda funny. I guess gospel singers drink just like we do and ball it up. We heard about a party they gave for all the celebrities in Vegas when they raised so much hell they had to call the law and they took guys to jail. This was a week before we got to town. Can you figure gospel singers doing this?

We had a cute little Dachshund puppy, and whenever we had the chance we'd take Snoopy with us. She used to love to go out and get the paper with me. You had to walk about half a block down the motel drive and then she'd lead the way back to our apartment with the paper in her mouth. Harry Mills and the Mills brothers would sit out there waiting for me and Snoopy to go by; they thought it was one of the funniest things, seeing that dog prancing along with that big paper in her mouth.

Then we left on that tour of Europe. That was the first time I'd been all round Europe but I still didn't get the chance to see enough. We went to Zurich and Berlin, then we rehearsed in Rome for a TV show we were going to do with Hazel Scott the pianist and the Peters Sisters. That was 18th April 1962. I'll never forget Hazel Scott. She was still a beautiful woman, been married to a New York preacher and congressman. She had a young Italian hairdresser, young enough to be her grandson, and the whole time we were making this TV film this little cat was taking care of her hair. All the Peters Sisters was married to some kind of royalty over there. If you ask me they was all hustling guys; one was a count, like Louis would say "no-count." Dukes or whatever. The guys had nothing, but these broads was making good money over there. On April 28th we played the Royal Festival Hall in London and that's the time I first met Peter Vacher and started thinking about this book. We stayed at the Washington Hotel and I could walk to Piccadilly, all of the places I had read about. I used to go to the Cathay Restaurant all the time. We traveled by train for our English dates so that was my chance to see the English countryside. Then we went all over Scotland and to Ireland where they had the biggest crowds that I ever seen. In fact they declared it "Louis Armstrong Day" in Belfast and people was lined up the whole way from the airport, 15 miles out, on top of buildings, up trees, on telephone poles, just as if the president had come to Ireland. When we got into Belfast the traffic couldn't move. It was one of the most wonderful things. Louis just smiled and said, "These cats sure like you cats."

We came back to New York on May 29th. We were off one day and then we flew to South America, to Valparaiso and Santiago, Chile; we flew 8000 miles to do those two dates. The cause of that was the Russians sending the Bolshoi Ballet over to Chile for political purposes and the USA wanting to counter with somebody they thought the Chilean people would like, so we went over behind them to play in these two cities. That's when the band had to play under a circus tent because they didn't have an auditorium big enough to accommodate the crowd. In fact we had a dressing room that was in the old circus wagon with the elephants and lions in the background. It reminded me of my old circus days. We outdrew the Bolshoi Ballet by three to one and that made Louis awful happy.

We went into a restaurant in one of those cities and Billy Kyle ordered meatballs and spaghetti. Those restaurants close at about two in the afternoon and we got in there just under the deadline. Just as Billy ordered this delicious food he had to get up and go to the little boys' room. As soon as he got up one of these Chilean waiters sits down and starts eating his food. When Billy got back he wanted to know where in hell his food was and these two waiters started apologizing. The head waiter said, "I'm sorry sir, that's something people don't do here. When you get up the waiters think you're through eating and that's the way they get most of their food." To make it doubly worse, the kitchen had closed; it was siesta time. After two nothing happens and they wouldn't serve him any more.

When we came back from Chile the first place they booked us was Lake Placid, New York, for some kind of celebration for July 4th. A lot of retired rich people and theatrical people lived in Lake Placid; their homes was on an island, like a resort, and it was interesting sightseeing around that lake. The entertainer Kate Smith had a beautiful home there. But the thing I remember mostly about that place was our living accommodation. Instead of being booked into a first-class hotel we wound up in an old-folks home. They stuck us down in the basement, gravel for the floor, all because Frenchie had screwed up the reservations.

Then we played the Newport Jazz Festival. I liked the New England states, particularly Vermont, where we met some people that had a big spread where they had maple trees, made their own maple syrup. The guy gave us all six jars of syrup to put on our hot cakes. We carted that back to Los Angeles and then gave it away. Folks back there would take us to their houses and have lobster bakes for us. That's what is good about being a musician, especially working with somebody like Louis, you get to meet such wonderful people.

The Newport Festival was very interesting. Old Charles Mingus, the great bass player that died, was there and he started raising hell on stage, ranting and raving about something somebody did to him, threatening not to play. He was a salty guy anyway. We had got into Newport just in time to play and had to get away right afterwards to go back to New York. We was traveling by bus, and soon as we got there all the musicians that was already there came round to see Louis. I run into my old friend Jimmy Rushing, and Duke Ellington was there, too. I talked a long time with another old friend, Lawrence Brown, the trombone player with Duke. They had Yank Lawson and J. C. Higginbotham for guests with Louis. I hadn't seen Higgie in years, not since Louis was with the Luis Russell band. I remember one of the tunes they had to do – *Panama* or something – Yank or Higgie couldn't remember, so we had to sit on the bus and try to rehearse the damn thing. The concert went fine and Higgie rode back with us. At the time barely no one would hire him to play because he was drinking a lot of wine, he was a kinda wino. He was disorganized and couldn't find much work. Anyway, him and Louis had a lot of fun talking.

Then we went into Harrah's club in Lake Tahoe and that was another great scene. Any time we played there or Las Vegas, Helen was raring to go because she loves to gamble. In this business a lot of places is bad to play or the accommodation is poor, but Harrah's had to go down as one of the greatest places in the world for an entertainer. Harrah's income is from gambling and he owns most of Lake Tahoe. He treated his entertainers like nobody in the world. When you get through playing an engagement there he always gives you something special and one thing that's done is that all your expenses is paid. He owns the Rolls Royce and Chevrolet agencies so each of us had a new Chevvy to use, with the gas furnished. Louis and George Gobel, who was the other headliner, each had a Rolls Royce and a chauffeur at their disposal. All your long-distance calls was paid and you was given a gold courtesy card which entitled you to everything in the casinos and the hotel – everything but gambling, that is. All your food and drink, and you could bring as many guests as you wanted. It was fabulous and he still does it now. I was talking to Bob Havens not long ago; he was up there with the "Lawrence Welk Show" and he told me Harrah's still do the same things. Like, if you're playing and there's tons of your friends and relatives with you you can take them to dinner every night, and when they bring you the bill you just sign it and show them your gold card.

George Gobel was a real nice guy. Him and Billy Kyle was particularly good friends. George was also a guitar player, kept his guitar in its case on the stand. We put a pornographic picture in the case, right on top of his guitar. When he opened it he broke up and he says, "Which of you bastards put this picture in here?" right on the stage. He held it up and showed it to the audience. Him and Billy used to correspond and one time George told Billy, "I thought you might be interested in this menu from the Cocoanut Grove in Los Angeles." They had Rhode Island Red chickens on the menu and for some reason they called them "Special Southern Fried *Colored* Chicken" and he had it circled. George invited us all to his house when we was playing the Cocoanut Grove ourselves over New Year's Eve, so the whole band and their wives went up there on New Year's Day. George lived at that time at Encino, close to where we live now in Woodland Hills. When we drove up to his house he lived on a kinda hillside. It was easier to go in the back part of the house, so he said to Billy, "You used to going in back doors anyway." That was the kind of crack he made. Him and Billy was always kidding each other about different things. Man, George was funny. Billy asked him where the men's room was and George said, "I got a special room for you, Billy." This damn room was all made up in black tiles, black toilet and tub, so Billy went in there and, seeing all that, he just broke up. George told Billy, "This kinda fits your personality, I knew you'd love this." George told Helen, whenever I was out on the road she had a standing invitation from his wife Alice to come over. You know to this day I've never seen George again.

We left Los Angeles after coming from Lake Tahoe and we went on to the

Roaring Twenties club in San Diego. On the way we went to Idaho Falls, Boise, Lewiston and Moscow, Idaho; then Sterling, Denver and Colorado Springs, Colorado; and then to Marion, Illinois. That was one of the places I knew from the Charles Berger days; in fact he had a road-house there. I started shivering when I got to Marion, thinking about those damn times. From there, it was Skokie, Illinois, then on to Albion, Minnesota, then we played South Bend, Indiana, for the University of Notre Dame. I think there's only one organization that traveled more than Louis and this was the Harlem Globetrotters. We used to run into them everywhere we went. South Bend was where we went into this Chinese restaurant which served the worst Chinese food we ever ate. Louis happened to be sitting at the table facing the kitchen, so finally he says, "No wonder this food is so bad, they got a bunch of soul brothers back in there cooking this Chinese food." Sure enough, they had a bunch of colored folk in there. Louis said, "These guys can make pork shops and chittlin's but they sure as hell can't cook Chinese food." We laughed like hell.

I think it was in 1962 that we played at the Waldorf Astoria for President Kennedy's birthday party and that's a story in itself. Like I said before, Joe Glaser was a real excitable guy and when you got something like this he was apt to make a damn big production out of it. The road manager says to us, "We all gotta meet in Joe's office 'cause we have to brief you up on this thing. All kinds of celebrities gonna be there." The fighter Sugar Ray Robinson, Leslie Uggams, Carol Channing, Jimmy Durante, Van Johnson, Henry Fonda, Eddie Fisher, Debbie Reynolds, you name 'em, they were there. Must have been about 30 top entertainers in that room. Anyway, Joe says, "We gotta get this thing all straightened out. Everybody's got to carry a special card for security purposes, and you won't be able to get close to the hotel unless you have this special red card with your name on it to show that you have cleared security." I was living almost within walking distance of the Waldorf Astoria. No automobiles was allowed within three square blocks of the hotel, so I got a cab, had my red card in my vest top pocket all ready to show. I had my clarinet case under my arm and I'm waiting to be stopped any minute. You could see security men, FBI talking in bunches, and policemen standing around smoking cigarettes, yet I just walked through the police lines into the hotel. Nobody stopped me. I could have had a pistol or a machine gun in my case, could have killed the president right there. I went into the lobby of the Grand Ballroom where we was gonna play and still nobody said a word to me. Any other time you might stick your nose in there and you'd get shot. They was sleeping on the job! Anyway, it was a big event. First thing we had to do was play *Happy Birthday*. Kennedy was up on a balcony in this big ballroom with his family and we all faced him and sang, got him applauded. For the finale we was all lined up, with Louis leading and us following, our hands on each other's shoulders, Carol Channing directly at the back of me, marching around the room singing *When the saints* – that was one of his favorites.

Some time before I had played a thing here when he was campaigning to be president. He came to Los Angeles and he was going to speak at one of the shopping centers. We was all on a flatbed truck, me and Nappy, Eddie Miller, Nick Fatool and Ziggy Elman, the trumpet player that used to be with Benny

Goodman. Kennedy and his sister, the one that married Peter Lawford, they was on that truck with us. He impressed me as being a nice guy right then and there. Had a picture taken with him. I liked him and I voted for him. What a tragedy it was when he got killed like that. We was in Terre Haute, Indiana, stopped over to get a rest on the way to Indianapolis. I was laying in bed half asleep, heard the newsflash come on. That was one of the sad times of my life.

We also played for Ted Kennedy's birthday party in Hyannisport. This was in a hall, quite a lot of people there, and they had a great big cake with Ted's name on it. Louis and the band played *Happy Birthday* for him and then we all went over and shook hands, got a piece of cake, too. Afterwards they took us all out to a lobster dinner in a prominent restaurant. That was the first and only time I met the fine trumpet player Clark Terry. He was doing a date in Hyannisport and joined us for dinner, along with some other celebrities.

Talking about politicians, a couple of times we went up to Washington to play before the whole US Senate, had some other actors and musicians along with us. Actually it wasn't a real big deal for me; we never thought too much of the politicians, anyway. In Washington you see extremes like nowhere else. Within calling distance of the White House, two blocks away, it was the darndest slums you ever seen in your life, old beat-up houses, people living on welfare. It reminded me of coming out of Central Park in New York, going out east on Seventh Avenue through Harlem and seeing a helluva lot of misery. The contrast I used to notice in the early days when I first went there with Joe Liggins and Kid Ory, you'd be so happy sometimes, and you'd look at that misery and then you'd be damn sad to see how a lot of people lived. Then you'd go out to Sugar Hill, that was the most exclusive section, like a suburb of Harlem, where Duke, Count and all the guys had big homes. Louis was an exception, he didn't live on Sugar Hill like most of your top entertainers; he lived in Corona, Long Island, in a quiet residential section.

Louis called us when we was in New York one time, to go out to the house for his birthday party. It was July 4th, and so hot there was steam coming off the sidewalks. I told him I didn't know whether we could get a cab on a holiday, so Louis said to see and then call him back. No cab driver would take us out as far as Corona, so we called Louis back and he said, "Thats OK, stay right there, I'm sending a limousine for you." About 30 minutes later this long, black limousine pulls up at the hotel and takes us out to Corona for the party. Lucille was barbecuing. Dizzy Gillespie and his wife were there, Doc Pugh and his wife, Trummy, so many people. Right away Trumpet, Louis's little dog, jumped up in Helen's lap 'cause she loves animals. Anyhow, the limousine and the driver sat in front of the house from two o'clock and we didn't leave until 11 o'clock at night. They took a plate of food out to him – he never joined the party – and then he took us right back to the hotel. We don't know how much that cost. Louis was so considerate like that. Louis had a big cake with the US flag and his name on it. His house was something else: you couldn't walk on the floor, the carpets were so thick; they had a bathroom all done in black, with purple towels and soap; all the furniture was beautiful.

When it came to the guys in the band, it was like family in every way. I knew Trummy before, but I never worked with him until I went with Louis. Trummy would always come around where Ory was playing, not to sit in but to hang out. One time in San Francisco he came around and we all got drunk together. Trummy was a real family man. You wouldn't think it, but Billy Kyle was one of the funniest guys, had a helluva great sense of humor. He was a terrific cartoonist, drew a picture of me playing my clarinet. When we went to Japan and somebody would ask him for his autograph, he'd write it in Japanese and they'd be flabbergasted. He was from Virginia and he told me when he was young his people was awful poor. They lived on a farm and he said they couldn't afford shoes, always ate good but they just couldn't afford shoes. If they was going out on a Saturday night, they'd dress up in the best clothes they had and get a bottle of shoe polish, apply that polish to their feet and shine 'em up. He said they looked real good. That story would kill me, it was so funny. Billy had an aunt in Detroit and, whenever we got ready to leave, she would always give Billy two shoe boxes of fried chicken and biscuits and honey. Delicious. We all looked forward to that.

I think it was in 1962 that we worked with Louis on the "Mike Douglas Show" for TV that was out of Cleveland. He was on that show for the whole week. First off, they would have a little round-table discussion, and they got Louis on there along with a news commentator named Alex Lomax that was originally from Georgia but came to live in Los Angeles. He had practically called Louis an Uncle Tom and Louis resented that. Lomax always said he would show Louis up for what he was and, sure enough, we was all anticipating this debate between the two of them. From the start they pretended to be the best of friends, wasn't no animosity shown, talking and laughing, shaking hands, when Lomax says, "I gotta ask you something, Louis. What about your younger days in New Orleans? I've heard you say you got along well with them white folks and you never had a lick of trouble. Seems to me you the only one that ever fooled with white folks down South and didn't have any trouble. I'm from down there and I know they give me and all other black men a lot of headaches. How come you could get along with them so good?" Louis says, "Well, they hired us for their lawn parties and different things. I just played my music and got along with them white people. They had nothing to say to me but they paid me. I got right in there with them." So Lomax looked at Louis and he says, "Well, let me ask you something else. Suppose you was playing at the Louisiana Country Club, exclusive for Louisiana society. Now, I'm acquainted that you can go in those clubs by the back door, but could you and your wife have walked in the front door, whatever was going on?" Louis looked at him straight in the eye and he says, "Alex, I don't know, I wasn't married then." Louis got out of that clean. People applauded and Alex must have been cursing under his breath. We was backstage digging all this.

The girl on the "Mike Douglas Show" was always looking for people that did unusual things to make the show different, and she asked Louis if any of the musicians had any unusual hobbies. "I gotta lot of them likes to drink whiskey and chase women, but my clarinet man is a good cook. He cooks for me all the time, New Orleans style." It seemed to them it might be a good idea to have me cooking on the show. I made them out a list of ingredients, came out at 300 dollars, and that was their budget for the whole month. I put about 20 pounds of lobster meat on it, to make some real gumbo. They put me in a chef's hat and in a long white apron. Had a great big bowl cooking. I'd cook and then they'd call me to go join the band and I'd be playing still dressed like a chef. Then I'd run back, cut up some stuff, cook some more and then play another song. Just before the show was due to finish I had the stuff all cooked and it dawned on me I better get my share right now, along with some for Louis, before they pass it out to the audience and the stage hands. So I got a big bowl and a choice piece of lobster, some crab and gumbo, and I was eating fast, my back to the audience. Suddenly I hear everybody laughin' like hell and I happened to turn round real slow; seems they had the goddam cameras beamed in on me while I was there eating like crazy. Man, I was wailin' on that stuff. Louis said, "Look at that cat go. Damn, home boy, you look out for yourself, save me some."

Helen saw the show up in Ohio where she was visiting her folks, said it was a fabulous thing. I run into Hamp afterwards, out at Lake Tahoe, and he says, "I saw you on TV. My mouth was watering, man. Now, you ain't never paid me the money for breaking that head on my drum at the Vernon Country Club and here I am in this little old place playing and I'm hungry. I'm watching that show and you made all that gumbo and stuff on there, I could have killed you right then. I couldn't get nothing to eat and you was up there pulling all that shit!" They've shown that show on a rerun about five times since.

People ask me where the cooking started. It comes from when I was a kid when we'd go camping. These old gals would be cooking and I could cook better than them. I always did like cooking, even though the other kids called me a sissy a few times and I had to whale in on 'em. They never called me that no more. When I played violin I got in some fights; they'd say the violin was a girl's thing. When I went out on the road, the cooking came in handy. This was one thing that helped seal my friendship with Louis, he liked my cooking. Every time I went to New York I'd go out to his house and cook.

We worked on Ed Sullivan's TV show a couple of times, but from Germany. Some people didn't like Ed, thought he was kinda stuffy, but I found out he was one of the nicest guys. We was over there with Maureen O'Hara and that girl vocalist Connie Francis, plus some current big singers and these comedians Rowan and Martin. I was impressed by how much Louis was liked in Europe. Every place we played there'd be crowds, and usually at the airports they'd have a dixieland band. We got to Berlin and we could see a bunch of people out by the runway. The guys in the band start laughin' and Danny says, "Lord, there's old Lady Goldenlocks with the same flowers we have all the time." I couldn't figure out what they was saying about these flowers. She was the German promoter, had booked all of Louis's tours and every time she'd be at the airport to meet him with a big bouquet of artificial flowers – same bunch all the time – to give to Louis. After they'd taken pictures she'd take the flowers back and put them in mothballs until the next time. She had the biggest diamond on her finger I'd ever seen and a million dollars in the bank!

Of course we did a lot of TV and made that Goodyear commercial in New York in 1962, but during my time Louis did less recording than at any stage of his career. In three years we made only one album and that was the *Hello Dolly* album. We also did *The Real Ambassadors* record with Dave Brubeck that featured the combined bands, plus Carmen McRae. Dave and his wife Iola wrote this musical based on Louis's life, and, by them being booked by ABC (Joe Glaser), too, that was a means of them producing it. They talked to Joe about it and he was all for it. The first thing we did was to make the album. I thought it was pretty good, and then we played some parts of it at the Monterey Festival in September 1962 and it was well received. I think it would have been a great play if Louis had lived. They would have probably eventually produced it on Broadway. Of course Dave Brubeck played an altogether different type of music from what I was playing. He had his own style.

The rest of the time we just went on playing one-nighters. Had some pretty crazy distances to travel. I know one time we flew from New York to Copenhagen for a few days just to play at the Tivoli Gardens for their anniversary, but the biggest jump we ever made was from Tokyo, Japan, to Houston, Texas, for some big oil tycoon's daughter's party at the Shamrock Hotel in Murchison. Then we played out at the Anheuser-Busch family estate for a big party. They're the ones that own Budweiser, which is probably the biggest selling beer in the USA – in the world for that matter. There's several brothers and it was Auguste Busch that hired Louis. He had set aside his trophy room for the band and he had four or five waiters there just to take care of us. Had a big buffet dinner set up. When we got there the head waiter says, "Welcome, Satchmo, to the Anheuser-Busch Estate on behalf of Mr Auguste Busch. His instructions are that you are to have the run of the place, anything you want. Your least wish is my command. We got all kind of liquor here." They had a bar like you'd find in an embassy, every kind of liquor you could mention. It was the summertime and you can get hotter than hell in St Louis in summer, so Louis says, "All I want is a cold bottle of Bud." The waiter went in back of the bar and he's searching. Pretty soon he comes out and says, "Satchmo, I don't know how to tell you this, that damn bus-boy forgot to put any Budweiser in here. Mr Busch will fire us all if he finds out about this. We'll get some." Louis let out a big belly laugh. "I'll be damned, here's this cat tells me I can have anything that's my heart's desire and they ain't got a bottle to give me, and this is the biggest brewery in the world." Louis never got over that.

In 1963 we went to New Zealand and Australia and I was thrilled to go. We caught a plane to Los Angeles and flew from there to New Zealand. Helen was home so I had a chance to spend a day with her. The next day we left for Auckland, had to stop over in Hawaii, and that's where I met Danny Barcelona's mother and brother. We had just about three hours on the ground. We flew into Christchurch, played the Theatre Royal, then we played Wellington for three days, then on to Dunedin City Hall. We met a lot of great musicians there before we went to Auckland for four days. From there we went to Brisbane, Australia, on March 24th. I went to one of the sanctuaries they have for those cute koala bears and I had a picture taken with a little koala. I wrote Helen I'd be bringing one back home; she said to forget it.

Then we went to Perth, which is one of the prettiest cities in the world to my idea. Imagine my surprise when we got off the plane at Sydney and we ran into Acker Bilk. He was just finishing up a tour. We had quite a time, so much so that Acker almost missed his plane. He was telling me how much he liked my *Lou-easy-an-ia*, recorded it a couple of times. We really had a ball, that was the first time I met Acker.

The Australian tour was wonderful. We met Graeme Bell and a lot of other musicians, prominent guys, and Graeme took us out for dinner. We really had a great time in Sydney, stayed there several days. We sat in with quite a lot of Australian musicians and I was very impressed. Great guys. From there we went on to Singapore, where we stayed overnight but didn't play, although we found a bunch of good musicians and jammed. Then we flew to Hong Kong and from there to Korea, where we stayed for about nine days. Every place we went the musicians just loved Louis. They couldn't have picked a better ambassador. Through being with Louis, we got VIP treatment. You tell somebody you work with Louis Armstrong and that was it. You was respected, people took care of you. No doubt about it, it was a peak.

Korea was something special. We stayed in Seoul almost two weeks. Pugh and I were down-town one day picking up some souvenirs at a department store and one of the English-speaking girls that was writing articles on us started asking us where we was from, so to amuse ourselves I said, "We're from the United States but I have here a very distinguished Korean doctor. I would like you to meet Dr Kim Lee." See, we tried to fit the name to the country we were in so, naturally, everybody in Korea is Kim or Lee or something. I got a kick out of the expressions on these people's faces. The girls started bowing and then Doc starts talking Korean – anyway, it sounded like Korean. Pretty soon everybody in this store had gathered round Doc and I. The people was trying to make out what the hell he was saying so they followed us out in the street and, believe me, we stopped the traffic. Pugh was still talking and a couple of traffic cops was trying to understand what he was saying; he almost got put in one of those Korean jails. Funnier than hell.

I don't know if you ever heard of the Walker Hill Hotel in Seoul? America had a lot of servicemen stationed over in Korea and one of their big bases was right out of Seoul. When the servicemen would have time off they'd save up some money and fly over to the Japanese mainland to spend their loot. Park Lee and the politicians and some of the army brass figured that they would build a Vegas-type spread in Korea. That way they could probably keep the servicemen there. They got an appropriation from the US Government of something like 50 million dollars and this Walker Hill spread was built on about 100 acres of land, just like Vegas – a complex of hotels and motels. They built roads and they even brought in gamblers from Vegas to teach the Koreans; had slot machines, too. Have you heard of the Kim Sisters, which is one of your top acts in America? They're from Seoul and they had a whole gang of brothers still living in Korea. One of them was the choreographer at the hotel. They had a pit band of about 15 terrific musicians, some of them pretty good jazz players. We all used to have sessions together.

Still, this was one of the big rip-offs of the American Government and a real unhappy experience for us. For one thing, this spread was supposed to have been built for all servicemen, but only officers could get in; you had to be an officer or somebody with influence to get in the damn place. They had a big scandal in Congress about this. What disgusted us was playing for the Korean and the army brass. We hardly got any applause at all. Usually every place Louis played you know the applause he'd get, but we'd be playing our hearts out and these damn officers would be too busy talking to each other. I've never seen Louis so disgusted and finally he said, "I'll be glad when this goddam job is over with. I'm gonna quit going on these American Government things. We have to be crazy to be doing this."

A guy took us out to a place where they had a lot of Korean call-girls. Everything was on the house, except the girls. If you wanted a girl you had to pay by the hour to take her upstairs. I won't call the musician's name but he took one of the girls with him back to the hotel and, like I said, you paid by the hour and he kept her the rest of the night. We had left the place at four in the morning and he kept her until six o'clock in the afternoon, until just before we had to go to work. The next thing I know, nine of the biggest pimps in Seoul came out to the hotel and got this guy from the band and threatened to throw him in the river or else pay for what he got. Cost him over a hundred dollars.

One thing about Korea which was a pleasant surprise was the food in the hotel, which was out of this world. Next to New Orleans, Korea has the best seafood we ever tasted. They had fire-cooked oysters, trout, even beautiful cat-fish, which is my favorite fish – all white meat and no bones. They had lobster and great big shrimps, about eight inches long. That was about the only thing I enjoyed about this whole damn trip. About two years after I left Louis I read that the US Government had stopped all the funds for Walker Hill and they showed everything was closed. Grass was growing ten feet high around the place that was so beautiful when I was there. One of the real bad things.

After Korea we went to Tokyo, which is real nice. I had been to Tokyo and Hong Kong when I used to ship out on the ocean liners in the thirties, but there'd been quite a change. We had a press conference in the Latin Quarter in Tokyo and that's where Louis had a ball dancing with a little Japanese princess. They had a band there called the Glenn Miller of Japan led by a white American; sounded exactly like Miller, used all Miller's book, tunes like String of Pearls. Then we went to Nagoya and a bunch of one-nighters, including Yokohama. From there we flew to Hawaii, where I had a reunion with Eddie Cole of the Two Hot Coles, which was a big attraction in Honolulu. Trummy was well known there, too, because he'd been living there just before he went with Louis. He had this disc-jockey show where he used to sign off "Aloha, you-all." We came back to San Francisco, Helen met us there, and then we went on some more one-nighters.

Billy Kyle was a great collector of pornographic pictures and he had a mass of them coming back from the Orient. When you get to Honolulu you have to go through customs and they ask if you have anything to declare. Billy said, no, but he had forgotten all about these books and pictures, right on top of his luggage. When they opened his suitcase they saw this stuff and Billy says, "I forgot about that." The customs official was a funny guy and he just took his time looking at every picture until finally he looked at Billy and shook his finger. "Naughty, naughty, naughty," he says, but he kept the pictures.

We made Hello Dolly in New York in December 1963 before starting out on tour again. We had a lead sheet, Billy wrote some backgrounds for Trummy and me, we made the record and completely forgot about it – didn't play it again.

About three weeks later we wound up in San Juan, Puerto Rico, around Christmas, and while we were there *Hello Dolly* started making the charts in America. The office called and told the road manager to get Louis to start playing *Hello Dolly* if he wasn't already doing it. We'd all forgot it. Bob, the band boy, had lost the lead sheet, so Louis says, "Any of you guys remember this damn tune?" Billy could only remember some parts, so we had to run all around San Juan trying to find the single. Couldn't find it, so they had to fly one out of New York to us and we listened to it. Then we started playing it and the very first time Louis did it on stage in Hotel San Juan he had to take about eight curtain calls, so he knew right then he had a hit. They wouldn't let him off the stage. It was his big number from then on and he started liking it, singing it, kept improvising on it and he'd even do a little dancing to it.

A lot of people thought *A Lot of Living* was a better number than *Hello Dolly*. Matter of fact, I did, too. At the recording session Jack Kapp, the owner of the record company, and his son were there and they wasn't satisfied with *Dolly*. "You know what we ought to do on this thing? It needs something to pep it up or perk it up a little." Somebody in the band said, "Why don't you try banjo, put something in there in front that's unusual, might fit in." They had a banjo player that lived close and they got hold of him. That's how that banjo part happened to come in there – just a second thought. I think it helped the record some.

We closed at the Hotel San Juan for New Year's Day 1964, and that was Trummy's last night with the band. His wife Sally was from Honolulu and she had gone back there to live because they had a little girl and she wanted to raise her in Honolulu. She practically gave Trummy an ultimatum but Joe Glaser wanted to keep him. Although Trummy was making a lot of money in that band, he wanted to go home. Joe kept saying he couldn't get anybody, that it was for Trummy to stay just two more weeks, but finally he left the band. He rode back on the plane with us and he said, "This is it." He had talked on the phone with Sally and made up his mind that night. "I just want to tell you guys goodbye. I won't see you in New York." That was the last time I seen Trummy for a long time. I think he had put in his notice six months before.

About three months after *Hello Dolly* was definitely a hit we made the balance of the album in Las Vegas with Big Chief Russell Moore on trombone. I had met the Chief before when he was with Louis's big band and then he was around Los Angeles for a while. He was also a pretty good piano player, something like Meade "Lux" Lewis. He could play jazz, dixieland or ragtime. He also said he had a brother that was very good, but I didn't know him. Chief played with Luis Russell, too; good trombone man. He had been working with Lester Lanin's society orchestra in New York and he more or less joined Louis as a spite deal. He asked Lanin for a raise and Lester wouldn't give it to him, so the Chief told Lanin he was gonna leave the band. In the meantime he was offered the chance to go with Louis. The Chief didn't really want to go on the road 'cause he was a little too heavy, it was uncomfortable for him to travel. He weighed like 350 to 400 pounds, believed in eating! We'd get off work at night, and he carried a little electric pot in which you could heat soup or chili so we'd eat in the room after the show. We always had a ball eating that stuff. "Our little picnic," says the Chief. We used to get a lot of cheese, crackers and canned goods. Billy Kyle would come back with two whole bags of shopping. When Billy quit drinking he started eating a lot. When I was in the band Billy didn't drink at all, on account he had been sick.

Anyway, after the Chief left Lanin's band Lester really missed him 'cause he was an asset to the band. He did things in that band which people liked – little comedy routines. Finally Lester Lanin gave him the money he wanted, and Chief went back shortly after I left Louis. He was still working with Lanin the last I heard. Lanin just plays dances and he has several bands that he sends out under his name. He's the biggest booker of bands in New York; in fact he sends bands clear to California.

The Chief is a full-blooded Pima Indian and we got a booking in Window Rock, Arizona, which is a reservation for the Pimas. You never seen so many Indians; they turned out in droves to see this guy. He's a kind of hero among his people for being a top-rated musician. They come to see the Chief and the Chief really performed. They brought him a big headdress, put it on him, made him a honorary chief – and Louis, too, for that matter. That was the Chief's night. Louis never cared about that, it never bothered him; all he wanted you to do was to be on that stage and play. The Chief had played around St Louis and he knew Arvell Shaw when he was real young, about 17 or 18 years old.

I'd have stayed with Louis longer than I did if I hadn't got sick. I got some sort of bladder infection and it developed into a large prostate deal. One time in London my water just stopped and Doc Schiff had to rush me into hospital. After that I was all right until we got to Stockholm and it happened again. Doc said I should see a neurologist when I got home, and when I did they said I had to have an operation. Joe Glaser wanted me to take off, have the operation and come back, but I told him, no. By this time I was tired of the road, so I turned in my notice in Sparks, Nevada, at a place called The Nugget, but I must have worked another six or eight weeks after that. It was three months before I could make my move. See, if Louis got along with you, Joe never wanted you to leave the band. If Louis was happy, Joe would do anything to keep the band like it was.

We were set to play the New York World's Fair in July, on the Singer exhibit, and I had told Joe to have a replacement clarinet player, but he didn't believe me. I got up there and he said he'd been talking to a couple of guys but couldn't get them, so would I stay for a couple of weeks. I had become friends with Kenny Davern when we run into him in Vegas, when he was with the Dukes of Dixieland; so I brought Kenny over to see Joe, but they couldn't get on friendly terms. And then Joe talked to Tony Parenti, but he wanted 900 dollars a week. Joe said that was more than he paid Jack Teagarden, so no deal. After that I just flat out told Joe, "I said, when I got to New York it was my last job." First off, Joe said, "If you're not gonna play this job I'm not gonna pay your transportation back home," so I told him to go to hell and I would pay my own fare. "Although I can go to the Musicians' Union and they'll make you pay it." That's the rules, 'cause I had given him legitimate notice three months before. I had given Louis notice and the office, so it wasn't one of those spur of the moment deals. Joe knew it and he says, "Well, I'm just kidding. You know I'm gonna send you back home. We love you." All that shit. Later they got Eddie Shu. He was actually a tenor man, did some stuff with Gene Krupa – hadn't played any of our music at all. I found out afterwards that Eddie's dad was a friend of Joe's or some connection like that. Joe says, "Would it be all right if Eddie brought his clarinet up there and you give him some pointers on the show?" Of course, I was glad to do that.

It hurt me to leave the band but in a way I was glad 'cause I was tired and sick. At first I signed up for a year but stayed on account of Louis. I liked him and I thought about the financial security, too. I wasn't a guy to go out and drink and that made me useful in the band. In fact I only got drunk once, in Baltimore, when I met a bartender I knew in Seattle: I was sick for three days. Anyway, I left finally and came home, three years almost to the day after I joined.

After I came out of the band it seemed as though Louis went pretty good for a while and then he started getting sick himself. We went to see him a couple of times in Las Vegas and up to Lake Tahoe where we had dinner with him. The last time I seen him he was pretty sick, looked bad, just skin and bones. I put my arms around him and he was so skinny. That was sad.

This was at the big "Seventieth Birthday Tribute" here in Los Angeles which they put on for Louis. They had Hoagy Carmichael, Johnny Green – the guy that wrote *Body and Soul* – the mayor, Joe Bushkin, Maxim Saury and a whole band from France. We had a cake for him ten feet tall; you had to get a ladder to get to the top. The French cats had brought Louis a bottle of wine that was bottled in 1890. Louis was hurtin', but you wouldn't know it when he came out on stage. Him and Hoagy did a little thing together on *Rockin' Chair*, both of them sitting in rocking chairs. Louis thanked the people. He still had the same bright disposition when he got on the stage. He was a hard guy to show emotion but we went backstage and he was emotionally affected, no doubt about that. Naturally, the house was packed.

I had seen him, when he was working with Pearl Bailey, walk out on stage and almost fall down before trying to play. Sad. I didn't want to see him that way but that's actually what he wanted to do, to cut out still blowing, and a few months later he was gone. People said I should go to his funeral and Buddy Burns wanted to pay my way, but I didn't want to go.

My time with Louis gave me security, like I said before, the chance to pick my spots. I didn't *have* to go back to Disneyland if I didn't want to. So as quickly as I got back to Los Angeles I talked to my doctor and arranged to have the operation. It seems as though 80 percent of men after a certain age will get that kind of problem. After that I went to work for an old craftsman named Dominick Colicio. I had decided I wanted to learn how to repair instruments. Really I preferred to learn about reed instruments, but I didn't find anybody that was interested in teaching me. I knew Dominick slightly and he says, "Why don't you let me learn you how to make horns?" Dominick had a fully fledged factory in Hollywood, so I decided to go to work with him. I don't know why, I just wanted something different. I quit playing music, except for a few gigs on the side whenever something good came up. Dominick made trumpets and trombones; some musicians said they was the best in the business. In fact LeBlanc offered him a lot of money to come take care of their plant, designing trumpets. So I worked around Dominick, learning how to make horns and the basics of repairing them.

Dominick was quite a funny guy. The first thing he says to me was, "Now, Joe, you coming to work for me, I'm gonna teach you the business and I want you to learn the customer is *never* right. Remember that." He repaired horns for other different music stores, some from as far away as New York, San Francisco and Seattle. In their eyes Dominick was the only man they wanted to work on them. This poor guy that had a music store in Fullerton, not far from Disneyland, brought in seven horns for Dominick to repair and relacquer, buff, replace the springs, take care of the valves, that sort of thing. Of course he had a list of these horns, that included a Conn, a Buescher and a Benge, which is a helluva good instrument. We had these big vats of pure acid where you dipped the horn for about half a minute to strip the old lacquer off. Anyway, Dominick stuck the Benge in the vat, which was right by the phone. The phone rang, and, instead of counting to 30, he forgot this horn was in the acid and went home. The next day, when Dominick came to look, all that was left was the little mother-of-pearl inlays from the valves. It didn't seem to worry him, 'cause when I got there he says, "D'you wanta buy a trumpet?" and he had these inlays in his hand. Sure enough, the fellow from Fullerton that brought in the seven horns came back a week later and he says, "Well, here's the Beuscher, the Conn, the Martin, the York . . .," and so forth. "Six horns, but where's the Benge?" So Dominick says, "What Benge?" and the guy wants to show him his list but Dominick repeats his story, "It's a mistake, you know I wouldn't do anything like that. Ask Joe here, he's got an honest face, he ain't gonna tell anything wrong." When he got through bullshitting that man, he put a doubt in his mind about this Benge, a 400-dollar trumpet, convinced him that he never brought that trumpet in there. They guy left and paid, thanked Dominick, who says, "That's all right, you gonna find that horn when you get back to your store."

Dominick made horns from scratch, had all the lathes and everything to cut the sheets of brass and shine 'em, all the benders to bend all these shapes. The only thing we bought was the springs and the valves; they was already made up. All the trumpet players knew Dominick. Conrad Gozzo, one of the greatest trumpet men you ever heard, was an alcoholic, and Dominick used to have to loan him horns to play. Always had a bunch of trumpets around there. Gozzo's horn would be in hock, even though he was in demand; he used to make 75,000 dollars a year in the studios, but he died flat broke. He was rated over Mannie Klein when he was in his prime. Dominick would almost cry to see him. He loved Gozzo 'cause he was Italian. We had to play a benefit for him.

I was with Dominick for over a year and I got so I could repair horns, could have opened me a repair store. Finally Harvey Brooks came in one day wanting to buy a trumpet for his nephew – called him Li'l Louie – and he says, "I told Li'l Louie you used to work with Louis and would pick him out a good trumpet." And that's when Harvey starts talking to me about coming back to Disneyland, to work with the Young Men from New Orleans.

I lost sight of Dominick from then on. The last time I seen him they had made a story of his life on film, called it *The Last of the Great Craftsmen*. He was always on to me to come back and manage the store. Then he died a few years back. His daughter and her husband run the store and the factory now. They called me up, I guess they were surprised that I wasn't at the funeral, told me that Dominick thought a lot of me and asked me to come and see the remodeled factory.

I went back to work on the *Mark Twain*. They had a bass player by then. Johnny St Cyr had died and they never put a banjo back in, and when Monette Moore died they put a trombone in there, too. Either that or they had a trombone when they didn't have a bass, 'cause Streamline Ewing worked with us sometimes. Mike was still there and when he got sick we used Blakeney on trumpet. Harvey got sick, too, and then we used Purnell for a while. Old Redd was still there all this time. After Sammy Lee they had Polo Barnes; he used to come up here and play during the season, then go back to New Orleans after the season ended. I took Polo's place.

The band wasn't too good. In the first place, when Johnny St Cyr was there he played a six-string guitar-banjo, which had a tone like beating on a washtub – one of the loudest tones you ever heard in your life. Harvey was a kinda pain in the ass playing piano, wanted to play the lead all the time and didn't play enough rhythm, so, with Redd on drums, sometimes these guys almost drove me nuts. But I had made up my mind. "Oh well, I'll stay here and get me a little security." I wanted to be doing something. I had got tired at Dominick's, working in the daytime, going round there. At first it was kinda fun and I learned a lot, but I needed a change.

The Disneyland hours was the same; same old bullshit, only the personnel changed. The season ran from June 20th to around September 20th. That was when they would have the "Dixieland at Disneyland" for one day and then the season would end, but we'd always have something to do at Disneyland every week, even during the off-season. A lot of organizations, like the Elks, or some bank chain, like the Bank of America, would lease the park out for the day. They would take it over, everybody would pay like ten dollars and then the rides and everything was free after that. They had to guarantee a minimum number of 10,000 people. If you wanted something to eat, then you would have to pay for it. Through this kind of thing we'd work out at the park two or three days a week for these specials, which paid pretty good, and with the other gigs I got that carried me in the off-time. Anyway, once you were out there you could file for your unemployment and be paid like 60 or 70 dollars a week. I stayed at Disneyland from 1966 to 1969. We never did make records, though we talked about it. They was on the verge of doing it several times but something always happened to stop it. I think they was waiting on Disney having his own label. They could have sold a lot of records.

Harvey died in 1968 and they put Redd in as the leader of the group. I didn't like that. Redd wasn't a musician; you put a note as big as a clock up there in front of him and he didn't know what it was. He wanted me and him to be co-leaders, but I said, "With me, I'll either be the leader or nothing. I ain't gonna be any co-leader. You call the tunes." In fact Redd told the guys in charge, "I don't think I'm the guy for the job." However, he stayed there.

When they brought Kid Ory back to play with us at Disneyland, it was like hell. Ory couldn't do nothing, couldn't blow his nose. He was senile even, and I remember that goddam Barbara bawling there, she was just as nutty as a fruitcake herself. He had on one black sock and one brown one. Poor guy, he asked me to tie his shoes and I started telling him to tie his own goddam shoe, 'cause I really had lost all respect for him. I was thinking of the things he did to Dort; it wasn't just because he fired me, I had forgot all about that. Dort was nice to everybody and she told Barney that Ory would get mad at her just before he left her; just as an excuse to try to justify to her that he was leaving for a reason he accused her of having an affair with us, that's Barney and me. Now when I first went to work with Ory I had access to a lot of money, 'cause I was going with Gladys, but Ory didn't have a shitting ass thing and Dort had to go out to work just to make ends meet. You'd think that sonofabitch, after he was making a little money, would want to make her comfortable in her old age when she wasn't well. Instead he walked off, took all the money and tried to take the house away from her; he sure did. Him and Barney was bosom buddies but Barney got so he wouldn't speak to him. I wouldn't go to his funeral. Ory tried to be chummy with me at Disneyland but he'd got so his mind was wandering. The night he played with us Helen came out there, and, as well as he knew her, he couldn't recognize Helen. God knows, he couldn't play anything. It was a helluva sad situation, yet, regardless of what a sonofabitch he was, that Ory name still sold, had some value. People didn't know the shit he had dished out to other people.

Then they started making changes at Disneyland, put a new director in and he had his own ideas; he took the band out altogether. I was gonna leave anyway, I had got tired. Then Sonny Anderson called me to organize a new band to take out to Disneyland. This was a six-piece and he just wanted me to pick whoever I wanted. They built New Orleans Square in the meantime and they needed a band for that. Disneyland always named things according to what they wanted, so we were the Delta Rhythm Kings. Since the guys from the Young Men wasn't working, I said I'd bring part of that band in there. I had Mike, Purnell, Jake Flores on trombone and Redd on drums. I never would have had him but they asked me to try to fit him in. See, the *Mark Twain* was still going but they didn't have regular musicians on it like they had before. They'd pick musicians out of the concert big band, guys that played dixieland, the good ones that had a feeling for it, call them the Strawhatters and put them in the *Mark Twain*. Once in a while they'd ask me to play. They usually had a parade every day but my band never marched. We rode on a little fire truck while other musicians like Jackie Coon had to march and blow in that hot sun. Dick Cary had a combo, marching, and some guy hit his lip; it got sore and never healed up. Wherever they wanted you to play they would tell you to play, but mostly our deal was for New Orleans Square. That went along for most of a whole season.

On bass I had a guy called Irv for a while, then Bernie Miller came in; he'd been with Artie Shaw and all those bands. Adolphus Morris, who's with Barry Martyn now, played with us for quite a while, as did Bernard Carriere. Adolphus is from Chicago, plays pretty good. Bernard is from New Orleans, had an awful lot of trouble with his legs. I played with him in August 1979 at the Festival in MacArthur Park. Jake Flores is pretty good; played a long time with Wingy and I think in the early days he played with Paul Whiteman. He used to do a little floorshow. He's Mexican. Mike is a good guy to have with you; there's not many trumpet players can outblow him and he can play a little piano, plus he's a good bass player. I just wish he'd tend to business and not talk so goddam much. He'd just as like do anything for you – nice guy. Mike's been having a helluva lot of trouble with his legs, phlebitis, just like Louis. His legs is hot all the time.

Then I got in a big humbug with Disneyland about the sun. This was in the summertime, hotter than hell, so I told them I wanted a canopy up over the bandstand to shield the men in the band. Old Redd and Purnell almost had a stroke a couple of times 'cause the sun was so hot. It would beam down on you and we couldn't take it. In the end I went and put a suit against them at the International Federation of Musicians. They got mad at me and wanted to give us two weeks' notice right away. They had agreed for us to play a certain length of time but somehow or other we didn't sign a contract, but I told them it was a verbal deal and I wouldn't let them let us go. Finally we worked out our time and I left.

I went to talk to Tranchitella, used to be president of Local 47, but the suit failed for the simple reason that I couldn't get Mike or any of them to sign the complaint. They said, "No, they might want to rehire us some time." Disneyland has a sheet where they put the names of guys they don't want back. Behind your name they write "NR: No Rehire." I was sick with it anyway. I was simply trying to make conditions better for the next musicians that came in behind me. I had got tired of that long drive but I stayed friends with them anyway. Sonny Anderson, him and I always got along fine, it was just the big wheels that didn't treat musicians too good.

Every Tuesday and Friday the people at Disney's studio, the animators and cartoonists that can play music, they have a session for about an hour. We got out there sometimes – Pete Daily, Nappy, Roy Brewer – had fun and made a lot of friends. I came out of Disneyland and started just gigging around with Nappy and different guys, going out of town once in a while. Nappy and I worked steady together from 1970 on. We went into the Calabassas Inn with a trio. That was Nappy's job. That's a beautiful place, like a big restaurant out near the motion picture actors' homes. We had a real nice deal out there, just for three nights a week. Bill Campbell was on piano, Art Anton was the drummer, and then we changed, had several good drummers. All the best musicians would come and sit in – guys like Matty, Barney, Eddie Miller – had a lot of great jam sessions. We got all we wanted to eat and drink, made like 150 dollars for the three nights, plus tips. We were there a long time, around eight months I guess. From then we never did look for a steady job, although I got a group together with Dick Cary and Nick Fatool to play at Howard Rumsey's "Concerts by the Sea." Howard was a bass player that used to be with Stan Kenton; he had a place called The Lighthouse with the drummer Shelly Manne, then he opened his own club at Redondo Beach. I used different guys: Ray Sherman played piano sometimes, and Bill Campbell; Abe Lincoln was on trombone and I had a drummer named Rich Parnell. It was a full band. For some reason we always had problems with that damn place.

Around that time Nappy and I worked for Mike Riley again. We was hired to play a couple of nights a week at his place in Pasadena, along with Rico Valese. Mike wanted us to come in as partners – me, Nappy and Rico – but we found out he had a couple of lawsuits going, a couple of gals was sueing him, and we knew we'd have to help pay the damages if he lost these suits so we told him, no. We just simply went to work for him and that's all it was. Mike was still one of the funniest comedians you ever seen. He would start playing *The Saints* and march right into the women's dressing room and goose them with the end of his trombone slide. Mike had some damn good musicians working for him at one time or another, guys like Jackie Coon on trumpet and a little piano player, used to be with Pete Daily, named Bugs Eye Skippy Anderson. Terrific musician, he was the chief arranger, had big eyes that kinda bugged out. On drums we had Charlie Lodice, he worked with us a lot; he's with Pete Fountain now. The last I heard of Mike Riley was when I played with him at the Musicians' Festival in MacArthur Park in August 1979. Amazing talent.

After that Warren Smith, who had played with me in the Dixie Flyers, got a gig down at Del Mar for the race season. Del Mar is the racetrack that Bing Crosby and another movie star owned at one time in the 1930s. A friend of Smitty's was managing a place there called the Steak House and they wanted a band to play during the race meeting. We went down there for the whole season; lasted about eight weeks. On that job Marvin Ash was the piano player, with Lou Diamond on drums, Smitty on trombone, Nappy and me; no trumpet – just Smitty and me in the front line. When that finished we went back to gigging around Los Angeles. The following year the guy decided he didn't want Smitty back and he asked me to get a group. That's when I got a trio with Lou and Bob Marquis, a good piano player out of Tucson, Arizona. As to Lou, I'd been working with him off and on for a long time. In the Dixie Flyers, he came in instead of Alton Redd and then Alton came in after Lou. He had played with Gus Arnheim, Teagarden and Red Nichols. Lou was one fine drummer, among the best. He died in 1973. Nappy played with us just on weekends. Originally I wasn't called for the job because they got a good trumpet player named John Findlay and he was due to put a band in there. John used to sit in, in fact he played with Smitty's band regularly on the weekends. Anyway, he got hooked up at Disneyland and he couldn't get away, so I got the job. It was wonderful. We'd go out to the racetrack every day, gamble and lose all our money!

One of the conditions for me to go there was that Helen and I would have a nice place to stay. She couldn't come and stay all week 'cause she didn't want to leave our animals, but she would come weekends with Nappy's wife, Alice. Don, the manager of the Steak House, leased this mansion for us from some people that was in Europe for the summer. It overlooked the bay, you could almost see San Diego only 15 miles away, and they had great iceboxes which Don stocked with filet mignon steaks, lobsters and everything good to eat. Lou was a helluva big eater, but after we'd been there about two weeks he says, "Goddam, I'm tired of all this lobster and stuff. I gotta have something simple to eat." To tell you the truth, I felt the same way. Up to that time I hadn't cooked any red beans and rice 'cause we thought we'd have a ball on all that lobster and steak, but finally I told Don, "Look, Don, quit bringing us all this lobster, just bring us some hot dogs and hamburger." And he did! Around San Diego is terrific for crawfish; you could go out and catch a ton of crawfish in no time. We'd boil 'em, make gumbo, get some beer and have a lot of fun.

The Steak House was an eating place where they had like a club with its own dance floor. We got a lot of the big-name jockeys in there, including Willie Shoemaker. The whole deal was owned by a couple of jockeys and Don made money all right, but he'd go play the horses and lose everything. The owners wasn't paying no attention to all this, and when they come to find out, the whole damn place was bankrupt.

The first time I ever remember talking to Barry Martyn was when we brought Louis to Los Angeles for that 70th birthday celebration. Barry was there with his band of Englishmen and I had organized a group with Mike DeLay and Alton Redd. Barry asked if I'd be interested in going to Europe and I told him, yes. The next thing I know I got this call from Barry and Floyd Levin telling me they was organizing this band, calling it the Legends of Jazz, intending to go to Europe. Their first choice for clarinet really was Albert Nicholas, since he was already over in Europe. I don't know why he didn't join. In the first place I told Barry I wasn't particular about going over there on one-nighters, but if he got anything here in the States I would work it, for a while anyway. However, I agreed to tour with him and it was very enjoyable, except the first trip which was almost a tragedy. I got pneumonia in England and a guy named Dave Bennett happened to be there and practically saved my life, took me into his home and into hospital, which I really appreciated. Did me a heck of a favor in fact. I'll always think of him and be grateful. Dave has been a good friend. I stayed with him a couple of weeks and since then we've been back to Europe, taken a trip to Belgium together, and I stayed with him again. The second European concert tour with the Legends was very nice. I was OK then.

I already knew everybody in the Legends band and had played with them, except Louis Nelson and Barry himself. I knew of Louis – good trombone player and a very nice guy. Of course, I'd been knowing old Tudi since I was a kid around New Orleans when he used to drive a barrel-wagon. In those days, all beer used to be in wooden barrels and his job was to pick up the empties, take them back to the brewery and get them refilled. Later I worked with Tudi in Los Angeles at the taxi-dance, and we had those years with Ory, so, naturally, we was friends. In fact I worked a job with Tudi just recently in a band called Roger Jamieson's New Orleanians. Roger's a nice guy, plays trombone like Kid Ory. He had Billy Hadnott on bass and that great guitar player Everett Barksdale. That was the first time I had played with Everett and I'm looking forward to working with him again. It's a pleasure to run into musicians like that. I've played with a lot of guitar players, like George Barnes, Lonnie Johnson and even T-Bone Walker. I played around Los Angeles with T-Bone just before I went with Joe Liggins. I played every type of music you can think about.

With the Legends, we never had a signed contract. Barry would tell me how many weeks we had and that was it. I wasn't too bothered about any contracts 'cause they can always be broken. They had a policy I liked where Barry always paid you ahead of time. On every tour we took, the checks was made out and post-dated in advance and left right here with Helen. When I got sick in England they just took me to the hospital, and you don't have all the red tape like we have in the United States. The first thing they want to know in a hospital over here is how much money you got, while you could be there dying. They didn't do that in England; just took me in. England is my favorite country of all the places I've ever been. Anyway, these checks was all made out and when Barry and them came back to Los Angeles I went to the airport and met them. By then I was getting along pretty good and the first thing Barry told me when I asked about the checks was to say I could keep them. I didn't expect that because he had to hire Sammy Rimington, a great reed man, to take my place for the rest of the tour. I paid 300 dollars for my transportation home but, outside of that, I had over 2000 dollars, and he said to keep it. I liked Barry because, whatever he told me, he did. I told Barry after I left the band in 1975 that I probably wouldn't go back to Europe on tour with anybody for any amount of money. If I ever do go it'll be on my own, but only if I can work at a location for a week or so.

The Legends had a pretty good band. We rehearsed and we knew what we were doing. To me that's the way to everything: preparedness, knowing what you're going to do. That's why, bands for bands, in Europe, in Japan, on the whole they're helluva lot better than bands here. I hate to say it, because we was born with the music, but we take it for granted over here. You put six guys together, start blowing, but a lot of times nothing happens. One of the biggest snarl-ups I ever seen was with a band that Frank Bull and Gene Norman brought in for the Dixieland Jubilee. This had Bud Freeman, Albert Nicholas, Wild Bill Davidson, Vic Dickenson and all these hell-fired musicians, along with Joe Sullivan on piano and Monk Hazel on drums. They never prepared their tunes and they got into something like *That's a plenty* and didn't know when to end the damn thing – a helluva mess. What I'm saying is, I've heard these European bands play and most of them know exactly what they was doing. They did a whole lot more ensemble, and that's what dixieland is. In New Orleans you never heard all these individual solos; even with Kid Ory's band with Papa Mutt it was togetherness, and the same with George Lewis's band.

With Barry's band it was fine, we had nice little arrangements. I certainly did more solos than anybody because I was a little better known from being with Ory and Louis so long, and for *Yellow Dog Blues*. You always got a lot of requests for that, but in the Legends everybody had a chance to shine. We got a lot of deals around Los Angeles playing private parties and we played some of the schools around here, too. As far as playing in a nightclub three or six nights a week goes, that's a thing of the past for any band in Los Angeles. You don't have bands playing steady any place here. People just don't support 'em. What you have here is your jazz clubs. Now San Francisco is different, much better, you got a couple of places where they use bands. The Legends played a lot of schools in little towns in the Middle West but never done any of the big schools. It looks like the Preservation Hall Jazz Band has all that sewed up. Still, we had some nice tours in the Midwest and we all got along fine; no problems there.

I did two seasons with the Legends. I really hated to leave because I liked Barry and the guys. The pay was good but I couldn't take any more of that road. From then, me and Nappy fell right back in together, along with Nick Fatool, Abe Lincoln and all of them.

We'd play a lot of guest shots or put together bands for special gigs, whatever came along. Like when I got a call to work for a riding club called the Capuleros, which is a bunch of very influential, more-or-less wealthy people. They'll pick on some big ranch and go on a four-day outing. They always bought bands in. These Capuleros is divided into about ten chapters and each would have their own individual entertainment, different bands and groups riding with them. On the last day they would have a contest to see who had the best group, something similar to the battles of the bands. The first thing they'd do would be to put up their bar and they'd bring in chuck wagons, all motorized, like portable kitchens with all their supplies. They had tents and everybody would usually sleep out in the open air or in a trailer. Some of them brought mobile homes. Capuleros came from all over the world for this four-day deal where they didn't do nothing but eat and get drunk. One time I played for them was out at the Wrigley Estate on Catalina Island, which was a tremendously big estate owned by the chewing gum people. On that island they got one of the few herds of wild buffalo still around; also they have many wild goats and wild boar. Once in a while they do let them go over and get the goats or have a boar-hunt, but it's against the law to kill the buffalo so they just keep breeding there. The last time I worked for the Capuleros was in 1976 where they had my old friend Phil Harris as the grand marshall and a band with Pee Wee Erwin, Nick Fatool and me.

Then I had the chance to go on the CETA (Comprehensive Employment Training Act) program, which was a very good paying job. This was a wonderful thing for the kids. The idea was to take a dixieland band to the schools and show them what the music was like. Usually, when we first got on the stand, the kids would look at us and they seemed uncomfortable as if this was something they was made to do, wanted to get it done and forget about it. "What in hell is these old bastards going to do for us?" But we told a story, had Gordon Mitchell as a narrator with us, and we told how this stuff started back in Africa, got to New Orleans, the funerals, the riverboats, the whole bit, and then we played a graduated thing from the tom-toms up to dixie, and Nappy sang the blues, which was terrific. I did some singing, too; it was a grand show. After that the kids loved it and we got a standing ovation. That's very unusual for kids. They always wanted us back. And that's when I had my first heart attack.

I had to go to Zeno's in Denver for three days in the dead of winter, to play some concerts. The altitude is too high there and I never should have gone. I had been on a couple of tough tours after leaving the Legends, going to Vancouver for three days and then on to Seattle, Portland and Eugene, also during the cold weather. Probably the heart attack was a blessing in a way, telling me to slow down. I had two other heart attacks after that. Doctor said I was in pretty good shape but every one of them was my own fault really, overdoing it. I don't think horn-blowing has anything to do with it. I just fooled around, didn't watch my diet, didn't take my medicine when I was supposed to take it. Blowing the horn really helps strengthen the heart, in a way of speaking. You don't feel it when you play. The musicians was wonderful. When I got sick they just fell head over heels wanting to do things for me. Max Herman from the musicians' union called me and I got letters and calls from all over the world, people I didn't know and guys I hadn't heard from in years. That's one thing that showed me how many friends I had.

I was off the CETA program for about six weeks and then I came back. I haven't done any heavy touring since then. I go to Sacramento for the festival, to the Pismo Beach Festival, been back to Denver a couple of times, but those are things I can do any time I want. I do some recording, overdubbing with different bands, like with John Fahey. I recorded with him three times, different groups.

John was a real nice guy but I don't know too much about him. The loot was pretty good and the work was fairly easy. You always knew you was gonna make a certain amount of money, damn near 200 dollars if you record one tune or if you record four.

These days I play with all kinds of groups but I'm living quietly. I've done some things with the Resurrection Brass Band, which was run by my old friend Gordon Mitchell. He was one of the founders of the Southern California Hot Jazz Society and quite a critic. He himself was a trombone player but also a promoter, bandleader and MC. His wife Dixie played in his bands, 'cause Gordon also had a jazz band with which we played dances and other functions. The guitar Dixie plays now was owned at one time by Bud Scott. The Resurrection Band was a marching band and I played with them a few times, but I didn't do any marching, you can be sure of that. Gordon took the band to Sacramento almost every year and I played with them the year Helen and I was made Empress and Emperor of the whole festival. One of the tunes we played was *Sacramento Jubilee*, the tune I wrote as the theme song for the festival. After Gordon died in 1981 his widow said she'd keep the band going; she put Al Reiman, another trombone player, in charge. They got all kinds of good musicians in that band, people like George Orendorff the great old trumpet player, Syl Rice the drummer, Billy Hadnott for the bass drum, and Gideon Honore as the sergeant of arms. Gordon always used the best musicians he could for his small band – guys like Nick Fatool, Nappy, Barney, Ray Leatherwood, Ray Sherman, Dick Cary, Mannie Klein and Abe Lincoln – and we played a lot of Christmas parties and church charity deals.

Another band I work with is Chuck Conklin's Angel City Jazz Band. I do guest appearances with them and we made records, too. I went to Pismo Beach for their jazz festival; had about 16 bands there, all more or less local. The guy that hired me for Pismo Beach is K. O. Ecklund, a piano player which was once with the Firehouse Five Plus Two. He's an old friend and he leads a band called the Desolation Jazz Ensemble Mess Kit Repair Battalion. Recently he called me up to go to Santa Maria to talk to the Chamber of Commerce as their guest speaker. They wanted to hear about Louis and my early days in New Orleans. I had them rolling in the aisles after I told them some of the stories from this book. Then I played with K. O.'s band. He's real humorous himself and a good writer. I first got to know him in about 1953 or 1954 when he called me and Mike DeLay about this big job he had at Newport Beach, which is where all the millionaires have their yachts. He said he was gonna play on a yacht, have lots of eats and drinks, so we was all prepared to board one of the big yachts when we come to find out it was only a goddam fishing barge with a canvas top on it. It started drizzlin' rain as soon as we got on the barge for this fishing party. Anyway, we all got drunk and the banjo player fell in the water. This thing was a helluva mess. I remind K. O. about it when I see him. It's always good for a laugh.

Recently I taped a three-hour radio show for Scott Ellsworth. They call his show "Scott's Place" and it comes out of Palm Springs on Station KFI. We talked and played all my records. Then I shot a funeral scene for a TV series called "The White Shadow" which is about a team of colored basketball players who have a white coach. Ella Fitzgerald was one of the principals on the film; I think she was meant to be a relative of one of the players. Me, Jake Porter, and a banjo player from Mandeville, Louisiana, played *When the saints* at the graveside – just did one tune. Of course, Jake is a fine trumpet man himself and he's the guy that wrote *Kokomo*, which Perry Como uses for his theme song. I was glad to see Ella, 'cause I knew her from years before when we did a couple of things together while I was with Louis and even when I was with Kid Ory.

Talking about funerals, I been playing too many damn funerals lately, they're kinda catching; you have to watch out for that. Like this lawyer I met when I was with Ory in the forties. Him and I got to be friends and his last wish was for me to play *Just a closer walk with thee* in the low register at his funeral. It was sad how he died. His wife was in the hospital for a heart operation and he was on his way to see her when they found him dead in his car in the hospital car park. His daughters called me up and I got a band out for the funeral with Bill Stumpp on trumpet, Bill Campbell on piano, Nappy and me; just four, that's all. This lawyer was a collector of old automobiles so they used a motorized hearse made in 1915, followed by a 1918 Chalmers with the top down, and that's what we rode on behind the hearse. He loved George Lewis's *Burgundy Street Blues*, so we played that going to the burial plot at Forest Lawn. The funeral lasted about two hours and we played at the chapel, then by the graveside and when they was leaving. They say it was the greatest funeral they ever had there, so many people came along. They had a big deal at their house in Brentwood, that's a kinda exclusive section, but I couldn't make it. I was too damn tired.

Outside of these different music jobs we have wonderful friendships with each other and I can't say too much for people like Nappy, Eddie and Nick. We are what they call pioneers of jazz now and we can make more money if we wanted to travel than we ever made before. There's more demand for our kind of music 'cause, as Louis said, "We cuttin' out fast, there ain't many of us left."

That's why the Preservation Hall Jazz Band do so well. They was in town playing at UCLA recently and I was invited to go. I took Nappy with me and, naturally, we went back in the dressing room. I was glad to see Willie Humphrey, his brother Percy, Cie Frazier, Sing Miller, Jaffe, the manager of the band, and Frank Demond. I know Frank from way back when we worked together in Fullerton in a place called the Latin Quarter. He played banjo then, but when Jim Robinson died Frank took his place in the band on trombone. So we was sitting out in the audience, Nappy and me, along with Willie's son who lives in Los Angeles, when they start playing *Lou-easy-an-ia*. Right in the middle of the tune they stopped and announced that the writer of the tune was in the house, and asked me to come up on the stand and made me do the vocals. Naturally, I hammed it up good, almost had a standing ovation. Well, about two-thirds of the house stood up; I guess the other third was too damn lazy or tired. Anyway, it made me feel good, I know that.

Right now I do about as much as I feel like doing, but I know I'll be playing until I cut out. I don't ever want to stop. I pick up my horn every day. I still love to play, blow something, and once in a while I'll go round the clubs and blow for free.

Discography

This discography represents the first attempt to identify the recordings of Joe Darensbourg and to list them in chronological order. Inevitably there are omissions – for example, the session with Louis Prima in the early 1960s has not been documented – and it is my hope that future editions of *Telling it Like it is* will incorporate revisions as they are made. I have been greatly assisted by Joe's own recollections and by access to his record collection. Others who have helped are Floyd Levin, who has been indefatigable in his efforts to locate rare copies of Darensbourg's records, Sid Bailey, who has researched Joe's Ory period and made copies and references available to me, and Dave Bennett, who has allowed me to check the discography against items in his collection. To these gentlemen and many others goes my gratitude.

A similar acknowledgement must be made to the standard works of discography, namely J. G. Jepsen's *Jazz Records, 1942–67* and W. Bruyninckx's *60 Years of Recorded Jazz, 1917–1977*. Additional source material has come from *The AFRS "Jubilee" Transcription Programs: an Exploratory Discography* by R. E. Lotz and E. Neuert (Frankfurt am Main, 1985) and *Boy from New Orleans: Louis "Satchmo" Armstrong, on Records, Films, Radio and Television* by H. Westerberg (Copenhagen, 1981), and to these authors I extend my particular thanks. Where the data shown here differs from previously published information, it may be assumed that the new information is correct.

Abbreviations

ah	alto horn		g	guitar
as	alto saxophone		ldr	leader
bb	brass bass		p	piano
bj	banjo		ss	soprano saxophone
bs	baritone saxophone		t	trumpet
c	cornet		tb	trombone
cl	clarinet		v	vocals
d	drums		vib	vibraphone
db	double bass		vn	violin
ens	ensemble			

(1) **1925**
Autumn   Jazzland Club, St Louis
Charlie Creath's Jazz-o-Maniacs
Unidentified big band including Creath (t) and Joe Darensbourg (as)

Dinah	OKeh (unissued)	
Spanish Shawl		
Ballin' the Jack		
Don't bring me posies (it's shoesies I need)		

NB: At various times Darensbourg has listed other titles for this session including *Goodnight, I'll see you in the morning, Sister Kate, St Louis Blues, Careless Love* and *Clap hands, here comes Charlie*; however, he has always included *Dinah* and *Spanish Shawl* among the songs recorded and maintained that there were only four sides involved.

(2) **1944**
Sept 26   Station KOL, Seattle
John Wittwer Trio
Joe Darensbourg (cl); John Wittwer (p); Keith Purvis (d)

3889 Joe's Blues (JD:v)		Exner 1
3890 Wolverine Blues		Exner 1
3891 Come back, sweet papa		Exner 2
3892 Tiger Rag		Exner 2

(3) **1945**
Feb 12   C. P. McGregor Studio, Hollywood
Kid Ory's Creole Jazz Band
Mutt Carey (t); Kid Ory (tb); Joe Darensbourg (cl); Buster Wilson (p); Bud Scott (g); Ed Garland (db); Alton Redd (d)

EX 5 Dippermouth Blues		Exner 3
EX 6 Savoy Blues		Exner 3
EX 7 High Society		Exner 4
EX 8 Ballin' the Jack (JD:v)		Exner 4

(4) **1945**
March 21   Los Angeles
Kid Ory's Creole Jazz Band
Mutt Carey (t); Kid Ory (tb); Joe Darensbourg (cl); Buster Wilson (p); Bud Scott (g); Ed Garland (db); Minor Hall (d); Cecile Ory (v)

L 3754 High Society   Decca 25134
L 3755 Muskrat Ramble   Decca 25133
L 3756 The girls go crazy   Decca 25133
L 3757 Blanche Touquatoux (KO, CO:v)   Decca 25134
NB: Cecile Ory was Kid Ory's sister-in-law.

(5) 1945
Spring Standard School Broadcasts, Hollywood
Kid Ory's Creole Jazz Band
Mutt Carey (t); Kid Ory (tb); Joe Darensbourg (cl); Buster Wilson or Fred Washington* (p); Bud Scott (g); Ed Garland (db); Minor Hall or Charlie Blackwell* (d)
Creole Song (KO:v)   *Jazz Panorama LP8, Folklyric 9008*
Blues no. 1*   *Jazz Panorama LP8*   "
Lonesome Road*   "
High Society   "
Blues no. 2*   "
NB: These titles were recorded for use in the weekly Standard (Oil Company) School Broadcasts on NBC to illustrate Afro-American music as part of a series entitled "Music From Other Lands," broadcast in spring 1945; the announcer is Frank Barton.

(6) 1945
cMay   C. P. McGregor Studio, Hollywood
Red Fox and his Ding Dong Daddies
Abe Filman (t); Joe Darensbourg (cl); Johnny Wittwer (p); Virgil Ireland (g); unknown (db); Red Fox (d, v)
Dark Eyes   V-disc (unissued)
I love my baby
Dippermouth Blues (1)
If you knew Susie
Ballin' the Jack (1, 2)
Royal Garden Blues
Shut the door
They're sending the judge to jail
(1) *Wittwer plays tb*
(2) add *Joe Venuti (vn)*
NB: According to *V-discs: a History and Discography* by R. S. Sears (Westport, CT, 1980), no V-discs by Red Fox are listed or known. However, Joe Darensbourg possessed the test-pressings and tape transcriptions that are listed above. Joe Venuti is known to have recorded for the Standard transcription series with Kay Starr and Les Paul (later issued on V-disc) in Hollywood around May 1945.

(7) 1945
Autumn   Los Angeles
Joe Liggins and his Honeydrippers
Joe Darensbourg (cl); Little Willie Jackson (ss, as, bs); James Jackson (ts); Joe Liggins (p); Frank Pasley (g); Red Callendar (db); Peppy Prince (d)
1015 Boddle-do-da-deet   Exclusive 219
1016 Sugar Lump (JL, ens:v)   Exclusive 219
NB: Two other titles, 1017 Goin' to heaven no how and 1018 Caravan, were recorded at this session; Darensbourg's playing is inaudible.

(8) 1947
Aug 9 "This is Jazz" broadcast, Mutual Studios, Hollywood
Kid Ory's Creole Jazz Band
Andrew Blakeney (t); Kid Ory (tb); Joe Darensbourg (cl); Buster Wilson (p); Bud Scott (g); Ed Garland (db); Minor Hall (d)
       Oh, didn't he ramble (KO:v)   *Dawn Club DC10001*
LA1 Snag it (BS:v)   Circle J12001
       Maryland, my Maryland   *Dawn Club DC10001*
LA2 Savoy Blues   Circle J12001
LA3 Down among the sheltering palms (BS:v) Circle J12002
       C'est l'autre can-can (KO:v)   *Dawn Club DC10001*
LA4 Weary Blues   Circle J12002

(9) 1947 or 1948
Rendezvous Ballroom, Santa Monica, California
Kid Ory and his Band
Andrew Blakeney (t); Kid Ory (tb); Joe Darensbourg (cl); Buster Wilson (p); Bud Scott (g); Ed Garland (db); Minor Hall (d)

Oh, didn't he ramble (ens:v)   *Vault LP 9006*
Down Home Rag
South
Dippermouth
High Society Rag
My Gal Sal
Tiger Rag
NB: Other titles on Vault LP 9006 feature Archie Rosate, who replaced Darensbourg for some of the Rendezvous Ballroom sessions; both Rosate and Blakeney remember the date as 1947, although other references state 1948.

(10) 1949
Station KGFJ broadcasts for the US Armed Forces Radio Service, Beverly Cavern, Hollywood
Kid Ory and his Creole Jazz Band
Andy Blakeney (t); Kid Ory (tb); Joe Darensbourg (cl); Buster Wilson (p); Ed Garland (db); Minor Hall (d); Alan Jeffries (compère)
Theme: Without you for an inspiration dear   USAFRS KO 3
Panama
Sister Kate
Mahogany Hall Stomp
Margie
Chinatown, my Chinatown
Black and Blue
12th Street Rag (fade)
Panama (fade)

(11) As for no.10
Theme   USAFRS KO 4
1919 Rag
Yellow Dog Blues
That's a plenty
Maryland, my Maryland
At a Georgia Camp Meeting
Muskrat Ramble
Margie
Yellow Dog Blues (fade)

(12) As for no.10
Theme   USAFRS KO 5
Panama
Storyville Blues
Sweet Georgia Brown
Carolina in the Morning
Mississippi Mud
Tiger Rag
Chinatown, my Chinatown (fade)

(13) As for no.10
Theme   USAFRS KO 6
Chinatown, my Chinatown
Four or Five Times
I'm with you where you are
Oh, didn't he ramble
Indiana
Original Dixieland One-step
12th Street Rag
Chinatown, my Chinatown (fade)

(14) As for no.10
Theme   USAFRS KO 12
Mississippi Mud
Yellow Dog Blues
Joshua fit de battle of Jericho
Jazz me Blues
Savoy Blues
Four or Five Times
Alexander's Ragtime Band
Mississippi Mud (fade)

(15) As for no.10
Theme   USAFRS KO 17
Oh, didn't he ramble
Bucket's got a hole in it
High Society
Do you know what it means to miss New Orleans?

Sugarfoot Stomp
Original Dixieland One-step
Ory's Boogie
Oh, didn't he ramble (fade)

(16) As for no.10
Theme   USAFRS KO 21
Alexander's Ragtime Band
Bucket's got a hole in it
Blues for Jimmy
At the Jazz Band Ball
Careless Love
Muskrat Ramble
Savoy Blues
Theme (fade)

(17) 1949
Broadcast, Beverly Cavern, Hollywood
Kid Ory and his Creole Jazz Band
Same personnel as for no.10

I am busy and you can't come in	Sounds 1208

Wang Wang Blues
Down in Jungle Town
Tuxedo Junction
The world is waiting for the sunrise
After you've gone
I'm with you where you are

(18) 1949
Beverly Cavern, Hollywood
Kid Ory and his Creole Dixieland Band
Same personnel as for no.10

ORY-8	All the girls go crazy 'bout the way I walk	AFRS Jubilee 343
ORY-9	Creole Song	Jubilee 341
ORY-10	Dippermouth Blues	Jubilee 343
ORY-11	Down among the sheltering palms	Jubilee 343
ORY-12	Mahogany Hall Stomp	Jubilee 341
ORY-13	Medley: I'm with you where you are / Near you	Jubilee 343
ORY-14	Royal Garden Blues	Jubilee 341
ORY-15	Snag it	Jubilee 341
ORY-16	South	Jubilee 341
ORY-17	South Rampart Street Parade	Jubilee 343
ORY-18	That's a plenty	Jubilee 343
ORY-19	Tiger Rag	Jubilee 343
ORY-20	What did Ory say?	Jubilee 343
ORY-21	When the saints go marching in	Jubilee 341

(19) 1949
Beverly Cavern, Hollywood
Kid Ory and his Creole Dixieland Band
Same personnel as for no.10

ORY-22	Bill Bailey, won't you please come home	Jubilee 346
ORY-23	Eh là bas	Jubilee 346
ORY-24	I'm looking over a four-leaf clover	Jubilee 348
ORY-25	I'm with you where you are	Jubilee 348
ORY-26	1919 Rag	Jubilee 348
ORY-27	Original Dixieland One-step	Jubilee 348
ORY-28	Ory's Boogie	Jubilee 346
ORY-29	Royal Garden Blues	Jubilee 346
ORY-30	Savoy Blues	Jubilee 348
ORY-31	South Rampart Street Parade	Jubilee 346
ORY-32	12th Street Rag	Jubilee 348
ORY-33	Wabash Blues	Jubilee 346
ORY-34	Yellow Dog Blues	Jubilee 348

(20) 1949
Beverly Cavern, Hollywood
Kid Ory and his Creole Dixieland Band
Same personnel as for no.10

ORY-35	Alexander's Ragtime Band	Jubilee 354
ORY-36	Baby won't you please come home	Jubilee 351
ORY-37	Blues for Jimmie Noone	Jubilee 354
ORY-38	Careless Love	Jubilee 354
ORY-39	Carolina in the Morning	Jubilee 351
ORY-40	Creole Song	Jubilee 351
ORY-41	Muskrat Ramble	Jubilee 354
ORY-42	Original Dixieland One-step	Jubilee 354
ORY-43	Savoy Blues	Jubilee 351
ORY-44	Some of these days	Jubilee 351
ORY-45	South Rampart Street Parade	Jubilee 351
ORY-46	12th Street Rag	Jubilee 351
ORY-47	What did Ory say?	Jubilee 354

(21) 1949
Beverly Cavern, Hollywood
Kid Ory and his Creole Dixieland Band
Same personnel as for no.10

ORY-48	Baby won't you please come home	Jubilee 358
ORY-49	Blues for Jimmie Noone	Jubilee 362
ORY-50	Careless Love (incomplete)	Jubilee 362
ORY-51	Jazz me Blues	Jubilee 362
ORY-52	Joshua fit de battle of Jericho	Jubilee 362
ORY-53	Medley: Cuddle up a little closer / Ole Miss	Jubilee 358
ORY-54	Mississippi Mud	Jubilee 362
ORY-55	Royal Garden Blues	Jubilee 358
ORY-56	San	Jubilee 358
ORY-57	Savoy Blues	Jubilee 362
ORY-58	South	Jubilee 358
ORY-59	12th Street Rag	Jubilee 358

(22) 1949
Oct 7 Dixieland Jubilee, Shrine Auditorium, Los Angeles
Kid Ory's Creole Jazz Band
Teddy Buckner (t); Kid Ory (tb); Joe Darensbourg (cl); Lloyd Glenn (p); Ed Garland (db); Minor Hall (d)

MM1360	12th Street Rag (1)	Dixieland Jubilee 213, Decca 9-11068
MM1361	Tiger Rag	Dixieland Jubilee 212, Decca 9-11067
MM1362	Savoy Blues	Dixieland Jubilee 213, Decca 9-11068
MM1363	Eh là bas (KO:v)	Dixieland Jubilee 212, Decca 9-11067

(1) add *Albert Nicholas (cl)*
Add: Castle Jazz Band
Don Kinch (c); George Phillips (tb); Bob Gilbert (cl); Larry DuFresne (p); Bob Short (bb); Homer Welch (d)
Pete Daily's Chicagoans
Pete Daily (c); Warren Smith (tb); Stan Storey (cl); Bernie Billings (ts); Don Owens (p); Nappy Lamare (bj); George Defebaugh (d)
Charlie Lavere's Chicago Loopers
Andy Secrest (c); Joe Yukl (tb); Rosy McHargue (cl); Charlie Lavere (p); George van Eps (g); Fred Whiting (db); Country Washburn (bb); Nick Fatool (d)

80037	Who's sorry now	Decca 9-11065

Add: Firehouse Five Plus Two
Danny Alguire (c); Ward Kimball (tb); Clarke Mallery (cl); Frank Thomas (p); Ralph Goff (bj); Erdman Penner (bb); John Mountjoy (d)
Also: *Muggsy Spanier, Red Nichols (c); Mannie Klein (t); Brad Gowans, Lou McGarity, King Jackson, Irvin Verrett (tb); Matty Matlock, Albert Nicholas (cl); Bud Freeman, Eddie Miller (ts); Joe Rushton (bass sax); Marvin Ash, Stan Wrightsman, Bob Hammack (p); Artie Shapiro (b); Rollie Culver, Smoky Stover, Zutty Singleton (d)*

80039	Muskrat Ramble	Decca 9-11066
80040	South Rampart Street Parade	Decca 9-11066

(23) 1950
June 27 Los Angeles
Kid Ory's Creole Jazz Band
Teddy Buckner (t); Kid Ory (tb); Joe Darensbourg (cl); Lloyd Glenn (p); Julian Davidson (g); Morty Corb (db); Minor Hall (d); Lee Sapphire (v)

RHCO4109	Glory of Love (LS:v)	Columbia 38956
RHCO4110	Savoy Blues	Columbia 38955
RHCO4111	Georgia Camp Meeting	Columbia 38957
RHCO4112	Mahogany Hall Stomp	Columbia 38956

(24) **1950**
July 6   Los Angeles
Kid Ory's Creole Jazz Band
*Teddy Buckner (t); Kid Ory (tb); Joe Darensbourg (cl); Lloyd Glenn
(p); Ed Shrivenak (g); Morty Corb (db); Minor Hall (d); Lee Sapphire
(v)*

RHCO4126-1	Blues for Jimmie	Columbia 38957
RHCO4127-1	Go back where you stayed	
	last night (LS, JD:v)	Columbia 38958
RHCO4128-1	Creole Song (KO:v)	Columbia 38955
RHCO4129-1	Yaaka hula hickey dula	Columbia 38958

(25) **1950**
Dec 5   Los Angeles
Burt Bales and the Gin Bottle Four
*Joe Darensbourg (cl); Burt Bales (p); George Bruns (bb); Minor Hall
(d); Jeanne Gayle (v)*

LK185	Angry (JG:v)	Good Time Jazz 35
LK186	Doodle Doo-doo (JG:v)	Good Time Jazz 35
LK187	Down among the sheltering	
	palms	Good Time Jazz 36

(26) **1950**
Dec 20   Los Angeles
Pete Daily and his Chicagoans
*Pete Daily (c); Burt Johnson (tb); Joe Darensbourg (cl); Pud Brown
(ts); Skippy Anderson (p); Jack Coss (g, bj); Bud Hatch (bb, db); Hugh
Allison (d)*

6927	Walkin' the dog	Capitol 1486
6928	Johnson Rag	Capitol 1370
6929	Chicken Rag	Capitol 1820
6930	Lou-easy-an-ia	Capitol 1370

(27) **1951**
May 5   Concert, Pomona, California
Kid Ory's Creole Jazz Band
*Teddy Buckner (t); Kid Ory (tb); Joe Darensbourg (cl); Lloyd Glenn
(p); Ed Garland (db); Minor Hall (d)*

LK229	St Louis Blues	Good Time Jazz 48
LK230	Ory's Boogie	Good Time Jazz 48
LK313	Blues for Jimmie, pt. 1	Good Time Jazz 55
LK314	Blues for Jimmie, pt. 2	Good Time Jazz 55

(28) **1951**
May 10   Dixieland Jubilee, Shrine Auditorium, Los Angeles
Kid Ory's Creole Jazz Band
Same personnel as for no.27

Shine	Mode (F) 9666
Maryland, my Maryland	

(29) **1951**
May 14   Los Angeles
Pete Daily and his Chicagoans
Same personnel as for no.26

7554	Gramophone Rag	Capitol 2302
7555	Take me out to the ball game	Capitol 1588
7556	Harmony Rag	Capitol 1588
7557	Peggy O'Neil	Capitol 1820

(30) **1951**
December   Los Angeles
Brother Bones, supported by the Joe Darensbourg Quintet
*Teddy Buckner (t); Joe Darensbourg (cl); Gerry Wiggins (p); Frank
Pasley (g); Billy Hadnott (db); Brother Bones (Freeman Davis) (bones,
whistling)*

Me and my shadow	Theme P166
Lou-easy-an-ia (JD, ens:v)	Theme P166
Charleston	Theme P168
Coquette	Theme P168

(31) **early 1952**
Los Angeles
Brother Bones and the Joe Darensbourg Quintet
*Teddy Buckner (t); Joe Darensbourg (cl); Harvey Brooks (p); Dave
Bryant (db); Frank Pasley (g); Brother Bones (bones, whistling)*

Monkey Snoots and Dumplin's (1)		
(LDD, ens:v)		Tempo TR1286
Bye Bye Blues		Tempo TR1286
Black Eyed Susan Brown		Tempo ?
Running Wild		Tempo ?

(1) add *Little Darlynne Devenny (v); Brooks plays celeste*
NB: Other titles listed in discographies as having accompaniment by Joe Darensbourg are in error.

(32) **early 1952**
Los Angeles
Joe Darensbourg and his Flat Out Five
*Teddy Buckner (t); Joe Darensbourg (cl); Gerry Wiggins (p); Frank
Pasley (g); Dave Bryant (db); Scat Man Crothers (v)*

Hot Rod Harry (The Coolest Cat	
in Town)	Hot Rod 1001
Hot Rod Cowboy	Hot Rod 1001
Saturday Night Drag Race, pt. 1	Hot Rod 1003
Saturday Night Drag Race, pt. 2	Hot Rod 1003

NB: Hot Rod Records was a division of Trend Inc, publishers of
Hot Rod magazine. The recordings were commissioned by Bob
Peterson, owner of the magazine, and distributed to new
subscribers; they were never sold through commercial channels.

(33) **1952**
April 6   Concert, Shrine Auditorium, Los Angeles
Kid Ory's Creole Jazz Band
*Teddy Buckner (t); Kid Ory (tb); Joe Darensbourg (cl); Lloyd Glenn
(p); Ed Garland (db); Minor Hall (d)*

Milenberg Joys	Vogue (F) CMDGN9666
Muskrat Ramble (KO:v)	

(34) **1953**
May 9   Broadcast, Club Hangover, San Francisco
Kid Ory's Creole Jazz Band
*Teddy Buckner (t); Kid Ory (tb); Joe Darensbourg (cl); Harvey Brooks
(p); Ed Garland (db); Minor Hall (d)*

Theme	Dawn Club DC12013
Clarinet Marmalade	
Down in Jungle Town	
Savoy Blues	
Sugar Blues	
Maple Leaf Rag	

(35) **1953**
May 16   Broadcast, Club Hangover, San Francisco
Kid Ory's Creole Jazz Band
Same personnel as for no.34

Theme	Dawn Club DC12013
Milenberg Joys	
All the girls go crazy 'bout the way I walk	
Snag it	
Fidgety Feet	
Theme	

(36) **1953**
May 23   Broadcast, Club Hangover, San Francisco
Kid Ory's Creole Jazz Band
Same personnel as for no.34

Theme	Dawn Club LC12016
Shine	
Aunt Hagar's Blues	
Muskrat Ramble	
Just a closer walk with thee	
Panama Rag	
Theme	

(37) **1953**
May 30   Broadcast, Club Hangover, San Francisco
Kid Ory's Creole Jazz Band
Same personnel as for no.34

The world is waiting for the sunrise	Dawn Club LC12016
At a Georgia Camp Meeting	
Creole Love Call	
Birth of the Blues	
Way down yonder in New Orleans	

(38) **1953**
December   Dayton, Ohio
Dixieland Rhythm Kings
Bob Hodes (t); Charlie Sonnanstine (tb); Joe Darensbourg (cl); Robin
Wetterau (p); Jack Vastine (bj); Gene Mayl (db, bb)
Irish Black Bottom   *Riverside RLP2505*
Ory's Creole Trombone
Melancholy (JV:v)
Come back sweet papa
St James Infirmary
Bill Bailey (JV:v)
Blue Mama's Suicide Wail (JV:v)
Darktown Strutters Ball (JV:v)   *Riverside RLP12-210*
Sunset Cafe Stomp
Muskrat Ramble
Weary Blues
Roll, Jordan, roll (JV:v)
Sweet Georgia Brown
Red River Valley
Blues my naughty sweetie gives to me
Big Butter and Egg Man

(39) **1953**
Dec 28–30   Turf Club, Dayton, Ohio
Dixieland Rhythm Kings
Same personnel as for no.38
Maple Leaf Rag   *Riverside RLP12-259 Empirical EM102*
Chattanooga Stomp
Wabash Blues
Buddy's Habits
Skid-dat-de-dat
Panama Rag
Trouble in Mind   *Riverside RLP12-259 Empirical EM105*
Careless Love Blues
Ain't gonna give you none of my jelly roll
Bourbon Street Parade
High Society
Dippermouth Blues
Yellow Dog Blues

(40) **1954**
January   Dayton, Ohio
Gene Mayl's Band
Same personnel as for no.38
Bill Bailey   *Audiophile AP-18*
Blue Mama's Suicide Wail
Sweet Georgia Brown
St James Infirmary
Red River Valley
Weary Blues

(41) **1955**
Feb 6   Concert, Los Angeles
Teddy Buckner and his Dixieland Five
Teddy Buckner (t); William Woodman, Sr (tb); Joe Darensbourg (cl,
ss); Harvey Brooks (p); Art Edwards (db); Jesse Sailes (d)
Martinique   *Dixieland Jubilee DJ104*
Do, Lord (WW, ens:v)   *Gene Norman Presents GNP-11*
West End Blues
When the saints
Honky Tonk Parade (HB:v)
Oh, didn't he ramble
Battle Hymn of the Republic
Just a closer walk with thee

(42) **1955**
July 16   Station KCBS broadcast, Club Hangover, San
Francisco
Teddy Buckner and his All-Stars
Same personnel as for no.41, with Bob Gerner (announcer)
Dear Old Southland (theme)   *Aircheck No 10*
Mahogany Hall Stomp
I want to linger
Dippermouth Blues
Bluin' the Blues
Tiger Rag
NB: This complete 30-minute broadcast includes a solo track
by Joe Sullivan (p).

(43) **1955**
Aug 6   Station KCBS broadcast, Club Hangover, San
Francisco
Teddy Buckner and his All-Stars
Same personnel as for no.42
Theme   *Aircheck No 10*
Big Butter and Egg Man
Mood Indigo
12th Street Rag
Memphis Blues
Royal Garden Blues
NB: Aircheck has further broadcasts by Buckner from Club
Hangover awaiting release, dating from July 23, July 30, Aug 20,
Aug 27 and Sept 3, 1955.

(44) **1955**
Oct 15   Dixieland Jubilee, Shrine Auditorium, Los Angeles
Teddy Buckner and his Band
Same personnel as for no.41
Sweet Georgia Brown   *Dixieland Jubilee DJ104*
That's my home   *Dixieland Jubilee DJ503*
Tailgate Ramble
Chinatown, my Chinatown
Dear Old Southland
Chimes Blues
How ya gonna keep him down on the farm?
Bluin' the Blues

(45) **1956**
June 20   Concert, Civic Auditorium, Pasadena, California
Louis Armstrong and the All Stars
Louis Armstrong (t); Trummy Young (tb); Edmond Hall (cl); Billy
Kyle (p); Arvell Shaw (db); Barrett Deems (d)
Teddy Buckner and his Band
Teddy Buckner (t); William Woodman, Sr (tb); Joe Darensbourg (cl);
Harvey Brooks (p); Art Edwards (db); Jesse Sailes (d)
Oh, didn't he ramble   *Gene Norman Presents GNPS11001*
NB: All other titles on this album are by Louis Armstrong's
band only.

(46) **1956**
Sept 17   San Francisco
Teddy Buckner and his Band
Same personnel as for no.41
Honky Tonk Parade   *Calliope CAL3004*
Mood Indigo
When the saints go marching in
Just a closer walk with thee

(47) **1956**
Club Hangover, San Francisco
Teddy Buckner and his Band
Same personnel as for no.41
12th Street Rag   *Vogue (F) LA527-30*
Snag it
Milenberg Joys
Winin' Boy Blues
Panama
Farewell Blues
I want to linger
Dippermouth Blues
I found a new baby

(48) **1956**
Oct 8   Los Angeles
Teddy Buckner and his Dixieland Band
Teddy Buckner (t); John "Streamline" Ewing (tb); Joe Darensbourg
(cl, ss); Harvey Brooks (p); Art Edwards (db); Jesse Sailes (d)
Wang Wang Blues   *Dixieland Jubilee DJ504*
Every night
Lassus Trombone
Struttin' with some Barbecue

(49) **1956**
Los Angeles
Teddy Buckner and his Band
Teddy Buckner (t); John Ewing (tb); Joe Darensboug (cl, ss); Chester
Lane (p); Art Edwards (db); Jesse Sailes (d)

Potato Head Blues *Dixieland Jubilee DJ505*
My bucket's got a hole in it
My Monday Date
Big Butter and Egg Man
Savoy Blues
Someday (TB:v)
High Society

(50) 1957
Aug 12   TV broadcast, Bobby Troup's "Stars of Jazz," Los Angeles
Joe Darensbourg and his Dixie Flyers
Mike DeLay (t); Warren Smith (tb); Joe Darensbourg (cl, ss); Harvey Brooks (p); Al Morgan (db); George Vann (d); Bobby Troup (announcer)
Milenberg Joys *Red Stick LP5080*
Just a closer walk with thee (GV:v)
NB: Red Stick was a label operated by Joe Darensbourg; LP5080, *Joe Darensbourg remembers his Dixie Flyers*, was its only release.

(51) 1957
September   Capitol Studios, Hollywood
Joe Darensbourg and his Dixie Flyers
Mike DeLay (t); Warren "Smitty" Smith (tb); Joe Darensbourg (cl); Harvey Brooks (p); Al Morgan (db); George Vann (d)
LM-0957-1 Just a closer walk with thee (GV:v) Lark LS-451
LM-0957-2 Lou-easy-an-ia (1) (JD:v) Lark LS-451
LM-0957-3 Martinique Lark LS-452
LM-0957-4 Yellow Dog Blues Lark LS-452
LM-0957-5 Stardust Lark LS-453
LM-0957-6 Stumbling Lark LS-453
LM-0957-7 Four or Five Times (GV, ens:v) Lark LS-454
LM-0957-8 Go back where you stayed last night (JD:v) Lark LS-454
(1) *Darensbourg plays ss*

(52) 1957
Oct 12   Station KMLA broadcast, The Lark, Los Angeles
Joe Darensbourg and his Dixie Flyers
Same personnel as for no.51
Lou-easy-an-ia (theme) *Red Stick LP 5080*
Bourbon Street Parade (JD:v)
Blues for Al
Royal Garden Blues
Savoy Blues

(53) 1957
November   Capitol Studios, Hollywood
Joe Darensbourg and his Dixie Flyers
Mike DeLay (t); Warren Smith (tb); Joe Darensbourg (cl); Harvey Brooks (p); William Newman (bj, g); Al Morgan (db); George Vann (d)
LM1157-1 Yellow Dog Blues *Lark LLP331*
LM1157-2 Just a little time to stay here
LM1157-3 How Long Blues
LM1157-4 That Da-da Strain
LM1157-5 When my dreamboat comes home
LM1157-6 Martinique
LM1157-7 Dixie Flyer March
LM1157-8 Careless Love
LM1157-9 Copenhagen
LM1157-10 Rockin' in Dixie
LM1157-11 Winin' Boy Blues
LM1157-12 Sweet Georgia Brown
NB: album title: On a Lark in Dixieland

(54) 1958
January   Capitol Studios, Hollywood
Joe Darensbourg and his Dixie Flyers
Same personnel as for no.51
LM-0158-1 Sassy Gal Lark LS-455

(55) 1958
Feb 11–12   Capitol Studios, Hollywood
Joe Darensbourg and his Dixie Flyers
Same personnel as for no.51

LM-0258-9 Snag it (1) Lark LS-455
LM-0258-12 Chimes Blues (2) Lark LS-456
LM-0258-13 Huggin' and Kissin' Lark LS-456
(1) *Darensbourg also plays ss*
(2) *Brooks also plays celeste; add unknown (g)*

(56) 1958
cFeb/March   Los Angeles
Joe Darensbourg and his Dixie Flyers
Mike DeLay (t); Warren Smith (tb); Joe Darensbourg (cl); Harvey Brooks (p); Al Morgan (db); Lou Diamond (d)
St Louis Blues *Lark EP-1451*
Careless Love
Beale Street Blues

(57) 1958
March   Capitol Studios, Hollywood
Joe Darensbourg and his Dixie Flyers
Same personnel as for no.51
LM-0358-21 Sleepy Time Gal (1) Lark LS-457
LM-0358-22 Lazy River Lark LS-457
NB: It is known that sufficient material was recorded by the Dixie Flyers to make up a second album on the Lark label; no date or further details have been confirmed.
(1) *add unknown (g)*

(58) 1958
July   Capitol Studios, Hollywood
Eddie Cole and Betty Cole, accompanied by Joe Darensbourg and Rene Hall's orchestra
John Ewing (tb); Joe Darensbourg (cl); Bill Green (ts); Floyd Turnham (bs); Eddie Cole, Betty Cole (p, v); unknown (vib); Rene Hall (g); Red Callender (db); Bill Douglass (d); unidentified chorus
LM-0758-37 Cling to me (1) Lark LS-458
LM-0758-38 You took your love from me (2) Lark LS-4512
LM-0758-39 You and I (1) Lark LS-458
LM-0758-40 Sweet Someone (3) Lark LS-4512
Label details: (1) *Betty Cole with Eddie Cole conducting orchestra and chorus*
(2) *Eddie and Betty Cole with orchestra*
(3) *Eddie and Betty Cole featuring Joe Darensbourg and orchestra with Rene Hall chorus*

(59) 1959
January   Capitol Studios, Hollywood
Joe Darensbourg Quintet
Joe Darensbourg (cl); Vic Feldman (vib); Laurindo Almeida (g); Red Callender (db); Bill Douglass (d)
LM-0159-41 Petite fleur Lark LS-4510
LM-0159-42 Over the waves Lark LS-4510

(60) 1961
Sept 2   Broadcast
Louis Armstrong and the All Stars
Louis Armstrong (t); Trummy Young (tb); Joe Darensbourg (cl); Billy Kyle (p); Irving Manning (db); Danny Barcelona (d); Jewell Brown (v)
Royal Garden Blues
C'est si bon (LA:v)
La vie en rose (LA:v)
Crazy Otto Rag
Bill Bailey
When it's sleepy time down South

(61) 1961
Sept 19   New York
Louis Armstrong–Dave Brubeck
Louis Armstrong (t); Trummy Young (tb); Joe Darensbourg (cl); Billy Kyle, Dave Brubeck (p); Gene Wright, Irving Manning (db); Joe Morello, Danny Barcelona (d); Dave Lambert, Jon Hendricks, Annie Ross (v) -
CO68006 Since love had its way (LA:v) *Columbia OL5850*
CO68007 Nomad (LA:v) Columbia 42832
CO68008 Cultural Exchange (LHR, LA, TY:v) *Columbia OL5850*
CO68009 Remember who you are (LA, TY:v)
King for a Day (1) (LA, TY:v)
(1) *Armstrong, Young, vocals only*

(62) **1961**
Oct 7 Broadcast
Louis Armstrong and the All Stars
Same personnel as for no.60
Way down yonder in New Orleans
Give me a kiss to build a dream on
High Society Calypso
Now you has jazz
When the saints go marching in (incomplete)

(63) **1961**
Dec 8 Broadcast, ?New York
Louis Armstrong–Duke Ellington
Louis Armstrong (t); Trummy Young (tb); Joe Darensbourg (cl); Duke Ellington (p); Irving Manning (db); Danny Barcelona (d)
Don't get around much anymore
I'm beginning to see the light
Solitude
I got it bad
Just squeeze me
It don't mean a thing
Azalea

(64) **1961**
Dec 17 CBS TV broadcast, "Ed Sullivan Show," New York
Louis Armstrong–Duke Ellington
Same personnel as for no.63
Duke's Place   *Pumpkin 109*
In a mellotone
Nobody knows the trouble I've seen (LA:v) (1)
(1) *add unknown strings*

(64a) **1961**
Dec 19 New York
Louis Armstrong–Dave Brubeck
Same personnel as for no.61, with Carmen McRae (v)
CO67990 Good Reviews (CMR, LA:v)   *Columbia OL5850*

(65) **1962**
January TV broadcast, "Westinghouse TV Show," Sun Valley, Idaho
Louis Armstrong and the All Stars
Louis Armstrong (t); Trummy Young (tb); Joe Darensbourg (cl); Billy Kyle (p); Billy Cronk (db); Danny Barcelona (d)
Struttin' with some Barbecue
Lazy River (LA:v)
On the sunny side of the street
When it's sleepy time down South
NB: Telecast on Feb 23, 1962

(66) **1962**
Feb 16–20 TV broadcast, concert, Stockholm
Louis Armstrong and the All Stars
Same personnel as for no.65, plus Jewell Brown, Monica Zetterlund (v)
When it's sleepy time down South (LA:v)
Indiana
My bucket's got a hole in it (LA, TY:v)
Tiger Rag
Blueberry Hill (LA:v)
All of me (JB:v)
St Louis Blues
When the saints go marching in
My man (MZ, LA:v)
After you've gone
NB: Telecast on Sept 29, 1962

(67) **1962**
Feb 24 Broadcast, concert, Musikhalle, Hamburg, Germany
Louis Armstrong and the All Stars
Same personnel as for no.65, minus Monica Zetterlund (v)
When it's sleepy time down South
Indiana
Give me a kiss to build a dream on (LA:v)
My bucket's got a hole in it (LA, TY:v)
Mack the Knife (LA:v)
Lover come back to me (JB:v)
Bill Bailey (JB:v)

When the saints go marching in
Struttin' with some Barbecue
Nobody knows the trouble I've seen (LA:v)
Blueberry Hill (LA:v)
The Faithful Hussar (LA:v)
When it's sleepy time down South
St Louis Blues (JB:v)
Have you heard about Jerry? (JB:v)

(68) **1962**
Feb 26 CBS TV broadcast, "Ed Sullivan Show," US Army post, West Berlin
Louis Armstrong and the All Stars
Same personnel as for no.67
When it's sleepy time down South (LA:v)
Royal Garden Blues
Blueberry Hill (LA:v)
The Faithful Hussar (LA:v)
When the saints go marching in (LA:v)

(69) **1962**
?Feb 26 Concert, Sportspalast, West Berlin
Louis Armstrong and the All Stars
Same personnel as for no.67
Indiana
My bucket's got a hole in it
Tiger Rag
Now you has jazz
High Society
Unidentified title featuring Young
Yellow Dog Blues
Mack the Knife
Lover come back to me (JB:v)
Can't help lovin' that man of mine (JB:v)
When the saints go marching in (LA, JB:v)

(70) **1962**
?Feb 27 TV broadcast, concert, Liederhall, Stuttgart, Germany
Louis Armstrong and the All Stars
Same personnel as for no.67
Basin Street Blues
Adios muchachos
I get ideas
Mack the Knife
Stompin' at the Savoy
Stompin' at the Savoy (encore)
When the saints go marching in
The Faithful Hussar

(71) **1962**
?Feb 28 TV broadcast, concert, Munich, Germany
Louis Armstrong and the All Stars
Same personnel as for no.67
When it's sleepy time down South
Tin Roof Blues
Basin Street Blues
Mahogany Hall Stomp
Indiana
Mack the Knife
High Society

(72) **1962**
March Concert, Manchester, England
Louis Armstrong and the All Stars
Same personnel as for no.67
Ole Miss
When I grow too old to dream
Tin Roof Blues
Yellow Dog Blues

(73) **1962**
April 24 TV broadcast, concert, Rome
Louis Armstrong and the All Stars
Same personnel as for no.67
Blues (1)
Ohi, Mari (LA, CV:v) (2)

Some of these days (LA, PS:v) (3)
When it's sleepy time down South
Indiana
New Orleans Function
Where the blues was born in New Orleans
Someday (LA:v)
C'est si bon (LA:v)
When it's sleepy time down South (LA:v)
Have you heard about Jerry? (JB:v)
Nobody knows the trouble I've seen (LA:v)
(1) *add Nunzio Rotondo, Nino Rosso (t)*
(2) *add Claudio Villa (v)*
(3) *add Peters Sisters (v)*

(74) **1962**
May 22   Concert, Nice, France
Louis Armstrong and the All Stars
Same personnel as for no.67
Tin Roof Blues
Yellow Dog Blues
All of me (JB:v)
Georgia on my mind (JB:v)
Bill Bailey (JB:v)
When the saints go marching in
Struttin' with some Barbecue
C'est si bon (LA:v)
Jazz me Blues
Basin Street Blues (LA:v)
Blueberry Hill (LA:v)
The man I love
Mack the Knife (LA:v)
Stomping at the Savoy
Lover come back to me (JB:v)
St Louis Blues (JB:v)
After you've gone
When it's sleepy time down South

(75) **1962**
Summer–autumn   Film soundtrack, "The Good Years of
Jazz," New York
Louis Armstrong and the All Stars
Same personnel as for no.67
When it's sleepy time down South (LA:v)   *Storyville SLP236*
C'est si bon (LA:v)
Someday (LA:v)
Have you heard about Jerry? (JB:v)
Nobody knows the trouble I've seen (LA:v)
When the saints go marching in (JB:v)
Now you has jazz (LA, TY:v)
Yellow Dog Blues

(76) **1962**
July 7   Newport Jazz Festival, Newport, Rhode Island
Louis Armstrong and the All Stars
Same personnel as for no.67
When it's sleepy time down South
Indiana
Give me a kiss to build a dream on (LA:v)
My bucket's got a hole in it (LA, TY:v)
Tiger Rag
Struttin' with some Barbecue
Stomping at the Savoy
Blueberry Hill (LA:v)
Canal Street Blues
Dippermouth Blues
Dear Old Southland
St Louis Blues (JB:v)
Can't help lovin dat man of mine (JB:v)
All of me (JB:v)
When the saints go marching in (LA, JB:v)
NB: Yank Lawson (t) and J. C. Higginbotham (tb) played with
the All Stars on this set and may appear on some titles.

(77) **1962**
Aug 1   Concert, Chicago
Louis Armstrong and the All Stars
Same personnel as for no.67

When it's sleepy time down
South (LA:v)   *Fox American Retrospectives
MF 208/5*
Indiana
Give me a kiss to build a dream on (LA:v)   "
My bucket's got a hole in it (LA, TY:v)   "
Tiger Rag   "
Struttin' with some Barbecue
When I grow too old to dream
Yellow Dog Blues
All of me (JB:v)
Can't help lovin dat man of mine (JB:v)
St Louis Blues (JB:v)   *Storyville SLP4101*
When the saints go marching in
When it's sleepy time down South
New Orleans Function/Flee as a bird   *MF 208/5*
New Orleans Function/Oh, didn't he ramble   "
C'est si bon (LA:v)   "
Ole Miss
La vie en rose (LA:v)   *Fox American Retrospectives
MF 208/5*
The Faithful Hussar (LA:v)   "
Once in a while
Mack the Knife (LA:v)   "
Stomping at the Savoy
Bill Bailey (JB:v)
Have you heard about Jerry? (JB:v)
After you've gone
When it's sleepy time down South   *Storyville SLP4101*
Blueberry Hill   "

(78) **1962**
Dec 14   CBS TV broadcast, Guantanamo Naval Base,
Guantanamo, Cuba
Louis Armstrong and the All Stars
Same personnel as for no.67
When it's sleepy time down South
Indiana
Blueberry Hill (LA:v)
Mack the Knife (LA:v)

(79) **1962**
Dec 31   NBC broadcast, Cocoanut Grove, Los Angeles
Louis Armstrong and the All Stars
Same personnel as for no.67
When it's sleepy time down South
Blueberry Hill (LA:v)
Struttin' with some Barbecue
Mack the Knife
Have you heard about Jerry? (JB:v)
When the saints go marching in (LA, JB:v)

(80) **1963**
March   BP TV broadcast, Sydney
Louis Armstrong and the All Stars
Same personnel as for no.67
When it's sleepy time down South
Now you has jazz
High Society Calypso
Basin Street Blues
Perdido
Blueberry Hill
How high the moon
Mack the Knife
Sweet Georgia Brown
Have you heard about Jerry?
I left my heart in San Francisco
When the saints go marching in

(81) **1963**
Between April 24 & May 3   Concert, Tokyo
Louis Armstrong and the All Stars
*Louis Armstrong (t); Trummy Young (tb); Joe Darensbourg (cl); Billy
Kyle (p); Arvell Shaw (db); Danny Barcelona (d); Jewell Brown (v)*
When it's sleepy time down South (LA:v)
Indiana
My bucket's got a hole in it (LA, TY:v)

Tiger Rag
Now you has jazz (LA, TY:v)
High Society Calypso
Ole Miss

(82) 1963
Dec 3   New York
Louis Armstrong and the All Stars
Louis Armstrong (t); Trummy Young (tb); Joe Darensbourg (cl); Billy Kyle (p); Tony Gattuso (g, bj); Arvell Shaw (db); Danny Barcelona (d); unknown strings
K7424 Hello Dolly (LA:v)   Kapp573
K7452 I've got a lot of living to do (LA:v)   Kapp573

(83) 1964
Jan 13   ABC TV broadcast, "Mike Douglas Show," Cleveland
Louis Armstrong and the All Stars
Louis Armstrong (t); Big Chief Russell Moore (tb); Joe Darensbourg (cl); Billy Kyle (p); Arvell Shaw (db); Danny Barcelona (d); Jewell Brown (v)
When it's sleepy time down South
My bucket's got a hole in it
Struttin' with some Barbecue
Rockin' Chair
Lazy Bones
Gone Fishin'

(84) 1964
Jan 14   ABC TV broadcast, "Mike Douglas Show," Cleveland
Louis Armstrong and the All Stars
Same personnel as for no.83
Blueberry Hill
Now you has jazz
High Society Calypso
Indiana
St Louis Blues

(85) 1964
Jan 15   ABC TV broadcast, "Mike Douglas Show," Cleveland
Louis Armstrong and the All Stars
Same personnel as for no.83
Ain't misbehavin'
Wabash Blues
Yellow Dog Blues
Someday

(86) 1964
Jan 16   ABC TV broadcast, "Mike Douglas Show," Cleveland
Louis Armstrong and the All Stars
Same personnel as for no.83
Basin Street Blues
Old Man Mose

(87) 1964
Jan 17   ABC TV broadcast, "Mike Douglas Show," Cleveland
Louis Armstrong and the All Stars
Same personnel as for no.83
I'll be glad when you're dead you rascal you
I cover the waterfront
Muskrat Ramble
I can't give you anything but love

(88) 1964
April 18   New York or Las Vegas
Louis Armstrong and the All Stars
Same personnel as for no.83, with Glen Thompson (g, bj)
          Jeepers Creepers (LA:v) (1)   Kapp KL1364
          Hey look me over (LA:v)   "
          I still get jealous (LA:v)   "
K3106 Someday (LA:v) (1)   Kapp597
          Give me a kiss to build
             a dream on (LA:v) (1)   Kapp KL1364
          Blueberry Hill (LA:v) (1), (2)   Kapp KL1364
          Be my life's companion (LA:v) (1)   "
          It's been a long, long time (LA:v) (1), (3)   "

K8142 You are woman, I am man (LA:v) (3)   Kapp K901
          Moon River (LA:v)   *Kapp KL1364*
(1) *add unknown strings*
(2) *Armstrong, vocals only*
(3) *add unknown reeds*

(89) 1972
Los Angeles
John Fahey and his Orchestra
Jack Feierman (t); Ira Nepus (tb); Joe Darensbourg (cl); Joanne Grauer (p); Nappy Lamare, Allan Reuss (bj); John Fahey (g); Joel Druckman (db)
Lord have mercy   *Reprise MS 2089*
NB: The album title is *Of Rivers and Religion*; remaining tracks do not feature Darensbourg.

(90) 1972
Sept 10   Columbia, South Carolina
Joe Darensbourg
Ernie Carson (c); Charlie Borneman (tb); Joe Darensbourg (cl); Ralph Goodwin (p); Bill Rutan (bj); Hal "Shorty" Johnson (bb); Joe O'Neal (d)
Yellow Dog Blues   GHB GHB-90
They're diggin' Willie's grave (EC:v)
Cake Walkin' Babies
Lou-easy-an-ia (JD:v)
Blues my naughty sweetie gives to me (1)
Floatin' down that old Green River (EC:v)
Dr Jazz
Just a little while to stay here
Winin' Boy Blues
Meet me tonight in dreamland
(1) *Darensbourg plays ss*
NB: Album title is *Barrelhousin' with Joe*.

(91) 1973
Los Angeles
John Fahey and his Orchestra
Jack Feierman (t); Britt Woodman (tb); Joe Darensbourg (cl); Johnny Rotella (as); Dick Cary (p, ah); Allan Reuss (bj); John Fahey, Peter Jameson (g); Joel Druckman (b)
New Orleans Shuffle   *Reprise MS2145*
I wish I knew how it would feel to be free (2)
After the ball (1), (3)   *Reprise MS2145*
(1) *Darensbourg plays ss*
(2) *Rotella and Cary out*
(3) *add unknown mandolin (possibly Chris Darrow)*
NB: Album title is *After the Ball*; remaining tracks do not feature Darensbourg.

(92) 1973
October   Emporium of Jazz, Mendota, Minnesota
The Legends of Jazz
Andy Blakeney (t); Louis Nelson (tb); Joe Darensbourg (cl); Alton Purnell (p); Ed Garland (db); Barry Martyn (d)
Conti Street Parade   *Crescent Jazz Productions CJP-1*
Out in the cold again
Legends Boogie
Apex Blues
Down among the sheltering palms
Lou-easy-an-ia (JD:v)
Just a little while to stay here
Old Man Mose (AP:v)
Red man Blues
Do you know what it means to miss New Orleans? (AB:v)

(93) 1974
May 30   Hollywood
The Legends of Jazz
Same personnel as for no.92
Black and White Rag   *Crescent Jazz Productions CJP-2*
Yellow Dog Blues
Creole Love Call (1)
High Society (1)
Where or when (1)
(1) *add Barney Bigard (cl)*

(94) 1975
Hollywood
John Fahey and his Orchestra
Jack Feierman (t); Britt Woodman (tb); Joe Darensbourg (cl); Johnny Rotella (as); Dick Cary (p); Allan Reuss (bj); John Fahey (g); Ira Westley (bb); unknown (d)
Old Fashioned Love   *Tacoma C-1043*
Boodle am Shake (2)
Keep your lamp trimmed and burning (1), (3)
(1) *Darensbourg plays ss*
(2) *add Bobby Bruce (vn, v), Fahey (jug, g)*
(3) *Feierman out*
NB: Album title is *Old Fashioned Love*; remaining tracks do not feature Darensbourg.

(95) 1977
April 15   Los Coyotes Country Club, Buena Park, California
The New Orleanians
Mike DeLay (t); Roger Jamieson (tb); Joe Darensbourg (cl); Gideon Honore (p); Adolphus Morris (db); Syl Rice (d)
Tipperary (SR:v)   Private tape
I'm confessing
Lou-easy-an-ia (JD:v)
Lazy River
NB: The remainder of this session is in the possession of Mr D. H. Ross.

(96) c1977
Encino, California
Chuck Conklin's Angel City Jazz Band
Chuck Conklin (c); Dan Snyder, Gordon Mitchell (tb); Joe Darensbourg (cl); Joe Ashworth (cl, ss, ts); Elaine Mitchell (p); Red Murphy (g); Dolph Morris (db); Ike Candioti (d); Marge Murphy (v)
Mournin' Blues   *Angel City Records LP*
Blue Prelude (EM:v)   (unnumbered)
Dippermouth Blues
Bury me on Basin Street (MM:v)
Creole Love Call
Happy days and lonely nights (MM:v)
My bucket's got a hole in it (JD:v)
Big Butter and Egg Man (EM:v)
As long as I live
Dardanella
Mama's gone, goodbye (MM:v)
NB: Album title is *Jazz: South by Southwest, vol. 1.*

(97) 1978
April   Encino, California
Chuck Conklin's Angel City Jazz Band
Chuck Conklin (c); Dick Cary (t); Dan Snyder, Gordon Mitchell (tb); Joe Darensbourg (cl); Wayne Songer (ts); Elaine Mitchell (p); Red Murphy (g); Dolph Morris (db); Ike Candioti (d); Marge Murphy (v)
Sacramento Jubilee (MM, JD:v) Angel City Records ACR4501
Swing down from New Orleans (MM:v)   ACR4501

(98) 1978
July 12   Encino, California
Buddy Burns's New Orleans Creole Gumbo Zave
Mike DeLay (t); John Ewing (tb); Joe Darensbourg (cl); Bill Campbell (p); Nappy Lamare (bj); Buddy Burns (db); Ray Hall (d)

Indiana (JD:v)   *Froggie Bottom Records FBR 1001*
Alice Blue Gown
Lou-easy-an-ia (JD:v)
You tell me your dream
Honeysuckle Rose
Bourbon Street Parade (JD:v)
Basin Street Blues (JD:v)
Who's sorry now
Poor Butterfly
Fidgety Feet

(99) 1979
June 29   Los Angeles
Art De Peer (t); Phil Gray (tb); Joe Darensbourg (cl); others unknown
Overdubbing for disco record
Unknown titles   Mike Garson Productions

(100) 1983
Jan 9   UCLA, Los Angeles
The Eagle Brass Band
Leo Dejan, Andy Blakeney, Herbert Permillion (t); Alex Iles, John Ewing (tb); Joe Darensbourg (E flat cl); Floyd Turnham (as); Sam Lee (ts); Benny Booker (bb); Teddy Edwards (snare d); Barry Martyn (bass d, ldr)
Just a little while to stay here   *GHB GHB-170*
Our Director
Fallen Heroes
All because we had that thing called jazz
High Society
S'wonderful
Sweet Sue
Abide with me
St Louis Blues
Bourbon Street Parade
NB: Album title is *The Last of the Line.*

(101) 1983
Aug 16   Film Soundtrack "All of Me," Los Angeles
Teddy Edwards and his New Orleans Dixieland Band
Leo Dejan, Herbert Permillion (t); John Ewing (tb); Joe Darensbourg (cl); Benny Booker (bb); Gus Wright (snare d); Teddy Edwards (bass d); Alton Purnell (grand marshall)
Oh, didn't he ramble
Just a closer walk with thee
When the saints go marching in

(102) 1984
Feb 6–10   New Orleans
Clive Wilson (t); Waldren "Frog" Joseph (tb); Joe Darensbourg (cl); Stan Mendelson (p); Danny Barker (g, bj); Lloyd Lambert (db); Freddie Kohlman (d)
Unidentified titles   Art of Jazz
                                                 (unissued)

(103) 1984
Nov 13   UCLA, Los Angeles
UCLA Music Class
Leo Dejan (t); Joe Darensbourg (cl); Alden Ashforth (p) plus unidentified student musicians
Unidentified titles   GHB (?)
                                                 (unissued)

Supplement to Discography

A listing of private tapes held by Joe Darensbourg

(1) **1945**
Red Fox and his Ding Dong Daddies (see discography)
Dark Eyes, Royal Garden Blues, Eventually, Dippermouth Blues, Shut the Door, They're sending the Judge to jail, If you knew Susie

(2) **1951**
April Station KFI Broadcast, Los Angeles
George Barclay interview with George Lewis, Joe Darensbourg and Alton Purnell
Unidentified music titles

(3) **1951**
Sept 15 Station KFI Broadcast, Los Angeles
George Barclay interview with Alphonse Picou and Joe Darensbourg

(4) **1955**
Oct 29 Station KFI Broadcast, Los Angeles
George Barclay interview with George Lewis (cl); Joe Darensbourg (ss); Alton Purnell (p)
Nobody knows the way I feel this morning/Jerusalem/Old Rugged Cross, Lou-easy-an-ia, Sweet Georgia Brown, Jambalaya/Oh Mr Trombone Ain't you Ashamed/Washington and Lee Swing/Jack Carey/Tiger Rag

(5) **1961**
Dec 17 CBS TV broadcast, "Ed Sullivan Show," New York (see discography)
Louis Armstrong–Duke Ellington

(6) **1962**
Feb 16–20 TV soundtrack, concert, Stockholm (see discography)
Louis Armstrong and the All Stars

(7) **1962**
Feb 24 Broadcast, concert, Hamburg (see discography)
Louis Armstrong and the All Stars

(8) **1962**
Summer–autumn Film soundtrack, "The Good Years of Jazz," New York
Louis Armstrong and the All Stars

(9) **1963**
March BP TV broadcast, Sydney (see discography)
Louis Armstrong and the All Stars

(10) **1970**
July 2 Station KFI broadcast, "Tribute to Louis," Los Angeles
Barney Bigard, Joe Darensbourg (cl); Earl Hines, Alton Purnell (p); Lionel Hampton (vib)

(11) **1970**
July Party at Floyd Levin's home, Studio City, California
Barney Bigard, Maxim Saury, Joe Darensbourg (cl); others unknown

(12) **1972**
April 12 Club New Orleans, Fullerton, California
Andy Blakeney (t); Frank Demond (tb); Joe Darensbourg (cl); Alton Purnell (p); Mike Faye (db); Teddy Edwards (d)

(13) **1972**
July 9 Cliff House, Malibu, California
Joe Darensbourg's birthday party

(14) **1973**
Aug 12 Concert at MacArthur Park, Los Angeles
Unidentified musicians

(15) **1974**
Jan 7 Mayfair Music Hall, Santa Monica, California
Legends of Jazz
Andy Blakeney (t); Louis Nelson (tb); Joe Darensbourg (cl); Alton Purnell (p); Ed Garland (db); Barry Martyn (d)

(16) **1974**
Aug 23 Basingstoke, Hampshire
Joe Darensbourg (cl); Dick Cook (cl); Terry Knight (bs); Dave Carey (vib); Dave Evans (d)

(17) **1974**
Aug 24 Basingstoke, Hampshire
Pat Halcox (t); Chris Barber (tb; on some tracks); Joe Darensbourg (cl); Richard Simmons (p); Terry Knight (db); Dave Evans (d)

(18) **1974**
Aug 25 John R. T. Davies's garden
Dick Sudhalter (c); Joe Darensbourg (cl); J. R. T. Davies (as, bs); Keith Ingham (p); Neville Skrimshire (g); Peter Ind (db)

(19) **1974**
Aug
Cuff Billett (t); Tony Hurst (tb); Joe Darensbourg (cl); Terry Knight (bs); Pat Hawes (p); Lennie Hastings (d)

(20) **1976**
Feb 2 Blue Angel Jazz Club, Los Angeles
Joe Darensbourg (cl); Nick Fatool (d); others unidentified

(21) **1976**
June 12 Vancouver, Canada
Joe Darensbourg (cl) with Vancouver Hot Jazz All Stars

(22) **1978**
Jan CETA program, unidentified location, Los Angeles
CETA Dixieland Band
Al Latour (tb); Joe Darensbourg (cl); Gideon Honore (p); Walt Yoder (b); Ray Hall (d); Bud Matlock (unidentified instrument)

(23) Unknown date and location
Abe Lincoln (tb); Joe Darensbourg (cl); Ray Sherman (p); Ray Leatherwood (b); Nick Fatool (d)

Test pressings held by Joe Darensbourg
(1) **1945**
May
Red Fox and his Ding Dong Daddies (see discography) V-disc tests
Dark Eyes, Ballin' the Jack, I love my baby, If you knew Susie, Dippermouth Blues

(2) **1953**
Dayton, Ohio
Joe Darensbourg (cl); unidentified (p), (bj)
Nobody's sweetheart now, Who's sorry now, Coney Island Washboard, High Society etc

(3) **c1957** unknown label
Unknown female singer acc Joe Darensbourg (cl); Harvey Brooks (p); unidentified (g), (b), (d)
Bill Bailey, A good man is hard to find

List of compositions by Joe Darensbourg

Joe's Blues (recorded 1944)
Hot Rod Harry (*The Coolest Cat in Town*) by Joe Darensbourg & Tom Medley
  (recorded 1952)
Hot Rod Cowboy by Joe Darensbourg & Tom Medley (recorded 1952)
Saturday Night Drag Race by Joe Darensbourg & Tom Medley (recorded 1952)
Just a little time to stay here by Joe Darensbourg & Milly Nichols © 1957
Rockin' in Dixie by Joe Darensbourg & Milly Nichols © 1957*
Lou-easy-an-ia words and music by Joe Darensbourg © 1960
Monkey Snoots and Dumplin's by Joe Darensbourg & Harvey Brooks (copyright
  secured)
The Chipperoo Song words and music by Joe Darensbourg © 1965
Sacramento Jubilee words and music by Joe Darensbourg © 1978

Joe Darensbourg was elected to ASCAP on 28 June 1979

---

* Although the text shows this song to have been written by Darensbourg and Harvey Brooks, in this case the copyright is in the name of Milly Nichols, which is believed to be the pseudonym of Mrs Harvey Brooks.)

The film appearances of Joe Darensbourg

The Road to Ruin, USA, 1928, directed by N. S. Parker: with Mutt Carey's Liberty Syncopators: Carey (t); Darensbourg (as); L. Z. Cooper (p); Minor Hall (d)

Legion of the Condemned, USA, 1928, directed by W. A. Wellman: with Mutt Carey's Liberty Syncopators

Mahogany Magic, USA, 1950, directed by W. Cowan: with Kid Ory's Creole Jazz Band: Teddy Buckner (t); Ory (tb); Darensbourg (cl); Lloyd Glenn (p); Ed Garland (db); Minor Hall (d)

Imitation of Life, USA, 1959, directed by D. Sirk: with marching band including Mike Delay (t) and Darensbourg (cl)

March of Dimes: Louis Armstrong, USA, mid-1960: TV short, with Armstrong and the All Stars (Darensbourg as substitute for Barney Bigard)

The Good Years of Jazz: Louis Armstrong and the All Stars, USA, 1961, produced by Mike Bryan for the Good Years of Jazz: with Louis Armstrong's All Stars: Armstrong (t); Trummy Young (tb); Darensbourg (cl); Billy Kyle (p); Billy Cronk (db); Danny Barcelona (d); Jewel Brown (v)

Winter Carnival in Sun Valley, USA, Jan 1962, ABC TV Special with Louis Armstrong and the All Stars

The Great White Hope, USA, 1970, directed by M. Ritt: with Andy Blakeney (t) and John Ewing (tb)

Elvis, USA, 1979, directed by J. Carpenter: with Gene Washington and Sammy Lee

The White Shadow, USA, Feb 1981, MTM Enterprises for CBS: episode with Ella Fitzgerald and Jake Porter (t)

All of Me, USA, 1984, directed by C. Reiner: with Teddy Edwards and his New Orleans Dixieland Band: Leo Dejan, Herbert Permillion (t); John Ewing (tb); Darensbourg (cl); Benny Booker (tuba); Gus Wright (snare d); Edwards (bass d); Alton Purnell (grand marshall)

Darensbourg also appeared in several movies, their identities now forgotten, as part of Satchel McVea's Howdy Band, and in others with Carey and as a member of various white and Mexican bands; he then appeared in two of Fatty Arbuckle's pictures. It is assumed that all of these films, made in the late 1920s, were silent.

Acknowledgement: to David Meeker, and to his book *Jazz in the Movies* (Talisman Books, London, 1981)

Career chronology

1906
Joseph Wilmer Darensbourg born in Baton Rouge, Louisiana, July 9th. As a child inspired musically by uncle, Willie Darensbourg, circus trombonist; first experiments with violin and piano.

1916
Clarinet lessons from Manuel Roque; plays occasionally with Roque's band.

1918
Takes lessons from Alphonse Picou in New Orleans and hears pioneer jazzmen at Perseverance Hall. Starts first band with violinist brother Frank. Plays for church socials, family parties and school dances.

1920
Plays professional jobs with Toots Johnson's jazz band in Baton Rouge, also odd dates with Buddy Petit and Guy Kelly. Occasionally works with Tody Harris's band. Runs away several times to join circus; visits California with the Al G. Barnes Circus.

1922
Runs away to Los Angeles, taking work as dishwasher and pattern-maker. Stays six months; plays occasionally with Mexican bands. Returns to Baton Rouge to work in father's shoe shop and resumes playing with family band.

1923–4
Band plays for Knights of Columbus convention in Opelousas, Louisiana. Darensbourg sits in with Martels family orchestra before joining full-time to tour extensively. Thereafter is committed to music professionally. Marries Hillary Martel. Works briefly with Rogers's Sunshine Minstrels, touring to Mississippi and Tennessee. Commences playing C-melody saxophone in after-hours clubs in Opelousas.

1925
Joins Doc Moon's Medicine Show as saxophonist, entertainer and medicine-mixer. Plays with small ballyhoo group to attract customers. Stays with Moon for four or five months. While in St Louis, plays Sunday sessions with Charlie

Creath's Jazz-o-Maniacs at Jazzland Club, recording for Okeh. Also works briefly with Jelly Roll Morton in East St Louis and with minstrel and carnival bands. Is occasionally with Fate Marable for riverboat excursions. Joins four-piece combo at Shady Rest road-house in Harrisburg, Illinois; remains three or four months but is shot twice and beaten up. After hospital stay, joins Al G. Barnes Circus sideshow band and realizes life-long ambition by parading with circus in Baton Rouge. Returns home to work with Tody Harris.

1926

Recruited for Hill and Vesthon's ODJB with Victor Spencer (t) and Gus DeLuce (tb). Travels to Houston, then to California. Band breaks up in Los Angeles; from then Darensbourg makes West Coast his home.

1927

Takes dance-hall work with DeLuce and then joins Mutt Carey's band to play at Liberty Dance Hall. Appears in silent films with band. Learns to repair instruments.

1928

Leaves Carey's Liberty Syncopators after a year to work with Freda Shaw's band aboard SS *HF Alexander* from May to October; boat runs from Los Angeles to Seattle.

1929

Settles in Seattle, plays second season with Shaw. Works in various nightclubs and after-hours spots with Palmer Johnson and Freddy Vaughn.

1930

With Johnson at Jungle Temple in Seattle; takes over leadership of house band. Teaches saxophonist Dick Wilson, who commences career (on alto saxophone) with Darensbourg's band. Plays occasionally with Gene Coy's big band and takes saxophone lessons from Frank Weldon. Leaves Jungle Temple to join Gerald Wells's seven-piece band, one of the best in Seattle. Plays in top clubs; also works on boats to Alaska.

1931

At Black and Tan Club with Phil Moore. Plays with Ceele Burke and then takes a trio to Green River, Wyoming. Stranded for the winter.

1932

Joins Gennessee Street Shufflers. Sustains severe injuries, including broken back, in automobile accident and develops tuberculosis; bedridden for 12 months. After recovery travels to Portland and then to Phoenix to continue recuperation. Plays with local dance bands.

1934

Is stranded in Prescott, Arizona, then rejoins Vic Sewell's band. Back in Seattle, plays with Oscar Holden at Blue Rose; also teaches children for WPA program. Works regularly on ocean liners, traveling to the Orient.

1935–8
Spends several years working at clubs in Bremerton, Washington. Meets Louis Armstrong for the first time.

1938
Back in Seattle, resumes work in clubs and operates a restaurant with Eddie Swanson. Rejoins Vic Sewell for season at Lyon's Music Hall and at Spinning Wheel. Short engagement in Bakersfield, California, with Al Riley (d), then resumes work in Bremerton.

1939–40
With Sewell at Follies Theater in Seattle, then travels to Spokane with pick-up band.

1941
Joins Tommy Thomas's big band on alto saxophone. Broadcasts regularly, plays at service camps in Pacific North West; also appears in clubs with Palmer Johnson.

1943–4
While with Al Pierre at 908 Club in Seattle meets Johnny Wittwer and Doc Exner. Joins Wittwer for year-long residency at China Pheasant near Tacoma, Washington. Following record recitals at Exner's house, recordings by Wittwer's trio are made and released on Exner's own label.

1945
Darensbourg is encouraged by Exner to arrange band recordings by Kid Ory. Replaces Red Mack (t) with Ory's quartet at Tip Toe Inn; also plays gigs with full Ory band. Appears with Red Fox's novelty band at Ken Murray's Blackouts in Los Angeles. With Ory for Jade Palace residency, starting April 1st; leaves August 14th to return to Seattle. Briefly with Thomas again before returning to Los Angeles to work in clubs and tour with Joe Liggins and Honeydrippers (on clarinet). Stays three months; concerts at Apollo Theater and other major venues.

1946
Returns to Seattle, is injured in automobile accident then recalled to Los Angeles by Ory. Plays short engagements with Fox, Red Nichols, Jack Teagarden, Pete Daily and Wingy Manone, all on clarinet. Fills in, on saxophone, with Ceele Burke, at Bal Tabarin. Rejoins Ory's Creole Jazz Band permanently for opening at Billy Berg's in Hollywood. Plays two-month engagement at Green Room, San Francisco.

1947
Green Room job finishes in March; plays in trio with Ory in Los Angeles club before returning to San Francisco. During summer, Ory's band plays weekends at Rendezvous Ballroom. Appears on "This is Jazz" broadcast with Ory's band before working again in San Francisco.

1948
Ory's band plays residency at Swing Club in San Francisco, then undertakes national concert tour, appearing at Carnegie Hall, April 30th. After casual dates around Los Angeles, band starts residency at Beverly Cavern and plays for First Dixieland Jubilee at Pan Pacific Auditorium, October 30th. Plays six-week residency at Venus Cafe in San Francisco with Bob Scobey (t) substituting for Andy Blakeney.

1949
Ory's band opens January 15th for nine-month residency at Beverly Cavern. Teddy Buckner (t) joins the band. Ory opens his own club in December.

1950
Lengthy residency at Royal Room; appears in film *Mahogany Magic*. Takes charge at Sunday jam sessions at Royal Room when Ory's band moves on to Lyman's Hollywood Grill in August. Back at Beverly Cavern in December.

1951
Band continues at Beverley Cavern before commencing similar residency at 331 Club, also in Los Angeles. Darensbourg heads Sunday jam sessions at Sardi's.

1952
Further periods at Beverly Cavern. Records for Hot Rod. Marries Helen on September 1st.

1953
Is dismissed by Ory in July, then works as a freelance before moving to Dayton, Ohio, with Gene Mayl's band; stays six months.

1954–7
Moves back to Los Angeles in June 1954; joins Teddy Buckner's new traditional band for 400 Club engagement which lasts three years. Records regularly; also makes concert appearances.

1957
Is offered opportunity to lead own band at Lark Restaurant in Los Angeles; forms Dixie Flyers. Appears as guest on "Stars of Jazz" TV show and records for Lark label. His version of *Yellow Dog Blues* becomes national jukebox hit. Band closes at Lark then plays local gigs and club dates.

1958

Dixie Flyers continue to appear in Los Angeles; also plays engagement at Easy Street, San Francisco, in September.

1959

Band plays residencies at Club Jazzville and, from August, at Zucca's in Pasadena. Opens at Armantrout's, Sherman Oaks, on December 16th, for three months.

1960

Dixie Flyers disband. Darensbourg takes local freelance jobs with Mike Riley, Buddy Burns and Ed Garland. Fronts all-star sextet at Club Hangover, San Francisco, for eight weeks from October 7th.

1961

Forms own trio for residency at Gilded Rafters, Sepulveda. Is then approached to join new jazz combo Young Men from New Orleans on Disneyland riverboat. Joins Louis Armstrong's All Stars on July 17th; plays first job at Bala, Canada. Band tours continuously; appears on "Ed Sullivan Show" from Germany, September 5th, before breaking attendance records at Basin Street East, New York, from December 1st.

1962

Band makes TV Special "Winter Carnival in Sun Valley" in January; continues road tour, which includes engagements at Riviera, Las Vegas. Makes film for Goodyear, April 2nd, then leaves for European tour, which closes on May 29th. To Chile, June 1st–2nd, then Newport Jazz Festival, July 7th, with J. C. Higginbotham and Yank Lawson. Band continues to tour USA for remainder of years, playing residencies at Las Vegas. Appears on "Ed Sullivan Show" from Cuba, December 14th.

1963

On March 6th band leaves for two months in Australia, New Zealand, Hong Kong, Korea and Japan. Plays for President Kennedy at Waldorf Astoria, New York, on May 22nd, then resumes usual touring schedule. Records *Hello Dolly* in December; huge chart success.

1964

Week-long residency on "Mike Douglas Show" from Cleveland in January, before national one-nighter tour. Darensbourg leaves band in New York on June 30th. Returns to Los Angeles and learns to repair musical instruments with Dominick Colicio. Works for Colicio for next 12 months, taking few playing jobs.

1965

Completes "sabbatical" and rejoins Young Men from New Orleans in June. Kid Ory plays annual engagement with band, September 24th–25th.

1965–9
Continues to appear with YMNO for annual seasons. Plays for "Dixieland at Disneyland" concerts and selected events organized by Southern California Hot Jazz Society.

1969
YMNO is disbanded but Darensbourg is invited to form new band for Disneyland. Takes Delta Rhythm Kings into New Orleans Square but engagement is terminated after dispute over working conditions. Leads own group at Steak House, Solana Beach, and continues to play locally with Nappy Lamare.

1970–72
Freelance engagements continue, including special concert "Hello Louis" at Shrine Auditorium, 3rd July 1970. From June 1971, plays with own trio at Calabassas Inn, Calabassas Park, for three months and then at Cafe De Rex in Beverly Hills. Records with John Fahey in 1972 and plays many local dates.

1973
Plays a season at Steak House with Warren Smith (tb) for Delmar race-goers. Works as freelance until approached to join new Legends of Jazz, which first performs at Wilshire Ebell Theater in "A Night in New Orleans" on September 8th. Legends undertake first European tour from October, then tour American Midwest.

1974
Darensbourg continues affiliation with Legends of Jazz. Tours Europe from March 6th but is taken ill in London. Resumes work with band in USA from April. Returns to Britain for solo dates in August, then tours extensively in the USA with Legends.

1975
Continues American tour until start of European tour, April 22nd. Upon return, leaves Legends to play as a freelance, working with Nappy Lamare and Nick Fatool. Also commences association with Roger Jamieson's New Orleanians.

1976–7
With Jamieson's band for casual dates; also appears as guest with dixieland clubs. Plays concerts and takes short out-of-town tours. With Chuck Conklin's Angel City Jazz Band from October 1977 before joining CETA Program as leader of the Dixieland Band, starting December 16th.

1978
Following guest season in Denver, suffers first heart attack. Resumes with CETA in March; program is completed at end of May. Returns to freelance schedule, playing many concerts; second heart attack in November.

1979
Third heart attack in February. Is back to active performance from April, playing occasional concerts and private parties.

1980–81
Considers himself semi-retired but takes occasional jobs, including wedding receptions and funerals.

1982
Helen Darensbourg has operation for cancer in January. Joe has a fall in August and is admitted to hospital in intensive care. No further appearances before year end.

1983–5
Records with Eagle Brass Band, January 1983. Is made "Jazzman of the Year" by *Jazz Forum*, July 17th; honored by City of Baton Rouge and Governor of Louisiana. Occasional film work and concerts. Visits New Orleans, February 1984, to record.

1985
Is appointed to Trials Board, AFM Local 47, January 15th. Suffers crippling stroke, February 5th, and dies of cardiac arrest in hospital in Van Nuys on May 24th. His ashes are scattered over the Pacific Ocean. An all-star "Tribute to Joe Darensbourg" is held at The Limelight, Saugus, on June 9th, with Joe Darensbourg's Dixie Flyers directed by Abe Most.

A bibliography of articles about Joe Darensbourg

Ashforth, Alden, and Gushee, Larry: "An Interview with Joe Darensbourg," *Footnote*, xv (1984), no. 3, p. 4; no. 4, p. 4

Bentley, John: "Joe Darensbourg," *Coda*, iii/8 (1960), 22 (also in *Eureka*, i/5 (1960), 21)

Biderman, John: "Emperor of Jubilee Traces all the Notes," *Sacremento Bee* (24 May 1980)

Buchanan, John: "Jazz Clarinet Legend to Play," *Denver Post* (18 Jan 1978)

Griffin, Stuart: "Meeting the People: Joe Darensbourg," *Mainichi Daily News* (Japan, 14 May 1963)

Hawthorn, Maggie: "A Jazzman Looks at Yesterday," *Seattle Post-Intelligencer* (12 June 1976), 12

Jones, Max: "There's Nobody I'd Rather Work For," *Melody Maker*, xxxvii (5 May 1962)

Laine, George: "Darensbourg is New Orleans," *The Independent* (Los Angeles, 10 Aug 1957), 7

Melinsky, Dorothy: "Darensbourg Joys," *Mississippi Rag*, v/2 (1977), 10

Mills, Ken, and Gordon, William B.: "The Great Joe Darensbourg: an Unknown Soldier Makes Good," *The Iconoclast*, i/1

Patch, Derek Whitmore: "Joe Darensbourg: Jazzman of the Year," *Jazz Forum*, no. 82 (1983), 3

Spenker, T. J.: "Joe Darensbourg," *Jazz Music*, iii/5 (1947), 14

Umphrey, Wallace: "New Orleans in Seattle," *Jazz Record*, no. 27 (1944), 10

Vacher, Peter: "A New Orleans Clarinettist: Joe Darensbourg," *Jazz News* (14 Jan 1961), 6

——: "Joe Darensbourg," *Melody Maker*, xlix (30 March 1974), 62

——: "Darensbourg: Creole King," *Melody Maker*, l (10 May 1975) 42

——: "Joe Darensbourg and the Legends of Jazz," *Footnote*, vi/4 (1975), 4

——: "Joe Darensbourg: Obituary," *Jazz Journal International*, xxxviii/9 (1985), 27

——: "My Louisiana Story," *Jazz Monthly*, ix/8 (1963), 4

Valdespino, Anne: "Saugus Dixieland Jam Honors Memory of Joe Darensbourg," *Los Angeles Times* (10 June 1985), 12

Walsh, Tom: "The Dixie Flyer," *Jazz Forum*, no. 56 (1978), 4

Walton, Clarence: "No People-eating for Joe, Just Good, Solid Jazz," *Norfolk-Ledger Star* (12 July 1958)

Wittwer, John: "A Tribute to Joe Darensbourg," *Jazz Record*, no. 36 (1945) (reprinted in *Selections from the Gutter: Jazz Portraits from "The Jazz Record"*, ed. Art Hodes and Chadwick Hansen, Berkeley, CA, and London, 1977)

Index